UNDERSTANDING
EATING DISORDERS

UNDERSTANDING EATING DISORDERS: ANOREXIA NERVOSA, BULIMIA NERVOSA, AND OBESITY

Edited by

LeeAnn Alexander-Mott
D. Barry Lumsden
*Department of Counseling, Development,
and Higher Education
College of Education
University of North Texas
Denton, Texas, USA*

Taylor & Francis
Publishers since 1798

USA	Publishing Office:	Taylor & Francis
		1101 Vermont Avenue, N.W., Suite 200
		Washington, DC 20005-3521
		Tel: (202) 289-2174
		Fax: (202) 289-3665
	Distribution Center:	Taylor & Francis
		1900 Frost Road, Suite 101
		Bristol, PA 19007-1598
		Tel: (215) 785-5800
		Fax: (215) 785-5515
UK		Taylor & Francis Ltd.
		4 John St.
		London WC1N 2ET
		Tel: 071 405 2237
		Fax: 071 831 2035

UNDERSTANDING EATING DISORDERS: Anorexia Nervosa, Bulimia Nervosa, and Obesity

2 3 4 5 6 7 8 9 0   BRBR   9 8 7 6 5

This book was set in Times Roman by Princeton Editorial Associates. The editors were Deena Williams Newman and Bernadette Capelle; the production supervisor was Peggy M. Rote. Cover design by Michelle Fleitz. Printing and binding by Braun-Brumfield, Inc.

A CIP catalog record for this book is available from the British Library.
 ∞ The paper in this publication meets the requirements of the ANSI Standard Z39.48-1984 (Permanence of Paper)

Library of Congress Cataloging-in-Publication Data

Understanding eating disorders : anorexia nervosa, bulimia nervosa, and obesity /
    LeeAnn Alexander-Mott and D. Barry Lumsden.
        p.   cm.
    Includes index.

    1. Eating disorders.   I. Alexander-Mott, LeeAnn.   II. Lumsden, D. Barry.
RC552.E18U53 1994
616.85′26—dc20   94-8719
ISBN 1-56032-294-2 (case)   CIP
ISBN 1-56032-295-0 (paper)

To Larry, my husband and best friend, with love and appreci-
ation for being who you are and for sharing your life with
me. To my parents, with love and appreciation for believing
in me and for loving me unconditionally—L. A.-M.

Contents

vii

Contributors

LEEANN ALEXANDER-MOTT, M.S.
Department of Counseling, Development,
   and Higher Education
College of Education
University of North Texas
Denton, TX 76203-3857

DAVID B. ALLISON, Ph.D.
Obesity Research Center
Columbia University College of
   Physicians and Surgeons
411 W. 114th Street, #3D
New York, NY 10025

BARTON J. BLINDER, M.D., Ph.D.
Department of Psychiatry and
   Human Behavior
University of California, Irvine
Irvine, CA 92664

C. LAIRD BIRMINGHAM, M.D.,
   F.R.C.P. (C)
Department of Medicine
University of British Columbia
Vancouver, British Columbia V6Z 1Y6
Canada

RACHEL CALAM, Ph.D.
University Department of Clinical
   Psychology
University of Manchester
Withington Hospital
West Didsbury
Manchester M20 8LR
United Kingdom

KARIN H. CHAO
College of Medicine
University of California, Irvine
Irvine, CA 92664

SCOTT J. CROW, M.D.
Department of Psychiatry
School of Medicine

University of Minnesota
Twin Cities Campus
Box 393 Mayo Memorial Building
420 Delaware Street, S.E.
Minneapolis, MN 55455-0392

JOANNE EVERILL, Ph.D.
University of Birmingham
Edgbaston
Birmingham B15 2TT
United Kingdom

ELLIOT M. GOLDNER, M.D.,
    F.R.C.P.
Department of Psychiatry
University of British Columbia
St. Paul's Hospital
1081 Burrard Street
Vancouver, British Columbia
    V6Z1Y6
Canada

MELANIE KATZMAN, Ph.D.
New York Hospital Cornell Medical
    Center
525 East 68th Street
New York, NY 10021

MICHAEL P. LEVINE, Ph.D.
Department of Psychology
Kenyon College
Samuel Mather Hall
Gambier, OH 43022-9623

RUSSELL D. MARX, M.D.
Department of Psychiatry
University of California, San Diego
345 Saxony Road, Suite 201
Encinitas, CA 92024

JAMES E. MITCHELL, M.D.
Department of Psychiatry
University of Minnesota
Minneapolis, MN 55455-0392

COLLEEN S.W. RAND, Ph.D.
Department of Psychiatry
J. Hillis Miller Health Center
College of Medicine
University of Florida

Box J-256-JHMHC
Gainesville, FL 32610

LORI A. SANSONE, M.D.
College of Medicine
University of Oklahoma
Tulsa, OK 74129-2808

RANDY A. SANSONE, M.D.
Department of Psychiatry
College of Medicine
University of Oklahoma
2802 Sheridan
Tulsa, OK 74129-2808

SARAH C. SITTON, Ph.D.
Department of Psychology
New College-St. Edwards University
Austin, TX 78704-6489

LINDA SMOLAK, Ph.D.
Department of Psychology
Kenyon College
Samuel Mather Hall
Gambier, OH 43022-9623

GLENN WALLER, M. Clinic Psychology,
    D. Phil.
School of Psychology
University of Birmingham
Edgbaston
Birmingham B15 2TT
United Kingdom

LILLIE WEISS, Ph.D.
Department of Psychology
Arizona State University
4202 N. 32nd Street, Suite H
Phoenix, AZ 85018

SHARLENE WOLCHIK, Ph.D.
Department of Psychology
Arizona State University
4202 N. 32nd Street, Suite H
Phoenix, AZ 85018

HAROLD E. YUKER, Ph.D.
Psychology Department
Hofstra University
Hempstead
Long Island, NY 11550

Preface

The three most commonly discussed eating disorders are anorexia nervosa, bulimia nervosa, and compulsive overeating/obesity. *Anorexia nervosa,* identified as a psychiatric syndrome for more than 100 years, was recognized in the American Psychiatric Association's *Diagnostic and Statistical Manual of Mental Disorders* (*DSM-III,* 1980) as a mental disorder. The DSM-III also recognized bulimia as a distinct diagnostic category, distinguishing it from anorexia nervosa; in 1987, the revised *Diagnostic and Statistical Manual of Mental Disorders* (*DSM-III-R,* 1987) changed the term to *bulimia nervosa.* Both anorexia nervosa and bulimia nervosa represent distinct diagnostic categories of eating disorders. The same cannot be said of either compulsive overeating or obesity.

Compulsive overeating is a term that has been used to designate the pattern by which typically overweight patients binge but do not purge. Compulsive overeaters often have a history of sustained overeating for a prolonged period of time. They do not attempt to counter the effects of the binges with vomiting or by using laxatives, diuretics, or exercise, and obesity results. Defined as an accumulation of excess body fat, obesity is used to designate a physical condition caused quite often by compulsive overeating. Currently, the Eating Disorders Work Group of the American Psychiatric Association's Task Force in a revised edition of *DSM-*

III-R (to be called *DSM-IV*) has set up tentative criteria for a binge-eating disorder, criteria that will encompass those individuals who have a significant problem with binge eating but who do not purge, thus not meeting criteria for bulimia nervosa.

Most theorists realize that neither compulsive overeating nor obesity has been formally recognized as an eating disorder per se. Many, however, still include one or both in the context of discussions of eating disorders, with the idea that there are common areas of interest among these various categories of eating problems and that research and work in one area might benefit the others.

In recent years, the incidence of these eating disorders has increased. In addition to this increase in prevalence, there has been a corresponding increased awareness of the eating disorders, which has resulted in a tremendous amount of research and literature in the eating disorders field. This book has been assembled with the aim of providing one volume that presents current knowledge on anorexia nervosa, bulimia nervosa, and obesity, and examines issues relevant to these disorders individually and collectively.

This book will be of interest to those working directly with people with eating disorders, including counselors, psychologists, nurses, medical practitioners, psychiatrists, and individuals working in eating disorders clinics and programs. Chapters in each of the three sections on anorexia nervosa, bulimia nervosa, and obesity contain discussions relevant to the etiology, course, and treatment of these eating disorders. Social workers and teachers will also find vital information necessary for understanding eating disorders and for dealing with victims of eating disorders.

Understanding Eating Disorders is an excellent source of current information on anorexia nervosa, bulimia nervosa, and obesity for the researcher. The contributors in individual chapters identify current research areas and suggest topics and fruitful areas for further research. Authors of the individual chapters are experts in their area of contribution. Thus, the book is a compilation of research from a group of experts who offer insight and guidance into the understanding, treatment, and prevention of eating disorders.

The book is divided into four parts. Part 1 includes four chapters. The first chapter, "Eating Disorders: A Historical Perspective," provides a foundation for the remainder of the book. Blinder and Chao show the gradual evolution of anorexia nervosa as a specific disease entity and point out current advances in the understanding and treatment of this disorder. They also discuss references throughout history to bulimia and trace the gradual acceptance of bulimia nervosa as a distinct syndrome. Finally, in their overview of the history of obesity, they note the effect of societal customs on attitudes toward obesity, the adverse health consequences of profound obesity, and the development of numerous slimming techniques. In the next chapter, "Critical Issues in the Developmental Psychopathology of Eating Disorders," Smolak and Levine identify and discuss five critical issues in the emerging field of developmental psychopathology that need to be considered in models of eating disorders. Consideration and application of these developmental principles will lead to greater insights into etiology and into prevention, a relatively neglected area. The developmental approach raises important questions for further research; developmental psychology and psychopathology will provide paradigms to guide the work of clinicians treating eating disorders patients. In "Parenting and Family Factors in Eating Problems," Waller and Calam warn that seeking typical parenting styles that provide for an eating disorder at-risk group and searching for particular risk factors (such as early food refusal) are inadequate. Waller and Calam suggest that family function should be viewed as only one factor interacting with other factors that contribute to eating psychopathology and toward or away from the development of eating disorders. This section ends with a chapter that examines a very timely and important topic in the eating disorders field, "Sexual Abuse and the Eating Disorders." Waller, Everill, and Calam consider the methodological and practical issues in determining the generalizability of any link between sexual abuse and eating psychopathology. Furthermore, the authors consider the nature of this link and discuss implications for treatment. For the present, the relevance of sexual abuse to the eating disorders must be understood in terms of individual cases. For those cases where sexual abuse is judged relevant, the authors offer guidelines for treatment. Judging the relevance of sexual abuse to the eating disorders is a fruitful area for clinical research. The development of psychological measures that would validate these formulations is also a very promising research area.

Part 2 focuses specifically on anorexia nervosa. In "Anorexia Nervosa: Definition, Diagnostic Criteria, and Associated Psychological Problems," the various ways in which anorexia nervosa has been defined since the first detailed description of this eating disorder are examined. Such issues as the division of anorexia nervosa into two distinct subgroups (restricting anorexics and bulimic anorexics), the difference between anorexia nervosa and weight preoccupation, and anorexia nervosa's differentiation from other psychiatric illnesses are examined. Viewing anorexia nervosa as a distinct subgroup will further research and treatment of this eating disorder. The next chapter, "Anorexia Nervosa: Theories of Etiology," contains a discussion by Marx of three areas of interest in the etiology of anorexia nervosa: factors that predispose, factors that precipitate, and factors that perpetuate the disorder. Marx shares insights concerning male anorexics, individuals often ignored or lightly passed over in discussions of etiology of anorexia nervosa. In the final chapter in this part, "Anorexia Nervosa: Methods of Treatment," Goldner and Birmingham suggest that the "best" treatment approach to anorexia nervosa has not been verified. However, they do review a widely agreed-upon set of primary treatment components. Current controversies in the treatment of anorexia nervosa, including the right to refuse treatment, inpatient versus outpatient treatment, the prevalence of childhood sexual abuse in anorexia nervosa, and pharmacotherapy in anorexia nervosa are discussed. Finally, the authors summarize the current information on treatment efficacy derived from clinical investigations.

Part 3 consists of three chapters, all dealing with bulimia nervosa. In "Bulimia Nervosa: Definition, Theories of Etiology, and Associated Psychological Problems," Weiss, Katzman, and Wolchik define and describe bulimia nervosa. They offer a review of the theories of etiology, maintain that the differences among theories of etiology are the result of emphasis rather than exclusion, and suggest common themes in models. Next, the authors propose an empirically based model of bulimia nervosa composed of two interacting, positive feedback loops that contribute to the bulimic cycle. Finally, Weiss, Katzman, and Wolchik offer suggestions for treatment and identify two areas for further research: the relationship between bulimia nervosa and depression, and the integration of existing models of bulimia nervosa into a comprehensive theory of etiology. In their chapter "Bulimia Nervosa: Medical Complications," Sansone and Sansone describe the numerous medical complications that result from binge eating or from the method of compensation following a massive caloric ingestion; they outline treatment methods for these complications. Interestingly, Sansone and Sansone report two cases of adenocarcinoma of the esophagus in bulimic women, supposedly related to the epithelial change in the esophagus that results from the repeated reflux of digestive juices. The authors suggest that this relationship, theorized about in the past, warrants further investigation. In the third chapter in this section, "Bulimia Nervosa: Methods of Treatment," Crow and Mitchell review the current status of psychotherapeutic and psychopharmacologic intervention strategies for bulimia nervosa and offer practical guidelines concerning the clinical management of bulimia nervosa patients, with their focus on the outpatient setting. Thus far, attempts to examine the relative effects of psychopharmacologic and psychotherapeutic treatments have been limited; the authors cite three studies that have attempted to do so. Although the studies cited offer conflicting results, the authors conclude that psychotherapy seems to be more effective, at least on a short-term basis. However, this area is one for further research.

Part 4 consists of three chapters that examine issues related to compulsive overeating/obesity. The first chapter, "Obesity: Definition, Diagnostic Criteria, and Associated Health Problems," includes a discussion of how obesity is defined and measured because of the effect that these two factors have on prevalence studies and morbidity and mortality associated with obesity. Rand, the author, examines the conflicting studies on relationships between obesity and morbidity and mortality (with some studies showing a positive relationship and other studies showing negative results, weak associations, or no results) and concludes that the relationship between obesity and health is complex and is influenced by gender and by environmental/behavioral characteristics of populations studied. Rand discusses the impact and implications of cultural attitudes on the evaluation of medical health risks for mild to moderate forms of obesity. She identifies current research as focusing on genetic and environmental/behavioral factors of populations studied in determining relationships between health and obesity. In "Obesity:

Sociocultural Perspectives," Yuker and Allison report that attitudes toward obesity and obese persons are quite negative, especially for women. Furthermore, they discuss factors influencing these negative attitudes and the harmful consequences of such attitudes. Most importantly, they identify and discuss several methodological issues that have arisen in studies of attitudes toward obesity and obese persons. For future research, Yuker and Allison suggest that studies of attitudes toward obesity and obese persons move beyond mere description of negative attitudes. Instead, studies should investigate moderators of the effects of these attitudes (both interpersonal and intrapersonal) and evaluate the efficacy of theory-based interventions to improve attitudes toward obese people. In "Obesity: Methods of Treatment," Sitton examines various methods of treatment for obesity and offers insight into current treatment methods, focusing on behavioral approaches and relapse prevention. As for future research, Sitton urges the need for research techniques that do not rely on self-reports.

We hope this volume will give a true picture of the relatedness of the eating disorders, will increase research in the individual disorders and in eating disorders collectively, and will facilitate interactions among those working with eating-disordered patients.

LeeAnn Alexander-Mott
D. Barry Lumsden

Part One

General Issues

The chapters in part one consider issues related generally to eating disorders. "The Eating Disorders: A Historical Perspective," the chapter on the history of eating disorders, considers anorexia nervosa, bulimia nervosa, and obesity. The remaining chapters focus on the more commonly paired anorexia nervosa and bulimia nervosa. These chapters, "Critical Issues in the Developmental Psychopathology of Eating Disorders," "Parenting and Family Factors in Eating Problems," and "Sexual Abuse and the Eating Disorders" focus on critical issues in the development of anorexia nervosa and bulimia nervosa.

Chapter 1

Eating Disorders: A Historical Perspective

Barton J. Blinder
Karin H. Chao

ANOREXIA NERVOSA

The word *anorexia,* derived from the Greek, means lack of appetite or avoidance and loathing of food. However, as used clinically in the eating disorders literature, this term is partially a misnomer. For a patient with anorexia nervosa, global appetite is not diminished; rather, it is modified, distorted, and initially, forcefully controlled. It is not until the advanced stage of the clinical disorder that the appetite may be significantly diminished. Hungry or not, the patients starve themselves to a point where the illness can progress to fatality.

Anorexia nervosa is a disorder that most commonly affects females in their teenage and young adult years. On some college campuses (Leichner & Gertler, 1988; Yu, 1986), it is estimated that as many as 20% of the young women demonstrate anorexic behaviors. Although the clinical occurrence of the illness is uncommon before age 10 and after age 30, anorexia nervosa may occur throughout the life cycle and affects males also (Anderson & Mickalide, 1983; Leichner & Gertler, 1988; Sibley & Blinder, 1988). Preadolescent occurrence of anorexia nervosa may begin as young as age 6; it is usually associated with childhood depression, anxiety, or trauma and involves a relatively higher proportion of boys (female to male ratio is 6 to 1). Male predominance is characteristic of atypical cases of anorexia nervosa occurring in the geriatric age group (Morley & Castel, 1983). Overall, women are afflicted by anorexia nervosa more frequently than men (Anderson & Mickalide, 1983; Gislason, 1988; Goodman, Blinder, Chaitin, & Hagman, 1988; Jones, Fox, & Babigian, 1980; Morley & Castel, 1983), with the ratio as high as 20 to 1. In past reports, the mortality rates were as high as 19% (Halmi, Broadland, & Rigas, 1975; Hsu, 1980). More commonly, the mortality rate is 5% and possibly much lower in the past decade (1980 to 1990) because of earlier recognition of the illness and improved comprehensive therapeutic approaches with advanced technical and medical support. Prognosis of treated anorexia nervosa patients 4 years after onset of illness are as follows (APA Practice Guideline for Eating Disorders, 1993): 44% had a good outcome (weight restored to within 15% of recommended weight for height and regular menstruation established); 24% had a poor outcome (weight never approached 15% under recommended weight for height and menstruation was absent or at best sporadic); 28% had an intermediate outcome (between that of the good and poor group); and fewer than 5% had died.

Prehistory

As early as the 9th century, a Persian boy, the son of the reigning Khalifah of the Islamic empire, developed rapid weight loss after he refused to eat or drink. He was diagnosed with a secondary condition of somatic complications. With a behavioral approach emphasizing rewards for eating, the court physician was able to help the boy to gradually restore his weight and health (Hajal, 1982; Sibley & Blinder, 1988).

The first recorded case of anorexia nervosa in a historical text was found in 895 A.D. (Habermas, 1986; Yates, 1989). Friderada, a serf, reportedly would first gorge and "eat(s) like a cow," then she would totally restrict food intake. However, even during fasting, some saw her eat in secrecy, and in fact, she often did so at night. Friderada's personality traits parallelled those found clinically in anorexia nervosa: an apparent fierce independence, denial of debility, piousness, and intense industriousness.

These early accounts of eating disorders were not confined to individuals. The legend of St. Wilgefortis (Lacey, 1982), the bearded medieval female saint, led to the development of cults based on rejection of sexuality, asceticism, and wasting of the body. St. Wilgefortis was suspected to be anorexic. Her hirsutism was likely the result of lanugo (long, fine, dark hair) found in chronic patients with anorexia nervosa.

Isolated Medical Accounts (Nonreligious)

The author of the first medical account of anorexia nervosa was Richard Morton (Bliss & Branch, 1960), a fellow of the College of Physicians in London and the appointed physician in ordinary to the King of England. (See Silverman's [1983] biography of Morton.) In his *Phthisologia, or, a Treatise on Consumptions* in 1696, Morton called anorexia nervosa a nervous disorder with an emotional or psychic basis. Labeling the disease a "nervous consumption," Morton noted that it was due to a disturbance of animal spirit.

Morton's first case involved a 20-year-old woman with the symptoms of diminished appetite and decreased menses. Upon examination, Morton was in awe to see the girl "so wasted . . . like a skeleton only clad with skin (Silverman, 1988, p. 83)." He concluded the disease was caused by sadness and anxious care and attributed it to excessive studying. This case was significant in the understanding of anorexia nervosa because, for the first time, this disease was differentiated from tuberculosis (Trail, 1970); Morton did not find other somatic symptoms except wasting and amenorrhea. Furthermore, despite the patient's physical condition, Morton noted she was indifferent to her own malnutrition and continued to be very hyperactive. She died 2 years later from weight loss.

Morton's second case involved a young adult son of a clergyman (Silverman, 1988). As with his first case, Morton noted his patient was not afflicted with tuberculosis since there was no cough, fever, or other symptoms of the lung. Morton concluded his patient suffered from anorexia and "passion of the mind" due to excessive study. For treatment, Morton suggested abandonment of studies, country air, and a milk diet. In addition, Morton encouraged a psychological treatment plan. The patient recovered in great measure.

Other early accounts of anorexia nervosa were written by Whytt in 1767. Whytt, a distinguished physician and president of the Royal College of Physicians of Edinburgh (Beumont, 1991; Silverman, 1987; Strober, 1986), conceived of anorexia nervosa as "wasting of body from morbid states of nerves" and a type of hypochondria or hysteria. Whytt found patients usually alternate between having an uncommon hunger (fames canina or dog hunger) and starvation. In one of Whytt's cases, a 14-year-old boy lost his appetite and had bad digestion. During one examination, Whytt noted the boy's pulse to be 40 per minute. However, 3 months later, the boy's appetite increased, he craved large meals every 2 or 3 hours, and his pulse went up to 110. As did Morton, Whytt concluded this patient suffered from nervous atrophy, which he defined as a morbid disease that affected the nerves of the stomach and was associated with nausea.

De Valangin, a fellow of the Royal College of Physicians, encountered a noteworthy case in which the patient developed anorexia from deliberate dieting (Beumont, 1991; De Valangin, 1768). He wrote, "A young lady who was inclined to be fat, was advised to make use of vinegar to reduce her fat; she lived accordingly on pickled mangoes, and only upon tea, with the smallest quantity of bread and butter, till at last prevailed upon by her physician to take a more nourishing diet."

Physicians of the 18th and 19th centuries often thought of anorexia nervosa as a female disease, attaching terms such as "nymphomania," "hysteria," and "the wandering womb disease." Giorgio Baglivi, chair of Medical Theory in Collegio Della Sapienza in Rome, concluded that anorexia affected young females of "genteel breeding" who were unrequited in love. Baglivi stated that it was the passion of the mind that led to the various physical ailments, and that anorexia nervosa was a mental illness that resulted in gastrointestinal symptoms. His treatment plan included getting the patient well by encouragement and persuasion (Bell, 1985).

Religious Fasting Women, Holy Anorexia

Food refusal, a characteristic of holy women of the Middle Ages in Western Europe, was associated with passionate devotion to the Holy Communion. Such prolonged abstinence from food was often undertaken for religious motives. St. Jerome stated in the 4th century: "Let your companion be pale and thin with daily fast" (Beumont, 1991, p. 9)

Asceticism, defined as "a spiritual or religious foundation for the practices of its devotees" (Rampling, 1985, p. 89), was the central theme among the anorexic religious fasting women of this period. These religious women used starvation as a measure to unite themselves with God. By refusing food and by practicing other acts of penance, the holy women believed they were on their way to salvation, eternal life, and God's love. Bell (1985) noted that these women believed they were becoming more acceptable in God's eyes by fasting. An individual gained spiritual liberation and merged herself with God through mortification of the flesh. Additionally, these religious women appeared to have used starvation as a way to rebel against societal mores and its patriarchal structure. For example, St. Catherine of Siena used self-starvation to defy church authority (Rampling, 1985).

In Bell's monograph, *Holy Anorexia,* three types of religious fasting women were defined. Catherine of Siena believed that bodily urges such as hunger and sexual desires were obstructions to holiness. By control through starvation, Catherine tried to decrease her bodily demands so she could free herself to commune with God. Catherine believed she was a bride of Jesus Christ, thereby a servant to God. The starvation implied the perfection of the soul, which elevated self-esteem through the resulting euphoria of union with God. Catherine eventually died of starvation; even death, she claimed, was a sweet liberation from flesh. (For further information on Catherine of Siena, see Bank and Kahn [1982], Blinder [1972], Freud [1936], and Rampling [1985].)

The second type of religious fasting women was typified by Veronica Giuliani (Bell, 1985). Unlike Catherine, Veronica recovered from her anorexia and gained a sense of self. Brought up by a very religious mother and three older sisters, all of whom became nuns, Veronica spent the major part of her life proving her autonomy and contesting her will and freedom from the male-dominated society.

Veronica believed that to be one with God implied starvation and other harsh austerities. Fed by the church and the elders, however, Veronica ultimately ate a limited diet. Furthermore, Veronica renewed her faith in the Virgin Mary as her mother and nurturer.

Reactions to these religious fasting women were numerous. Some saw them as miraculous and saintly; others, however, said they were the devil's agents or a fraud. In the Middle Ages, it was left to the responsibility of the church to examine the veracity of the miraculous origin of behaviors or events. By the late 19th century, these decisions were made by scientific and medical investigators (Brumberg, 1988).

A third type of religious fasting women were the married penitents (Bell, 1985; van der Eycken, 1988). They were women who married at a very young age and who never had the opportunity to contest their identity and find a sense of autonomy. It was when widowhood or other life crises occurred that they started to rebel and developed anorexia nervosa.

The Franciscan church appealed to most married penitents. It was St. Francis himself who displayed compassion for women developing a calm immunity to their sexuality. Most of the married penitents joined the church after the death of their husbands. A majority of them were more than 25 years old; a few may have already undergone menopause.

Bell [1985] stated that religious fasting women were seen as docile, uncomplaining, and servile; in the spiritual world their accomplishments were important in rescuing their souls and in paying debt for mortal sins. Religious fasting women suppressed their physical urges and basic feelings, therefore freeing their bodies to perform heroic feats and to commune with God. They believed themselves to be Christ's brides and his servants; they believed saintly austerities, starvation, and even death intensified the ultimate reward of uniting with God.

When comparisons are made between the holy anorexics and 20th century, modern-day anorexics, many similarities are found (Bell, 1985; Beumont, 1991; Brumberg, 1988; Bynum, 1987). Both carried the internal pseudodynamic theme of decreased sexuality. Both were trapped in their highly valued societal goals, such as thinness, self-control, and self-denial. They were also champions for perfection. Both had enhanced their confidence by achieving through starvation a newly won, but fragile, self-esteem. However, from this self-esteem, a sense of insecurity soon arose, provoking an even more relentless pursuit of starvation, the characteristic feature of which was often an obsessional march toward death.

For these women, the essential self-functioning capacity of will and autonomy was at stake. Suppression of hunger and restriction of food intake created the paradoxical facade of simultaneous iron will and dangerous vulnerability. Ultimately, the loss of conscious control of the body led to physical disregulation and damage, despite the appearance of prodigious activity.

However, what inspired the holy anorexics to undertake their fasting was different from that of 20th-century anorexics. The religious fasting women's behavior stemmed from a desire to unite with God. Their starvation was holy and altruistic; they strove for spiritual beauty and perfection in God's eyes (Bynum, 1987). In contrast, the actions of modern-day anorexics are secularized, representing a transformation of values from the fundamental sense of ascetic/spiritual toward a striving for physical, not spiritual, beauty (Bruch, 1977; Brumberg, 1988).

Fasting Girls (Miraculous Maids)

In the 1800s, the term *anorexia mirabilis* emerged to describe young women or girls in their teens who were apparently able to sustain life without food. The term *mirabilis* (miraculous) conveyed the uncertainty and bewilderment about the etiology and intention of the fasting. The issue of the fasting girls sparked a controversy between laws of science and traditional religion, with those from the church viewing the anorexic girls' behavior as a miracle-working process (Brumberg, 1988; van der Eycken & Lowenkopf, 1990; Habermas, 1991). (For further information on fasting girls, see Brumberg [1988], Fowler [1871], and van der Eycken and Lowenkopf [1990].)

Beard (1839–1889), a neurologist, stated that girls who boasted themselves as miraculous maids were fraudulent and ignorant. Beard noted that there were no men who claimed to be miraculous because the male body works in a more logical and rational manner; the male body functions according to the laws of metabolism, whereas the female body does not (Brumberg, 1988).

Clinical Description of Anorexia Nervosa

William Gull (1810–1880), a physician at Guy's Hospital in London and the appointed physician to the Queen, first used the clinical term *anorexia nervosa* in 1874 (Bruch, 1973; Garfinkel & Garner, 1982; Lucas, 1981; Strober, 1986; Tolstrup, 1990). This designation persisted even though true loss of appetite was not a feature of the illness. Gull believed the lack of appetite was nervous (nervosa) in origin; he noted that anorexia nervosa was "essentially a failure of the power of the gastric branches of the vagus nerve" (Brumberg, 1988, p. 121). Those who were afflicted by this disease were teenage or young women, mostly from rich families, and they all suffered from emotional distress. Earlier in 1868 Gull had used the term *hysteric apepsia* to describe the same clinical syndrome. However, Gull thought this term was not appropriate because hysteric was derived from the Greek word *hysteros,* meaning uterus, suggesting it was exclusively a female disease. Gull mentioned that "the subjects of this affliction are mostly of the female sex . . . but I have occasionally seen it in males at the same age" (Brumberg, 1988, p. 120). However, Gull never formally presented cases of male anorexia nervosa. Also, Gull noted that apepsia, meaning indigestion, was not appropriate because food that was eaten was also digested, except in the later stage of the disease.

Gull described anorexia nervosa as "a perversion of the ego" (Brumberg, 1988, p. 121). He did not believe it was an organic disease, and he called it "a morbid mental state" (p. 121). Gull diagnosed anorexia nervosa by noting the symptoms of amenorrhea, decreased body weight, decreased respiration rate, and increased motor activities. At the same time, he noted the absence of tuberculosis or other mesenteric diseases. The hyperactivity of the patient was characteristic of anorexia, especially in the early stage of the disease, he stated, "for it seemed hardly possible that a body so wasted could undergo the exercise which seemed agreeable" (p. 125). Gull used this hyperactivity to distinguish these patients from those suffering from tuberculosis.

Gull defined anorexia as an independent disease to be treated outside the mental asylum. He noted, "there is no greater amount of hysteria than in anorexia nervosa, but it could hardly be called insanity" (p. 125). In terms of treatment, Gull believed that moral control of the patient and a change in her family or domestic environment were crucial to a cure. He recommended force feeding, warm baths, electric shock, and sending the patient away from home because "relations and friends are generally the worst attendants" (p. 123). Gull did not prescribe any medication.

Three of Gull's cases were documented as Miss A, B, and C (Beumont, 1991; Brumberg, 1988). These cases were important because Gull took drawings of these girls before and after the treatment. Before the treatment, these girls, who ranged in age from 16 to 23, appeared gaunt and sullen. After the treatment, they seemed more pleasant with roundness of the face. In all three cases, Gull noted the minute amount of food taken by his patients, the occurrence of amenorrhea, and hyperactivity. None of the three girls were suffering from any organic disease. These girls recovered; however, in other instances, Gull claimed that "a fatal termination of the malady" (p. 119) was possible.

Charles Lasegue (1816–1883), a contemporary of Gull, studied anorexia nervosa and called it *anorexia hyserique* (Bruch, 1973; Brumberg, 1988; Garfinkel & Garner, 1982; Lucas, 1981; Russell, 1985; Strober, 1986; Tolstrup, 1990). Like Gull, Lasegue believed the disease was a disturbance of the central nervous system. In Lasegue's studies, he documented eight women, ranging in age from 18 to 32. Lasegue noted that anorexia was not the same as hysterical emaciation or acute depression. None of his patients fasted totally, but all had aversion to some types of food. He believed anorexia began with emotional trauma ". . . which she avows or conceals. Generally it relates to some real or imaginary marriage project, to a violence done to some sympathy, or to some more or less conscious desire" (p. 129). Like Gull, Lasegue believed that family played a large part in this disease, and he advocated separation in treating the patients; unlike Gull, Lasegue believed the disease did not terminate in death. Furthermore, Lasegue keenly recognized the patient's denial of physical debility and the significant psychodynamic stages of patient–family interaction.

In the first stage of the disease, girls expressed feelings of uneasiness after meals with "vague sensations of fullness" (Brumberg, p. 129). Their health remained satisfactory without emaciation, restriction, or diminishment in physical or social activities. Parents expressed concern and offered their child favorite foods, implying that eating in response to this expression of their affection would be proof of love for them. Stage 2 of the disease was characterized by the dominance of parents' attention to restricted eating aggravated by the patient's denial and indifference and the emergence of a phobic-inhibiting position with respect to food. At the same time, the patient's paradoxical presumed activity and compliance with other requests continued. Physical deterioration was the hallmark of stage 3 of anorexia. Lasegue noted emaciation, amenorrhea, constipation, and syncope. Separation from family became the imperative of treatment.

Louis-Victor Marce, a French psychiatrist, also studied anorexia nervosa in the second half of the 19th century (Beumont, 1991; Marce, 1860; Silverman, 1989). Marce gave accounts of young girls who had "delirious ideas of hypochondriacal nature" (Silverman, 1989, p. 834) and thought they could not or ought not to eat. In spite of physical debility, some willingly refused food and died of hunger. Marce called this refusal of food a "gastric nervous disorder" that affected the cerebral nerves. Marce noted that his patients concentrated obsessively on the function and the state of the stomach. However, in a post-mortem examination, the structural integrity of the stomach was perfectly healthy. Marce noted that "the stomach digests perfectly what is committed to it, but in the end it comes to content itself with the feeblest doses of nourishment, until one is surprised that life should survive so long with such slender means of reparation" (p. 833). In treating these girls, Marce advised doctors to pay attention to their psychological as well as physical well-being. Marce mentioned that one of his patients did show some insane patterns of behavior. He prescribed forced feeding, sending the girls away from home and "[entrusting] the patients to the care of strangers" (p. 834).

The French psychiatric pioneer, Pierre Janet, linked the loss of appetite to emerging adolescent sexuality (Beumont, 1991; Brumberg, 1988; Habermas, 1991). Janet called this disease "hysterical anorexy" and labeled it as "an outer expression of psychological disturbance and underlying emotional difficulty" (Brumberg, 1988, p. 214). Food refusal was a result of a delusion or mental disturbance that became an obsessive idea (idee fixe); the aim was to keep the body small and childlike and not grow up. The overwhelming demands of their appetite could lead not only to diminished attractiveness but also to an exposure of the patient to something immoral. Furthermore, in 1895, Janet and De La Tourette differentiated the term *anorexie mentale,* a form of hysteria with fixation on thinness, from the term *anorexie gastrigue,* a voluntary abstention from food because of an assumed stomach spasm. Of interest is the fact that modern research has verified delayed gastric emptying as a clinical consequence of anorexia nervosa accounting for bloating and discomfort, as well as possibly modifying appetite (McCallum, Grill,

Lange, Planky, Glass, & Greenfield, 1985; Russell, Freedman, Feiglin, Jeejeebhoy, Swinson, & Garfinkel, 1983).

Janet delineated three stages of the illness (over 18 months to 10 years), ranging from abdominal complaints to conflicts with family over eating behavior and finally to a driven hyperactivity, false euphoria, and morbid deterioration.

No study of anorexia nervosa could be complete without mentioning the green sickness or chlorosis (Parry-Jones, 1985; Russell, 1985; Sibley & Blinder, 1988). Chlorosis puzzled physicians for centuries, and many wondered if it was a manifestation of anorexia nervosa. In the 1500s, Johannes Lange called it "morbis virgineus" or "maiden's sickness," and its main features included paleness, avoidance of food, and amenorrhea. Physicians attributed chlorosis to unrequited love, uteral dysfunction, or hypochromic anemia. Particularly in 18th-century and 19th-century England, chlorosis was so common that it was considered an epidemic. However, by the early 20th century, medical reports of chlorosis virtually disappeared. Anorexia nervosa and chlorosis shared many clinical features, notably amenorrhea. Both affected adolescent girls around puberty; many suspected that earlier cases of anorexia might be mislabeled as chlorosis. Loudon (1980) said that anorexia nervosa and chlorosis were analogous and were on the "same psychopathological continuum" (Beumont, 1991, p. 15). However, two clinical characteristics of chlorosis not initially apparent in anorexia nervosa were the green-yellowish tinge of the skin and hypochromic anemia.

In 1859 in the American Journal of Insanity, William Chipley published an article on sitomania (Brumberg, 1988; Kelly, 1912; van der Eycken & Lowenkopf, 1990). Sitomania, he wrote, was a phase of insanity caused by either mental or digestive derangement. Sitomanics did not eat because of their fear of poison in food or their belief in the divine command and other supernatural direction telling them not to eat. These patients may have suffered from schizophrenic or other delusional disorders that modified appetite or distorted cognition sufficiently to cause malnutrition (Blinder, 1991).

When parents brought their emaciated daughters to Chipley, he concluded they were not crazy as were other food refusers labeled sitomanics. These girls were not delusional, heard no voices, and did not act indecently. They claimed they "had no appetite . . . and eating distressed" them (Brumberg, 1988, p. 107). Chipley concluded these patients were capable of living "on the outside," and therefore were "not asylum clientele" (p. 109). Furthermore, according to Chipley, these girls were from a higher walk of society and had very protective parents; they resorted to food refusal to extract sympathy and to exert power within their families and friends. Chipley documented one case of an "amiable" and "delicate" young woman, who was "not slow in perceiving that wonder and amazement grew inversely to the amount of food taken" (p. 108). Chipley called these girls manipulative; he believed they used food refusal to satisfy vanity. In treating these girls, Chipley recommended private "nervous homes," therapeutic spas, and recuperative travel to serene environments.

William Smoult Playfair (1836–1903) disagreed with others and called anorexia a variant of *neurasthenia*. Neurasthenia was a form of nervous exhaustion or deficiency of nervous energy with symptoms such as headache and insomnia (Casper, 1983; Playfair, 1888; Stainbrook, 1952). Playfair noted that anorexia was a juvenile form of neurasthenia, precipitated by stressful life events such as loss of love, loss of money, or domestic bereavement. According to Playfair, the increase in the number of young women refusing food resulted from the fact that for the first time they were allowed too much civilization such as higher education. He proposed no easy cure for this disease.

Confusion with Pituitary Insufficiency   In 1914 and 1916, Morris Simmonds, a pathologist at the University of Hamberg, published two papers that described a form of emaciation or pituitary cachexia due to destruction of the anterior lobe of the pituitary (Beumont, 1991; Bruch, 1973; Garfinkel & Garner, 1982; Lucas, 1981; Sibley & Blinder, 1988). Simmonds' (1914, 1916) discovery resulted from the autopsy of a severely emaciated woman who died after progressive signs of pituitary failure. Simmonds sparked new interests in the study of the endocrine system to provide a new explanation of anorexia nervosa. For the next 20 years, little attention was paid to Gull or Lasegue or alternative theories of anorexia; concentration on the endocrinologic causality of the illness narrowed. Simmonds' treatment plan of injecting pituitary extract into anorexia patients was widely practiced. Although the approach had much appeal, it led to misdiagnosis of many individuals who were malnourished from starvation, not from pituitary insufficiencies. In 1942, Berkman conducted extensive research to find that only 101 out of Simmonds' original 595 patients had true pituitary lesions (Berkman, Weir, & Kepler, 1947; Beumont, 1991; Brumberg, 1988; Yates, 1989).

Rediscovery of Anorexia Nervosa As a Disease Entity and Clinical Entity
Sheehan and Summers' studies in 1948 showed that anorexia nervosa patients had decreased basal metabolic rate and amenorrhea (Yates, 1989). They concluded that these were the only two symptoms anorexia nervosa and Simmonds' disease had in common. A true anorexic had extreme loss of weight, increase in activity, hirsutism, and a relentless desire to be thin. However, only one fourth of Simmonds' patients lost extreme amounts of weight. Berkman also documented 117 patients who had a reversible insufficiency of anterior pituitary function as a consequence rather than a cause of their starvation. He also found that anorexia nervosa affected both men and women, old and young. Berkman's research concentrated on the relationship between thyroid and body weight. Along with colleagues from the Mayo Clinic, he treated anorexia nervosa as if it were a general metabolic disorder; he also acknowledged the role of "psychic disturbance" or the "nervous cause" in anorexia nervosa. In 1936 and 1939, Ryle published two papers refuting the theory that anorexia nervosa was merely a form of Simmonds' disease: "I believe, however . . . that the origins of the disease are,

as Gull maintained, to be sought in a disturbance of the mind and a prolonged insufficiency of food and nothing more" (Brumberg, 1988, p. 212).

Psychoanalytic Era

Between 1895 and 1905, Freud and Janet linked the anorexic's aversion to food to conflicts in psychosexual development (Brumberg, 1988; Mount Sinai Seminar Group, 1964; Schwartz, 1990; Wilson, Hogan, & Mintz, 1992; Wilson, Hogan, & Mintz, 1985). These girls refused to eat to force their bodies to stay thin and childlike, thereby retarding normal sexual development and delaying their transformation to sexual adults. Freud and Janet concluded that anorexic girls feared adult womanhood and heterosexuality. In *Fasting Girls* (1988), Brumberg stated that "clinicians confirm the direction of the Freudian interpretation: anorectics generally are not sexually active adolescents" (Brumberg, 1988, p. 28). In addition to the psychosexual theory of anorexia, Freud also concluded that patients did not eat because of early memories of disgust toward food, and that some patients during childhood were forced to eat under threat of punishment. He saw anorexics using food as a contest of wills and self-mastery. Freud wrote:

> "The neurosis concerned with eating disorders parallel to melancholia is anorexia nervosa. The famous anorexia nervosa of young girls seems to me (on careful observation) to be a melancholia where sexuality is undeveloped. The patient asserts she has not eaten simply because she had no appetite and for no other reason. Loss of appetite—in sexual terms—is loss of libido" (Masson, 1985).

In 1940, Waller, Kaufman, and Deutsch proposed that symptoms of anorexia nervosa were based on unconscious fantasies. From detailed psychoanalytic data emerging in treatment, they concluded that female patients who rejected food were unconsciously rejecting a wish for oral impregnation by their fathers. The psychoanalytic era sparked the psychosomatic movement, which attempted to bridge the gap between the mind and the body. This movement showed that both current emotional stress and developmental, psychological conflicts could trigger physical changes.

Psychosocial Era

Hilde Bruch pioneered the psychosocial era in 1962 with her published description of three perceptual and conceptual disturbances in anorexia nervosa: disturbance of body image, in which the anorexic girl overestimated her body size; interoceptive disturbance, in which the patient was not able to interpret hunger and satiation signals; and a disorder of personal control, in which the anorexic girl had an overwhelming sense of ineffectiveness. Furthermore, Bruch emphasized the anorexic's relentless pursuit of thinness. The sense of ineffectiveness was central to the psychopathology of the illness, and the anorexic acted in response to external demands (Shapiro, Blinder, Hagman, & Pituck, 1993).

Bruch (1962) viewed societal changes and pressures as a determinant of anorexia nervosa. For example, females of the 20th century had many more educational, occupational, and sexual options available to them. Bruch profiled the clinical presentation of a female anorexic personality type appearing in increasing numbers after the 1940s. The patient demonstrated a pseudomaturity with driven academic overachievement and social compliance that compensated for an underlying sense of inadequacy, low self-esteem, and rejection sensitivity. The clinical features of anorexia nervosa then represented a misguided thrust for individuality and exercise of will that finally unmasked the true deficit in self-regulation (Gordon, 1988; Wilson, Hogan, & Mintz, 1992; Wilson, Hogan, & Mintz, 1985).

In 1978, Salvador Minuchin and colleagues published studies on the family structure of an anorexia nervosa patient. The first characteristic of the family was enmeshment; each member of the family was overly involved with the others' feelings and thoughts. Parents advocated family loyalty; they did not allow children to develop individuality and independence. Second, parents of the anorexic were overprotective. Gradually, parental control became the norm of the family. Next, the anorexic family avoided conflicts; the members of the family did not confront issues, and they denied there were any problems. Parents exercised total autonomy to maintain the apparent harmony and normality of the household. The anorexic girl who grew up in such a family had been held back from adulthood and its responsibilities; she was told to conform to all rules. Eventually, the girl developed anorexia nervosa because she strove for identity and autonomy. Minuchin attributed a similar pattern of family interactional conflicts to several psychosomatic disorders of childhood and adolescence (Minuchin, Rosman, & Baker, 1978).

Biopsychosocial Era

In 1981, Lucas proposed the biopsychosocial model to describe the multifactorial influences in patients with anorexia nervosa. Societal influences and expectations along with family developmental experiences coalescing in genetically vulnerable young women produced a perpetuated cycle of dieting, weight loss, malnutrition, and psychobiologic impairment. Facing increasing competition, the overachieving, perfectionistic young woman turned inward to a magnified and perverse sense of autonomy that led to self-injurious behavior.

In saying that "no woman can ever be too thin or too rich" (Casper, 1983, p. 3) the Duchess of Windsor echoed the sentiment of a society whose ideal female body image was shifting toward thinner and smaller sizes. Garner and Garfinkel's research on the women in Playboy centerfolds and contestants for the Miss America title demonstrated that weight decreased steadily from 1959 to 1979. Furthermore, successive title winners of the Miss America contest weighed less than their competitors (Garfinkel & Garner, 1982). At the same time mean weight of American women under 30 years of age was increasing, the weight of the idealized models was decreasing at the same rate. Thus, tension was created. At this point, at least 60% of high school senior girls and 80% of college girls were dieting (Gordon, 1988; Hawkins & Clement, 1980; Heunemann, Shapiro, Hampton, & Mitchell, 1966).

Neurobiologic Research

With the advent of modern technology, scientists could readily examine the relationship between anorexia nervosa and brain function. Anorexia nervosa had long been associated with hormonal and neuroendocrine mechanisms, especially with the hypothalamic-pituitary axis (Blinder, 1980; Walsh, 1980; Weiner & Katz, 1983); the etiology of anorexia nervosa was partially attributed to hypothalamic immaturity. Disturbances were generally reversible, and certain ones related directly to degree of weight loss, such as thyroid stimulating hormone (TSH) response to thyrotropin-releasing hormone (TRH), resting gonadotropin levels, and luteinizing hormone (LH) responses to provocative tests (Beumont, Burrow, & Caspar, 1987; Blinder, Chaitin, & Goldstein, 1988; Gwirtzman, Holstein, & Boy-Byrne, 1988; Walsh, 1980). Other hypothalamic dysfunctions were secondary to caloric deprivation. Some of these were changes in the resting plasma growth hormone (GH), triiodothyronine (T_3), and rT_3. Other physiologic alterations appeared related to the psychological stress and affective arousal to which the patients were subjected, for example, the amenorrhea that can precede weight loss or persist after weight restoration (Blinder, 1980).

Other researchers used brain imaging techniques to visualize the role of neuroanatomical structure and brain metabolism in eating disorders. Studies (Hagman, Buchsbaum, Wu, Rao, Reynolds, & Blinder, 1990; Kaye & Gwirtsman, 1985; Morley, Levine, & Krahn, 1988) of patients with anorexia and bulimia showed they had decreased levels of cerebrospinal fluid (CSF) norepinephrine, and that serotonin and corticotropin-releasing factor (CRF) played a significant role in eating disorder pathology. Other findings (Andreason, Altemus, Zametkin, King, Lucinio, & Cohen, 1992; Wu, Hagman, Buchsbaum, Blinder, Derfler, Tai, Hazlett, & Sicotte, 1990) concluded that bulimic patients have an asymmetric metabolic rate in the temporal lobe (left hemisphere greater than the right) and that this specific hypermetabolism is independent of the mood state. Furthermore, hypermetabolism in the orbitofrontal lobes in obsessive compulsive disorder (OCD) patients and hypometabolism in the left anterolateral prefrontal cortex in depression have been reported by different groups (Andreason, et al., 1992; Baxter, Schwartz, Phelps, Mazziotta, Mazziotta, & Guze, 1987; Baxter, Phelps, Mazziotta, Guze, Schwartz, & Selin, 1983; Nordahl, Benkelfat, Semple, Gross, King, & Cohen, 1989). Patients with anorexia nervosa were found by positron emission tomography (PET) scan to have relative hypermetabolism of the caudate nucleus and quantitative hypometabolism of other brain structures (Krieg, Pirke, Lauer, & Backmund, 1988). Computed tomography (CT) and magnetic resonance imaging (MRI) studies showed anorexia and bulimia patients had ventricular enlargement and sulcal atrophy related to emaciation, with a reasonably good chance of reversal following weight gain (Hagman, 1992).

Throughout history, anorexia nervosa has gradually evolved to be a specific disease entity. Numerous etiologies and manifestations have been associated with this eating disorder. Anorexia nervosa appeared in a religious context, where it became an act of faith in the life of Catherine of Siena. Subsequently, the existence of this illness reinforced superstition and belief in miracles. Finally, the contemporary clinical core of anorexia nervosa became secularized in its surface connections to the satisfaction of vanity and the ultimate pursuit of thinness as a gender-related issue. The biopsychosocial model identifies multiple determinants in the causation and consequences of the eating disorders. Advances in the understanding of the neurobiology of appetite and eating, comorbidity with other psychiatric disorders, principles of nutritional rehabilitation, and the complexity of developmental psychopathology and the family system have all led to improved diagnosis and more effective treatment (Andersen, 1985; APA Practice Guidelines for Eating Disorders, 1993; Beumont et al., 1987; Blinder, Chaitin, & Goldstein, 1988; Casper & Offer, 1990; Fluoxetine Bulimia Nervosa Collaborative Study Group, 1992; Hollander, 1993; Minuchin, Rosman, & Baker, 1978; van der Eycken, Kog, & van der Linden, 1989; Walsh, Stewart, Roose, Gladis, & Glassman, 1984; Wilson et al., 1985; Yates, 1989; Blinder, 1991; Yager, 1991).

BULIMIA NERVOSA

Bulimia, derived from the Greek, means ravenous hunger; it most commonly affects teenage or young women. The patient practices binge eating that consists of uncontrollable, recurrent overeating, most often outside of normal meal time in a driven pre-preemptory pattern-disrupting routine daily activity. The compensatory behavior that occurs subsequent to binge eating can include purging (mechanical or chemical self-induced vomiting, ruminatory regurgitation, and laxative and diuretic abuse) and nonpurging (prolonged abstinence from food, extreme vigorous exercise, and the use or abuse of anorexic medication) techniques. The patient's weight fluctuates, and unlike an anorexic, a bulimic may not necessarily be underweight. Studies show 70% of bulimics are within the normal weight range, while 15% are overweight and 15% are underweight (De Zwaan & Mitchell, 1991).

Historical Accounts of Bulimia Nervosa

Bulimia nervosa is not a new disorder (Russell, 1979). Scattered historical references suggest bulimia, and detailed case histories have been written over the last 60 years (Blinder & Cadenhead, 1986; Casper, 1983; Ziolko & Shrader, 1985).

Entries compatible with bulimia nervosa can be seen in the Latin writings of Aulus Gellius and Sextus Pompeius Festus, grammarians of the 2nd and 4th centuries A.D., respectively, and with the description of canine hunger in the works of Theodorus Priscianus, a 5th-century physician (Smith, 1866; Lewis & Short, 1900). Romans were known to tickle their throats with feathers after each meal to induce vomiting, thus allowing them to return to gluttonous feasting (Fischer, 1976). The Romans did so to enhance the enjoyment of a wider selection of palatable foods. (In contrast, bulimic patients have a narrow, stereotyped food selection, usually carbohydrates, with repetitive eating of the same item.) Galen, a 2nd-century Greek physician, noted that an abnormal acid humor in the stomach was the cause of "bulimis," which resulted in an exaggerated, but false, signal of hunger (Siegel, 1973; Stein & Laakso, 1988). Powdermaker (1973) noted gluttony was an acceptable behavior for primitive cultures. After months of enduring hunger, then hunting for food and finally preparing the feast, one Trobriand Islander declared: "We shall be glad, we shall eat until we vomit" (Boskind-White & White, 1986). In the Talmud (400 to 500 A.D.), the term *boolmut* was used to describe an overwhelming hunger that impaired a person's judgment about food and about external events (Blinder & Cadenhead, 1986; Kaplan & Garfinkel, 1984; van der Eycken, 1985).

However, the earliest English language example of bulimia nervosa occurred in 1398 in the English translation of Bartholomeus by John Trevisa in Glanville's encyclopedic 13th-century work, De Proprietativus Rerum (Parry-Jones, 1991). James (1743) described "true boulimus," which was characterized by intense preoccupation with food and overeating at very short intervals, terminated by vomiting (Stein & Laakso, 1988). Motherby (1785) studied three types of bulimia nervosa: bulimia of pure hunger, bulimia associated with swooning, and bulimia terminated by vomiting (Stunkard, 1990). Furthermore, bulimia nervosa was recognized in the 1797 edition of the Encyclopedia Britannica (Stunkard, 1990).

Case Histories of Bulimia Before 1900

In the 18th and 19th centuries, binge eating and vomiting was considered worthy of medical attention only if the overeating could be seen as a symptom of another disease. Gull (1873) noted one anorexic patient: "occasionally for a day or two, her appetite was voracious, but this was rare and exceptional." He also saw another anorexic patient who, in order to induce vomiting, would think of "putrid cat pudding" (Blinder & Cadenhead, 1986, p. 232).

Lesegue (1873) noted that many anorexics reactively vomited after they had been forced to eat. Janet (1929) commented that Lasegue's second phase of illness occurred when the patient learned to vomit what she swallowed. Briquet (1859) studied a woman who for months ate normally, but then went into a phase of vomiting everything she ate (Habermas, 1989). Casper, Eckert, Halmi, Goldberg,

& Davis (1980) and Garfinkel and Garner (1982) noted a significant occurrence of bulimic behaviors and symptoms in approximately 40% of anorexia nervosa patients.

During this period, different terms were coined to describe the overwhelming urge to overeat and vomit (Habermas, 1989). However, none of them associated bingeing and purging with weight control (Ziolko & Schrader, 1985). Blanchez (1869) used the term *cynorexia* to mean a cycle of overeating and vomiting. The cynorexic was literally possessed by the thought of food and insatiable hunger. Stiller (1884) described *hyperorexia* as a constant eating of small amounts of food in order to counteract feelings of faintness. Soltmann (1894) documented a 17-year-old boy who ate massive amounts of food when he returned home from school and was outraged when kept from eating. Soltmann called the symptom *polyphagia,* in which there was an absence of a feeling of fullness, leading to a rather constant devouring of huge amounts of food. Speculatively, this might have been a variant Klein-Levin syndrome (Orlowsky, 1982; Sugar, Khandelwal, and Gupta, 1990).

Secret Eating and Food Stealing

Bingeing in secret and stealing food have been patterns seen frequently in bulimics (De Zwaan & Mitchell, 1991; Habermas, 1989). Janet (1908) noted his patient Nadia "from time to time forgets herself to the point of devouring gluttonously anything she can get hold of. At other times, she cannot resist the urge to eat something; she then secretly eats biscuits" (Stunkard, 1990, p. 264). Wulff's (1932) Patient A claimed she secretly binged on foods such as sweets, pastries, and bread that were restricted because of her obesity (Stunkard, 1990). She categorized foods by saying, "This is good; the worst, the better" (Habermas, 1989, p. 347). Bergmann (1934) documented a young thin woman who hoarded food from the pantry at night. Stunkard Grace and Wolff (1955) coined the term *night feeders* to describe obese patients who consumed large amounts of food during the night. Other authors noted secret eating and stealing food often associated with binge eating and suggested such activities fell in the same category as binge eating (Casper, Ecker, Halmi, Goldberg, & Davis, 1980; Densmore-John, 1988). Secret eating, usually planned in advance and carried out late in the day, was all part of the isolating nature of bulimia nervosa. From a developmental and psychodynamic perspective, secret eating and stealing food were suspected to express impulsiveness, ambivalence, or rebelliousness (De Zwann & Mitchell, 1991; Habermas, 1989; Schwartz, 1990; Wilson, Hogan, & Mintz, 1992).

1900–1950

During the first half of the 20th century, many of the studies on eating disorders were overshadowed by Simmonds' observation of pituitary insufficiency. Nevertheless, Wulff (1932) described four cases of eating disorders in women characterized by uncontrollable and recurrent overeating, prolonged fasting, hypersomnia, depressed mood, and irritability (Blinder & Cadenhead, 1986; Habermas, 1989; Stunkard, 1990). All four went through the phase of binge eating, and two of the four vomited. Patient B described the binge episodes as "circumstances of animal eating" in that she devoured everything in sight, including orange peels and scraps of paper. Usually the patients binged on snacks or dessert foods, which were avoided at other times because they were fattening and calorie-rich. This phase alternated with the phase of prolonged fasting. Patient D often went through three to six day-long fasts that could extend to complete abstinence from food for the entire day. Patient C noted her motivation to fast was to lose weight. During fasting, these patients selected a constricted cuisine of fruits, vegetables, and milk. The fasting phase often ended with the onset of yet another phase of prolonged binge eating episodes; such cycles brought these women a strong sense of disgust with their own bodies and broken promises to never do it again.

Wulff (1933) characterized binge eating as an "oral symptom-complex" in which the patient regressed to obtain a "pure oral erotic satisfaction . . . almost a sexual perversion" (Stunkard, 1990, p. 267). He placed bulimia between melancholia and addiction. From a psychoanalytic perspective, what bulimia had in common with the above mental states was that they all encompass a sense of loss or detachment leading to an "insult to narcissism," the reaction to which culminated in binge eating (Blinder & Cadenhead, 1986; Habermas, 1989; Stunkard, 1990).

Binswanger (1944) described the case of Ellen West, a partially remitted anorexic who began to struggle with bulimia. Her symptoms included binge eating, violent vomiting, and laxative abuse. West's diary detailed her struggle for control over her emotions and her body weight (Beumont, 1991; Blinder & Cadenhead, 1986; Britt & Bloom, 1982; Casper, 1983; Stunkard, 1990).

Selling and Ferraro (1945) observed bulimia in refugee children between 1933 and 1939. Many of these children came to the United States from Europe without their parents, and they fed themselves frantically and excessively when they felt insecure. However, when these children found new homes, they reduced their food intake (Casper, 1983). Waller, Kaufman, and Deutsch (1940) described two women who overate on candies and then starved themselves in a defensive reaction to an incestuous pregnancy fantasy involving their fathers. Berkman (1930) reported that out of 177 anorexia patients, 66% vomited. Most said they did so to relieve the sensation of fullness. Schottky (1932) noted a female patient who used a hose to empty out what she ate and induce vomiting (Habermas, 1989). Nogue (1913) researched the prescriptive use of laxatives or thyroid for the purpose of weight control. This brought about changes in the kind of laxatives used to lose weight; earlier, anorexics used vinegar to control weight (Gungl & Stichl, 1892; Janet, 1908; Wallet, 1892).

Bulimia Nervosa and Anorexia Nervosa

Many authors have described bulimia nervosa in nonanorexic patients. Some characterized it as a rare neurotic condition. Janet (1908) studied a 26-year-old male who was "withdrawn with a bizarre character." This man's self-induced vomiting, as Janet noted, was a form of tic and not a part of anorexia (Habermas, 1989). Abraham (1916) described a patient who, instead of vomiting, binged only on vegetables during bulimic attacks to counteract the weight gain. Abraham called it a "neurotic hunger" in which the feeding and satiety signals originate from anxiety and internal psychological conflict, not the emptiness or fullness of the stomach (Blinder, 1980; Blinder & Cadenhead, 1986; Habermas, 1989). Abraham associated the bulimic condition with repression of libido and likened it to an addiction (dipsomania, alcoholism, or morphinism) (Blinder, 1980). Wulff (1932) characterized the somnolence that followed the binges as a kind of "sleep drunkenness" completing the bulimic cycle during which patients sought and fulfilled "oral erotic stimulation" (Stunkard, 1990, p. 267). Lindner (1955) noted the case of Laura who binged but did not vomit. Laura's father abandoned her and her family when she was young; Lindner suggested Laura's distended stomach represented her secret wish to be impregnated by her father (Blinder & Cadenhead, 1986). Kirshbaum (1951) used the term *hyperorexia* as a manifestation signifying hypothalamic insufficiencies.

The modern history of bulimia first appeared in connection with patients who also suffered from anorexia. Nemiah (1950) reported the case histories of 14 anorexia nervosa patients with this condition (Stunkard, 1990). Four of 14 patients were suspected of bulimia due to their abnormal eating pattern and vomiting. Many authors were aware of overeating, laxative abuse, and self-induced vomiting in anorexics, but considered bulimia nervosa to be a variant of anorexia nervosa rather than a distinct syndrome (Bond, 1949; Bruch, 1962; Nemiah, 1950). Abraham and Beumont (1982) viewed bulimia nervosa and anorexia nervosa as extremes of the same disorder; whereas Russell (1979) described bulimia nervosa as an indicator of chronicity of anorexia nervosa. In separate studies done by Casper et al. (1980) and Garfinkel, Moldofsky, and Garner (1980), about half of patients with anorexia demonstrated bulimic behavior; in Mitchell et al.'s study (1985), 30% to 80% of patients with bulimia had a history of anorexia. Blinder, Chaitin, and Hagman (1987) reported an increased history of anorexia nervosa preceding bulimia and more extensive current eating disorder symptoms in those bulimic patients who had comorbidity for depression. Katz and Sitnick (1982) considered bulimia nervosa as a manifestation of the constant core syndrome of eating disorder. Comparing bulimia and anorexia, a bulimic patient may not necessarily be underweight; about 15% of the time, she is overweight. Unlike anorexics, a bulimic patient may or may not have amenorrhea (although oligomenorrhea, anovulatory cycles, and occasional missed periods are common). A bulimic patient possesses a greater premorbid weight, more affective instability, and greater interpersonal sensitivity. She is more extroverted and is more likely to have a personality disorder diagnosis (Casper et al., 1980; Garfinkel et al., 1980; Russell, 1979; Strober, 1980, 1981).

After 1950

Some cases of bulimia nervosa before the 1940s mentioned the patient's concern with body shape and body weight. Janet (1908) noted one of Charcot's cases of a young girl who wore a rose-colored ribbon around her waist to ensure that her waist size never exceeded what she thought and measured it to be (Brumberg, 1988). However, not until after the 1940s did the overconcern of patients with body shape and self-image become a usual and constant feature (Casper, 1983). The desire for and pursuit of thinness theme started appearing more frequently in the literature, culminating in the 1970s with what Bruch called "the pursuit of thinness," and what Selvini-Palazzoli termed "the desperate need to grow thinner" (Casper, 1983, p. 10). The idea of thinness was becoming a virtue, and it was a symbol of independence, autonomy, self-control, and a moral grace. A combination of cultural, economic, and psychological factors may have contributed to the vast and rapid emergence of bulimia nervosa (Gordon, 1992). Following the years of the Great Depression, prosperity and increase in the availability of foods led more girls to worry about overeating and being overweight (Casper, 1983). Fat was deemed disgraceful and indicative of a lack of self-control. Waller et al. (1940) saw patients who were "ashamed of being fat" (Lucas, 1981, p. 3). Casper, Offer, & Ostrov (1981) noted this dread of fatness came from a critical self-image, which drove the patient to develop bulimia and to "escape into a controlled, desirable, however, distorted and isolated thin existence." (p. 656). Bruch (1973) saw this development as a compensatory mode of action covering feelings of pervasive inadequacy.

Bulimia Nervosa as a Distinct Syndrome

Toward the end of the 1970s, more focus was given the occurrence of gorging in patients of normal weight. Bruch (1957) described a case of a patient who binged and vomited, but he was neither obese nor emaciated (anorexia). Because these patients did not have an obvious weight disturbance, it seemed necessary to define a new syndrome to encompass their disorder. Boskind-Lodahl (1976) used the term *bulimarexia* to describe an eating disorder, usually in young women at a normal weight, in which the patient alternated between bingeing and strict fasting. Bulimarexics had low self-esteem, poor body image, and a fear of not being successful in heterosexual relationships. Boskind-Lodahl and White (1978) noted "the importance of sociocultural factors in female role definition and the view of bulimarexia as related to the struggle to achieve a 'perfect' female image in which women surrendered their self-defining powers to others" (p. 84).

With some initial caution, the concept of a distinct syndrome of bulimia nervosa came to be accepted. Russell (1979) designated the term *bulimia nervosa* to describe a subgroup of patients who, in contrast to eating restrictors, were found to have an older age of onset, a more chronic outcome, and a higher incidence of premorbid and family obesity (Beumont, George, & Smart, 1976; Casper, Eckert, Halmi, Goldberg, & Davis, 1980; Garfinkel, Moldofsky, & Garner, 1980; Strober, 1981; Strober, Salkin, Burroughs, & Morrel, 1982). These patients manifested greater anxiety and depression, reported a higher incidence of impulsive behavior (substance abuse and kleptomania), demonstrated more evidence of premorbid emotional instability, showed a greater body image dissatisfaction, and revealed more extensive family conflict (Casper, et al., 1980; Garfinkel, et al., 1980; Katzman & Wolchik, 1984; Strober, 1980). According to DSM-IV (American Psychiatric Association, 1993) the essential features of bulimia nervosa are recurrent and uncontrollable episodes of binge eating; self-induced vomiting; the use of laxatives or diuretics, strict dieting, fasting, or vigorous exercise to prevent weight gain; and persistent overconcern with body shape and weight. Self-evaluation is unduly influenced by body shape and weight and the disturbance does not occur exclusively during episodes of anorexia nervosa. The binge eating and inappropriate compensatory behaviors both occur, on the average, at least twice a week for 3 months. Bingeing usually precedes vomiting by about 1 year. Bulimia is usually diagnosed in teenage or young women, with the age of onset between 16 and 19; less than 10% of patients are men (De Zwaan & Mitchell, 1991). In surveys of college and high school populations (Halmi, Falk, & Schwartz, 1981; Hawkins & Clement, 1980; Johnson, Lewis, Love, Lewis, & Stuckey, 1984; Nagelberg, Hale, & Ware, 1984; Pyle, Mitchell, & Eckert, 1981; Russell, 1979), a range of 4.1% to 13% of college and high school students met the criteria for bulimia. In 1991, Kendler, MacLean, Neale, Kessler, Heath, and Eaves reported a 4% lifetime incidence of bulimia nervosa in all women. This disorder is not easily cured. Of the 45 patients with eating disorders reported by Bruch in 1973, 25% suffered from bulimic attacks; 12 years later, the number went up to 50% (Bruch, 1985).

OBESITY

Obesity is a condition characterized by the excessive accumulation of fat (when the body weight exceeds by 20% the standard weight listed in the usual height-weight tables) (Kaplan & Sadock, 1991). Step variations in the magnitude of excessive weight have been delineated according to increases in total body mass index (weight in kg/[height in m]^2). The latter statistic may be placed on a continuum so that a result over 25 (25 to 45) may signify the degree of obesity from moderate to morbid and reflect the level of accelerated mortality risk as a consequence of the morbidity of anticipated medical complications (hypertension, cardiac and circulatory disease, diabetes, orthopedic disorders). Fundamentally, obesity is a result of overnutrition.

Obesity existed in most primitive and ancient societies. Portrayals of human forms during the Aurignacian era, which dated some 20,000 years ago, showed rather plump and obese women. Some supposed fat was admired during this period; obesity in a woman was looked upon as a sign of enhanced fertility, capacity to bear children, and ability to endure the extremes of weather conditions (Beumont, 1991; Bruch, 1973).

Attitudes toward obesity showed concern beginning in the classical times when it became recognized as a functional and health problem. Aristophanes, a 5th-century B.C. Greek comedy writer, described in his work *Plutus* that obese men were "bloated, gross, and pre-senile . . . they are fat rogues with big bellies and dropsical legs, whose toes by the gout are tormented." The Greek goddesses such as Venus and Diana were plump and matronly with round bodices. They glorified and portrayed the mother earth image (Boskind-White & White, 1986). However, in their own daughters and wives, the Greeks emphasized slimness and beauty in order to look seductive in revealing clothes. The Greek physician Dioscorides described radish, caper, and vinegar as substances that disturbed the bowel system (Wellmann, 1914). These were prescribed as diuretics and emetics. Hippocrates described obesity in detail and advocated exercise and punitive measures such as sleeping on hard beds for losing weight. The Cretans also had drugs that allowed one to drink and eat as much as one wished and remain slender. In Sparta, people were customarily trained to survive in its military society. A Spartan writer, Xenophane, described diets as being sparse, strict at best, so its people could survive war times and could enjoy better health. Obese people were punished for their adiposity; youths were examined in the nude for excess weight gain, and those who gained weight were subjected to compulsory diets and scourging. The Romans frowned on obesity, and they were accredited for inventing the vomitorium, which allowed them to binge and to relieve themselves of the feeling of fullness. To preserve their youthful figures, Roman wives and daughters often starved themselves to the point of death. Galen prescribed diuretics to "make them thin as reeds" (Boskind-White & White, 1986, p. 353). Egyptian men also chose wives who were young and slender.

In some religious circles, gluttony was considered a sin. For example, in the painting "The Last Judgment," the sinners were fat, but the disciples were slender. Bible verses also discredited gluttony. Examples include the following: "For the drunkard and the glutton will come to poverty" (Proverbs 23:21); "He is a glutton and a drunkard, then all the men stoned him to purge evil from their midst" (Deuteronomy 21:20); "Behold a glutton and a drunkard—a friend of tax collectors and sinners" (Matthew 11:19). However, in an overtly ambivalent perspective, obesity was also viewed as the "grace of God." In works throughout the Renaissance, scenes of merry feastings were depicted with great joy and vitality. Botticelli's Venus and Da Vinci's works portrayed women who had round bodices and full figures (Bruch, 1973).

In other non-Western cultures, obesity was looked on as a favored trait. For some Polynesian people, it was a privilege to be so well fed and pampered that one could be at such leisure to get fat. Some Malayan kings were noted to be very large, and they were specially cared for with massages and exercises to preserve their good health (Bruch, 1973). The girls of Banyankole of East Africa underwent regimens to gain weight in preparation for marriage. It was a compliment to the men who married plump women; it showed the men off as good providers (Boskind-White and White, 1986).

Throughout the Victorian Age, obesity was associated with lower class status and poverty. Dress designs of the period stressed full breasts and tiny waistlines (for instance, the Gibson girl image of 19th-century America). Women stayed away from food in order to be slim and to create the hourglass shape. In 1864, Ebstein distinguished three types of obesity: stout, comical, and severe (Beumont, 1991). Some poor immigrant mothers during the 1930s who suffered from hunger in their childhood and youth did not see obesity in their children as a social or medical negative. To them, plumpness meant security and success. Slenderness was at its peak during the 1960s with the arrival of Twiggy (5'7", 92 pounds). Severe abstinence from food and various forms of weight control were used to achieve a type of malnourished figure that was heralded as the standard of beauty. It was of no surprise that during this time there was both an increase in medical and psychiatric recognition of eating disorders and more women diagnosed as anorexic or bulimic.

Cross-cultural studies of Caucasians' and minorities' views on body type showed that blacks and other minorities do not prefer the ultrathin body type (Huenemann et al., 1966; Levinson, Powell, & Steelman, 1986; Maddox, Black, & Liederman, 1968; Stern, Pugh, & Gaskill, 1982). Studies showed that black girls and their families were not as obsessed with being thin or losing weight (Dornbusch, Smith, & Duncan, 1984; Sobal & Stunkard, 1989; Striegel-Moore, Silberstein, & Rodin, 1986; Wadden, Foster, & Stunkard, 1989; Wadden, Stunkard, Rich, et al., 1990). The latter attitudes contributed to a twofold increased prevalence of obesity in blacks compared to Caucasian women (Van Itallie, 1985). In addition to attitudinal and social value determinants, differences in informed nutrition practices, opportunities for regular exercise, and poverty-determined adverse health practices contribute to the difference between blacks and whites. Kumanyika (1993) gave special attention to obesity as it occurs in and affects ethnic minorities (that is, black Americans, Hispanic Americans, Asian and Pacific Islander Americans, American Indians and Alaska Natives, and Native Hawaiians) in the United States. In most of these groups, the prevalence of obesity is substantially higher than in whites, especially among women. Black and Hispanic women have a higher prevalence of obesity than do whites, especially among women. Between 1960 and 1980, the prevalence of obesity among whites increased by 3% in women and by 6% in men. In blacks, however, the prevalence of obesity increased by 7% in women and by 28% in men. Diabetes mellitus and certain other obesity-related conditions occur to a markedly greater-than-average extent in many minority populations. According to the second National Health and Nutrition Examination Survey (NHANES II) (Jackson, 1993), the American Indian children weighed more, and had a statistically significant higher body mass index than the NHANES II reference population for nearly every age and sex group. The overall prevalence of obesity in American Indian children (exceeding the 85th percentile of the reference population) was 39.3% compared with the NHANES II population. Higher socioeconomic status in females correlated to lower body weight and less chance of becoming obese (Sobal & Stunkard, 1989). Other studies showed that decline in educational level was related to an increasing amount of body fat and obesity (Sonne-Holm & Sorensen, 1986; Teasdale, Sorensen, & Stunkard, 1992).

Obesity through the ages has been clearly influenced by prevailing social custom with both overvaluation of its presence and severe derision and social ostracism. A plethora of methods for slimming have been attempted and early observations were made of the adverse health consequences of profound obesity.

DISCUSSION QUESTIONS

1 Discuss epidemiology of anorexia nervosa and bulimia nervosa. Include age of onset, male/female ratio, atypical cases of anorexia nervosa, mortality rate, and prognosis.

2 Discuss contributions made by Richard Morton to the field of eating disorders. Include what Morton concluded was the cause of anorexia nervosa? What were some somatic symptoms describe? What was the treatment plan?

3 Define asceticism and discuss its importance as viewed by the *holy anorexics.*

4 In Bell's monograph on *holy anorexia,* 3 types of religious women who fasted were described. Discuss the different outcomes of these women, and common attitudes and behavioral traits in their personalities.

5 What are the similarities and differences between the *holy anorexics* and the 20th-century, modern-day anorexics?

6 Discuss William Gull's contribution to the field of anorexia nervosa. Include what Gull believed were important determinants of the illness. What symptoms of anorexics were described? What characteristic distinguished AN from TB? What was his treatment plan?

7 What were the stages that Charles Lasague recognized as the three psychodynamic significant stages of patient-family interaction with an anorexic?

8 Discuss major contributions made by Marce, Janet, Chipley, and Playfair to the study of anorexia nervosa.

9 In rediscovering anorexia nervosa as a disease in the 1930s and 1940s, what were some physiologic abnormalities found in anorexics?

10   Between 1885 and 1905, Freud and Janet linked the anorexics' aversion to food to conflicts in psychosexual development. How did these clinical theorists describe anorexics in developmental and psychodynamic terms?

11   What were the three perceptual and conceptual disturbances in anorexia nervosa described by Hilde Bruch?

12   Describe the biopsychosocial model of anorexics that Lucas proposed in 1981.

13   Examine the neurobiologic differences in patients with anorexia versus patients with bulimia (metabolic and CNS changes.)

14   Briefly discuss five descriptions of bulimia nervosa behavior from different historical epochs.

15   Compare the clinical and theoretical closeness or disparity of anorexia nervosa and bulimia nervosa.

16   Discuss the cultural, economic, and psychological factors which contributed to what Bruch called "the pursuit of thinness."

17   Discuss the different attitudes toward obesity, from the Romans, the Greeks, biblical Scriptures, non-western cultures, the Victorian Age, and the modern western culture.

18   Study the cross-cultural and ethnic differences on views of the body image.

REFERENCES

Abraham, K. (1916). Untersuchungen uber die fruheste pragenitale Entwicklungsstufe der Libido. In K. Abraham (Ed.), *Psychoanalytische studien* (Vol. 2, pp. 84–112). Frankfurt: S. Fischer.

Abraham, S. F. & Beumont, P. J. (1982). How patients describe bulimia or binge eating. *Psychological Medicine, 12,* 625–635.

American Psychiatric Association. (1993). *Diagnostic and statistical manual of mental disorders* (3rd ed., rev.). Washington, DC: Author.

American Psychiatric Association Practice Guidelines for Eating Disorders. (1993). *American Journal of Psychiatry, 150,* 212–228.

Andersen, A. E. (1985). Practical comprehensive treatment of anorexia nervosa and bulimia. Baltimore: John Hopkins University Press.

Andersen, A. E., & Mickalide, A. E. (1983). Anorexia nervosa in the male. *Psychosomatics, 24,* 1066–1074.

Andreasen, P. J., Altemus, M., Zametkin, A. J., King, A. C., Lucinio, J., & Cohen, R. M. (1992). Regional cerebral glucose metabolism in bulimia nervosa. *American Journal of Psychiatry, 149,* 1506–1513.

Bank, S. P., & Kahn, M. D. (1982). *The sibling bond.* New York: Basic Books.

Baxter, L. R., Phelps, M. E., Mazziotta, J. C., Guze, B. H., Schwartz, J. M., & Selin, C. E. (1987). Local cerebral glucose metabolic rates in obsessive compulsive disorder. *Archives of General Psychiatry, 44,* 211–218.

Baxter, L. R., Schwartz, J. M., Phelps, M. E., Mazziotta, J. C., Guze, B. H., Selin, C. E., Gerner, R. H., & Sumida, R. M. (1989). Reduction of prefrontal cortex glucose metabolism common to three types of depression. *Archives of General Psychiatry, 46,* 243–250.

Beard, G. (1871). *Eating and drinking: A popular manual of food and diet in health and disease.* New York: Putnam.

Bell, R. M. (1985). *Holy anorexia.* Chicago: University of Chicago.

Bergmann, G. (1934). Magerkeit und Magersucht. *Deutsche Medizinische Wochenschrift, 60,* 123–127, 157–160.

Berkman, J. M. (1930). Anorexia nervosa, anorexia, inanition, and low metabolic rate. *American Journal of Medical Science, 180,* 411–424.

Berkman, J. M. (1939). Functional anorexia and functional vomiting: Their relation to anorexia nervosa. *Medical Clinics of North America, 23,* 901–912.

Berkman, J. M., Weir, J. F., & Kepler, E. J. (1947). Clinical observations on starvation edema, serum protein and the effect of forced feeding in anorexia nervosa. *Gastroenterology, 9,* 357–390.

Beumont, P. J. (1991). The history of eating and dieting disorders. *Clinical Applied Nutrition, 1,* 9–20.

Beumont, P. J., Burrow, G. D., Casper, R. C. (Eds.). (1987). *Handbook of eating disorders, Part I: Anorexia nervosa and bulimia.* New York: Elsevier.

Beumont, P. J., George, G. C., & Smart, D. E. (1976). Dieters and vomiters and purgers in anorexia nervosa. *Psychological Medicine, 6,* 617–622.

Binswanger, L. (1944). The case of Ellen West: An anthropological-clinical study. In R. May, E. Angel, & H. Ellenberg (Eds.), *Existence* (pp. 237–264). New York: Basic Books.

Blinder, B. J. (1972). Sibling death in childhood. *Child Psychiatry and Human Development, 2,* 169–175.

Blinder, B. J. (1980). Developmental antecedents of the eating disorders: A reconsideration. *Psychiatric Clinics of North America, 3*(3), 579–592.

Blinder, B. J. (1991). Eating disorders in psychiatric illness. *Clinical Applied Nutrition, 1,* 73–85.

Blinder, B. J., & Cadenhead, K. (1986). Bulimia: A historical overview. *Annals of the American Society for Adolescent Psychiatry, 13,* 231–240.

Blinder, B. J., Chaitin, B. F., & Goldstein, R. (Eds.). (1988). *The eating disorders: Medical and psychological bases of diagnosis and treatment.* Great Neck, NY: PMA.

Blinder, B. J., Chaitin, B. F., & Hagman, J. O. (1987). Two diagnostic correlates of dexemethasone non-suppression in normal weight bulimics. *Hillside Journal of Clinical Psychiatry, 9*(2), 211–216.

Bliss, E. L., & Branch, C. H. H. (1960). *Anorexia nervosa: Its history, psychology, and biology.* New York: Hoeber.

Bond, D. D. (1949). Anorexia nervosa. *The Rocky Mountain Medical Journal, 46,* 1012–1019.

Boskind-Lodahl, M. (1976). Cinderella's stepsisters: A feminist perspective on anorexia and bulimia. *Signs: Journal of Women in Culture and Society, 2,* 342–356.

Boskind-Lodahl, M., & White, W. C. (1978). The definition and treatment of bulimarexia in college women—a pilot study. *Journal of the American College Health Association, 27,* 84–86.

Boskind-White, M., & White, W. C., Jr. (1986). Bulimarexia: A historical-sociocultural perspective. In K. D. Brownell & J. P. Foreyt (Eds.), *Handbook of eating disorders* (pp. 353–366). New York: Basic Books.

Briquet, P. (1859). *Traite de clinique et therapeutique de l hysterie.* Paris: Bailliere.

Britt, L. & Bloom, R. (1982). Portrait of Obsession [Film]. Venice, CA: Video Masters Production.

Brownell, K. E. & Foreyt, J. P. (Eds.). (1986). *Handbook of eating disorders.* New York: Basic Books.

Bruch, H. (1957). *The importance of overweight.* New York: Norton.

Bruch, H. (1962). Perceptual and conceptual disturbances in anorexia nervosa. *Psychosomatic Medicine, 24,* 287–294.

Bruch, H. (1973). *Eating disorders: Obesity and anorexia nervosa, and the person within.* New York: Basic Books.

Bruch, H. (1977). Psychological antecedents of anorexia nervosa. In R. A. Vigersky (Ed.), *Anorexia nervosa: A monograph of the national institute of child and human development* (p. 1010). New York: Raven Press.

Bruch, H. (1985). Four decades of eating disorders. In D. M. Garner & P. E. Garfinkel (Eds.), *Handbook of psychotherapy of anorexia nervosa and bulimia* (pp. 7–18). New York: Guilford.

Brumberg, J. J. (1988). *Fasting girls.* Cambridge: Harvard University Press.

Bynum, C. W. (1987). *Holy feast and holy fast: The religious significance of food to medieval women.* Berkeley: University of California Press.

Casper, R. C. (1983). On the emergence of bulimia nervosa as a syndrome. *International Journal of Eating Disorders, 2,* 13–15.

Casper, R. C., Eckert, E. D., Halmi, K. A., Goldberg, S. C., & Davis, J. M. (1980). Bulimia, its incidence and importance in patients with anorexia nervosa. *Archives of General Psychiatry, 37,* 1030–1044.

Casper, R. C., & Offer, D. (1990). Weight and dieting concerns in adolescents: Fashion or symptom? *Pediatrics, 86,* 384–390.

Casper, R. C., Offer, D., & Ostrov, E. (1981). The self-image of adolescents with acute anroexia nervosa. *Journal of Pediatrics, 98,* 656–661.

Coulon, V., & van Daele, M. (Eds.). (1930). *Aristophanes* (Vol. 5). Paris: Les Belles Lettres. (Original work published 1963)

Densmore-John, J. (1988). Nutritional characteristics and consequences of anorexia nervosa and bulimia. In B. J. Blinder, B. F. Chaitin, & R. S. Goldstein (Eds.), *The eating disorders* (pp. 305–314). New York: PMA.

de Valangin, F. (1768). *A treatise on diet.* London: J & W Oliver.

De Zwaan, M., & Mitchell, J. E. (1991). Bulimia nervosa. *Clinical Applied Nutrition, 1,* 40–48.

Dornbusch, S. M., Smith, J. M., & Duncan, P. D. (1984). Sexual maturation, social class, and the desire to be thin among adolescent females. *Journal of Developmental and Behavioral Pediatrics, 5,* 308–314.

Fischer, M. F. K. (1976). *The art of eating.* New York: Vintage.

Fluoxetine Bulimia Nervosa Collaborative Study Group. (1992). Fluoxetine in the treatment of bulimia nervosa: A multicenter, placebo-controlled, double blind trial. *Archives of General Psychiatry, 49,* 139–147.

Fowler, R. (1871). *A complete history of the Welsh fasting girl.* London: Publisher.

Freud, A. (1936). The ego and the mechanism of defense. New York: International Universities Press.

Garfinkel, P. E. & Garner, D. M. (1982). *Anorexia nervosa: A multidimensional perspective*. New York: Brunner/Mazel.

Garfinkel, P. E., Moldofsky, H., & Garner, D. M. (1980). The heterogeneity of anorexia nervosa: Bulimia as a distinct subgroup. *Archives of General Psychiatry, 37,* 1036–1040.

Gislason, I. L. (1988). Eating disorders in childhood (ages 4 through 11). In B. J. Blinder, B. F. Chaitin, & R. S. Goldstein (Eds.), *The eating disorders* (pp. 285–294). Great Neck, New York: PMA.

Goodman, S., Blinder, B. J., Chaitin, B. F., & Hagman, J. O. (1988). Atypical eating disorders. In B. J. Blinder, B. F. Chaitin, & R. S. Goldstein (Eds.), *The eating disorders* (pp. 393–404). Great Neck, New York: PMA.

Gordon, R. A. (1988). A sociocultural interpretation of the current epidemic of eating disorders. In B. J. Blinder, B. F. Chaitin, & R. S. Goldstein (Eds.), *The eating disorders* (pp. 151–163). New York: PMA.

Gordon, R. A. (1992). *Anorexia and bulimia: Anatomy of social epidemic.* London: Blackwell.

Gull, W. W. (1874). Anorexia nervosa (apepsia hysterica, anorexia hysterica). *Transactions of the Clinical Society, 7,* 22–28.

Gungl, H., & Stichl, A. (1892). *Neuropathologische studien.* Stuttgart: Enke.

Gwirtsman, H. E., Holstein, L. A., & Boy-Byrne, P. (1988). New neuroendocrine findings in anorexia nervosa and bulimia. In B. J. Blinder, B. F. Chaitin, & R. S. Goldstein (Eds.), *The eating disorders* (pp. 205–214). New York: PMA.

Habermas, J. (1986). Friderada: A case of miraculous fasting. *International Journal of Eating Disorders, 5,* 555–562.

Habermas, T. (1989). The psychiatric history of anorexia and bulimia: Weight fears and bulimic symptoms in early cases. *BASH Magazine, 8,* 342–358.

Habermas, T. (1991). The role of psychiatric and medical traditions in the discovery and description of anorexia nervosa in France, Germany, and Italy. *The Journal of Nervous and Mental Disease, 1979,* 360–365.

Hagman, J. O. (1992). Brain imaging and eating disorders. *The Biology of Feast and Famine, 17,* 285–298.

Hagman, J. O., Buchsbaum, M. S., Wu, J. C., Rao, S. J., Reynolds, C. A., & Blinder, B. J. (1990). Comparison of regional brain metabolism in bulimia nervosa and affective disorder assessed with positron emission tomography. *Journal Affective Disorders, 19,* 153–162.

Hajal, F. (1982). Psychological treatment of anorexia from the ninth century. In B. J. Blinder, B. F. Chaitin, & R. S. Goldstein (Eds.), *The eating disorders* (pp. 247–258). New York: PMA.

Halmi, K. A., Broadland, G., & Rigas, C. A. (1975). A followup study of 70 patients with anorexia nervosa: An evaluation of prognostic factors and diagnostic criteria. In R. D. Wirt, G. Winokur, & M. Roff (Eds.), *Life history research in psychopathology* (Vol. 4). Minneapolis: University of Minnesota Press.

Halmi, R. A., Falk, J. R., & Schwartz, E. (1981). Binge-eating and vomiting. *Psychological Medicine, 11,* 697–706.

Hawkins, R. C. & Clement, P. F. (1980). Development and construct validation of a self report measure of binge-eating tendencies. *Addictive Behaviors, 5,* 219–226.

Heunemann, R. L., Shapiro, L. R., Hampton, M. R., & Mitchell, B. W. (1966). A longitudinal study of gross body composition and body conformation and their association with food and activity in a teenage population. *American Journal of Clinical Nutrition, 18,* 325–338.

Hollander, E. (Ed.). (1993). *Obsessive compulsive related disorders.* Washington, DC: American Psychiatric Press.

Hsu, L. K. G. (1980). Outcome of anorexia nervosa: A review of the literature. *Archives General Psychiatry, 37,* 1041–1042.

Jackson, M. (1993). Height, weight, and body mass index of American Indian schoolchildren, 1990–1991. *Journal of the American Dietetic Association, 93,* 1136–1140.

James, P. (1743). *Medical dictionary.* London: Osborn.

Janet, P. (1908). *Les obsessions el la psychasthenie* (Vol. 1). Paris: Alcan.

Janet, P. (1929). Excerpts from the major symptoms of hysteria. In M. R. Kaufman & M. Haiman (Eds.), *Evolution of psychosomatic concepts* (pp. 156–164). New York: International Universities Press.

Johnson, C., Lewis, C., Love, S., Lewis, L., & Stuckey, M. (1984). Incidence of correlates of bulimic behavior in a female high school population. *Journal of Youth and Adolescents, 13,* 15–26.

Kaplan, A. S., & Garfinkel, P. E. (1984). Bulimia in the Talmud. *American Journal of Psychiatry, 141*(5), 721.

Kaplan, H. I., Sadock, B. J. (1991). *Synopsis of psychiatry.* Baltimore, MD: Williams and Wilkins.

Katz, J. L., & Sitnick, T. (1982). Anorexia nervosa and bulimia. *Archives General Psychiatry, 39,* 487–488.

Katzman, M. A., & Wolchik, S. A. (1984). Bulimia and binge-eating in college women: A comparison of personality and behavior characteristics. *Journal of Consulting and Clinical Psychology, 53*(3), 423–428.

Kaye, W. H. & Gwirtsman, H. E. (Eds.). (1985). *A comprehensive approach to the treatment of normal weight bulimics.* Washington, DC: American Psychiatric Press.

Kelly, H. A. (1912). *A cyclopedia of American Medical Biography* (Vol. 1). Philadelphia: W. B. Saunders.

Kendler, K. S., MacLean, C., Neale, M., Kessler, R., Heath, A., & Eaves, L. (1991). The genetic epidemiology of bulimia nervosa. *American Journal of Psychiatry, 148,* 1627–1637.

Kirshbaum, W. R. (1951). Excessive hunger as a symptom of cerebral origin. *Journal of Nervous and Mental Disease, 113,* 95–115.

Krieg, J. C., Pirke, K. M., Lauer, C., & Backmund, H. (1988). Endocrine, metabolic, and cranial computed tomographic findings in anorexia nervosa. *Biological Psychiatry, 23,* 377–387.

Kumanyika, S. (1993). Special issues regarding obesity in minority populations. *Annals of Internal Medicine, 119* 650–654.

Lacey, J. H. (1982). Anorexia nervosa and a bearded female saint. *British Medical Journal, 285,* 1816–1817.

Laseque, C. (1873). On hysterical anorexia by Dr. Laseque. *Medical Times and Gazette, 2,* 265–266, 367–369.

Leichner, P., & Gertler, A. (1988). Prevalence and incidence studies of anorexia nervosa. In B. J. Blinder, B. F. Chaitin, & R. S. Goldstein (Eds.), *The eating disorders* (pp. 131–149). New York: PMA.

Levinson, R., Powell, B., & Steelman, L. C. (1986). Social location, significant others and body image among adolescents. *Psychology Quarterly, 49,* 330–337.

Lewis, C. T. & Short, C. (1900). *A Latin dictionary.* Oxford: Claredon Press.

Lindner, R. (1955). *The fifty minute hour.* New York: Reinehart.

Loudon, I. S. L. (1980). Chlorosis, anaemia, and anorexia nervosa. *British Medical Journal, 281,* 1669–1675.

Lucas, A. R. (1981). Toward the understanding of anorexia nervosa as a disease entity. *Mayo Clinic Proceedings, 56,* 254–264.

Maddox, G. L., Black, L. W., & Liederman, V. R. (1968). Overweight as social deviance and disability. *Journal of Health and Social Behavior, 4,* 287–298.

Marce, L. V. (1860). On a form of hypochondriacal delirium occurring consecutive to dyspepsia, and characterized by refusal of food. *Journal of Psychological Medicine and Mental Pathology, 13,* 264–266.

Masson, J. M. (1985). *The complete letters of Sigmund Freud to Wilhelm Fliess: 1887–1904.* Harvard University: Belkmap Press.

McCallum, R. W., Grill, B. B., Lange, R., Planky, M., Glass, E. E., & Greenfield, D. G. (1985). Definition of a gastric emptying abnormality in patients with anorexia nervosa. *Digestive Diseases and Sciences, 30,* 713–722.

Minuchin, S., Rosman, B. L., & Baker, L. (1978). *Psychosomatic families: Anorexia nervosa in context.* Cambridge: Harvard University Press.

Mitchell, J. E., Pyle, R. L., & Eckert, E. D. (1985). Bulimia. In R. E. Hales and A. J. Frances (Eds.), *American Psychiatric Association Annual Review* (Vol. 4, pp. 464–480). Washington, DC: American Psychiatric Press.

Morley, J. E. & Castel, S. C. (1985). Death by starvation: The sepulveda Grecc Method, no. 6. *Geriatric Medicine Today, 4,* 76–78.

Morley, J. E., Levine, A. S., & Krahn, D. D. (1988). Neurotransmitter regulation of appetite and eating. In B. J. Blinder, B. F. Chaitin, & R. S. Goldstein (Eds.), *The eating disorders* (pp. 11–20). New York: PMA.

Morton, R. (1694). *Phthisiologia: Or, a treatise of consumptions.* London: Smith & Walford.

Motherby, G. (1785). *A new medical dictionary: Or a general respiratory of physic.* London: J. Johnson & J. Robinson.

Mount Sinai Seminar Group. (1964). In M. R. Kaufman & M. Heiman (Eds.), *Evolution of psychosomatic concepts* (pp. 78–103). New York: International Universities Press.

Nagelberg, D. B., Hale, S. L., & Ware, S. L. (1984). The assessment of bulimic symptoms and personality correlates in female college students. *Journal of Clinical Psychiatry, 40,* 440–445.

Nemiah, J. C. (1950). Anorexia nervosa: A clinical psychiatric study. *Medicine, 29,* 225–268.

Nogue, G. (1913). *L. anorexie mentale.* Toulouse: Dirion.

Nordahl, T. E., Benkelfat, C., Semple, W. E., Gross, M., King, A. C., & Cohen, R. M. (1989). Cerebral glucose metabolic rates in obsessive compulsive disorder. *Neuropsychopharmacology, 2,* 23–28.

Orlowsky, M. J. (1982). The Kleine-Levin syndrome: A review. *Psychosomatics, 23,* 609–610, 615–617, 621.

Parry-Jones, B. (1991). Historical terminology of eating disorders. *Psychological Medicine, 21,* 21–28.

Parry-Jones, W. L. (1985). Archival exploration of anorexia nervosa. *Journal of Psychiatric Research, 19,* 95–100.

Playfair, C. (1888). Note on so-called anorexia nervosa. *Lancet, 1,* 817–818.

Pyle, R. L., Mitchell, J. E., & Eckert, E. D. (1981). Bulimia: A report of 34 cases. *Journal of Clinical Psychiatry, 42,* 60–64.

Rampling, D. (1985). Ascetic ideals and anorexia nervosa. *Journal of Psychiatric Research, 2,* 89–94.

Russell, D. M., Freedman, M. L., Feiglin, D. H. I., Jeejeebhoy, K. N., Swinson, R. P., & Garfinkel, P. E. (1983). Delayed gastric emptying and improvement with domperidone in a patient with anorexia nervosa. *American Journal of Psychiatry, 140,* 1235–1236.

Russell, G. F. M. (1979). Bulimia nervosa: An ominous variant of anorexia nervosa. *Psychological Medicine, 9,* 429–448.

Russell, G. F. M. (1985). The changing nature of anorexia nervosa: An introduction to the conference. *Journal of Psychiatric Research, 19,* 101–109.

Ryle, J. A. (1936). Anorexia nervosa. *Lancet, 2,* 893–899.

Ryle, J. A. (1939). Discussion on anorexia nervosa. *Proceedings of the Royal Society of Medicine, 32,* 35–37.

Sagar, R. S., Khandelwal, S. K., & Gupta, S. (1990). Interepisodic morbidity in Klein-Levin syndrome. *British Journal of Psychiatry, 157,* 139–171.

Schottky, J. (1932). Uber ungewohnliche Triebhandlunge bei prozesshafter Entwicklungsstorung. *Zeitschrift fur das Gesamtgebiet der Neurologie und Psychiatrie, 143,* 38–55.

Schwartz, H. J. (Ed.). (1990). *Bulimia: Psychoanalytic treatment and theory.* CT: International Universities Press.

Selling, L. S., & Ferraro, M. A. (1945). *The psychology of diet and nutrition.* New York: Norton.

Shapiro, D. H., Blinder, B. J., Hagman, J. O., & Pituck, S. (1993). A psychological "sense-of-control" profile of patients with anorexia nervosa and bulimia nervosa. *Psychological Reports, 73,* 531–541.

Sibley, D. C. & Blinder, B. J. (1988). Anorexia nervosa. In B. J. Blinder, B. F. Chaitin, & R. S. Goldstein (Eds.). *The eating disorders* (pp. 247–258). New York: PMA.

Siegel, R. E. (1973). *Galen psychopathology and function and diseases of the nervous system.* New York: Karger.

Silverman, J. A. (1983). Richard Morton, 1637–1696, limner of anorexia nervosa: His life and times. *JAMA, 250,* 2830–2832.

Silverman, J. A. (1987). Robert Whytt, 1714–1766, eighteenth century limner of anorexia nervosa and bulimia: An essay. *International Journal of Eating Disorders, 6,* 143–146.

Silverman, J. A. (1988). Richard Morton's second case of anorexia nervosa: Reverend Minister Steel and his son—an historical vignette. *International Journal of Eating Disorders, 7*, 439–441.

Silverman, J. A. (1989). Louis-Victor Marce, 1828–1864: Anorexia nervosa's forgetten man. *Psychological Medicine, 19*, 833–835.

Simmonds, M. (1914). Ueber Hypophysisschwund mit fodlichem Ausgang. *Deutsche Medizinische Wochenschrift, 40*, 322–323.

Simmonds, M. (1916). Ueber Kachexie hypophysaren Ursprungs. *Deutsche Medizinisdre Wodenschrift, 1*, 190–191.

Smith, W. (1866). *A Latin-English dictionary.* London: J. Murray.

Sobal, J. & Stunkard, A. J. (1989). Socioeconomic status and obesity: A review of the literature. *Psychological Bulletin, 105*, 260–275.

Soltman, O. (1894). Anorexia cerebralis und Zentrale Nutritionsneurose. *Jahrbuch fur kinderheilkunde, 38*, 1–13.

Sonne-Holm, S., & Sorensen, T. I. A. (1986). Prospective study of attainment of social class of severely obese subjects in relation to parental social class, intelligence and education. *British Medical Journal, 292*, 580–589.

Stainbrook, E. (1952). Psychosomatic medicine in the nineteenth century. In M. R. Kaufman & M. Heiman (Eds.), *Evolution of psychosomatic concepts* (pp. 6–35). New York: International Universities Press.

Stein, D. M. & Laakso, W. (1988). Bulimia: A historical perspective. *International Journal of Eating Disorders, 7*, 201–210.

Stern, M. P., Pugh, J. A., & Gaskill, S. P. (1982). Knowledge, attitudes, and behavior related to obesity and dieting in Mexican Americans and Anglos: The San Antonio heart study. *American Journal of Epidemiology, 115*, 917–927.

Stiller, B. (1884). *Die Nervosen Magenkrankheiten.* Stuttgart: Enke.

Striegel-Moore, R. H., Silberstein, L. R., & Rodin, J. (1986). Toward an understanding of risk factors in bulimia. *American Psychology 41*, 246–263.

Strober, M. (1980). Personality and symptomatological features in young, nonchronic anorexia nervosa patients. *Journal of Psychosomatic Research, 24*, 353–359.

Strober, M. (1981). The significance of bulimia in juvenile anorexia nervosa: An exploration of possible etiological factors. *International Journal of Eating Disorders, 1*, 28–43.

Strober, M. (1986). History and psychological concepts. In K. D. Brownell & J. P. Foreyt (Eds.), *Handbook of eating disorders* (pp. 231–246). New York: Basic Books.

Strober, M., Salkin, B., Burroughs, G., & Morrell, W. (1982). Validity of the bulimia restrictor distinction in anorexia nervosa and parental personality characteristics and family psychiatric morbidity. *Journal of Nervous and Mental Disease, 170*, 345–351.

Stunkard, A. J. (1990). A description of eating disorders in 1932. *American Journal of Psychiatry, 147*, 263–268.

Stunkard, A. J., Grace, W. J., & Wolff, H. G. (1955). The night eating syndrome: A pattern of food intake among certain obese patients. *American Journal of Psychiatry, 19*, 78–86.

Teasdale, T. W., Sorensen, T. I. A., & Stunkard, A. J. (1992). Intelligence and educational level in relation to body mass index of adult males. *Human Biology, 64*, 99–106.

Tolstrup, K. (1990). Incidence and causality of anorexia nervosa seen in an historical perspective. *Acta Psychiatrica Scandivica, 82* (Suppl.), 1–6.

Trail, R. R. (1970). Richard Morton, the Gideon Delaune Lecture. *Medicine History, 2,* 166–174.

van der Eycken, W. (1985). Bulimia has different meaning. *American Journal of Psychiatry, 142,* 141–142.

van der Eycken, W. (1988). Anorexia nervosa in adults. In B. J. Blinder, B. F. Chaitin, & R. S. Goldstein (Eds.), *The eating disorders* (pp. 295–304). New York: PMA.

van der Eycken, W., Kog, E., & Vander Linden, J. (Eds.). (1989). *The family approach to eating disorders.* Great Neck, NY: PMA.

van der Eycken, W. & Lowenkopf, E. L. (1990). Anorexia nervosa in 19th century America. Journal of Nervous and Mental Disease, 178, 531–535.

Van Itallie, T. B. (1985). Health implications of overweight and obesity in the United States. *Annals of Internal Medicine, 103,* 983–988.

Wadden, T. A., Foster, G. D., & Stunkard, A. J. (1989). Dissatisfaction with weight and figure in obese girls: Discontent but not depression. *International Journal of Obesity, 13,* 89–97.

Wadden, T. A., Stunkard, A. J., & Rich, L. (1990). Obesity in black adolescent girls: A controlled clinical trial of treatment by diet, behavior modification, and parental support. *Pediatrics, 85,* 345–352.

Waller, J. V., Kaufman, M. R., & Deutsch, F. (1940). Anorexia nervosa: A psychosomatic entity. *Psychosomatic Medicine, 2,* 3–16.

Wallet, A. (1892). Deux cas d'anorexie hysterique. *Nouvelle Iconoraphie de la Salpetriere,* 276–280.

Walsh, B. T. (1980). The endocrinology of anorexia nervosa. *Psychiatric Clinics of North America, 3,* 299–312.

Walsh, B. T., Stewart, J. W., Roose, S. P., Gladis, M., & Glassman, A. H. (1984). Treatment of bulimia with phenelzine: A double-blind, placebo-controlled study. *Archives of General Psychiatry, 41,* 1105–1109.

Weiner, H. & Katz, J. L. (1983). The hypothalamic-pituitary-adrenal axis in anorexia nervosa: A reassessment. In P. L. Darby, P. E. Garfinkel, D. M. Garner, & D. V. Coscina (Eds.), *Anorexia nervosa: Recent developments in research* (pp. 249–270). New York: Alan R. Liss.

Wellmann, M. (Ed.). (1914). *Pedanii dioscoridis anazarbei de matenia medica libri gunigue* (Vol. 3). Berlin: Weidman.

Whytt, K. (1767). *Observation on the nature, causes, and cure of those disorders which have been commonly called nervous, hypochondriac, or hysteric to which are prefixed some remarks on the sympathy of the nerves.* Edinburgh: Becket, Deltondt, & Balfour.

Wilson, C. P., Hogan, C. C., & Mintz, I. L. (Eds.). (1985). *Fear of being fat: The treatment of anorexia nervosa and bulimia* (2nd ed.). Northvale, NJ: Jason Aronson.

Wilson, C. P., Hogan, C. C., & Mintz, I. L. (Eds.). (1992). *Psychodynamic technique in the treatment of eating disorders.* Northvale, NJ: Jason Aronson.

Wu, J. C., Hagman , J. O., Buchsbaum, M. S., Blinder, B. J., Derfler, M., Tai, W. Y., Hazlett, E., & Sicotte, N. (1990). Greater left cerebral hemispheric metabolism in bulimia assessed by positron emission tomography. *American Journal of Psychiatry, 147,* 309–312.

Wulff, M. (1932). Eine Interessante orale Symptomkomplex und Seine Beziehung zur Sucht. *Int Z Psychonanal, 18,* 281–302.

Yager, J. (1991). Bulimia nervosa. In B. D. Bietman & G. L. Klerman (Eds.), *Integrating pharmacotherapy and psychotherapy* (pp. 253–270). Washington, DC: American Psychiatric Press.

Yates, A. (1989). Current perspectives on the eating disorders: I. History, psychological and biological aspects. *Journal of the American Academy of Child Adolescent Psychiatry, 28,* 813–828.

Yu, J. (1986). Eating disorders: Anorexia and bulimia. *Vital Signs* (Vol. 6, No. 1). Ithaca, NY: Cornell University Health Services.

Ziolko, H. U. & Schrader, H. C. (1985). Bulimie [Bulimia]. *Fortschritte der Neurologie und Psychiatrie, 53,* 231–258.

Chapter 2

Critical Issues in the Developmental Psychopathology of Eating Disorders

Linda Smolak
Michael P. Levine

Most etiological models of anorexia nervosa and bulimia nervosa juxtapose numerous sociocultural, familial, personality, and biological factors (Garfinkel & Garner, 1982; Johnson & Connors, 1987). Developmental variables, such as genetic predispositions or puberty, are included in some of these multidimensional models, especially the more psychodynamically oriented ones. Nevertheless, with a few exceptions (e.g., Strober, 1991), eating disorder theorists have not treated these variables in a manner consistent with developmental psychology's tenets. Although proponents of the multidimensional models have demonstrated that diverse factors function as possible precursors and determinants of eating disorders, they have neglected the paths and processes by which predisposition (vulnerability) is transformed into disorder.

This chapter explores principles, theories, and data within the fields of developmental psychology and developmental psychopathology that might strengthen theory and research concerning the causes of eating disorders. Then, in light of these issues, two causal models that incorporate developmental variables are critiqued. Finally, suggestions for future research in accordance with a developmental perspective are offered. More general reviews of developmental factors and eating disorders are found in Attie and Brooks-Gunn (1992), Striegel-Moore (1993), and Thelen, Lawrence, and Powell (1992).

WHAT CAN DEVELOPMENTAL PSYCHOPATHOLOGY ADD TO THE STUDY OF EATING DISORDERS?

Developmental psychology and developmental psychopathology raise at least five broad issues that need to be addressed by models of eating disorders.

Paths of Development

The core principle of developmental psychopathology is that disordered behavior, like adaptive behavior, is a developmental process. Metaphorically, this process is a path that branches off from the multilane road known as normal adaptation (Cichetti & Schneider-Rosen, 1986; Sroufe, 1989). The path may or may not rejoin the main road, and there may be other paths leading to or from each branch. This concept of paths reminds us that: (1) pathology is related to normal development; (2) several developmental trajectories might result in a single category of disorder; and (3) pathology continues as a process affected by larger developmental processes, its symptoms, contributing factors, and severity changing over time. There is no known point in development at which a certain path becomes fixed or inevitable. Even the appearance of symptoms does not guarantee a single outcome.

This perspective calls attention to the limitations of theories and research (e.g., cross-sectional investigations of the correlation between life stress and eating disorder) that emphasize the static point known as symptom onset. Developmental psychopathologists accept the role of proximal stressors in the emergence of a full-blown disorder, but they shift the focus of study to processes that create the stressor or lead the person to interpret it in a pathological fashion (Cowan, 1988). For example, the incidence of bulimia nervosa and anorexia nervosa increases in adolescence, yet the prevalence rate is fairly low. This suggests interactions between adolescent changes (creating the increased risk) and some type of individual vulnerability (limiting the effect to a minority of girls) that lead to different developmental paths (e.g., no symptoms → some symptoms → full-blown disorder, or no symptoms → subclinical disorder → full recovery).

A Transactional Approach

Developmental psychopathologists view development as an ongoing process of mutual and reciprocal influence between the child and the environment (Cichetti & Schneider-Rosen, 1986). This transactional approach differs significantly from the more common additive or interactive models by emphasizing the reciprocal determinism found within the dynamic nature of development (Smolak, 1986). As the environment shapes her, the child shapes and selectively evokes an environment. Consequently, potentially negative effects within the environment (e.g., low expectations, hostility, lack of opportunity) can in some instances be construed as reactions, as well as contributors, to the child's behavior. As the child gets older, this type of pathological system becomes even more complex. Changes in the child (e.g., her abilities) and in her environment (e.g., cultural expectations) will likely provide her with greater choice in creating her environment (e.g., friends and activities). Her selections are likely to be consistent with and supportive of her characteristics, attitudes, and style (Scarr & McCartney, 1983).

Within this transactional perspective, developmental continuity of a particular behavior or personality structure may really reflect environmental continuity. This is true in two ways. First, there is often temporal consistency in the behavior of parents, teachers, and peers, as well as continued exposure to certain values, behaviors, and opportunities due to social class, religious affiliation, and so on. Second, the parents are often similar in their parenting expectations, techniques, and styles.

If either form of environmental continuity is disrupted, the child's behavior may change dramatically. The negative effects of such discontinuity have been demonstrated for a variety of events such as divorce and unemployment (Hetherington, 1989; McLoyd, 1989). However, it is important to examine how the timing and duration of discontinuity interact with the challenges and abilities of the child's developmental stage. What happens, for example, when a mother who was depressed throughout her son's infancy recovers when he becomes a toddler? Is the boy still at risk for developing problems? Is the risk as great as that of a boy whose mother continues to be depressed? What is the effect of the other parent, if one is present? Are there better or worse times, from the perspective of the child's development, for the parent to be depressed?

Questions like these, as well as the larger issue of developmental paths, are best addressed through longitudinal research. This methodology would provide much-needed natural histories of eating disorders and their subclinical variants. It would also avoid the confounding that arises from nonrecursive relationships between pathology and social interactions, self-perceptions, perceptions of stress, and other factors that might be considered causal factors. Moreover, longitudinal research is the only way to determine the existence and impact of continuities and/or discontinuities in potentially important environmental factors (e.g., family dynamics) and individual characteristics (e.g., the importance of attractiveness in the individual's self-system; Brooks-Gunn, Rock, & Warren, 1989).

Definitions of Normal and Abnormal

The definition of abnormal or pathological remains a confusing and controversial topic. The study of children adds a special dimension to the debates because developmental levels and environmental control may constrain or alter symptom expression (Cichetti & Schneider-Rosen, 1986; Thelen et al., 1992). Developmental psychology can provide age-related standards of normal behavior that consider the mixture of values, adaptability of functioning, and statistical normativeness that we rely on in making such judgments (Sroufe, 1989).

A very important issue here is whether certain pathological processes are even possible in a young child. The classic example is the question of whether a young child can actually experience the type of hopelessness that is a hallmark of postpubescent depression (Rutter, 1986). The same question needs to be raised about lack of interoceptive awareness, one of the central components of a true eating disorder (Bruch, 1973; Garfinkel & Garner, 1982; Polivy & Herman, 1987).

The process of learning to identify and describe emotions and needs begins in infancy. The child must learn, not only to distinguish one internal state from another, but also to integrate this information with linguistic (for labeling) and cognitive (for making causal attributions) information (Greenberg, Kusche, & Speltz, 1991). Indeed, it may be the inability to integrate these components that creates risk for the deficits in self-awareness and impulse control that are characteristic of eating disorders (Greenberg et al., 1991). The gradual development of interoceptive skills calls into question whether prepubertal children who are diagnosed as anorexic (Gowers, Crisp, Joughin, & Bhat, 1991; Thelen et al., 1992) can truly possess the nervosa of the disorder.

Molar and Molecular Levels of Analysis

Suppose an underlying personality or cognitive structure is the core of not only vulnerability for an eating disorder, but also the disorder itself. Developmental psychopathologists refer to such structures as the molar level of symptomatology, while manifestations of the core (i.e., actual signs and symptoms) are called the molecular level (Cichetti & Schneider-Rosen, 1986). As implied in the previous discussion of interoceptive awareness, it is possible that the molar level undergoes substantial reorganization from one phase of development to another. Our task is to identify the structures that are precursors to other structures. It is also possible that the molar level will remain fairly consistent across at least some phases of development, while the molecular level changes. Eating disorders researchers might look at how body esteem issues or emotional lability are expressed in elementary versus middle versus high school girls. The value of this approach for secondary prevention is clear.

Developmental Transitions

Finally, there is a growing literature regarding developmental transitions, including those in early and late adolescence (e.g., Barth, 1989; Montemayor, Adams, & Gullota, 1990), and the demands they place on coping resources. During transitions, there are substantial reorganizations in a variety of personality, cognitive, and relationship structures, as well as changes in social roles and cultural expectations. These periods are of interest to developmental psychopathologists because the person may lack the internal mechanisms and/or social support necessary to cope with the transitional challenges and any concomitant nonnormative stressors. Resultant changes in attitudes, emotions, and relationships may be a step toward developmental deviation.

Interest in developmental transitions is more than a simple extension of stressor-appraisal-coping models. The emphasis is on the effects of normative changes that are viewed as necessary and generally positive for development. Thus, the focus is not only on individual differences in coping with the stress, but also on the implications of the reorganizations that occur at this time for subsequent development.

SELF-OTHER DIFFERENTIATION IN JOHNSON AND CONNORS' (1987) MODEL OF BULIMIA NERVOSA

Disturbances of self have long been considered a core feature of the eating disorders (Bruch, 1973; Garfinkel & Garner, 1982; Johnson & Connors, 1987). Interoceptive awareness, defined as the ability to gauge one's own emotional and physical states, is impaired, resulting in an inability to regulate hunger and affect. This deficit is often interwoven with interpersonal mistrust to produce an extreme concern about who is controlling one's physical and psychological life. A sense of ineffectiveness and self-esteem low enough to be symptomatic of depression are common, as is a distorted impression of body shape and size. All of these problems reflect doubt, confusion, anxiety, and anger about one's sense of being, including autonomy and self-control.

It is not surprising, then, that many theorists and researchers have described eating disorders as basically a problem of self-other differentiation (Johnson, 1991). More specifically, it is hypothesized that failure to negotiate the infant separation-individuation process successfully (Mahler, Pine, & Bergman, 1975) makes it impossible for the child to cope with adolescent tasks concerning autonomy, sexuality, and self-control. Control/loss of control over food intake and over one's own body become ways of expressing one's emotional turmoil, as well as unconscious surrogates for management of self and relationships.

The Johnson and Connors (1987) Model

Craig Johnson and Mary Connors (1987) use separation-individuation disturbances to explain anorexia nervosa and bulimia nervosa. In keeping with psychodynamic tradition, mother-infant interaction within the early years is viewed as critical to, and perhaps deterministic of, adult outcome (Table 2-1).

Johnson and Connors (1987) begin with the assumption (Bruch, 1973) that interoceptive awareness develops through a mother's appropriate responses to her baby's signals of distress. If she fails to respond, or if maternal responses are not

Table 2-1   Mahler's Phases of Separation-Individuation

Stage	Age	Description
Forerunners of Separation-Individuation		
Autistic phase	0–2 months	The infant does not respond to external stimuli, physiological stimuli. The newborn is simply trying to establish homeostasis within his new environment. There seems to be a stimulus barrier between the newborn and the environment.
Symbiotic phase	2–5 months	The child is aware of the mother and her fulfillment of his physical needs, but he does not distinguish himself from her. He does not understand that he and his mother are distinct people. Instead, he acts as if he and his mother form one omnipotent system.
Subphases of Separation-Individuation Process		
Differentiation subphase	5–10 months	The child begins to "hatch" out of the symbiotic relationship. She begins to discriminate her mother from other people and develops a special attachment to her.
Practicing subphase	10–18 months	The infant becomes aware that his body is separate from his mother's. Locomotor development contributes to this realization. The child's concept of his mother is further differentiated and consolidated so that she becomes even more important to the baby.
Rapprochement subphase	15–22 months	Toddlers seem more attached to their mothers. There is often intense separation and stranger anxiety. Thus, after moving away from the mother in the practicing subphase, the child now seems more attached than ever to her mother. She still recognizes that she and her mother are separate, however.
Consolidation of individuality and the beginnings of emotional object constancy	24–36 months	The child has a well-formed concept of her mother. This includes understanding that her mother is a permanent entity with both positive and negative characteristics. The child can tolerate increasingly lengthy separations from the mother.

Reproduced from *Infancy* (p. 223) by L. Smolak, 1986, New Jersey: Prentice Hall. Copyright 1986 by Prentice-Hall. Reprinted by permission.

linked to the child's signals, the child will become confused about physical states, interpersonal interactions, and their connection. Johnson and Connors (1987) propose that the self-imposed starvation and other forms of restriction indicative of anorexia nervosa are an outgrowth of maternal overinvolvement, whereas the lack of impulse control indicative of bulimic behavior is an adaptation to maternal underinvolvement.

Johnson and Connors (1987) also link subtypes of eating disorders to Mahler et al.'s (1975) specific subphases. In keeping with their psychodynamic developmental perspective, Johnson and Connors postulate three subtypes of eating-disordered patients: psychotic, character disordered, and neurotic. As shown in Figure 2-1, they argue that the majority of eating-disordered patients fall within the character-disordered group. Character disorders reflect problems in the middle subphases of separation-individuation, while the more primitive ego resources of the psychotic person represent disruption during the initial separation. Despite their considerable anxieties and maladaptive behavior, neurotic people are seen as suffering from developmental disruptions that are less severe because they occurred after establishment of a separate sense of self.

Johnson and Connors subdivide character-disordered clients into borderline and false self/narcissistic. Borderline personality disorder is marked by significant ego deficits that result in serious self-regulatory problems. Intense anger and

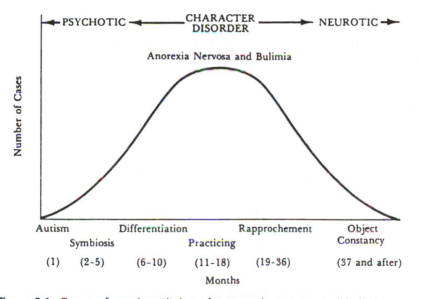

Figure 2-1 Range of psychopathology for anorexia nervosa and bulimia nervosa patients. This figure is from *The Etiology and Treatment of Bulimia Nervosa: A Biopsychosocial Perspective* (p. 103) by C. L. Johnson and M. E. Connors, 1987, New York: Basic Books. Copyright 1987 by Basic Books. Reprinted by permission.

anxiety are frequent experiences, and self-other relationships vacillate between idealization (clinging) and paranoid experiences of malevolent intrusion (withdrawal). Under stress, the borderline's self-other boundaries may virtually disappear, leading to extreme dedifferentiation. In a false self-narcissistic character disorder there are greater ego resources and less emotional torment, yet the narcissistic label is paradoxical because the person's fundamental experience of self is one of "nonexistence, fraudulence, and ineffectiveness" (Johnson, 1991, p. 185). To compensate for these feelings, the individual constructs a false front.

The intersection of the anorexic-bulimic and false self-borderline categories creates four subtypes. As shown in Table 2-2, each of the subtypes represents the effects of a different type of early mothering on separation-individuation (Johnson & Connors, 1987; Johnson, 1991). For example, nonmalevolent maternal intrusiveness during the differentiation and practicing subphases leaves the child with interoceptive deficits and an orientation toward self-regulation through accommodation to mother's needs. This sets the stage for the false self form of anorexia nervosa, the "best little girl in the world" (Levenkron, 1978), who as an adolescent becomes a defiant restrictor in order to establish (save) her self.

By their own admission, Johnson and Connors' (1987) theory is quite speculative and based heavily on their extensive clinical experience and on object relations theory. Although research does not support Johnson and Connors' sharp distinction between the mothers/families of anorexics versus those of bulimics (Wonderlich, 1992), there is some limited empirical evidence linking separation-individuation difficulties to bulimia nervosa and anorexia nervosa (Friedlander & Siegel, 1990; Rhodes & Kroger, 1991; Smolak & Levine, 1993). However, lack of comparability in measures and samples makes it impossible to draw many specific conclusions regarding the relationships. There is some evidence that females with restricting anorexia nervosa are less separated (i.e., more dependent) than those with bulimia nervosa (Rhodes & Kroger, 1991; Smolak & Levine, 1993). In addition, Friedlander and Siegel (1990) found that low scores on self-other differentiation are correlated with high scores on the Eating Disorder Inventory (EDI) subscales of ineffectiveness and interoceptive awareness. It is noteworthy that, to date, separation-individuation measures do not account for a large proportion of the variance in eating disorder scores.

Thus, the data are much less specific in regard to the relationship between eating disorders and separation-individuation. They also suggest this relationship has a less powerful influence than that proposed by Johnson and Connors (1987). Given the complex measurement issues, the limited use of clinical samples in research, and the absence of a direct test, it would be premature to dismiss the model on empirical grounds. Nevertheless, the principles of developmental psychopathology and developmental psychology can help clarify the limitations of Johnson and Connors' (1987) theory, as well as suggest needed expansions and revisions.

Table 2-2 Variations in Character Pathology for Anorexic and Bulimic Patients

Pathology	Borderline Malevolent	False self/narcisstic Nonmalevolent
Restrictor Overinvolvement	Malevolent intrusiveness (intentional) Attachment - hostile, controlling enmeshment Separation - retaliation by other, injury to self Self - repeatedly overwhelmed, in danger Other - punitive, controlling, harsh, critical Defenses - paranoid defenses used to establish and protect boundaries, splitting	Nonmalevolent intrusiveness (unintentional) Attachment - controlling but less hostile and punitive enmeshment Separation - depletion of both self and other, injury to other Self - extension of other, without identity, ineffective, reactive Other - fragile Defenses - less paranoid, more obsessive, phobic
Bulimic Underinvolvement	Malevolent neglect (intentional) Attachment - hostile disengagement resulting in clingy dependence Separation - abandonment, emptiness, fragmentation Self - worthless, unlovable Other - withholding, punitive Defenses - hysterical/impulsive used in effort to introject, projective identification	Nonmalevolent neglect (unintentional) Attachment - less hostile disengagement, wish for intimacy versus fear of disappointment, discovery, rejection, injury to other Separation - protective of self and other, pseudoautonomy, distant closeness Self - fraud, inadequate, destructively needy Other - incapable of adequate holding Defenses - schizoid defenses, avoidance, denial, isolation of affect, intellectualization, suppression

Reproduced from *The Etiology and Treatment of Bulimia Nervosa: A Biopsychosocial Perspective* (p. 105) by C. L. Johnson and M. E. Connors, 1987, New York: Basic Books. Copyright 1987 by Basic Books. Reprinted by permission.

Developmental Pathways

There is no doubt that negative early experiences can significantly contribute to abnormal development, but the effects are not deterministic or inevitable. Events as dramatic as maternal loss or child sexual abuse do not invariably have long-term negative effects (Browne & Finkelhor, 1986; Rutter, 1979). Much depends on other variables affecting development, such as the genetic predispositions of the child, the occurrence of later stressors, and the availability of social supports (Garmezy, 1983).

Similarly, disturbances in the mother-infant relationship do not always produce negative outcomes, much less a specific type of negative outcome. This is especially clear in the attachment literature. There are important similarities between current models of attachment and Johnson and Connors' theory. Ainsworth (Ainsworth, Blehar, Waters, & Wall, 1978), Bowlby (1977), and Sroufe (1989) have argued that the quality of attachment has a great impact on subsequent development, including pathological development. Bowlby (1977) even mentions eating disorders as a possible outcome of inadequate attachment. These researchers also maintain that maternal attentiveness to infant needs is the primary determinant of attachment. Indeed, research has demonstrated the following connections: (1) insensitive mothering with avoidant attachment; (2) maternal underinvolvement with ambivalent/resistant attachment; and (3) moderate stimulation and consistent responsivity with secure attachment (e.g., Ainsworth et al., 1978; Belsky, Rovine, & Taylor, 1984). These relationships are clearly similar to those postulated for Johnson and Connors' subtypes. In addition, recent research supports the long-held theoretical proposition that attachment is positively correlated with development of the self (Pipp, Easterbrooks, & Harmon, 1992). Thus, there is reason to believe that attachment and separation-individuation processes during infancy and childhood are both components of self development, and that which promotes one, promotes them all.

However, even a cursory analysis of the attachment outcome literature confirms the principle of multiple pathways. For example, Fagot and Kavanagh (1990) found that insecure attachment at 18 months was unrelated to teacher-rated or parent-rated behavior problems at age 4. Even when a correlation between insecure attachment and subsequent disorder does appear, it is far from a perfect relationship. A recent cross-sectional study of preschoolers found that 20% of a clinical sample had secure attachments, while about 25% of the nonclinical comparison sample had insecure attachments (Greenberg et al., 1991). Furthermore, changes in family or childcare circumstances reduce the relationship between early attachment and later outcome (Erickson, Sroufe, & Egeland, 1985).

Certainly, continuity in the environment (e.g., family interactions), and in modes of coping that are selectively reinforced, will typically produce considerable continuity in development. Thus, children whose mothers consistently report higher levels of family stress are more likely to show behavioral disorders across the entire 3-year-old to 9-year-old period (Campbell, 1991). Nonetheless, in evaluating models like that of Johnson and Connors (1987), we should bear in mind that environments can and do change in ways that mediate the effects of early experience.

We should also be reminded that developmental psychologists have increasingly insisted that no one phase of development is the key or primary or determinant stage (Hetherington & Baltes, 1988). A deviant beginning does not doom one to psychopathology any more than a normal or superior infancy guarantees lifelong mental health (Sroufe, 1989). Although discontinuity in the form of stressors (e.g., death of parent) is potentially very significant, it is the continuity of experience that encourages a child to continue on a "negative path." These issues of early experience, plasticity, and continuity call our attention to the need for longitudinal research on eating disorders.

More recently, Maine (1991) examined the overlooked role of inadequate fathering in eating disorders. Most theories highlighting separation-individuation difficulties as a precursor of eating disorders focus on the effects of early mothering. Although developmental research suggests that mothers and fathers are similar in some ways, such as in importance as attachment objects (Fox, Kimmerly, & Schafer, 1991), there are some significant differences in paternal versus maternal influences (Lamb, 1986). A potentially important example is that fathers are more likely to endorse and enforce sex role stereotypes (Jacklin & Maccoby, 1983), which have been implicated in the development of eating problems (Timko, Striegel-Moore, Silberstein, & Rodin, 1987). Furthermore, it is not clear that the effects of mothers are independent of the effects of fathers (Phares, 1992). Does insensitive mothering have the same impact regardless of the father's emotional connection and style of interacting with the child? Similarly, extrafamilial support may reduce the impact of pathological parenting (Garmezy, 1983).

In summary, Johnson and Connors (1987) present a biopsychosocial perspective emphasizing the role of inadequate separation-individuation in the production of eating disorders. In light of the attachment literature, Johnson and Connors' approach does not seem to be sufficiently developmental. Applying the developmental principles of multiple pathways, transactionalism, and longitudinal research would help refine this (and any) multidimensional approach by acknowledging the interactive effects of personal and environmental factors and by encouraging the study of aspects of familial and extrafamilial relationships that typically remain constant across the lives of girls and women who develop eating disorders.

Molar Versus Molecular Analysis

What might a child who is at risk for the development of eating disorders look like at different ages or stages? This question forces us to distinguish the core (or molar) features of eating disorders from the symptomatic (or molecular) reflections of the core at various stages of development (Cichetti & Schneider-Rosen,1986).

Borderline Disorder in Children   According to Johnson and Connors (1987), the core structure of most eating disorders is the ego deficit (e.g., lack of interoceptive awareness) that underlies the character types discussed above. The developmental perspective, then, directs us to examine whether young children are capable of possessing this molar structure, and, if so, in what form.

Looking for evidence of borderline behaviors in children seems a reasonable place to begin. In fact, several researchers have recently claimed that there are borderline children (Cauwels, 1992; Cicchetti & Olsen, 1990). These children are very anxious, emotionally overreactive in response to perceived threats, and so dependent as to be labeled symbiotic. They also have minipsychotic episodes, e.g., brief periods of autistic withdrawal or uncontrollable rage.

At the molecular level, these symptoms are quite similar to those seen in adults with borderline personality disorder. But are the structures underlying these manifestations really the same? Phenotypic (molecular) similarity is no guarantee of isomorphism in underlying structures of self. Developmental psychologists are quite familiar with the fact that similar behaviors in adults (especially the elderly) and children may actually reflect very different levels of organization and competency (see, e.g., research on Piagetian tasks by Hornblum & Overton, 1976).

Do borderline children become borderline adults? Although there is no straightforward answer to this question, three sets of limited findings offer more support for the principle of multiple paths. First, according to retrospective accounts, it is questionable whether even a majority of adolescents or adults with borderline personality disorder exhibited such maladaptive behavior as children (Cauwels, 1992). Second, Wergeland's (1979, cited in Cicchetti & Olsen, 1990) study of 29 children, ages 2 to 13, hospitalized for borderline psychosis found that 11 (38%) were symptom-free at a follow-up assessment 5 to 20 years later. The others had problems ranging from frank psychosis to moderate neurosis; only 5 (17%) were still borderline. Third, most borderline children are male, whereas in adulthood the diagnosis is given far more commonly to females (Cauwels, 1992).

Temperament   The lack of any clear relationship between borderline children and borderline disorder in adulthood suggests that the molar (core) structures develop and change throughout childhood and adolescence. There is little available research concerning childhood predictors of personality disorders (Johnson, 1993); thus, we must examine personality vulnerabilities that may lead to the dysfunctional core structure.

One feasible source of vulnerability for personality and eating disturbances is temperament (Johnson & Connors, 1987; Strober, 1991). In general, temperament refers to a fairly stable disposition to react in certain ways to external and internal demands. Threshold and intensity of emotional reactivity, preferred levels of sociability and activity, typical responses to novelty, and general resilience in the face of stress are the sorts of characteristics that comprise temperament. Temperament influences the organization and management of self and others, thereby contributing to the transactions emphasized by developmental psychopathologists (Bates, 1987). At least some temperament characteristics appear to have a genetic basis (Buss & Plomin, 1984).

Johnson and Connors (1987) have proposed that the affective instability associated with bulimia nervosa is constitutional. Since affective qualities are frequently considered to be an important dimension of temperament (e.g., Bates, 1987), our understanding of affective instability may be increased by understanding models of temperament. Again, the developmental literature on temperament would encourage us to recognize the dynamic interplay of child and environment. For example, there are demonstrations of how environment may moderate or exacerbate temperament (Gandour, 1989) as well as evidence of temperament's influence on parental and teacher behavior (Bates, 1987). Strober (1991) recently provided an example of how temperament might be helpful in understanding anorexia nervosa.

Self Development   Temperament suggests an inborn structure that is exacerbated or moderated by the environment. The self-development literature, on the other hand, raises the possibility of a structure that changes with both maturation and social experiences. Children as young as 3½ have concepts of self that involve general dispositions instead of specific memories or expectations (Eder, 1989; Miller & Aloise, 1989). Furthermore, by age 7½ these self concepts appear to be organized into personality clusters resembling the adult structures of neuroticism and extraversion (Eder, 1990). There is considerable variation between children on these traits, but within children there is at least some stability. Such personality structures might operate similarly to the socially oriented temperament characteristics proposed by Strober.

Research by Greenberg et al. (1991) points to another aspect of self that may provide clues to the development of eating problems. They argue that the integration of behavioral, linguistic, and cognitive skills crucial for self-control and interoceptive awareness may be thought of as an identifiable structure that shows variability across individual children. All of these findings suggest that various forms of vulnerability in self structure may be measurable in young children. This raises the possibility of charting developmental pathways for children with different early personality vulnerabilities.

Summary of the Implications of Developmental Psychopathology for the Johnson and Connors (1987) Model

Johnson and Connors (1987; Johnson, 1991) have presented a multidimensional model that incorporates developmental factors. Their use of Mahler's stage theory and of research on family dynamics to distinguish among different forms of eating disorders is an important recognition of different developmental paths. Overall, however, Johnson and Connors (1987) make insufficient use of developmental principles and research. This is most evident in lack of attention to factors that might, over the long run, mediate the effects of the mother-infant relationship. The literature on attachment provides a paradigm for investigating such effects, including emphasis on the importance of ongoing transactions between the child and the environment, including the father.

Several ways in which developmental psychology and developmental psychopathology might contribute to a resolution of these problems have been suggested. Longitudinal studies of borderline or depressed children would be very useful, as would continued study of the development of self in nonclinical children. Careful review of the attachment and temperament literature might be helpful in identifying the variety of personal and social forces that produce continuity and change in the molar and molecular aspects of self. More generally, the developmental approach will help to identify those circumstances in which the interaction of vulnerabilities (whether constitutional or created by experience) and stressors is particularly likely to create the paths related to eating problems. This is the focus of the second developmental model to be discussed.

DEVELOPMENTAL TRANSITIONS AND LEVINE & SMOLAK'S (1992) MODEL OF RISK FOR EATING DISORDERS

Recently, we presented a model that attempts to explain the partial continuum of nonpathological dieting, subclinical eating disturbances, and full-blown eating disorders (Levine & Smolak, 1992). The model emphasizes normal developmental transitions, such as puberty or pregnancy, that increase the salience of three (at times interrelated) issues: body weight and shape, heterosocial demands, and achievement. Given the modal ages for onset of eating disorders, early adolescence and college transitions are viewed as particularly important (see also Attie & Brooks-Gunn, 1992).

Developmental Transitions

During a developmental transition, existing structures (of personality, self, cognition, etc.) are partially or completely dissolved and then reorganized in order to cope more effectively with the challenges of the next developmental phase (Levinson, 1986). Old structures, including relationships, are no longer completely adequate to handle new demands, while the new structures have not yet been consolidated. This transition leaves the individual more vulnerable than usual to the effects of stressors.

By definition, everyone faces normative challenges as he or she moves through a developmental transition. During the early adolescence transition the challenges include puberty, the beginning of heterosocial relationships, movement toward a career choice, and, in general, a gradual increase in adultlike responsibilities. With the support of family and friends, the majority of teens cope quite effectively (Harter, 1990; Offer, Ostrov, & Howard, 1984).

According to our model, these challenges may be overwhelming if they occur simultaneously. Simmons and her colleagues have shown that junior high girls facing three or more stressors have significant declines in grade point average, extracurricular activities, and self-esteem (e.g., Simmons, Burgeson, Carlton-Ford, & Blyth, 1987). Boys were not as negatively affected. Due to an earlier onset of puberty, girls are more likely than boys to face the co-occurrence of puberty, dating, and transition to middle school or junior high.

How might these cumulative stressors contribute to eating problems? Many young girls come to the early adolescence transition already believing that being slender is important (Thelen et al., 1992). We hypothesize that this belief is part of a broader schema that includes information about the importance of thinness to attractiveness, the importance of attractiveness to social and career success for women, the many methods for becoming thin, and the relevance of attractiveness for one's own self-esteem. This schema is similar to, and possibly a precursor of, those hypothesized to occur in restrained eaters (King, Polivy, & Herman, 1991) and eating disorder patients (Vitousek & Hollon, 1990).

This thinness schema would cause the girl to selectively assimilate media, parental, and peer messages as supporting her assessment of attractiveness and its importance. It is activated by events that threaten maintenance of the ideal shape. Furthermore, since the girl believes the idealized slender shape is important for maximizing the likelihood of success in the social and career arenas, threats in these areas will also activate the thinness schema. Again, these beliefs are reinforced by her biased attention to, and interpretation of, cultural stereotypes (Silverstein, Perdue, & Kelly, 1986).

Our model proposes that disordered eating attitudes and behaviors can be created when weight gains, changes in heterosocial demands, and threats to achievement are filtered through the thinness schema (Levine & Smolak, 1992). If either weight gains or heterosocial demands occur alone, the outcome is an intensification of weight and shape concern and the development of nonpathological dieting. If these challenges occur simultaneously and the thinness schema is severe, then the risk of subclinical eating disturbances rises. If there are also threats to her sense of achievement, and if the young woman possesses a particular self-definition emphasizing success in multiple roles in order to secure an identity through external approval (superwomanness; Steiner-Adair, 1986), the risk of frank eating disorders increases. Without the thinness ideal or the superwoman complex, this combination of stressors will result in a different disorder (e.g., depression), adjustment problems, or successful coping.

In early adolescence the weight (fat) gains are caused by pubertal development (Faust, 1983), while heterosocial demands arise from the concurrence of biological changes and the rituals of dating. Achievement threats appear as children move from supportive elementary environments to the more competitive middle school setting (Bush & Simmons, 1987; Eccles & Midgley, 1990). Note that these three changes (stressors) are all normative events in the United States. Future research must establish whether they are also normative in other cultures which commonly report cases of eating disorders. However, it is reasonable to expect that comparable, though not necessarily identical, events do occur in other cultures. The timing of menarche is fairly universal. Other cultures do increase the pressure for adult behavior, which we would expect would include both career (academic) and heterosocial demands. So, for example, both the British and Japanese school systems involve important testing (to determine future education) during this period.

Thus, consistent with the goals of developmental psychopathology, our model attempts to demonstrate how normal development may be channeled into deviant paths. Both cross-sectional and longitudinal data supporting the model have been reported (Levine, Smolak, Moodey, Shuman, & Hessen, 1994; Smolak et al., 1993). Other studies relating the tasks of puberty to dieting, body dissatisfaction and disordered eating are reviewed in Attie and Brooks-Gunn (1992) and Levine and Smolak (1992).

Relation to Developmental Psychopathology

Our model incorporates the principles of developmental psychopathology in several ways. It demonstrates how a particular developmental event (or set of events) might result in normal development, eating problems or disorders, or some other form of psychopathology such as depression. In keeping with the transactional perspective, our model acknowledges the interplay of (a) stressors, (b) the timing of stressors, (c) social variables (e.g., family and peers), and (d) characteristics of the individual (thinness and superwoman schemata). These features, coupled with the variety of outcomes explained, are consistent with the principle that classes of psychopathology should be conceptualized as a set of developmental pathways related to paths of normal development (Sroufe, 1989). Our model also has the flexibility to suggest several potential points of onset of the core features of eating disorders instead of emphasizing one particular path.

At this time, the model's principal shortcoming is its inability to account for individual differences in vulnerability to the effects of developmental transitions that increase the salience of weight, shape, achievement, and control. The paths we postulate are incomplete because the model does not explain how girls develop the thinness and superwoman schemata that mediate reactions to individual or simultaneous developmental events. As is the case for Johnson and Connors' (1987) model, there is much to be gained from the developmental literature.

Analysis of Molar Structure

The literature on self-development seems particularly relevant to an account of the development of schemata incorporating the importance of being slender and/or appearing successful in multiple roles. Elementary school-age children have a self-concept in which physical self and social self are differentiated (Harter, 1990). The physical self-concept is further subdivided into competence (e.g., in sports) and attractiveness. In general, children with lower body esteem tend to have lower self-esteem (Mendelson & White, 1985). More interesting for our purposes is the fact that, at least among girls, body esteem drops considerably during the middle school years, even as other components of self-esteem increase (Abramowitz, Petersen, & Schulenberg, 1984). Overweight girls may suffer especially pronounced drops in body esteem during the adolescent years (Mendelson & White, 1985).

It appears that at least some components of the thinness schema develop normatively during elementary school. A variety of researchers have demonstrated that some nonobese third through sixth graders would like to be thinner and have tried to lose weight (Maloney, McGuire, Daniels, & Specker, 1989; Thelen et al., 1992). Even younger children demonstrate a preference for thin people (e.g., Lerner & Jovanovic, 1990). However, it is not clear how and to what extent components of the thinness schema are integrated with the broader self schema. Weight and body shape have not been clearly demonstrated to be important determinants of self-esteem or peer relationships among young elementary school children (Cohen, Klesges, Summerville, & Meyers, 1989; Mendelson & White, 1985). This is consistent with broader developmental research suggesting that social standards only begin to be applied to self during elementary school and that such comparison intensifies during adolescence. What is clear is that existing developmental theory and research can contribute much to our attempts to design studies that address the schemata underlying eating problems.

As was true of Johnson and Connors' (1987) theory, our model would also benefit from a greater recognition of the possible contribution of temperament and other genetic predispositions. For example, Strober's (1991) theory suggests that a girl will be more susceptible to developing a stringent thinness schema if she is constitutionally inclined to minimize novelty and stimulation, avoid harm through withdrawal and worry, and be painfully sensitive to social mediators of approval and security. Research on sex role schema development (e.g., Bem, 1981) is also clearly applicable to our superwoman construct and to the more general issue of the relationship between the thinness schema, female roles, and self-concept.

Dangers of Overnormalizing Normative Development

As theorists interested in psychopathology turn to developmental psychology for potential variables and models, there is the risk that concepts of development will be oversimplified. For example, our model emphasizes the fat gains associated with female pubertal development. But what about individual differences in the timing of these fat gains? Although most girls accumulate fat throughout puberty, especially in the middle and late phases of the process, a few put it on even before the onset of their growth spurt. Are these girls especially at risk for eating problems (Attie & Brooks-Gunn, 1992)? And what of that minority of girls who actually lose weight as they go through puberty? Are they immune to eating problems? Similar questions could be raised about the middle school transition, since not all children move out of elementary school at the end of fifth grade. Simmons and her colleagues (Simmons & Blyth, 1987) have demonstrated that those who stay in an elementary school setting are at less risk for self-esteem problems, but questions concerning how (or if) they might develop eating problems remain unaddressed.

The point here is that we need to be careful not to overnormalize normative development. Doing so reduces our understanding of the multiple pathways that lead to adolescent or adult outcomes. Overgeneralization also tends to divert us from the important analysis of contexts of development. Research has already begun to demonstrate that career and school contexts influence eating attitudes and behaviors (Attie & Brooks-Gunn, 1992; Richards, Boxer, Petersen, & Albrecht, 1990). The issue of how the features of the dominant culture might interact with other factors to alter an individual's risk for eating disorders deserves more attention (Root, 1990). Research on the development of minority children (e.g., McLoyd & Spencer, 1990) can provide a model for such work.

Summary of the Implications of Developmental Psychopathology for Levine & Smolak's (1992) Model

Our model includes multiple pathways to a continuum of outcomes, a transactional approach, and an emphasis on developmental transitions. Thus, it is more clearly rooted in developmental psychology than most other models of eating disorders. Yet, we still see numerous ways in which the model would be strengthened by developmental psychopathology and developmental psychology. Most notably, greater attention needs to be given to the development of psychological (molar) structures that set the stage for a potentially pathological interpretation of transitional events. Greater awareness of individual differences in normal development is also needed.

DISCUSSION AND CONCLUSIONS

Although developmental variables have long played a role in etiological models of eating disorders, application of developmental principles has usually been minimal or absent. The emerging field of developmental psychopathology offers five core principles that address these shortcomings: developmental pathways, transactional analyses, molar versus molecular structures, definitions of normal versus abnormal development, and developmental transitions. All areas of psychopathology can benefit from a developmental perspective, but three characteristics of eating disorders make it particularly likely that application of developmental principles will lead to important insights into etiology and thus to much needed guidance in the relatively neglected area of prevention.

First, there appears to be at least a partial continuum of attitudes and behaviors ranging from normal eating to eating disorders (Levine & Smolak, 1992; Polivy & Herman, 1987). In many Western countries body dissatisfaction and dieting are common in nonclinical samples of adolescent girls and women. Indeed, they are virtually normative. The relationship of body dissatisfaction and dieting to the morbid fear of fat, the drive for thinness, and body image distortion seen in eating-disordered patients is unclear, but there is good reason to believe that dieting per se contributes to some forms of eating disorders. This continuum is consistent with developmental psychopathology's contention that abnormal development represents a path off the road of normal development such that the two share at least some common roots.

Second, eating disorders are overwhelmingly more common among women than among men. No one has yet uncovered a special innate biological female vulnerability to account for this sex difference. Hence, the sex difference in risk for eating disorders must be based in large part on environmental influences that affect and transact with personality structures and cognitive schema. The immense developmental sex-role literature can provide theoretical and methodological guidance here. We believe the issue of gender role development to be of paramount importance for an understanding of eating disorders and the continuum mentioned earlier. The process not only exemplifies the principle of multiple pathways, but it also demonstrates the transactional model of development. Girls often experience different cultural contexts than boys do simply because of their biological sex. This differential treatment may contribute to the development of gender schema, which in turn create biases in the interpretation of the environment (Liben & Signorella, 1993), which then shape the influence of the environment on the child's development.

Third, eating disorders tend to emerge during the early adolescence and early adult transitions (Attie & Brooks-Gunn, 1992). Developmental psychology can provide a clearer understanding of why these transitions are periods of heightened vulnerability. For example, greater attention to loss of social support during these two (but perhaps not other) normative transitions may provide a basis for prevention programs (DuBois, Felner, Brand, Adan, & Evans, 1992). The surge of eating problems during these transitions also draws our attention to the molar structures of body image or self that are evaluated, and perhaps restructured.

The developmental approach raises many questions for future research. Clinicians working with adolescents and adults have identified core personality and cognitive features of eating disorders. It is now critical to document what the early forms of these features look like, what their roots are, and how they evolve toward or away from eating disorders. Developmental psychology and developmental psychopathology provide important paradigms to guide this work.

DISCUSSION QUESTIONS

1 Discuss three implications of the developmental psychopathology concept of "paths of development."

2 What is the distinction between molar and molecular structures? How is this distinction relevant to the development of eating disorders?

3 Describe the relationship between parenting styles and eating disorders as outlined by Johnson and Connors.

4 The developmental literature on attachment suggests several problems with Johnson and Connors model of infant development's relationship to eating disorders. Discuss two of these problems.

5 Discuss the relationship of borderline personality in children to the molar/molecular structure distinction.

6 What is the role of normative cumulative stressors in Levine and Smolak's model? How do these reflect the developmental psychopathology principle of multiple pathways?

7 Discuss the possible relationship of Levine and Smolak's notion of a thinness schema to self-development.

8 What does it mean to suggest that overnormalizing normal development may be risky for our understanding of the development of eating disorders?

9 Consider why a developmental psychopathology approach is particularly valuable in understanding eating disorders.

REFERENCES

Abramowitz, R. H., Petersen, A., & Schulenberg, J. E. (1984). Changes in self-image during early adolescence. In D. Offer, E. Ostrov, & K. I. Howard (Eds.), *Patterns of adolescent self-image* (pp. 19–28). San Francisco: Jossey-Bass.

Ainsworth, M. D. S., Blehar, M., Waters, E., & Wall, S. (1978). *Patterns of attachment.* Hillsdale, NJ: Erlbaum.

Attie, I., & Brooks-Gunn, J. (1992). Developmental issues in the study of eating problems. In J. H. Crowther, D. L. Tennenbaum, S. E. Hobfoll, & M. A. P. Stephens (Eds.), *The etiology of bulimia nervosa: The individual and familial context* (pp. 35–58). Washington, DC: Hemisphere.

Barth, F. D. (1989). Separation-individuation, sense of self, and bulimia in college students. *Journal of College Student Psychotherapy, 3,* 135–149.

Bates, J. (1987). Temperament in infancy. In J. Osofsky (Ed.), *Handbook of infant development* (2nd ed., pp. 1101–1149). New York: Wiley.

Belsky, J., Rovine, M., & Taylor, D. (1984). The Pennsylvania Infant and Family Development Project III: The origins of individual differences in infant-mother attachment: Maternal and infant contributions. *Child Development, 55,* 718–728.

Bem, S. L. (1981). Gender schema theory: A cognitive account of sex-typing. *Psychological Review, 88,* 354–364.

Bowlby, J. (1977). The making and breaking of affectional bonds. *British Journal of Psychiatry, 130,* 201–210.

Brooks-Gunn, J., Rock, D., & Warren, M. P. (1989). Comparability of constructs across the adolescent years. *Developmental Psychology, 25,* 51–60.

Browne, A., & Finkelhor, D. (1986). Impact of child sexual abuse: A review of the research. *Psychological Bulletin, 99,* 66–77.

Bruch, H. (1973). *Eating disorders: Obesity, anorexia nervosa, and the person within.* New York: Basic Books.

Bush, D. M., & Simmons, R. (1987). Gender and coping with entrance into adolescence. In R. C. Barnett, L. Biener, & G. K. Baruch (Eds.), *Gender and stress* (pp. 185–217). New York: Free Press.

Buss, A. H., & Plomin, R. (1984). *Temperament: Early developing personality traits.* Hillsdale, NJ: Erlbaum.

Campbell, S. B. (1991). Longitudinal studies of active and aggressive preschoolers: Individual differences in early behavior and in outcome. In D. Cicchetti & S. Toth (Eds.), *Internalizing and externalizing expressions of dysfunction: Rochester symposium on developmental psychopathology* (Vol. 2, pp. 57–90). Hillsdale, NJ: Erlbaum.

Cauwels, J. M. (1992). *Imbroglio: Rising to the challenges of borderline personality disorder.* New York: W. W. Norton.

Cichetti, D., & Olsen, K. (1990). Borderline disorders in childhood. In M. Lewis & S. Miller (Eds.), *Handbook of developmental psychopathology* (pp. 355–370). New York: Plenum.

Cichetti, D., & Schneider-Rosen, K. (1986). An organizational approach to childhood depression. In M. Rutter, C. E. Izard, & P. B. Read (Eds.), *Depression in young people: Developmental and clinical perspectives* (pp. 71–134). New York: Guilford.

Cohen, R., Klesges, R., Summerville, M., & Meyers, A. (1989). A developmental analysis of the influence of body weight on the sociometry of children. *Addictive Behaviors, 14,* 463–476.

Cowan, P. A. (1988). Developmental psychopathology: A nine-cell map of the territory. In E. D. Nannis & P. A. Cowan (Eds.), *Developmental psychopathology and its treatment* (pp. 5–29). San Francisco: Jossey-Bass.

DuBois, D., Felner, R., Brand, S., Adan, A., & Evans, E. (1992). A prospective study of life stress, social support, and adaptation in early adolescence. *Child Development, 63,* 542–557.

Eccles, J., & Midgley, C. (1990). Changes in academic motivation and self-perception during early adolescence. In R. Montemayor, G. Adams, & T. Gullota (Eds.) *From childhood to adolescence: A transitional period?* (pp. 134–155). Newbury Park, CA: Sage.

Eder, R. (1989). The emergent personologist. The structure and content of 3½-, 5½-, and 7½-year-olds' concepts of themselves and other persons. *Child Development, 60,* 1218–1228.

Eder, R. (1990). Uncovering young children's psychosocial selves: Individual and developmental differences. *Child Development, 61,* 849–863.

Erickson, M. F., Sroufe, L. A., & Egeland, B. (1985). The relationship between quality of attachment and behavior problems in preschool in a high-risk sample. In I. Bretherton

& E. Waters (Eds.), *Growing points of attachment theory and research. Monographs of the Society for Research in Child Development, 50,* 147–166.

Fagot, B., & Kavanagh, K. (1990). The prediction of antisocial behavior from avoidant attachment classifications. *Child Development, 61,* 864–873.

Faust, M. S. (1983). Alternative constructions of adolescent growth. In J. Brooks-Gunn & A. C. Petersen (Eds.), *Girls at puberty: Biological and psychosocial perspectives* (pp. 105–125). New York: Plenum.

Fox, N., Kimmerly, N., & Schafer, W. (1991). Attachment to mother/attachment to father: A meta-analysis. *Child Development, 62,* 210–225.

Friedlander, M. L., & Siegel, S. M. (1990). Separation-individuation difficulties and cognitive-behavior indicators of eating disorders among college women. *Journal of Counseling Psychology, 37,* 74–78.

Gandour, M. (1989). Activity level as a dimension of temperament in toddlers: Its relevance for the organismic specificity hypothesis. *Child Development, 60,* 1092–1098.

Garfinkel, P. E., & Garner, D. M. (1982). *Anorexia nervosa: A multidimensional perspective.* New York: Brunner/Mazel.

Garmezy, N. (1983). Stressors of childhood. In N. Garmezy & M. Rutter (Eds.), *Stress, coping, and development in children* (pp. 43–84). New York: McGraw-Hill.

Gowers, S., Crisp, A., Joughin, N., & Bhat, A. (1991). Premenarcheal anorexia nervosa. *Journal of Child Psychology and Psychiatry, 32,* 515–524.

Greenberg, M., Kusche, C., & Speltz, M. (1991). Emotional regulation, self-control, and psychopathology: The role of relationships in early childhood. In D. Cicchetti & S. Toth (Eds.), *Internalizing and externalizing expressions of dysfunction: Rochester symposium on developmental psychopathology* (Vol. 2, pp. 21–56). Hillsdale, NJ: Erlbaum.

Harter, S. (1990). Issues in the assessment of the self-concept of children and adolescents. In A. LaGreca (Ed.), *Through the eyes of a child* (pp. 292–325). Boston: Allyn & Bacon.

Hetherington, E. M. (1989). Coping with family transitions: Winners, losers, and survivors. *Child Development, 60,* 1–14.

Hetherington, E. M., & Baltes, P. B. (1988). Child psychology and life-span development. In E. Hetherington, R. Lerner, & M. Perlmutter (Eds.), *Child development in life-span perspective* (pp. 1–20). Hillsdale, NJ: Erlbaum.

Hornblum, J., & Overton, W. (1976). Area and volume conservation among the elderly: Assessment and training. *Developmental Psychology, 12,* 68–74.

Hsu, L. K. G. (1990). *Eating disorders.* New York: Guilford.

Jacklin, C., & Maccoby, E. (1983). Issues of gender differentiation in normal development. In M. Levine, W. Carey, A. Crocker, & R. Gross (Eds.), *Developmental-behavioral pediatrics* (pp. 175–184). Philadelphia: Saunders.

Johnson, C. (1991). Treatment of eating-disordered patients with borderline and false-self/narcisstic disorders. In C. Johnson (Ed.), *Psychodynamic treatment of anorexia nervosa and bulimia* (pp. 165–193). New York: Guilford.

Johnson, C., & Connors, M. E. (1987). *The etiology and treatment of bulimia nervosa: A biopsychosocial perspective.* New York: Basic Books.

Johnson, J. (1993). Relationship between psychosocial development and personality disorder symptomology in late adolescents. *Journal of Youth and Adolescence, 22,* 33–42.

King, G. A., Polivy, J., & Herman, C. P. (1991). Cognitive aspects of dietary restraint: Effects on person memory. *International Journal of Eating Disorders, 10,* 313–321.

Lamb, M. (Ed.). (1986). *The father's role: Applied perspectives.* New York: Wiley.

Lerner, R. M., & Jovanovic, J. (1990). The role of body image in psychosocial development across the life span: A developmental contextual perspective. In T. F. Cash & T. Pruzinsky (Eds.), *Body images: Development, deviance and change* (pp. 110–127). New York: Guilford.

Levenkron, S. (1978). *The best little girl in the world.* Chicago: Contemporary Books.

Levine, M. P., & Smolak, L. (1992). Toward a model of the developmental psychopathology eating disorders: The example of early adolescence. In J. H. Crowther, D. L. Tennenbaum, S. E. Hobfoll, & M. A. P. Stephens (Eds.), *The etiology of bulimia nervosa: The individual and familial context* (pp. 59–80). Washington, DC: Hemisphere.

Levine, M. P., Smolak, L., Moodey, A., Shuman, M., & Hessen, L. (1994) Normative developmental challenges and dieting and eating disturbances in middle school girls. *International Journal of Eating Disorders, 15,* 11–20.

Levinson, D. (1986). A conception of adult development. *American Psychologist, 41,* 3–13.

Liben, L., & Signorella, M. (1993). Gender-schematic processing in children: The role of initial interpretations of stimuli. *Developmental Psychology, 29,* 141–149.

Mahler, M. S., Pine, F., & Bergman, A. (1975). *The psychological birth of the human infant.* New York: Basic Books.

Maine, M. (1991). *Father hunger.* Carlsbad, CA: Gurze.

Maloney, M. J., McGuire, J., Daniels, S. R., & Specker, B. (1989). Dieting behavior and eating attitudes in children. *Pediatrics, 84,* 482–489.

McLoyd, V. (1989). Socialization and development in a changing economy. *American Psychologist, 44,* 293–302.

McLoyd, V., & Spencer, M. (Eds.). (1990). Special issue on minority children. *Child Development, 62,* 263–589.

Mendelson, B., & White, D. (1985). Development of self-body esteem in overweight youngsters. *Developmental Psychology, 21,* 90–96.

Montemayor, R., Adams, G., & Gullota, T. (1990). *From childhood to adolescence: A transitional period?* Newbury Park CA: Sage.

Offer, D., Ostrov, E., & Howard, K. (1984). The self-image of normal adolescents. In D. Offer, E. Ostrov, & K. Howard (Eds.), *Patterns of adolescent self-image* (pp. 5–18). San Francisco: Jossey-Bass.

Phares, V. (1992). Where's poppa? The relative lack of attention to the role of fathers in child and adolescent psychopathology. *American Psychologist, 47,* 656–664.

Pipp, S., Easterbrooks, M. A., & Harmon, R. (1992). The relation between attachment and knowledge of self and mother in one- to three-year-old infants. *Child Development, 63,* 738–750.

Polivy, J., & Herman, C. P. (1987). Diagnosis and treatment of normal eating. *Journal of Consulting & Clinical Psychology, 55,* 635–644.

Rhodes, B., & Kroger, J. (1991, April). *Parental bonding and separation-individuation difficulties among late adolescent eating disordered women.* Paper presented at the Biennial Meeting of the Society for Research in Child Development, Seattle, Washington.

Richards, M. H., Boxer, A. M., Petersen, A. C., & Albrecht, R. (1990). Relation of weight to body image in pubertal girls and boys from two communities. *Developmental Psychology, 26,* 313–321.

Root, M. P. (1990). Disordered eating in women of color. *Sex Roles, 22,* 525–536.

Rutter, M. (1979). Maternal deprivation, 1972–1978: New findings, new concepts, new approaches. *Child Development, 50,* 283–305.

Rutter, M. (1986). The developmental psychopathology of depression: Issues and perspectives. In M. Rutter, C. E. Izard, & P. B. Read (Eds.), *Depression in young people: Developmental and clinical perspectives* (pp. 3–30). New York: Guilford.

Scarr, S., & McCartney, K. (1983). How people make their own environments: A theory of genotype-environment effects. *Child Development, 54,* 424–435.

Silverstein, B., Perdue, L., & Kelly, E. (1986). The role of the mass media in promoting a thin standard of bodily attractiveness for women. *Sex Roles, 14,* 519–532.

Simmons, R. G., & Blyth, D. A. (1987). *Moving into adolescence: The impact of pubertal change and school context.* Hawthorne, NJ: Aldine.

Simmons, R. G., Burgeson, R., Carlton-Ford, S., & Blyth, D. A. (1987). The impact of cumulative change in early adolescence. *Child Development, 58,* 1220–1234.

Smolak, L. (1986). *Infancy.* Englewood Cliffs, NJ: Prentice-Hall.

Smolak, L., & Levine, M. P. (1993). Separation-individuation difficulties and the distinction between bulimia nervosa and anorexia nervosa in college women. *International Journal of Eating Disorders, 14,* 33–41.

Smolak, L., Levine, M. P., & Gralen, S. (1993). The impact of puberty and dating on eating problems among middle school girls. *Journal of Youth and Adolescence, 22,* 355–368.

Sroufe, L. A. (1989). Pathways to adaptation and maladaptation: Psychopathology as developmental deviation. In D. Cichetti (Ed.), *The emergence of a discipline: Rochester symposium on developmental psychopathology* (Vol. 1, pp. 13–40). Hillsdale, NJ: Erlbaum.

Steiner-Adair, C. (1986). The body politic: Normal female adolescent development and the development of eating disorders. *Journal of the American Academy of Psychoanalysis, 14,* 95–114.

Striegel-Moore, R. H. (1993). Etiology of binge eating: A developmental perspective. In C. G. Fairburn & G. T. Wilson (Eds.), *Binge eating: Nature, assessment, and treatment* (pp. 144–172). New York: Guilford.

Strober, M. (1991). Disorders of the self in anorexia nervosa: An organismic-developmental paradigm. In C. L. Johnson (Ed.), *Psychodynamic treatment of anorexia nervosa and bulimia* (pp. 354–373). New York: Guilford.

Thelen, M. H., Lawrence, C. M., & Powell, A. L. (1992). Body image, weight control, and eating disorders among children. In J. H. Crowther, D. L. Tennenbaum, S. E. Hobfoll, & M. A. P. Stephens (Eds.), *The etiology of bulimia nervosa: The individual and familial context* (pp. 81–101). Washington, DC: Hemisphere.

Timko, C., Striegel-Moore, R., Silberstein, L. R., & Rodin, J. (1987). Femininity/masculinity and disordered eating in women: How are they related? *International Journal of Eating Disorders, 6,* 701–712.

Vitousek, K., & Hollon, S. (1990). The investigation of schema content and processing in eating disorders. *Cognitive Therapy and Research, 14,* 191–214.

Wonderlich, S. (1992). Relationship of family and personality factors in bulimia. In J. H. Crowther, D. L. Tennenbaum, S. E. Hobfoll, & M. A. P. Stephens (Eds.), *The etiology of bulimia nervosa: The individual and familial context* (pp. 103–126). Washington, DC: Hemisphere.

Chapter 3

Parenting and Family Factors in Eating Problems

Glenn Waller
Rachel Calam

Family functioning was one of the earliest factors suggested to be relevant to the eating disorders (e.g., Lasegue, 1873). Since then, clinicians and researchers have proposed a number of models of family interaction that might explain a link with anorexia nervosa and bulimia nervosa (e.g., Minuchin, Rosman & Baker, 1978; Selvini-Palazzoli, 1974). Most of these models portray the family system or individual members as having a directly harmful effect upon the identified patient. However, it is also possible to see the family as a medium for transmitting pathological sociocultural values to the potential sufferer.

Hsu (1983) pointed out that many single cause models of eating disorders have been advanced, and that family dysfunction is only one of the possible factors that might explain anorexia nervosa and bulimia nervosa. It is important to recognize that no single cause model will be adequate to explain more than a small proportion of cases. Instead, the interaction of a number of factors should be considered. Such multiple cause models are useful in understanding the development and maintenance of individual cases. They all cite family dysfunction as one of the factors in the eating disorders. Some are relatively detailed in their description of the family features (e.g., Lacey, 1986), while others are less elaborate (e.g., Slade, 1982).

The family appears to have a pathological influence upon eating in two conceptual areas, although these areas are likely to overlap. First, it is necessary to consider the family's influence on the development of food preferences and fussiness in childhood and adolescence. Second, the family seems to be involved in the development of the control issues (including those relating to food) that are central to anorexic and bulimic eating disorders. This latter influence is likely to occur in adolescence and early adulthood, when establishing control is a particularly salient separation issue, but it can also be seen in late childhood in some cases.

It is appealing to assume that these areas of family influence overlap, so that family influence on food fussiness would continue into influences on formal eating disorders. However, there is no evidence for such continuity (Birch, 1987). Therefore, it is necessary to be cautious in assuming any relationship between parenting in early childhood and the later development of anorexic or bulimic eating disorders.

Parenting and family interaction are of particular importance when considering therapeutic techniques for food-related problems. Parental style and strategies have clinical relevance when treating early feeding problems (e.g., Harris & Booth, 1992; Iwaniec & Herbert, 1982). In treating anorexic and bulimic eating disorders, it has been shown that family therapy can be of value in some cases (Russell, Smukler, Dare, & Eisler, 1987). More generally, reviews and more scientific metaanalysis (e.g., Garner, 1985; Hartmann, Herzog, & Drinkmann, 1992) have suggested that individual psychotherapy is more likely to be effective if it includes consideration of relationship issues (including family relationships), regardless of the theoretical basis of the therapy.

In addition to any dysfunction in their family of origin, recent research has suggested there are difficulties in anorexics' and bulimics' relationships with their own spouses and children. Eating-disordered women report particular marital difficulties (Van den Broucke & Vandereycken, 1989; Van Buren & Williamson, 1988; Woodside & Shekter-Wolfson, 1990). These family dysfunctions might also merit therapeutic intervention, particularly in an effort to reduce cross-generational transmission of food-related psychopathology.

Constructing and targeting treatments that reduce the family-related psychopathology of childhood and adult eating problems obviously depends on having a coherent picture of the problematic patterns of interaction that underlie those problems. However, before considering those characteristic patterns, a number of methodological issues in studying family interaction and eating disorders need to be considered.

METHODOLOGICAL CONSIDERATIONS

Understanding the role of any factor in the eating disorders depends on understanding the methodological issues that are inherent in research into clinical and developmental psychology (e.g., Parry & Watts, 1989). While a full discussion of those issues is beyond the scope of this chapter, a number of methodological caveats should be kept in mind when considering the role of parenting and family interaction in eating problems.

First, the causality of any association between family function and eating psychopathology is certain to be complex. Slade (1982) and Lacey (1986) make this point clearly. They suggest that an eating disorder can be a consequence of (among other factors) characteristic patterns of family interaction, but that the eating disorder itself may have subsequent effects on the family. It is also unsafe to assume that any association of family function and eating patterns involves direct causality, since both might be products of other factors (e.g., peer influence, developmental level).

Second, because the methods of investigation differ, it is difficult to establish comparability or continuity in the findings of research into childhood and adult eating problems. The parenting factors behind eating behaviors in childhood have been studied largely through direct observation. In contrast, research into family function in anorexia nervosa and bulimia nervosa has generally involved more subjective measurement.

Finally, a number of different models of family function have been used to explain the development of eating disorders, particularly in adulthood. While these models have a degree of conceptual overlap, their comparability is limited. In particular, the measures that have been used to test these models are difficult to compare. This issue will be considered in greater detail below.

PARENTING AND THE DEVELOPMENT OF EATING DISORDERS

As has been noted above, the research into parenting factors in childhood eating problems has stressed an association with food preferences and fussiness. However, the links to more formal eating disorders are not yet established. Parenting is only one of a number of factors that influence food preference and refusal in children and adolescents. Other influences include: the provision of information, such as nutritional value (e.g., Eiser, Eiser, Patterson, & Harding, 1984; Gorn & Goldberg, 1982); gender of the child (e.g., George & Krondl, 1983); prior intake and experience (e.g., Birch & Marlin, 1982; Pangborn & Giovanni, 1984); and developmental stage (e.g., Harris & Booth, 1992). Parental influence is of particular interest because it appears to operate via a number of mechanisms in determining food choice, including those outlined above.

These mechanisms in determining food choice can be identified from an early developmental stage. Given the potential for childbirth to create a disabling depressive disorder (e.g., Cox, Connor, & Kendell, 1982), it is important to consider the effect of maternal mood on the infant's development. Hopkins, Marcus, and Campbell (1984) point out that there is a lack of systemic investigation into the effects of postnatal depression on child care. However, recent research has demonstrated that maternal mood around pregnancy is associated with infant feeding problems and practices. Using a prospective, longitudinal design, Hellin and Waller (1992) showed links between antenatal depression and mothers' difficulties in breast feeding and between postnatal anxiety and mothers' perception of the infant as fussy and demanding over food. This line of research requires extension to determine whether parental mood is linked to eating behaviors in older children and adolescents.

Later in the child's development, parental modeling may be a major factor in the effects of family function on food choice (e.g., Birch, 1987). The research evidence only partially supports this conclusion. In particular, parental preferences seem to have relatively little influence on the expressed food preferences of children and young adults (e.g., Rozin, Fallon & Mandell, 1984; Weidner, Archer, Healy, & Matarazzo, 1985). Weidner et al. (1985) found that the father's preference was important in determining what was served at meals, although there was no evidence that this fact influenced the child's preference for specific foods. There is better evidence for an association with family members' dislikes. Rozin et al. (1984) showed strong links between parents' and children's attitudes toward contamination and cleanliness of food.

Parental influence on children's eating behaviors has formed the basis of many clinicians' attempts to modify "fussy" eating. Such clinical management tends to take two forms. There are several relatively simplistic behavioral interventions (e.g., Bernal, 1972; Ireton & Guthrie, 1972; Larson, Ayllon, & Barrett, 1987; Thompson & Palmer, 1974) involving parents, caregivers, or teachers as the direct therapists. However, it has been suggested (Iwaniec, Herbert, & McNeish, 1985) that such behavioral work should be supplemented with therapeutic intervention aimed at improving the more general mother-child relationship. Birch (1987) has shown that by itself, positive and negative reinforcement from adults is poor at making children like foods, supporting the argument that any treatment of food fussiness may require more than a simplistic behavioral approach, whether or not it involves the parents.

The evidence shows that parental behavior can affect children's food preferences and fussiness. However, that influence can only be understood by considering the multiple mechanisms that may be involved in parenting and by relating those mechanisms to the other influences on food choice (outlined above). As with anorexia nervosa and bulimia nervosa, understanding chronic food refusal in children depends on using a multifactorial model of human behavior (Harris & Booth, 1992).

How might the problems of food fussiness and refusal be related to the subsequent development of anorexia nervosa and bulimia nervosa? As mentioned earlier, there is no research evidence of such a link (Birch, 1987), perhaps because such research would be enormously difficult to conduct. Given that the prevalence of childhood food refusal is high (e.g., Eppright, Fox, Fryer, Lamkin, & Vivian,

1969) while the prevalence of anorexia nervosa and bulimia nervosa are relatively low (e.g., Crisp, Palmer, & Kalucy, 1976; Rand & Kuldau, 1992), and allowing for the time span needed for any such research, it is possible that no definitive epidemiological study could be conducted. Such prospective, longitudinal research could be carried out, however, if it were based on a sensible carrier mechanism. In other words, early food refusal per se appears to be an inadequate risk factor for later anorexia nervosa or bulimia nervosa. Are there other factors, particularly involving the family, that would merit further scrutiny in any predictive research?

Two such family factors seem worthy of closer attention. First, it would be possible to use characteristic patterns of family interaction that seem to be pathological in the eating-disordered population (see below) and to look for early signs of those patterns in the families of young children. However, given the complex role of family function in the causality of anorexia nervosa and bulimia nervosa (Lacey, 1986; Slade, 1982), it would be risky to adhere to too tight a definition of pathological family function.

Second, it might be more productive to consider the long-term effects of a family style that makes food a focus for conflict from an early age, either following or prior to any actual food fussiness or food refusal. Control seems to be a core issue in the development of eating disorders (Rezeck & Leary, 1991; Slade, 1982). Anorexia nervosa or bulimia nervosa serves the function of reestablishing an individual's control over one aspect of life. Longitudinal research into early feeding problems and later eating psychopathology could consider an at-risk subgroup of cases where parental style (particularly high desire for control; e.g., Burger, 1992) and the infant's temperament contribute to a struggle for control for its own sake, rather than simply to ensure adequate nutrition.

This controlling parental style might be the strongest early factor in determining anorexic and bulimic tendencies. For example, childhood fussy eating itself may be a risk factor, but only in combination with a parenting style that makes such food fussiness a focus for control. Machan and Waller (1993) found that parents of anorexics and bulimics report using no greater level of control over fussy eating than parents of comparison women, but they describe using that control at an earlier age.

FAMILY INTERACTION IN ANOREXIA AND BULIMIA NERVOSA

The most influential clinical observations of the characteristic patterns of family interaction in the eating disorders have been reported by family therapists. In particular, Selvini-Palazzoli (1974) and Minuchin et al. (1978) described models of family function that are characterized by a rigid, enmeshed style with poor problem resolution skills. However, such observations should be treated with care, particularly because of potential biases in the samples concerned. For example, it might be argued that family therapy is only likely to be taken up by relatively enmeshed families, thus skewing these early descriptions of characteristic family style in the eating disorders.

There are several further reservations about interpreting any research into links between family function and the eating disorders. These are similar to the general methodological concerns discussed earlier. First, the causality is likely to be complex. While family functioning may cause eating psychopathology, it is also probable that family interaction will be impaired by having a member with an eating disorder. Second, to add to the complexity, both eating problems and family dysfunction may be separate products of other factors, such as poor self-esteem or external stressors. Finally, there is the issue of how one assesses family function. A number of measures exist (see below), with greater or lesser degrees of comparability. Given this variation, how does one get a useful picture of the family? While more objective observational measures may appear more satisfactory, subjective measures are more likely to relate to the sufferer's psychopathology. Similarly, the pictures of family interaction given by individual family members will differ, leaving the clinician or researcher to decide whose version should be considered accurate or clinically useful.

Research Evidence

Standardized measures of family function fall into three broad types that vary in objectivity, ease of application, and likely relevance to psychopathology. Those types are: relatively concrete measures (degree of relatedness, family structure), observational measures with objective criteria, and subjective self-report measures. As with other disorders, the nature of family interaction in anorexia nervosa and bulimia nervosa has been studied using all of these methods.

Concrete Measures   Concrete measures of family structure in anorexia are reasonably easy to establish. In an early study, Morgan and Russell (1975) described a number of family factors that appeared to be associated with the presence of anorexia nervosa, including evidence of psychiatric disorder and family disharmony (reflected in the rate of marital breakdown). These findings were taken to suggest both genetic and environmental family factors in anorexia. Birth order and family size have also been considered for any association with eating disorders (e.g., Lacey, Gowers, & Bhat, 1991). However, the results of these studies are either negative or yield results that are hard to interpret. A greater amount of research has focused on the possibility of a genetic link.

The evidence for a genetic component in the development of any disorder depends largely on research into the rates of concordance in relatives of different degrees of genetic similarity. In particular, comparison is made between monozygotic (MZ) and dizogytic (DZ) twins. The research evidence to date is very mixed, with conflicting patterns of association. Studying the proximal family,

Waters, Beumont, Touyz, & Kennedy (1990) showed no concordance for anorexia nervosa in twins of anorexics (MZ or DZ). Studies of the concordance for bulimia nervosa tend to show higher rates in MZ than DZ twins, but the rate of concordance varies widely across studies (e.g., Hsu, Chesler, & Santhouse, 1990; Fichter & Neogel, 1990).

When considering the extended family, Strober, Morrell, Burroughs, Salkin, and Jacobs (1985) found that anorexia nervosa and bulimia nervosa were more common than would be expected in the families of anorexics. Restrictive and bulimic subtypes of sufferer had relatives who had anorexia nervosa and bulimia nervosa, respectively. Strober, Lampert, Morrell, Burroughs, and Jacobs (1990) reached largely similar conclusions. To conclude, there may be a genetic component in the eating disorders, but this is likely to make only a small contribution in the great majority of cases. It remains important to understand the more direct impact of family environment on anorexic and bulimic disorders.

Observational Measures   Observational measures are more difficult to standardize than concordance. They are also more difficult to apply than other measures. However, they offer a picture of family functioning that is likely to reflect any real life disturbance. The expressed emotion measure, reflecting degree of warmth and criticism, has been used with anorexics and bulimics (e.g., Dare & Eisler, 1992). There seems to be little specific linkage with the eating disorders, although high levels of criticism are associated with poor short-term outcome and dropping out of therapy (Szmukler, Eisler, Russell & Dare, 1985). Humphrey (1987, 1989) has also used an observational method to assess family function in a multiaxial framework. While interpretation of her complex results is difficult, they appear to be compatible with theories of the eating disorders.

Subjective Measures   Compared to the objective and observational methods outlined above, subjective measures are relatively easy to use. Therefore, they have provided the bulk of the evidence for a link between family interaction and eating disorders. There are two principal drawbacks to such methods. First, there are many self-report measures of family function, tapping different dimensions of behavior. The disparity in dimensions makes comparison of studies difficult. The second drawback is that these subjective measures reflect perceived family function. However, this second drawback is perhaps less serious than it appears since the anorexic's or bulimic's perception of family dysfunction is likely to have the greatest relevance to psychological factors in the etiology and maintenance of the eating disorder. Some of the more widely used measures are outlined below.

In considering subjective descriptions of family dysfunction, most research has focused on the perspective of the individual sufferer, both for convenience and because this is intuitively the most appropriate viewpoint. However, some research has compared the descriptions of family function given by different family members. In general, the findings of these papers support the use of the sufferer's own perspective. Women with eating disorders describe their families in a more negative light than their parents do (Stern, Dixon, Jones, Lake, Nemzer, & Sansone, 1989), and the ratings of the sufferers are more accurate than those of parents in differentiating eating-disordered and comparison women (Waller, Calam, & Slade, 1988; Waller, Slade, & Calam, 1990a). Fathers' perceptions of family function are particularly poor at differentiating these groups.

The Parental Bonding Instrument (Parker, Tupling, & Brown, 1979) measures perceived parental care and overprotection. It has been used to distinguish eating-disordered from non-eating-disordered women and to differentiate diagnostic groups (Calam, Waller, Slade, & Newton, 1990; Palmer, Oppenheimer, & Marshall, 1988; Pole, Waller, Stewart, & Parkin-Feigenbaum, 1988). The results suggest that low parental care and high paternal overprotection distinguish eating-disordered from comparison women. This pattern of differences was most true for bulimics (particularly those with no history of anorexia), who reported particularly low levels of parental care (Calam et al., 1990).

The Family Assessment Device (Epstein, Bishop & Levin, 1983) has one general scale and six specific scales (measuring perceived problem solving, clarity of communication, differentiation of roles, experience of emotion, concern for each other, and clarity of rules). Waller, Calam, & Slade (1989) showed that eating-disordered women rate their families as functioning poorly on all of these scales. Again, this pattern was most true for the bulimics with no history of anorexia, while anorexics and bulimics with a history of anorexia had similar levels of perceived family dysfunction.

The Family Adaptability and Cohesion Evaluation Scale (Olson, McCubbin, Barnes, Larsen, Muxlen, & Wilson, 1982) reflects two of the dimensions of family interaction that Minuchin et al. (1978) highlighted. However, research using this measure has failed to support Minuchin's model unequivocally (Kagan & Squires, 1985; Waller, Slade, & Calam, 1990b). While these studies have confirmed that eating psychopathology is associated with poor adaptability, they have also shown that these families appear to have low levels of perceived cohesion (as opposed to Minuchin's description of them as enmeshed).

With 10 subscales, the Family Environment Scale (Moos & Moos, 1981) is another multidimensional measure of perceived family function. While designed for more general clinical purposes, it has been widely used with the eating-disordered population (Blouin, Zuro, & Blouin, 1990; Head & Williamson, 1990; Scalf-McIver & Thompson, 1989; Stern et al., 1989; Strober, 1981; Williams, Chamove, & Millar, 1990). All of these studies show abnormal family functioning in eating-disordered women. Unfortunately, they show very different patterns of abnormality, and the patterns do not appear to be specific for the eating disorders (Williams et al., 1990).

A number of other self-report measures have been used to test perceived family function in the eating disorders. As with the measures detailed above, these employ either a small number of scales, which are considered specific to the eating disorders (e.g., Kog & Vandereycken, 1989; Kog, Vertommen, & Degroote, 1985), or more general multidimensional measures (e.g., Dolan, Lieberman, Evans, & Lacey, 1990; Humphrey, 1987, 1988). Again, these measures tend to show a general trend toward perceived family dysfunction, but those patterns of dysfunction are hard to compare because the scales reflect different theoretical structures.

Summary and Critique of Research Evidence

It is impossible to summarize definitively the research evidence outlined above. This difficulty is principally due to the variety of measures used with their different scales. In addition, even when they use the same measure, there are differences in the outcome of studies, presumably due to variations in the samples used. Perhaps the best model available at present is that the families of women with eating disorders report abnormal patterns of family interaction characterized by low levels of cohesion, overprotectiveness, high levels of criticism, and low levels of emotional warmth. These are similar to the characteristics described as important by other clinical researchers (e.g., Strober, 1992). However, the exact nature of the abnormality varies with the type of eating disorder.

The categorical approach of comparing eating-disordered and non-eating-disordered women depends on the assumption that any difference between their family function is associated specifically with eating disorders. However, comparison of the findings in the papers outlined above with data from other clinical groups using the same measures (e.g., Miller, Kabacoff, Keitner, Epstein, & Bishop, 1986; Parker, 1983) is not reassuring. Taken as a whole, eating-disordered women report similar levels of poor interaction to those reported in other disorders. Taken from the most pessimistic viewpoint, these findings could be interpreted as showing simply that any family with a member with some psychological disorder will have poor interaction as a result of that member's presence.

It appears to be necessary to differentiate four groups (restrictive anorexics, bulimic anorexics, bulimia nervosa with a history of anorexia nervosa, bulimia nervosa without a history of anorexia) in order to develop approximate characteristic patterns for each group. If reduced to a single dimension, the degree of abnormality in family function appears to be lowest in restrictive anorexics and greatest in bulimics who have no history of anorexia (Waller et al., 1989).

An alternative to this categorical approach is to consider the association of family function with dimensional measures of eating psychopathology. It is surprising that relatively little research considers such potential associations. The existing publications show only moderate associations between family function and eating symptomatology (e.g., Kagan & Squires, 1985; Scalf-McIver & Thompson, 1989). However, recent research suggests that a clearer picture emerges when different features of eating psychopathology are considered. Waller (1994) has shown that frequency of bingeing is associated with low degrees of enmeshment and poor problem solving. In contrast, restrictive eating patterns tend to be linked to high enmeshment and good problem solving.

The difficulty in establishing a specific link between eating disorders and characteristic patterns of family interaction is due to the very diffuse nature of the literature to date. In particular, the existing research is based on different conceptual models, depends on different research models, and uses a variety of tools. Experience to date should assist in planning further research, which applies more informative research methods and tools.

Strategies for Future Research

It is clear that future research into the links between family function and eating disorders will need to establish better comparability before any conclusions about causality can be reached. The measures in use require some standardization, but that should be based on the development of a common theoretical model that is specific to the eating disorders. A number of measures have used Minuchin et al.'s (1978) model, but it should be remembered that this model was not devised with reference to the eating disorders alone but to psychosomatic families.

It is a matter of particular concern that these measures of family function do not differentiate eating disorder sufferers from other diagnostic groups. It has been suggested (Waller, 1994) that this lack of specificity might be resolved by developing measures of family function that correlate with the degree of eating psychopathology rather than attempting to discriminate the eating-disordered population. It is important to make such measures relevant to the eating disorders specifically rather than to psychological disturbance in general. The measures (and the models underlying them) should therefore be based on a theoretical understanding of the eating disorders.

It is unlikely that any family-based model of eating disorders will be successful in its own right because anorexia nervosa and bulimia nervosa are determined by the interaction of a number of factors (Hsu, 1983). It would be more productive to examine the mechanisms by which different factors, including family dysfunction, contribute to eating psychopathology. We suggest that Slade's (1982) functional analysis of the eating disorders would be a useful model to use as a basis for such further research. Slade suggested that family factors, adolescent conflict, and stressors can all contribute to the low self-esteem, perfectionism, and need for control that are high-risk characteristics for anorexia and bulimia. Future research should consider family patterns that contribute to generating poor self-esteem and perfectionist tendencies. For example, Waller and Hartley (1993) have demonstrated that parental noncontingent disapproval is associated with poor self-esteem. The effect of such parental disapproval is analogous to a learned helplessness effect. Similarly, Emmelkamp and Karsdorp (1987) have shown a role for parental handling in the development of a Type A style, including perfectionist tendencies. However, these measures need substantial elaboration before they can be of practical value.

In evaluating the validity of any such new measures, their clinical utility is paramount. They should be able to predict high-risk groups in the general population with greater specificity than existing family measures, while differentiating potential eating-disordered from other clinical groups. The measures should also be accurate in targeting and evaluating the use of family-oriented therapies or individual therapies that address relationship issues (Crisp, Norton, Gowers, Halek, Bowyer, Yeldham, Levett, & Bhat, 1991; Garner, 1985; Hartmann et al., 1992).

In order to be of use in evaluation, measures will probably need to be dimensional so they can be associated with dimensional measures of change in eating psychopathology. Such a quantitative approach to psychopathology is more useful than looking for categorical changes in the eating disorders, where positive change is gradual and dependent on a large amount of therapeutic input (e.g., Fairburn & Cooper, 1989; Hartmann et al., 1992). Most important, family function will be associated with the eating disorders only in some cases. The contribution of family function toward or away from the development of eating disorders will be understood only if it is seen as part of a multidimensional model of anorexia nervosa and bulimia nervosa.

Other factors may have an effect in combination with family dysfunction. One example that is of particular interest is sexual abuse. Intrafamilial abuse appears to have links to eating psychopathology (e.g., Calam & Slade, 1987), particularly where there is a greater level of bulimic symptomatology (e.g., Waller, 1992). However, Ray, Jackson, and Townsley (1991) demonstrated there is not a simple association of intrafamilial sexual abuse and disturbed family dynamics, since women reporting extrafamilial abuse showed a similar level of perceived family disturbance. This is a potential variable in understanding links between family interaction and eating disorders, but it requires further investigation.

CONCLUSIONS

It has been stressed that the literature to date does not allow us to describe typical patterns of parenting or family dysfunction in eating problems. Indeed, seeking for a typical pattern may detract from the crucial task of understanding the range of potentially psychopathological parental and family styles.

In the midst of these confusing findings, there is a risk of losing sight of the most important goals of such research. We identify two questions that should be used to guide future investigation. First, is it possible to establish continuity between parenting in childhood and the eating disorders of later life, or should we treat the two periods as separate? Second, is it possible to develop family therapies that successfully address unhealthy family functioning in appropriate cases of eating problems, or is the apparent effect of family therapy (e.g., Dare & Eisler, 1992) due simply to its addressing relationship issues (e.g., Garner, 1985; Hartmann et al., 1992)? Answers to these questions would allow for appropriate targeting of educational and clinical efforts and might even mean that all this research would be of practical benefit, reducing the distress caused by eating problems at all points across the life span.

DISCUSSION QUESTIONS

1   What psychological mechanisms are involved in parents' attempts to influence their young children's fussy eating? How effective and how ethical do those attempts seem to be?

2   Discuss the advantages and drawbacks of different methods of assessing family interaction. Is there a best method for use in clinical settings?

Exercise

Design a longitudinal study that would allow you to decide whether early childhood feeding difficulties are associated with adolescent and adult eating disorders and to assess how much of this association is due to parental style in childhood. In your design, allow for the conceptual and practical difficulties with longitudinal research (e.g., loss of subjects, number of children needed to ensure sufficient eating-disordered subjects in later life).

Write this piece as if it were a project proposal, including a title, a brief introduction to the relevant literature, aims and hypotheses, a method section, and an outline of the data analyses used to address each of the individual hypotheses. Normally, the whole exercise should be confined to no more than five sides (typed and double spaced). However, if it is conducted as a group exercise, the teacher may wish to set a different limit.

REFERENCES

Bernal, M. E. (1972). Behavioural treatment of a child's eating problems. *Journal of Behaviour Therapy and Experimental Psychiatry, 3,* 43–50.

Birch, L. L. (1987). The acquisition of food acceptance patterns in children. In R. A. Boakes, D. A. Poppelwell, & M. J. Burton (Eds.), *Eating habits: Food, physiology and learned behaviour.* Chichester: John Wiley and Sons.

Birch, L. L., & Marlin, D. W. (1982). I don't like it; I never tried it: Effects of exposure on two-year-old children's food preferences. *Appetite, 3,* 353–360.

Blouin, A. G., Zuro, C., & Blouin, J. H. (1990). Family environment in bulimia nervosa: The role of depression. *International Journal of Eating Disorders, 9,* 649–658.

Burger, J. M. (1992). *Desire for control: Personality, social and clinical perspectives.* New York: Plenum Press.

Calam, R., & Slade, P. (1987). Eating problems and sexual experience: Some relationships. *British Review of Bulimia and Anorexia Nervosa, 2,* 37–43.

Calam, R., Waller, G., Slade, P., & Newton, T. (1990). Eating disorders and perceived relationships with parents. *International Journal of Eating Disorders, 9,* 479–485.

Cox, J. L., Connor, Y. M., & Kendell, R. E. (1982). Prospective study of the psychiatric disorders of childbirth. *British Journal of Psychiatry, 140,* 111–117.

Crisp, A. H., Norton, K., Gowers, S., Halek, C., Bowyer, C., Yeldham, D., Levett, G. & Bhat, A. (1991). A controlled study of the effect of therapies aimed at adolescent and family psychopathology in anorexia nervosa. *British Journal of Psychiatry, 159,* 325–333.

Crisp, A. H., Palmer, R. L., & Kalucy, R. S. (1976). How common is anorexia nervosa? A prevalence study. *British Journal of Psychiatry, 128,* 549–554.

Dare, C., & Eisler, I. (1992). Family therapy for anorexia nervosa. In P. J. Cooper & A. Stein (Eds.), *Feeding problems and eating disorders in children and adolescents.* Chur: Harwood Academic Publishers.

Dolan, B. M., Lieberman, S., Evans, C., & Lacey, J. H. (1990). Family features associated with normal body weight bulimia. *International Journal of Eating Disorders, 9,* 639–647.

Eiser, J. R., Eiser, C., Patterson, D. J., & Harding, C. M. (1984). Effects of information about specific nutrient content on ratings of "goodness" and "pleasantness" of common foods. *Appetite, 5,* 349–359.

Emmelkamp, P. M. G., & Karsdorp, E. P. (1987). The effects of perceived parental rearing style on the development of Type A pattern. *European Journal of Personality, 1,* 223–230.

Eppright, E. S., Fox, H. M., Fryer, B. S., Lamkin, G. H., & Vivian, V. (1969). Eating behaviour of pre-school children. *Journal of Nutrition Education, 1,* 16–19.

Epstein, N. B., Bishop, D. S., & Levin, S. (1983). The McMaster family assessment device. *Journal of Marital and Family Therapy, 9,* 171–180.

Fairburn, C. G. & Cooper, P. J. (1989). Eating disorders. In: K. Hawton, P. M. Salkovskis, J. Kirk, & D. M. Clark (Eds.), *Cognitive-behaviour therapies for psychiatric populations: A psychiatric guide.* Oxford: Oxford University Press.

Fichter, M. M., & Neogel, R. (1990). Concordance for bulimia nervosa in twins. *International Journal of Eating Disorders, 9,* 255–263.

Garner, D. M. (1985). Individual psychotherapy for anorexia nervosa. *Journal of Psychiatric Research, 19,* 423–433.

George, R. S., & Krondl, M. (1983). Perceptions and food use of adolescent boys and girls. *Nutrition and Behaviour, 1,* 115–125.

Gorn, G. J., & Goldberg, M. E. (1982). Behavioral evidence of the effects of televised food messages on children. *Journal of Consumer Research, 9,* 200–205.

Harris, G., & Booth, I. (1992). The nature and management of eating problems in pre-school children. In P. J. Cooper & A. Stein (Eds.), *Feeding problems and eating disorders in children and adolescents.* Chur: Harwood Academic Publishers.

Hartmann, A., Herzog, T., & Drinkmann, A. (1992). Psychotherapy of bulimia nervosa: What is effective? A meta-analysis. *Journal of Psychosomatic Research, 36,* 159–167.

Head, S. B., & Williamson, D. A. (1990). Association of family environment and personality disturbances in bulimia nervosa. *International Journal of Eating Disorders, 9,* 667–674.

Hellin, K., & Waller, G. (1992). Mothers' mood and infant feeding: Prediction of problems and practices. *Journal of Reproductive and Infant Psychology, 10,* 39–51.

Hopkins, J., Marcus, M., & Campbell, S. B. (1984). Postpartum depression: A critical review. *Psychological Bulletin, 95,* 498–515.

Hsu, L. K. G. (1983). The aetiology of anorexia nervosa. *Psychological Medicine, 13,* 231–238.

Hsu, L. K. G., Chesler, B. E., & Santhouse, R. (1990). Bulimia nervosa in eleven sets of twins: A clinical report. *International Journal of Eating Disorders, 9,* 275–282.

Humphrey, L. L. (1987). Comparison of bulimic-anorexic and nondistressed families using structural analysis of social behaviour. *Journal of the American Academy of Child and Adolescent Psychiatry, 26,* 248–255.

Humphrey, L. L. (1988). Relationships within subtypes of anorexic, bulimic, and normal families. *Journal of the American Academy of Child and Adolescent Psychiatry, 26,* 248–255.

Humphrey, L. L. (1989). Observed family interactions among subtypes of eating disorders using structural analysis of behaviour. *Journal of Consulting and Clinical Psychology, 57,* 206–214.

Ireton, C. L., & Guthrie, H. A. (1972). Modification of vegetable-eating behaviour in preschool children. *Journal of Nutrition Education, 4,* 100–103.

Iwaniec, D., & Herbert, M. (1982). The assessment and treatment of children who fail to thrive. *Social Work Today, 13,* 8–12.

Iwaniec, D., Herbert, M., & McNeish, A. S. (1985). Social work with failure-to-thrive children and their families. *British Journal of Social Work, 15,* 375–389.

Kagan, D. M. & Squires, R. L. (1985). Family cohesion, family adaptability, and eating behaviours among college students. *International Journal of Eating Disorders, 4,* 269–279.

Kog, E., & Vandereycken, W. (1989). Family interaction in eating disorders patients and normal controls. *International Journal of Eating Disorders, 8,* 11–23.

Kog, E., Vertommen, H., & Degroote, T. (1985). Family interaction research in anorexia nervosa: The use and misuse of a self-report questionnaire. *International Journal of Family Psychiatry, 6,* 269–279.

Lacey, J. H. (1986). Pathogenesis. In L. J. Downey & J. C. Malkin (Eds.), *Current approaches: Bulimia nervosa.* Southampton: Duphar.

Lacey, J. H., Gowers, S. G., & Bhat, A. V. (1991). Bulimia nervosa: Family size, sibling sex and birth order. A catchment area study. *British Journal of Psychiatry, 158,* 491–494.

Larson, K., Ayllon, T., & Barrett, D. H. (1987). A behavioural feeding programme for failure-to-thrive infants. *Behaviour Research and Therapy, 25,* 39–47.

Lasegue, E. C. (1873). On hysterical anorexia. *Medical Times Gazette, 2,* 367–369.

Machan, J., & Waller, G. (1993). Maternal recall of management of childhood eating in anorexic and bulimic women: Maintaining food fussiness. *Eating Disorders Review, 1,* 32–40.

Miller, I. W., Kabacoff, R. I., Keitner, G. I., Epstein, N. B., & Bishop, D. S. (1986). Family functioning in the families of psychiatric patients. *Comprehensive Psychiatry, 27,* 302–312.

Minuchin, S., Rosman, B. L., & Baker, L. (1978). *Psychosomatic families: Anorexia nervosa in context.* Cambridge: Harvard University Press.

Moos, R. H., & Moos, B. S. (1981). *Family environment scale.* Palo Alto: Consulting Psychologists Press.

Morgan, M. G., & Russell, G. F. M. (1975). Value of family background and clinical features as predictors of long-term outcome in anorexia nervosa: Four-year follow-up study of 41 patients. *Psychological Medicine, 5,* 355–371.

Olson, D. H., McCubbin, H. I., Barnes, H., Larsen, A., Muxlen, M., & Wilson, M. (1982). *Family inventories.* Minnesota: Family Social Science.

Palmer, R. L., Oppenheimer, R., & Marshall, P. D. (1988). Eating-disordered patients remember their parents: A study using the Parental Bonding Instrument. *International Journal of Eating Disorders, 7,* 101–106.

Pangborn, R. M., & Giovanni, M. E. (1984). Dietary intake of sweet foods and of dairy fats and resultant gustatory responses to sugar in lemonade and to fat in milk. *Appetite, 5,* 317–327.

Parker, G. (1983). *Parental overprotection: A risk factor in psychosocial development.* New York: Grune & Stratton.

Parker, G., Tupling, H., & Brown, L. B. (1979). A parental bonding instrument. *British Journal of Medical Psychology, 52,* 1–10.

Parry, G., & Watts, F. N. (Eds.). (1989). *Behavioural and mental health research: A handbook of skills and methods.* Hove: Lawrence Erlbaum Associates.

Pole, R., Waller, D. A., Stewart, S. M., & Parkin-Feigenbaum, L. (1988). Parental caring versus overprotection in bulimia. *International Journal of Eating Disorders, 7,* 601–606.

Rand, C. S. W., & Kuldau, J. M. (1992). Epidemiology of bulimia and symptoms in a general population: Sex, age, race and socioeconomic status. *International Journal of Eating Disorders, 11,* 37–44.

Ray, K. R., Jackson, J. L., & Townsley, R. M. (1991). Family environments of victims of intrafamilial and extrafamilial child sexual abuse. *Journal of Family Violence, 6,* 365–374.

Rezeck, P., & Leary, M. (1991). Perceived control, drive for thinness, and food consumption: Anorexic tendencies as displaced reactance. *Journal of Personality, 59,* 129–142.

Rozin, P., Fallon, A., & Mandell, R. (1984). Family resemblance in attitudes to foods. *Developmental Psychology, 20,* 309–314.

Russell, G. F. M., Szmukler, G. I., Dare, C., & Eisler, I. (1987). An evaluation of family therapy in anorexia nervosa and bulimia nervosa. *Archives of General Psychiatry, 44,* 1047–1057.

Scalf-McIver, L. & Thompson, J. K. (1989). Family correlates of bulimic characteristics in college females. *Journal of Clinical Psychology, 45,* 467–472.

Selvini-Palazzoli, M. S. (1974). *Self-starvation: From the intrapsychic to the transpersonal approach to anorexia nervosa.* Haywards Heath: Human Context Books.

Slade, P. (1982). Towards a functional analysis of anorexia and bulimia nervosa. *British Journal of Clinical Psychology, 21,* 167–179.

Stern, S. L., Dixon, K. N., Jones, D., Lake, M., Nemzer, E., & Sansone, R. (1989). Family environment in anorexia nervosa and bulimia. *International Journal of Eating Disorders, 8,* 25–31.

Strober, M. (1981). The significance of bulimia in juvenile anorexia nervosa: An exploration of possible etiologic factors. *International Journal of Eating Disorders, 1,* 28–43.

Strober, M. (1992). Family factors in adolescent eating disorders. In P. J. Cooper & A. Stein (Eds.), *Feeding problems and eating disorders in children and adolescents.* Chur, Switzerland: Harwood Academic Publishers.

Strober, M., Lampert, C., Morrell, W., Burroughs, J., & Jacobs, C. (1990). A controlled family study of anorexia nervosa: Evidence of familial aggregation and lack of shared transmission with affective disorders. *International Journal of Eating Disorders, 9,* 239–253.

Strober, M., Morrell, W., Burroughs, J., Salkin, B., & Jacobs, C. (1985). A controlled family study of anorexia nervosa. *Journal of Psychiatric Research, 19,* 239–246.

Szmukler, G. I., Eisler, I., Russell, G. F. M., & Dare, C. (1985). Anorexia nervosa, parental "expressed emotion" and dropping out of treatment. *British Journal of Psychiatry, 147,* 265–271.

Thompson, R. J., & Palmer, S. (1974). Treatment of feeding problems: A behavioural approach. *Journal of Nutrition Education, 6,* 63–66.

Van Buren, D. J., & Williamson, D. A. (1988). Marital relationships and conflict resolution skills of bulimics. *International Journal of Eating Disorders, 7,* 735–741.

Van den Brouche, S., & Vandereycken, W. (1989). The marital relationship of patients with an eating disorder: A questionnaire study. *International Journal of Eating Disorders, 8,* 541–556.

Waller, G. (1992). Sexual abuse and the severity of bulimic symptomatology. *British Journal of Psychiatry, 161,* 90–93.

Waller, G. (1993). Perceived family interaction and bulimic symptomatology. *Psychological Reports, 74,* 27–32.

Waller, G., Calam, R., & Slade, P. (1988). Family interaction and eating disorders: Do family members agree? *British Review of Bulimia and Anorexia Nervosa, 3,* 33–40.

Waller, G., Calam, R., & Slade, P. (1989). Family interaction and eating disorders. *British Journal of Clinical Psychology, 28,* 285–286.

Waller, G., & Hartley, P. (1993). Perceived parental style and eating disorders. Manuscript submitted for publication.

Waller, G., Slade, P., & Calam, R. (1990a). Who knows best? Family interaction and eating disorders. *British Journal of Psychiatry, 156,* 546–550.

Waller, G., Slade, P., & Calam, R. (1990b). Family adaptability and cohesion: Relation to eating attitudes and disorders. *International Journal of Eating Disorders, 9,* 225–228.

Waters, B. G. H., Beumont, P. J. V., Touyz, S., & Kennedy, M. (1990). Behavioural differences between twin and non-twin female sibling pairs discordant for anorexia nervosa. *International Journal of Eating Disorders, 9,* 265–273.

Weidner, G., Archer, S., Healy, B., & Matarazzo, J. D. (1985). Family consumption of low fat foods: Stated preference versus actual consumption. *Journal of Applied Social Psychology, 15,* 773–779.

Williams, G., Chamove, A. S., & Millar, H. R. (1990). Eating disorders, perceived control, assertiveness and hostility. *British Journal of Clinical Psychology, 29,* 327–335.

Woodside, D. B., & Shekter-Wolfson, L. F. (1990). Parenting by patients with anorexia nervosa and bulimia nervosa. *International Journal of Eating Disorders, 9,* 303–309.

Chapter 4

Sexual Abuse and the Eating Disorders

Glenn Waller
Joanne Everill
Rachel Calam

Over the past decade, there has been a growing awareness of the extent of reported sexual abuse and its relationship to different forms of psychological disturbance. Many definitions of sexual abuse have been used in the literature, varying in how narrow or broad their criteria are (see "Methodological Issues" below). For the purposes of this review, a relatively broad definition will be used. Sexual abuse will be taken to mean acts that the victim has experienced as both sexual and unwanted.

Oppenheimer, Howells, Palmer, & Chaloner (1985) were among the first to draw attention to the links of meaning that might exist between sexual abuse and the eating disorders. They suggested that women who had been abused would be likely to experience particular feelings of disgust or inferiority about their own femininity and sexuality, and that those feelings were likely to manifest as concerns about weight, body shape, and size. Since that time, there have been a number of case reports citing sexual abuse as a critical causal factor in individual cases of anorexia nervosa and bulimia nervosa (e.g., Goldfarb, 1987; Schechter, Schwartz, & Greenfeld, 1987; Sloan & Leichner, 1986). However, Oppenheimer et al. (1985) carefully avoided concluding that there was any simple causal link between the phenomena of sexual abuse and eating disorders. They suggested that any such link would be complex, applying to different degrees in different cases.

This review considers the methodological and practical issues in determining the generalizability of any link between sexual abuse and eating psychopathology. It will then go on to consider the nature of that link and its implications for treatment. Because there are no studies that consider the role of sexual abuse in males with eating disorders (although the general psychopathological impact of sexual abuse on male victims is beginning to be described [e.g., Metcalfe, Oppenheimer, Dignon, & Palmer, 1990]), only female sufferers will be considered. Other forms of abuse will not be examined, as there is insufficient literature at present on the consequences of emotional and physical maltreatment in eating disorders.

LARGE-SCALE STUDIES

A number of large-scale studies have described rates of reported sexual abuse among women with eating disorders. Oppenheimer et al. (1985) reported a rate of 64% in their original sample and 58% in a subsequent report from an extension of that case series (Palmer, Oppenheimer, Dignon, Chaloner, & Howells, 1990). Several other case series and surveys have reported similar high rates of unwanted sexual experiences among anorexics and bulimics, including Hall, Tice, Beresford, Wooley, & Hall (1989; who reported a prevalence rate of 50%), Beckman & Burns (1990; 66%), Abramson and Lucido (1991; 69%), and Waller (1991; 48%). Other studies, using stricter criteria for defining abuse (e.g., only forms of abuse involving physical contact), have also shown considerable rates of sexual abuse among eating-disordered women, although at lower levels than in the studies cited above. Such studies include reports by Bulik, Sullivan, and Rorty (1989; 30%), McClelland, Mynors-Wallis, Fahy, and Treasure, (1991; 30%), Root and Fallon (1988; approximately 42%), Fairburn and Welch (1993; 21% overall), and Lacey (1990; 7%).

The prevalence figures vary substantially across studies. This variation is partly due to differences in diagnostic criteria used, but principally due to different methods of inquiry and definitions of abuse. This range of reported prevalences emphasizes the need to consider a number of methodological issues when determining the link between the phenomena of sexual abuse and eating psychopathology.

METHODOLOGICAL ISSUES

Many factors need to be understood when considering this research. Due to the extent of the literature, the following outline is not intended to be comprehensive. Peters, Wyatt, and Finkelhor (1986) and Briere (1992) give more detailed discussions of the methodological factors examined here and of other related issues.

Definitions of Sexual Abuse

Three general strategies are used to define sexual abuse. First, it can be defined in terms of legal categories (e.g., incest, rape). Studies that use this form of definition naturally report relatively low rates of sexual abuse (e.g., Lacey, 1990). Second, abuse can be defined as taking place when the abuser acts in order to achieve sexual gratification. However, neither of these two definitions is particularly useful in determining whether abuse is likely to have an impact on the psychological state of the victim. Therefore, the majority of studies have used a third definition: the victim should have experienced the event as both sexual and unwanted.

Within these broad strategies are further factors that should be taken into account in interpreting the results of large-scale research. Age at abuse and age relative to the abuser have both been considered. A number of studies have focused on childhood sexual abuse by older perpetrators (e.g., Abramson & Lucido, 1991; Bulik et al., 1989; McClelland et al., 1991) on the assumption that developmental factors influence the impact of the abuse. However, there is no *a priori* reason why abuse in adult life or by an abuser who is not substantially older should be discounted. Indeed, clinical experience suggests it would be counter-productive to do so. Therefore, other studies have considered abuse across the age range and without regard to the age of the abuser (e.g., Hall et al., 1989; Palmer et al., 1990; Waller, 1991).

The nature of the abuse also appears to be important. Some studies consider specific acts when defining sexual abuse (e.g., Hall et al., 1989). Others have narrow and broad criteria for abuse, which include particular sexual acts (e.g., Palmer et al., 1990). Most frequently, studies differentiate between noncontact and contact forms of abuse, with the latter producing predictably conservative prevalence rates.

Inquiring About Abuse

The questions asked and method of inquiry are key factors. Peters et al. (1986) suggest that asking several specific questions is likely to lead to a higher reported rate of abuse than asking a single general question (e.g., "Have you ever been sexually abused?"). They also suggest that interviews are likely to lead to greater reported rates of abuse than questionnaire measures, although the only study to compare the two methods (Waller, 1991) failed to find such a difference. The majority of studies drawn from large case series (e.g., Hall et al., 1989; Palmer et al., 1990; Waller, 1991) have used interviews alone, or in combination with questionnaire measures. The fact that retrospective reports are involved also needs to be considered. Brewin, Andrews, & Gotlib (in press) discussed the possible difficulties associated with the use of retrospective reports of early experience. However, they concluded that these difficulties are unlikely to explain differences in the reported experiences of psychiatric and nonpsychiatric populations.

To summarize, the pattern of prevalences of reported sexual abuse in studies of eating-disordered populations is likely to be at least partly a product of the definitions used and the issues around inquiry. However, other factors need to be considered when determining the link between the two phenomena.

COMPARISON WITH OTHER GROUPS

Before reaching any conclusions about the impact of sexual abuse on eating attitudes and eating disorders, it is important to consider whether the reported experiences of these women are any different from those of other groups. Two specific comparisons need to be made. First, Is the prevalence of sexual abuse any greater in women with eating disorders than in the remainder of the population with psychological/psychiatric disorders? Second, Is the prevalence of abuse any greater in eating-disordered women than in the general population?

A number of studies have reported rates of sexual abuse among different psychiatric groups, including eating-disordered women (e.g., Bushnell, Wells, & Oakley-Browne, 1992; Hall et al., 1989; Pribor & Dinwiddie, 1992). To date, the most valuable research into this question is that reported by Palmer and Oppenheimer (1992), Folsom, Krahn, Nairn, Gold, Demitrack, and Silk (1993), and Fairburn and Welch (1993). These authors compared eating-disordered women and women with other psychiatric disorders, using similar methodologies and criteria for the two groups. Each found that, overall, the eating-disordered women reported lower rates of abuse than the women with other diagnoses. Palmer and Oppenheimer (1992) concluded that any link that does exist between sexual abuse and the eating disorders is "unlikely to be specific or special" (p. 363), although they noted that this does not mean the link is always irrelevant. Pope and Hudson (1992) reviewed similar but less well-controlled studies. They also suggested there was insufficient evidence to conclude that eating-disordered women were abused more frequently than others in the general psychiatric population.

Only one study compares directly the rates of reported abuse in eating-disordered women and in the general population. In a preliminary report, Fairburn and Welch (1993) found that bulimic women reported abuse more often than normal comparison women. However, this greater prevalence was only found in bulimics recruited from the community and not in those who had been referred for treatment. Pope and Hudson (1992) and Connors and Morse (1993) reviewed prevalence rates in studies that gave less direct opportunities for comparison. They concluded there was no convincing evidence of higher rates of sexual abuse among eating-disordered women than among nondisordered women. A more definitive answer to this question should emerge over the next few years as the Fairburn and Welch (1993) data sets are completed.

To summarize, it appears the prevalence rate of sexual abuse is not necessarily greater among eating-disordered women than among either women with other psychiatric diagnoses or nondisordered women. This conclusion has led to a reinforcement of what might be labeled the "coincidence hypothesis." In other words, there has been little or no evidence that the apparent relationship between reported sexual abuse and the development of eating disorders is anything other than coincidental, given the prevalence of the two phenomena (Finn, Hartman, Leon, & Lawson, 1986). This hypothesis suggests that the sexual abuse found in case studies (e.g., Goldfarb, 1987; Schechter et al., 1987; Sloan & Leichner, 1986) is unlikely to be a causal factor. There will be an equal proportion of such experiences in the general population, yet these will not have had an impact on eating psychopathology. Alternatively, if there is any association between sexual abuse and subsequent psychological disturbance, there is no reason to suppose that this association will differ between women with eating disorders and women with other disorders.

The coincidence hypothesis is unlikely to be immediately acceptable to the majority of clinicians working with eating-disordered women who report sexual abuse. However, it should be remembered that clinicians are human. As such, they are prone to many of the information processing biases they recognize in their clients (e.g., Arkes, 1981). It is perfectly plausible that clinicians will make false assumptions about causality from coincidence or contiguity or that they will ignore evidence that does not agree with their existing beliefs.

The research evidence summarized to date does not allow the coincidence hypothesis to be discounted. The effectiveness of strategies that might be used for overcoming that hypothesis and for demonstrating the nature of any link between the phenomena of sexual abuse and eating psychopathology are considered in the next section.

OVERCOMING THE COINCIDENCE HYPOTHESIS

So far, the literature covered has considered the possibility of links between two very blunt phenomena: sexual abuse and eating disorders. However, in recent years interest in a more refined level of investigation has grown; this research will be considered here. It should allow for a clearer statement of the limitations and generalizability of the links between sexual abuse and eating psychopathology.

The clarification is required for two reasons. First, the research outlined above tends to use Diagnostic and Statistical Manual of Mental Disorders (DSM) criteria for anorexia nervosa and bulimia nervosa (American Psychiatric Association, 1980, 1987), and fails to consider more refined concepts of eating psychopathology (e.g., other subtypes of eating disorder, dimensions of eating attitudes). Second, it is important to consider the nature of any reported abuse. Does that nature differ between eating-disordered and non-eating-disordered women?

Four questions will be addressed in order to determine the limitations of the coincidence hypothesis. First, Are there differences in frequencies of reported abuse between subtypes of eating disorder? Second, Is the nature of any abuse important? Third, Is there a relationship between specific types of sexual abuse and dimensional measures of eating attitudes? Finally, Are there links between specific types of abuse and specific features of eating psychopathology?

Prevalence of Sexual Abuse in Different Eating Disorders

Studies have considered whether there are different rates of reported abuse between anorexics and bulimics. The findings of these studies are mixed. For example, both Bushnell et al. (1992) and Pribor and Dinwiddie (1992) reported associations of intrafamilial sexual abuse and bulimia nervosa, but no similar associations among anorexics. In contrast, using a broader definition of sexual abuse, Palmer et al. (1990) found no difference in the reported rates of abuse in anorexics and bulimics.

In an attempt to clarify this issue, Waller (1991, 1993a) and Waller, Halek, and Crisp (1993) have used different categories of eating disorder. Restrictive anorexics (i.e., those who were substantially underweight and who showed no bingeing or purging behaviors) displayed a very low prevalence. By contrast, there were significantly higher rates among bulimic anorexics, bulimics with a history of anorexia, and bulimics with no history of anorexia. In a study comparing obese binge eaters with obese nonbinge eaters, Kanter, Williams, and Cummings (1992) showed a similar trend. The binge eaters were more likely to report a history of sexual abuse, although the association failed to achieve significance.

While this pattern requires replication in other case series, it suggests there is an association between sexual abuse and disorders with a bulimic component, rather than with eating disorders per se. The finding of a nonrandom association between reports of sexual abuse and eating disorders is clearly incompatible with the coincidence hypothesis, which should predict random distribution across diagnostic categories (although the possibility of biases in reporting cannot be discounted). If using categories of eating disorders in such research, it is clearly important to define the disorders more clearly than by simply using standard diagnostic schemes.

Is the Nature of Sexual Abuse Important?

A number of studies of non-eating-disordered psychiatric groups have suggested it is important to consider the reported nature of any sexual abuse, rather than simply registering its occurrence (e.g., Bownes, O'Gorman, & Sayers, 1991; Briere & Zaidi, 1989; Carlin & Ward, 1992; Jacobson, 1989; Winfield, George, Swartz, & Blazer, 1990). A growing body of evidence shows that specific characteristics of abuse (age at abuse, identity of the perpetrator, multiple experiences, use of physical force) are associated with greater levels of psychopathology.

Similar evidence is emerging in the eating disorders. For example, Calam and Slade (1987, 1991) showed that eating-disordered women were more likely than comparison groups (depressed and nondisordered women) to have a number of specific unwanted sexual experiences (e.g., enforced intercourse, intercourse with an authority figure, abuse by a close male relative). Again, this finding is incompatible with the coincidence hypothesis. It is clearly important to understand the nature of any abuse when considering its possible link to the individual eating disorder.

Sexual Abuse and Measures of Eating Attitudes

Levels of eating psychopathology in the non-eating-disordered population also appear to be related to the occurrence and nature of sexual abuse. Calam and Slade (1987, 1989) reported higher Eating Attitude Test (EAT-26; Garner, Olmsted, Bohr, & Garfinkel, 1982) scores among women who reported abuse, particularly if it involved family members, force, or a young victim. Williams, Wagner, and Calam (1992) confirmed this association with EAT-26 scores, particularly where women reported a greater number of abusive experiences. Beckman and Burns (1990) showed similar (although generally weaker) links between the nature of any abuse and the degree of bulimic attitudes. Smolak, Levine, and Sullins (1990) reported that the women in their sample who reported sexual abuse had higher overall Eating Disorder Inventory (EDI; Garner, Olmsted, & Polivy, 1983) scores, although there were no differences on specific subscales.

The same pattern has not been found in eating-disordered women. Waller (1992a) showed that a reported history of sexual abuse was not associated with EAT-26 scores in this group. Similarly, Folsom et al. (1993) found no relationship between EDI scores and sexual abuse in an eating-disordered group.

The links between sexual abuse and levels of eating psychopathology are often only moderate in strength, and they vary according to the measures used and populations considered. However, at a general level, these studies confirm that reported sexual abuse has some associations with greater levels of eating psychopathology, whereas the coincidence hypothesis would predict there should be no such relationship.

The Nature of Sexual Abuse and Types of Eating Psychopathology

Having considered the relevance of specific forms of abuse and of the nature of any eating psychopathology, it is necessary to consider how the two interact. This seems to be the most promising line in understanding the nature of any links between the relatively blunt phenomena of sexual abuse and eating disturbance. In keeping with the concept of links of meaning, it is possible to hypothesize that particular eating behaviors might be more common among women who had experienced particular forms of abuse (e.g., an association between enforced oral intercourse and vomiting). To date, there has been little research into this field, but there is evidence of some linkage.

Calam and Slade (1987, 1989) showed that among non-eating-disordered women, different features of sexual abuse were associated with specific dimensions of eating psychopathology (using the EAT-26). In an eating-disordered population, Waller (1992a,b) concluded that the nature of any abuse (identity of abuser, age at abuse, use of force) was associated with the frequency of bingeing. In contrast, only the identity of the abuser was related to the frequency of vomiting, and none of these variables were related to EAT-26 scores. Other symptoms of the eating disorders have also been shown to be linked to the nature of any abuse. For example, more recent sexual abuse is associated with greater body image distortion among eating-disordered women (Waller, Hamilton, Rose, Sumra, & Baldwin, 1993).

It would be unwise to draw definitive conclusions on the basis of the few studies described above. Further research, particularly with eating-disordered groups, is needed to build on these initial findings. However, the results to date suggest that a complete picture of the link between sexual abuse and the eating disorders requires detailed understanding of both the nature of the abuse and the specific symptoms/dimensions involved.

Summary

While further research is obviously needed to support and extend these findings, it is clear there is considerable evidence that disconfirms the coincidence hypothesis. At the purely phenomenological level, there are links between sexual abuse and more bulimic behaviours in the eating-disordered population, especially where the abuse has particular characteristics. However, it would be unwise to discount the coincidence hypothesis entirely. Both clinical experience and statistical probability indicate there will be some coincidental overlap of the two phenomena (i.e., women with eating disorders who have also been sexually abused, but where the abuse has not contributed to the causation or maintenance of the disorder).

Two important topics remain. First, the research outlined above does not address the links of meaning between the phenomena. Second, it is necessary to determine when any reported abuse is relevant to the eating disorder (i.e., when any reported abuse is not coincidental), so that treatments can be used in a way that is appropriate to the individual. These topics will be addressed below.

LINKS OF MEANING: FACTORS MEDIATING THE EFFECTS OF UNWANTED SEXUAL EXPERIENCE UPON EATING PSYCHOPATHOLOGY

The mediators of the relationship between sexual abuse and eating disorders are certain to be complex. There is a need to identify these mediating factors, because they are likely to involve important cognitive, emotional, and behavioral targets for treatment. In general, the mediators include both psychological and interpersonal factors.

Psychological Variables

General Self-Esteem   It seems plausible that poor self-esteem consequent to sexual abuse would be relevant in the development and maintenance of eating disorders. However, following a review of studies that investigated the effects of abuse on self-esteem, Finkelhor (1986) concluded that evidence for such an effect was mixed at best. Waller (1992b) and Smolak et al. (1990) found that little or none of the relationship between abuse and eating psychopathology could be explained by any mediating effect of self-esteem.

Self-Blame   Self-blame for the abuse is an important psychological response, probably because it is more specific than poor general self-esteem. Jehu (1988) suggests a number of reasons why false perceptions of self-blame are present in abuse victims. In particular, the perpetrator's strategies for maintaining secrecy (Jehu, 1988, pp. 66–67; Andrews & Brewin, 1990) and the inability of the victim to control the circumstances of the abuse (Finkelhor & Browne, 1985) are important. Self-blame has been described in different ways in the literature, including self-denigratory beliefs and shame. Self denigratory beliefs include feelings of worthlessness, stigmatization, and inferiority (Jehu 1988, pp. 77–81). Andrews (1992) found evidence to suggest that shame over physical appearance acts as a mediator between abuse and bulimia.

Dissociation   Dissociation (including depersonalization, memory loss, etc.) has been linked to sexual abuse (Briere & Runtz, 1988; Coons & Milstein, 1986; Sanders, McRoberts, & Tollefson, 1989) and to the eating disorders (Abraham & Beumont, 1982; Heatherton & Baumeister, 1991; Johnson, Lewis, & Hagman, 1984; Russell, 1979). Dissociation is a relatively primitive defense mechanism. It appears to be related to the use of blocking, enabling escape from abusive or traumatic situations where physical escape is not possible (Sandberg & Lynn, 1992; Spiegel, 1986). Dissociation is used initially as a normal defense; however, it can become maladaptive if used over time and in less traumatic situations (Putnam, 1989). The blocking or escape from awareness is suggested to be critical in the development of bulimic symptoms (Heatherton & Baumeister, 1991; Lacey, 1986).

Control   Abuse victims are often made to feel powerless due to the repeated violation of personal boundaries (Finkelhor, 1986). Perceived levels of control are reported to be poor in those women who report abuse and for whom a high level of desire for control is likely (Brehm & Brehm, 1981). Control is an important aspect of eating disorder psychopathology. A number of writers have incorporated control into models of the psychopathology of the eating disorders (Duker & Slade, 1988; Johnson et al., 1984; Slade, 1982; Williams, Chamove, & Millar, 1990). Control over food is proposed to be an attempt to compensate for lack of control elsewhere. Rezek & Leary (1991) refer to this as displaced reactance. They suggested that eating-disordered women use calorie counting to stay in control when faced with threatening situations where food is not present.

Personality Disorders   Personality disorders are associated with both reported sexual abuse (Briere & Zaidi, 1989; Coons & Milstein, 1986; Herman, Perry, & Van Der Volk, 1989) and the eating disorders (Gartner, Marcus, Halmi, & Loranger, 1989; Shearer, Peters, Quaytman, & Ogden, 1990). McClelland, Mynors-Wallis, Fahy, & Treasure (1991) found that the three phenomena (sexual abuse, disordered personality, and eating disorders) were linked to some extent. Studies suggest that the cluster of behaviors associated with borderline personality disorder (American Psychiatric Association, 1987) is particularly relevant to the development and maintenance of eating disorders in victims of sexual abuse (Shearer et al., 1990; Wonderlich & Swift, 1990). These behaviors include impulsiveness, poor anger control, self-harm, unstable relationships, and affective disturbance.

In a recent study, Waller (1993b, 1994) found that reported sexual abuse, borderline personality symptoms, and specific bulimic symptomatology (i.e., bingeing and purging) were linked. These findings are compatible with a proposed model that suggests sexual abuse causes specific borderline symptoms to develop as consistent traits. In turn, this personality style influences the eating-disordered behavior (i.e., bingeing and purging). This study shares many of the difficulties inherent in this field (diagnostic issues, use of retrospective data, etc.). It will be impossible to verify the role of personality in the link between abuse and eating disorders without extensive longitudinal studies. However, this factor would merit such long-term investigation.

Interpersonal Factors

Family Interaction   It is difficult to determine the mediating effects of family interaction, as it could be argued that the effects of the nature of any abuse are likely to be related to family function. Waller (1992b) could find no evidence to suggest that perceived family dysfunction acted as a mediator between abuse and bulimic symptoms. However, it is possible that such experiences will contribute to the psychological consequences of abuse (Conte & Schuerman, 1987).

Disclosure   A key factor in determining the extent to which the victim feels responsible for the abuse is the experience of disclosing to significant others. It has been suggested that disclosure has a direct bearing on later psychological well-being (Jehu, 1988). In particular, adverse reactions to disclosure (e.g., blaming or ignoring the victim, disbelief, punishment) are likely to be detrimental to psychological functioning (Browne & Finkelhor, 1986; Waller, 1994).

Relatively little research has been done on the impact of disclosure experiences, but the evidence to date stresses its importance in psychopathology. Everill & Waller (in press) concluded that a perceived adverse response to disclosure served to reinforce perceptions of self-blame and dissociative experiences in nondisordered women. It was suggested that a possible causal link might exist between intensified feelings of self-blame and greater use of primitive defenses such as dissociation, which would allow relief from the negative emotional state. However, conclusions must be tentative due to the small number of participants who reported an adverse response to disclosure.

In a study of anorexic and bulimic women who reported sexual abuse, Waller and Ruddock (1993) showed that levels of psychopathology were highest in those women who reported adverse responses to disclosure. They binged and vomited more frequently and showed more of the symptoms of borderline personality disorder. Both of these studies suggest that an adverse response to disclosure of childhood sexual abuse increases the risk of psychological disturbance, including eating symptomatology.

To summarize, disclosure plays an important part in enhancing psychological disturbance, which contributes to the development of an eating disorder. However, it is difficult to determine whether this effect is partly a product of associated family dysfunction. Any disruption of the family following disclosure can have a negative effect on the child. Self-blame can be intensified if there is an adverse reaction to the disclosure, especially if the perpetrator was a family member and made the child believe she had a responsibility to keep the family together by remaining silent (Herman, 1981; Summit, 1983). An element of perceived betrayal by the nonabusing parent may also be present, leading the child to feel she has been rejected by both parents.

Developmental Level

The interactive or additive pattern between these psychological and interpersonal variables is complex. However, one important factor that seems to link some of the psychopathology of eating disorders and the effects of abuse is developmental level. There is some conflict as to whether the age of the victim at the time of the abusive experience is important. In his review of the literature, Finkelhor (1986) suggests that studies disagree as to whether abuse at a younger age leads to poorer psychological sequelae (e.g., Meiselman, 1978; Peters, 1985). Finkelhor concluded that overall the age at first abuse has little significant impact on later psychological function. In contrast, Everill & Waller (under consideration) found that abuse occurring at a younger age was associated with greater levels of psychopathology, particularly dissociation and self-denigration. Cole and Putnam (1992) suggested that abuse that begins in the preschool years (ages 2 to 5) may cause the victims to rely more strongly on denial or dissociation as coping strategies. Coons, Cole, Pellow, and Milstein (1989) and Putnam, Guroff, Silberman, Barban, and Post (1986) reported that women with multiple personality disorder had an early onset of abuse, with 95% reporting onset before the age of 9.

The use of primitive defense mechanisms or coping strategies is a potential link between abuse and the use of bulimic behaviors in the eating disorders (see above). Children who are abused for the first time in late childhood are more likely to blame others or to use rationalization or other defenses as a means of coping. Although the use of dissociation is reported to decrease in children abused for the first time in late childhood (Coons et al., 1989; Cramer, 1991; Putnam et al., 1986; Schibuk, Bond, & Bouffard, 1989), it does remain elevated in comparison with controls (Putnam & Trickett, 1991).

Cole and Putnam (1992) stressed the importance of not underestimating the effects of abuse in adolescence. Although they suggest most abuse begins in childhood, such experiences will continue in adolescence. They believe this is particularly traumatic for a girl as she tries to deal with her sexual identity and opposite-sex peer relationships. In particular, if the victim relies on denial and dissociation, the risk of worsening psychopathology increases, as relying on these primitive defenses increases the likelihood of acting impulsively when frustrated or angry.

A Preliminary Model of Mediating Variables

Each of the variables considered above is a possible contributing factor in the development and maintenance of an eating disorder. A preliminary model of the relationship between abuse and specific eating disorder symptomatology incorporating these mediating factors is proposed in Figure 4-1. It should not be assumed that this model describes any specific individual. Rather, it is intended to convey a more global picture of plausible associations, which may be relevant to different degrees in individual cases.

This model suggests that self-blame and loss of perceived control are both crucial psychological mediators. Both arise out of the nature of abuse and the circumstances surrounding it (age, support, etc.). These mediators have the common consequence of requiring the victim to use a relatively primitive defensive style based on dissociation. That style involves the use of attempts to block out the world. Bulimic behaviors are among the impulsive actions that help a victim who is in an inescapable emotional state escape from awareness (Heatherton & Baumeister, 1991).

Evidence exists for some components of this model, while other parts remain untested. It is hoped that this preliminary formulation will provide a framework

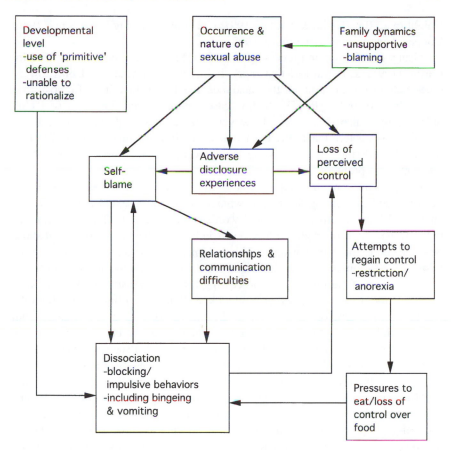

Figure 4-1 Preliminary model of the mediating variables in the relationship between sexual abuse and eating disorders.

for further research, with the aim of refining our understanding of the factors that mediate between sexual abuse and eating psychopathology.

JUDGING RELEVANCE

Little research has been done into judging the relevance of sexual abuse to psychopathology. The field is undoubtedly complex, but is a potentially fruitful area for clinical research. The ability to judge the relevance of sexual abuse to the individual case would assist clinicians in determining who needs treatment that focuses on such experiences. In addition, a wide body of research explores the cognitive processes associated with relevance to the individual. The best example of this in the eating disorders is the literature demonstrating that anorexics and bulimics are abnormally sensitive to stimuli relating to food, body shape, and weight (e.g., Ben-Tovim & Walker, 1991; Channon, Hemsley, & de Silva, 1988; Cooper, Anastasiades, & Fairburn, 1992).

Using an information-processing task, Foa, Feske, Murdock, Kozak, & Mc-Carthy (1991) demonstrated that rape victims have an attentional bias toward rape-related words, but only if they also meet the diagnostic criteria for post-traumatic stress disorder (PTSD). In this case, an associated diagnosis of PTSD indicates relevance to the case. However, most clinicians do not use such co-morbidity as a determinant of relevance. Instead, they rely more on their formulation of the individual case, stressing the antecedents and consequences that are relevant to the problem.

Using a similar methodology to Foa et al. (1991), Waller and Ruddock (1993) demonstrated that eating-disordered women who report sexual abuse show an attentional bias toward abuse-related words. However, this effect was substantially stronger in those women where it was judged that the history of sexual abuse was relevant to the eating disorder. This judgment of relevance was made on the basis of the formulation of the individual case and was always made prior to the administration of the information-processing task. Further studies (Waller, Ruddock, & Cureton, in press; Waller, Ruddock, & Pitts, 1993) suggest that both the clinician's judgment of relevance and the attentional bias are associated with scores on Jehu's (1988) inventory of self-denigratory beliefs consequent to abuse. This finding is in keeping with the conclusion (above) that such beliefs are strong mediators of the links between sexual abuse and the eating disorders.

There is little doubt that it is important to determine the relevance of any abusive experience upon eating psychopathology so that treatments can be targeted appropriately. However, it is still difficult to decide the best means of determining that relevance. While the use of information-processing measures in this field is in its infancy, such methods offer considerable promise. On the other hand, there is unlikely to be any acceptable substitute for clinicians' judgments of relevance to the formulation of the individual case (partly due to the complexities of cases and partly due to clinicians' preference for methods with high face validity). Neither measure of relevance can be validated absolutely, but they can be used to validate each other concurrently. Perhaps the best use for information-processing correlates of relevance would be as measures in evaluating the individual's cognitive changes during therapy. Further research would be needed to establish the utility of such an approach.

TREATMENT ISSUES

Having judged sexual abuse to be relevant to an individual with an eating disorder, the clinician needs to be aware of how to address the abuse therapeutically. There is little evidence to suggest that any unique clinical skills are required to treat psychological disorders when they involve a history of abuse (Beutler & Hill, 1992). Therefore, there is unlikely to be a need for the person to be referred to a specialist service. However, it seems reasonable to suggest that clinicians should use existing proven methods for reducing the psychological consequences of sexual abuse (e.g., Jehu, 1988). It remains to be shown whether treatment for such cases should focus first on the consequences of the abuse or the eating psychopathology. However, the authors' experience suggests that the two are best addressed in parallel.

Given the prevalence of sexual abuse in the case of the eating disorders, it is important to inquire sensitively about such a history in each case. However, particular psychological signs (e.g., dissociation, self-denigration) should help the clinician in making judgments about the relevance of that abuse. Having determined that the consequences of sexual abuse should be a target for treatment in the individual case, the research indicates there might be particular therapeutic benefits of addressing the psychological factors that act as links of meaning when treating eating disorders in women who report sexual abuse. Those factors can also be used in evaluation of the effectiveness of treatment.

CONCLUSIONS

This review began with an apparently simple question: Is sexual abuse related to the eating disorders? By now, it should be apparent that the question is not at all simple and that the answer is far from clear. The answer depends on a much clearer picture than we have at present of the links between specific forms of sexual abuse and particular aspects of eating psychopathology. The following conclusions can be reached:

1   At the crude phenomenological level, it is possible to say there is a relationship between sexual abuse and eating psychopathology and that the relationship is more than coincidental in many cases. In particular, the association between bulimic symptoms and the nature of any abuse merits further investigation.

2   An understanding of the psychological and practical factors that mediate between the two phenomena (i.e., the links of meaning) is developing. The psychological factors of self-denigration and dissociation seem to be particularly worthy of further research. They are closely allied (either causally or at a descriptive level) to the blocking or escape from awareness that are characteristic of bulimic behaviors (e.g., Heatherton & Baumeister, 1991; Lacey, 1986). Personality disorders (particularly borderline personality disorder) are also worth considering, although probably in terms of their symptoms rather than at the level of the syndrome. The impact of practical factors, such as developmental level and experiences of disclosure, also needs much more investigation.

3   For clinical purposes, the relevance of sexual abuse to the eating disorders can be understood only in terms of a formulation of the individual case. However, there is the potential for developing psychological measures that validate those formulations, and particularly for evaluating the effectiveness of treatment.

4   The relevance of sexual abuse to the treatment of the eating disorders remains to be tested. However, the two should be addressed in parallel rather than sequentially.

Future practice should be guided by these conclusions. Clinicians and researchers need to be able to determine when abuse has occurred, when it is relevant to the individual eating disorder, and what are the psychological mediators that underpin any link between abuse and the eating psychopathology. However, the professional's inquiry into any history of abuse needs to be sensitive and sympathetic to reduce the dangers associated with a perceived adverse response to disclosure (Waller & Ruddock, 1993; Everill & Waller, in press). The most important task for the future must be the development of treatment programs that address both the abuse and the eating disorder in as effective a manner as possible.

DISCUSSION QUESTIONS

1   What might be a typical pattern of psychological deficits arising from sexual abuse, and why might such a pattern be associated with a bulimic disorder rather than with restrictive anorexia?
2   What factors should a clinician bear in mind when attempting to assess whether a history of childhood sexual abuse is relevant to an eating disorder in an adult woman?

Exercise

Given the methodological, clinical, and ethical constraints, design a study that would yield prevalence rates for sexual abuse in two chosen clinical populations (*not* eating-disordered) and a nonclinical population. The study should allow meaningful comparison of the prevalence rates in the three groups.

Write this piece as if it were a project proposal, including a title, a brief introduction to the relevant literature, aims and hypotheses, a method section, and an outline of the data analyses used to address each of the individual hypotheses. Normally, the whole exercise should be confined to no more than five sides (typed and double spaced). However, if it is conducted as a group exercise, the teacher may wish to set a different limit.

REFERENCES

Abraham, S. F., & Beumont, P. J. V. (1982). How patients describe bulimia or binge eating. *Psychological Medicine, 12,* 625–635.

Abramson, E. E., & Lucido, G. M. (1991). Childhood sexual experience and bulimia. *Addictive Behaviours, 16,* 529–532.

American Psychiatric Association. (1980). *Diagnostic and statistical manual of mental disorders* (3rd ed.). Washington DC: Author.

American Psychiatric Association. (1987). *Diagnostic and statistical manual of mental disorders* (3rd ed., revised). Washington DC: Author.

Andrews, B. (1992, December). *Shame as a mediating factor between early abuse and psychiatric disorder.* Paper presented at the British Psychological Society Conference, London.

Andrews, B., & Brewin, C. R. (1990). Attributions for marital violence: A study of antecedents and consequences. *Journal of Marriage and the Family, 52,* 757–767.

Arkes, H. R. (1981). Impediments to accurate clinical judgment and possible ways to minimize their impact. *Journal of Consulting and Clinical Psychology, 49,* 323–330.

Beckman, K. A., & Burns, G. L. (1990). Relation of sexual abuse and bulimia in college women. *International Journal of Eating Disorders, 9,* 487–492.

Ben-Tovim, D. I., & Walker, M. K. (1991). Further evidence for the Stroop test as a quantitative measure of psychopathology in eating disorders. *International Journal of Eating Disorders, 10,* 609–613.

Beutler, L. E., & Hill, C. E. (1992). Process and outcome research in the treatment of adult victims of childhood sexual abuse: Methodological issues. *Journal of Consulting and Clinical Psychology, 60,* 204–212.

Bownes, I. T., O'Gorman, E. C., & Sayers, A. (1991). Assault characteristics and post-traumatic stress disorder in rape victims. *Acta Psychiatrica Scandinavica, 83,* 27–30.

Brehm, S. S., & Brehm, J. W. (1981). *Psychological reactance: A theory of freedom and control.* New York: Academic Press.

Brewin, C. R., Andrews, B., & Gotlib, I. H. (in press). Psychopathology and early experience: A reappraisal of retrospective reports. *Psychological Bulletin.*

Briere, J. (1992). Methodological issues in the study of sexual abuse effects. *Journal of Consulting and Clinical Psychology, 60,* 196–203.

Briere, J., & Runtz, M. (1988). Symptomatology associated with childhood sexual victimization in a non clinical adult sample. *Child Abuse and Neglect, 12,* 51–59.

Briere, J., & Zaidi, L. Y. (1989). Sexual abuse histories and sequelae in female psychiatric emergency room patients. *American Journal of Psychiatry, 148,* 55–61.

Browne, A. & Finkelhor, D. (1986). Initial and long-term effects: A review of the research. In D. Finkelhor (Ed.), *A sourcebook on child sexual abuse.* Newbury Park: Sage.

Bulik, C. M., Sullivan, P. F., & Rorty, M. (1989). Childhood sexual abuse in women with bulimia. *Journal of Clinical Psychiatry, 50,* 460–464.

Bushnell, J. A., Wells, J. E., & Oakley-Browne, M. A. (1992). Long-term effects of intrafamilial sexual abuse in childhood. *Acta Psychiatrica Scandinavica, 85,* 136–142.

Calam, R., & Slade, P. (1987). Eating problems and sexual experience: Some relationships. *British Review of Bulimia and Anorexia Nervosa, 2,* 37–43.

Calam, R., & Slade, P. (1989). Sexual experiences and eating problems in female undergraduates. *International Journal of Eating Disorders, 8,* 391–397.

Calam, R., & Slade, P. (1991). Eating patterns and unwanted sexual experiences. In B. Dolan & I. Gitzinger (Eds.). *Why women? Gender issues and eating disorders* (pp. 27–34). London: European Council on Eating Disorders.

Carlin, A., & Ward, N. (1992). Subtypes of psychiatric inpatient women who have been sexually abused. *Journal of Nervous and Mental Disease, 180,* 392–397.

Channon, S., Hemsley, D., & de Silva, P. (1988). Selective processing of food words in anorexia nervosa. *British Journal of Clinical Psychology, 27,* 259–260.

Cole, P. M., & Putnam, F. W. (1992). Effect of incest on self and social functioning: A developmental psychopathology perspective. *Journal of Consulting and Clinical Psychology, 60,* 174–184.

Connors, M. E., & Morse, W. (1993). Sexual abuse and eating disorders: A review. *International Journal of Eating Disorders, 13,* 1–11.

Conte, J. R., & Schuerman, J. R. (1987). Factors associated with an increased impact of child sexual abuse. *Child Abuse and Neglect, 11,* 201–211.

Coons, P. M., Cole, C., Pellow, T. A., & Milstein, V. (1989). Symptoms of post traumatic stress and dissociation in women victims of abuse. In R. P. Kluft (Ed.), *Incest related syndromes of adult psychopathology.* Washington DC: American Psychiatric Association.

Coons, P. M., & Milstein, V. (1986). Psychosexual disturbances in multiple personality: Characteristics, etiology and treatment. *Journal of Clinical Psychiatry, 47,* 106–110.

Cooper, M. J., Anastasiades, P., & Fairburn, C. G. (1992). Selective processing of eating-, shape-, and weight-related words in persons with bulimia nervosa. *Journal of Abnormal Psychology, 101,* 352–355.

Cramer, P. (1991). *The development of defense mechanisms: Theory, research and assessment.* New York: Springer-Verlag.

Duker, M., & Slade, R. (1988). *Anorexia nervosa and bulimia: How to help.* Milton Keynes: Open University Press.

Everill, J. T., & Waller, G. (in press). Disclosure of sexual abuse and psychological adjustment in female undergraduates. *Child Abuse and Neglect.*

Everill, J. T., & Waller, G. (under consideration). The nature of sexual abuse and its long-term psychological correlates in female undergraduates. *Journal of Interpersonal Violence.*

Fairburn, C. G., & Welch, S. (1993, April). *Sexual abuse and bulimia nervosa.* Paper presented at Eating Disorders '93: Update and Innovations, London.

Finkelhor, D. (Ed.). (1986). *A Sourcebook on Child Sexual Abuse.* Newbury Park, CA: Sage.

Finkelhor, D., & Browne, A. (1985). The traumatic impact of child sexual abuse: A conceptualization. *American Journal of Orthopsychiatry, 55,* 530–541.

Finn, S., Hartman, M., Leon, G., & Lawson, L. (1986). Eating disorders and sexual abuse: Lack of confirmation for a clinical hypothesis. *International Journal of Eating Disorders, 5,* 1051–1060.

Foa, E. B., Feske, U., Murdock, T. B., Kozak, M. J., & McCarthy, P. R. (1991). Processing of threat-related information in rape victims. *Journal of Abnormal Psychology, 100,* 156–162.

Folsom, V., Krahn, D., Nairn, K., Gold, L., Demitrack, M. A., & Silk, K. R. (1993). The impact of sexual and physical abuse on eating disordered and psychiatric symptoms: A comparison of eating disordered and psychiatric inpatients. *International Journal of Eating Disorders, 13,* 249–257.

Garner, D. M., Olmsted, M. P., Bohr, V., & Garfinkel, P. E. (1982). The Eating Attitudes Test: Psychometric features and clinical correlates. *Psychological Medicine, 12,* 871–878.

Garner, D. M., Olmsted, M. P., & Polivy, J. (1983). Development and validation of a multi-dimensional eating disorder inventory for anorexia nervosa and bulimia. *International Journal of Eating Disorders, 2,* 15–34.

Gartner, A. F., Marcus, R. N., Halmi, K., & Loranger, A. W. (1989). DSM-III-R personality disorders in patients with eating disorders. *American Journal of Psychiatry, 146,* 1585–1591.

Goldfarb, L. A. (1987). Sexual abuse antecedent to anorexia nervosa, bulimia, and compulsive overeating: Three case reports. *International Journal of Eating Disorders, 6,* 675–680.

Hall, R. C. W., Tice, L., Beresford, T. P., Wooley, B., & Hall, A. K. (1989). Sexual abuse in patients with anorexia nervosa and bulimia. *Psychosomatics, 30,* 73–79.

Heatherton, T. F., & Baumeister, R. F. (1991). Binge eating as escape from self-awareness. *Psychological Bulletin, 110,* 86–108.

Herman, J. L. (1981). *Father-daughter incest.* Cambridge, MA: Harvard University Press.

Herman, J. L., Perry, J. C., & Van der volk, B. A. (1989). Childhood trauma in borderline personality disorder. *American Journal of Psychiatry, 146,* 490–495.

Jacobson, A. (1989). Physical and sexual assault histories among psychiatric outpatients. *American Journal of Psychiatry, 146,* 755–758.

Jehu, D. (1988). *Beyond sexual abuse: Therapy with women who were childhood victims.* Chichester: Wiley.

Johnson, C., Lewis, C., & Hagman, J. (1984). The syndrome of bulimia: Review and synthesis. *Psychiatric Clinics of North America, 7,* 247–273.

Kanter, R. A., Williams, B. E., & Cummings, C. (1992). Personal and parental alcohol abuse, and victimization in obese binge eaters and nonbingeing obese. *Addictive Behaviours, 17,* 439–445.

Lacey, J. H. (1986). Pathogenesis. In L. J. Downey & J. C. Malkin (Eds.), *Current approaches: Bulimia nervosa.* Southampton: Duphar.

Lacey, J. H. (1990). Incest, incestuous fantasy and indecency: A clinical catchment area study of normal-weight bulimic women. *British Journal of Psychiatry, 157,* 399–403.

McClelland, L., Mynors-Wallis, L., Fahy, T., & Treasure, J. (1991). Sexual abuse, disordered personality and eating disorders. *British Journal of Psychiatry, 158 (Suppl. 10),* 63–68.

Meiselman, K. (1978). *Incest: A psychological study of causes and effects with treatment recommendations.* San Francisco: Jossey-Bass.

Metcalf, M., Oppenheimer, R., Dignon, A., & Palmer, R. L. (1990). Childhood sexual experiences reported by male psychiatric patients. *Psychological Medicine, 20,* 925–929.

Oppenheimer, R., Howells, K., Palmer, R. L., & Chaloner, D. A. (1985). Adverse sexual experiences in childhood and clinical eating disorders: A preliminary description. *Journal of Psychiatric Research, 19,* 357–361.

Palmer, R. L., Chaloner, D. A., & Oppenheimer, R. (1992) Childhood sexual experiences with adults reported by female psychiatric patients. *British Journal of Psychiatry, 160,* 261–265.

Palmer, R. L., & Oppenheimer, R. (1992). Childhood sexual experiences with adults: A comparison of women with eating disorders and those with other diagnoses. *International Journal of Eating Disorders, 12,* 359–364.

Palmer, R. L., Oppenheimer, R., Dignon, A., Chaloner, D. A., & Howells, K. (1990). Childhood sexual experiences with adults reported by women with eating disorders: An extended series. *British Journal of Psychiatry, 156,* 699–703.

Peters, S. D. (1985, August). Child sexual abuse and later psychological problems. Paper presented at the American Psychological Association, Los Angeles.

Peters, S. D., Wyatt, G. E., & Finkelhor, D. (1986). Prevalence. In D. Finkelhor (Ed.), *A sourcebook on child sexual abuse* (pp. 15–59). Newbury Park, CA: Sage.

Pope, H. G., & Hudson, J. I. (1992). Is childhood sexual abuse a risk factor for bulimia nervosa. *American Journal of Psychiatry, 149,* 455–463.

Pribor, E. F., & Dinwiddie, S. H. (1992). Psychiatric correlates of incest in childhood. *American Journal of Psychiatry, 149,* 52–56.

Putnam, F. W. (1989). *Diagnosis and treatment of multiple personality disorder.* New York: Guilford Press.

Putnam, F. W., Guroff, J., Silberman, E., Barban, L., & Post, R. (1986). The clinical phenomenology of multiple personality disorder: Review of 100 recent cases. *Journal of Clinical Psychiatry, 47,* 258–293.

Putnam, F. W., & Trickett, P. (1991, May). *Dissociation in sexually abused girls.* Paper presented at the Annual Meeting of the American Psychiatric Association, New Orleans.

Rezek, P. J., & Leary, M. R. (1991). Perceived control, drive for thinness, and food consumption: Anorexic tendencies as displaced reactance. *Journal of Personality, 59,* 129–142.

Root, M. P. P., & Fallon, P. (1988). The incidence of victimization experiences in a bulimic sample. *Journal of Interpersonal Violence, 3,* 161–173.

Russell, G.. F. M. (1979). Bulimia nervosa: An ominous variant of anorexia nervosa. *Psychological Medicine, 9,* 429–448.

Sandberg, D. A., & Lynn, S. J. (1992). Dissociative experiences, psychopathology and adjustment in child and adolescent maltreatment in female college students. *Journal of Abnormal Psychology, 101,* 717–723.

Sanders, B., McRoberts, G., & Tollefson, C. (1989). Childhood stress and dissociation in a college population. *Dissociation, 2,* 17–23.

Schechter, J. O., Schwartz, H. P., & Greenfield, D. G. (1987). Sexual assault and anorexia nervosa. *International Journal of Eating Disorders, 5,* 313–316.

Schibuk, M., Bond, M., & Bouffard, R. (1989). The development of defenses in childhood. *Canadian Journal of Psychiatry, 34,* 581–588.

Shearer, S. L., Peters,, C. P., Quaytman, M. S., & Ogden, R. L. (1990). Frequency and correlates of childhood sexual and physical abuse histories in adult female borderline inpatients. *American Journal of Psychiatry, 147,* 214–216.

Slade, P. (1982). Towards a functional analysis of anorexia nervosa and bulimia nervosa. *British Journal of Clinical Psychology, 21,* 167–179.

Sloan, G., & Leichner, P. (1986). Is there any relationship between sexual abuse or incest and eating disorders? *Canadian Journal of Psychiatry, 31,* 656–660.

Smolak, L., Levine, M. P., & Sullins, E. (1990). Are child sexual experiences related to eating disordered attitudes and behaviours in a college sample? *International Journal of Eating Disorders, 9,* 167–178.

Spiegel, D. (1986). Dissociating damage. *American Journal of Clinical Hypnosis, 29,* 123–131.

Summit, R. C. (1983). The child sexual abuse accommodation syndrome. *Child Abuse and Neglect, 7,* 177–193.

Waller, G. (1991). Sexual abuse as a factor in the eating disorders. *British Journal of Psychiatry, 159,* 664–671.

Waller, G. (1992a). Sexual abuse and bulimic symptoms in eating disorders: Do family interaction and self-esteem explain the links? *International Journal of Eating Disorders, 12,* 235–240.

Waller, G. (1992b). Sexual abuse and the severity of bulimic symptomatology. *British Journal of Psychiatry, 161,* 90–93.

Waller, G. (1993a). Association of sexual abuse and borderline personality disorder in eating disordered women. *International Journal of Eating Disorders, 13,* 259–263.

Waller, G. (1993b). Sexual abuse and eating disorders. Borderline personality disorder as a mediating factor? *British Journal of Psychiatry, 162,* 771–775.

Waller, G. (1994). Childhood sexual abuse and borderline personality disorder in the eating disorders. *Child Abuse and Neglect, 18,* 97–101.

Waller, G., Halek, C., & Crisp, A. H. (1993). Sexual abuse as a factor in anorexia nervosa: Evidence from two separate case series. *Journal of Psychosomatic Research, 37,* 873–879.

Waller, G., Hamilton, K., Rose, N., Sumra, J., & Baldwin, G. (1993). Sexual abuse and body image distortion in the eating disorders. *British Journal of Clinical Psychology, 32,* 350–352.

Waller, G., & Ruddock, A. (1993). Experiences of disclosure of child sexual abuse and psychopathology. *Child Abuse Review, 2,* 185–195.

Waller, G., & Ruddock, A. (under consideration). An information-processing approach to verification of reported sexual abuse in eating-disordered and comparison women. *Journal of Abnormal Psychology.*

Waller, G., Ruddock, A., & Cureton, S. (1993). Cognitive correlates of reported sexual abuse in eating-disordered women.

Waller, G., Ruddock, A., & Pitts, C. (1993). When is sexual abuse relevant to bulimic disorders? The validity of clinical judgments. *Eating Disorders Review, 1,* 143–151.

Williams, G. J., Chamove, A. S., & Millar, H. R. (1990). Eating disorders, perceived control, assertiveness and hostility. *British Journal of Clinical Psychology, 29,* 327–335.

Williams, H. J., Wagner, H. L., & Calam, R. M. (1992). Eating attitudes in survivors of unwanted sexual experiences. *British Journal of Clinical Psychology, 31,* 203–206.

Winfield, I., George, L., Swartz, M., & Blazer, D. (1990). Sexual assault and psychiatric disorder among a community sample of women. *American Journal of Psychiatry, 147,* 335–341.

Wonderlich, S. A., & Swift, W. J. (1990). Borderline versus other personality disorders in the eating disorders: Clinical description. *International Journal of Eating Disorders, 9,* 629–638.

Part Two

Anorexia Nervosa

Anorexia nervosa has been recognized in medical literature as a psychiatric syndrome for more than 100 years. In 1980, the American Psychiatric Association, in its *Diagnostic and Statistical Manual of Mental Disorders* (*DSM-III*), recognized anorexia nervosa as a mental disorder and defined it with the following diagnostic criteria:

1 An intense fear of becoming obese, which does not diminish as weight loss progresses.

2 Disturbance of body image, for example, claiming to "feel fat" even when emaciated.

3 Weight loss of at least 25% of original body weight or, if under 18 years of age, weight loss from original body weight plus projected weight gain expected from growth charts may be combined to make the 25%.

4 For women, amenorrhea.

In 1987, the American Psychiatric Association made additional changes in the criteria for anorexia nervosa in its revised *DSM-III,* named *DSM-III-R.* The necessity of a low body weight was specified, the controversial term *disturbance in body image* was deleted, and an additional criterion of amenorrhea for three consecutive menstrual cycles was used. The criteria are as follows:

1 Refusal to maintain body weight over a minimal weight for age and height (e.g., weight loss leading to maintenance of body weight 15% below that expected, or failure to make expected weight gain during period of growth, leading to body weight 15% below that expected).

2 Intense fear of gaining weight or becoming fat, even though underweight.

3 Disturbance in the way in which one's body weight, size, or shape is experienced (e.g., the person claims to "feel fat" even when emaciated, believes that one area of the body is "too fat" even when obviously underweight).

4 In females, the absence of at least three consecutive menstrual cycles when otherwise expected to occur.

Other changes in the diagnostic criteria, the most notable of which is the division of anorexia nervosa into bulimic and restricter subtypes, will be included in *DSM-IV.*

Chapters in this part consider the definition, diagnostic criteria, associated psychological problems, theories of etiology, and methods of treatment for anorexia nervosa.

Chapter 5

Anorexia Nervosa: Definition, Diagnostic Criteria, and Associated Psychological Problems

LeeAnn Alexander-Mott

In the literature on anorexia nervosa, considerable attention has been given to how this eating disorder should be defined. Those who have researched and written about the concept of anorexia nervosa have noted the difficulty in defining the disorder (Dally & Gomez, 1979; Theander, 1970), the confusion and change in the definition of anorexia nervosa (Bruch, 1966, 1973; Garfinkel, Moldofsky, & Garner, 1980; Lowenkopf, 1982; Lucas, 1981; Sibley & Blinder, 1988), and the need for anorexia nervosa to be strictly defined (Dally, 1969; Dally & Gomez, 1979; Hsu, 1990; Russell, 1970). This chapter will review various ways in which anorexia nervosa has been conceptualized since the first detailed description of this eating disorder (Morton, 1694).

EARLY DESCRIPTIONS OF ANOREXIA NERVOSA

Morton (1694), who published the first medical description of anorexia nervosa, noted the chief characteristics to include decreased appetite, amenorrhea, food aversion, hyperactivity, and emaciation. Morton called the condition a nervous atrophy and "attributed it quite unequivocally to psychological factors" (Selvini-Palazzoli, 1974, p. 9).

Nearly 200 years later, anorexia nervosa was "rediscovered" (Sholevar, 1987, p. 31) by Gull in England and Lasegue in France. In an address made at a meeting of the British Medical Association at Oxford in 1868, Gull first referred to the condition, using the term *hysteric apepsia* to describe it. Later, in 1874, Gull presented the case histories of patients with anorexia nervosa, defined the illness, and changed the name of the condition from apepsia hysterica to anorexia nervosa. Gull (1874) noted that the victims of anorexia nervosa were usually women between the ages of 16 and 23. He defined anorexia nervosa through a series of signs and symptoms that include emaciation, amenorrhea, constipation, loss of appetite, slow pulse, slow respiration, and the absence of somatic pathology to account for the condition. Gull (1874) attributed the loss of appetite to a "morbid mental state" and stated that its origin was "central and not peripheral" (quoted in Bliss & Branch, 1960, p. 14).

Almost concurrent with Gull's work were the observations of Lasegue in France. In 1873, Lasegue gave an account of self-starvation and extreme emaciation in young women. Emphasizing a hysterical origin, Laseque called the condition *hysterical anorexia* and noted the cardinal features of anorexia nervosa: occurrence in young women from 15 to 20 years of age, diminished food intake and food refusal (although some gorging did occur), severe constipation, overactivity, amenorrhea (in the late stages), and emaciation (quoted in Bliss & Branch, 1960, pp. 14–15). Lasegue also recognized the psychological origins of the disease; he attributed the onset to a peculiar mental state resulting from some emotional upset.

The psychological as well as the physical aspects of the disorder received attention in Gull and Lasegue's descriptions, and anorexia nervosa was recognized as a distinct clinical entity. As numerous case reports of anorexia nervosa followed, however, "there was a gradual widening of the original concepts of Gull and Lasegue" (Dally, 1969, p. 3), and the literature on anorexia nervosa became characterized by contradiction and confusion (Bruch, 1973, p. 211).

ANOREXIA NERVOSA AND SIMMONDS' DISEASE

One major source of confusion occurred following Simmonds' (1914) report of anterior pituitary lesions in a patient with cachexia. Simmonds' (1914) report resulted in a link between cachexia and pituitary failure; in the next few decades, numerous cases of weight loss of undetermined etiology (the majority of which were anorexia nervosa) were diagnosed and treated as cases of hypopituitarism, often with fatal results. No longer was anorexia nervosa a "psychological disorder with physical manifestations" (Garfinkel & Kaplan, 1986, p. 260) as described by Gull and Lasegue. The concept of anorexia nervosa became vague, lost its status as a discrete entity, and was "subsumed under pituitary failure, a rare condition" (Sibley & Blinder, 1988, p. 248).

In order for anorexia nervosa to regain its status as a distinct clinical entity and be reestablished as a disease of psychological origin (Dally, 1969, p. 3), it would first have to be distinguished from pituitary failure. In the 1930s and 1940s, such attempts were made. Agreeing with Gull (1874), Ryle (1936) noted that anorexia nervosa was a psychological disorder, the origins of which were "to be sought in a disturbance of the mind and a prolonged insufficiency of food and nothing more" (p. 893). Farquharson and Hyland (1936) noted that although the syndrome of anorexia nervosa "bears a superficial resemblance to that of Simmonds' disease, it is actually quite distinct and different" (p. 225). The authors maintained that the syndrome is based on a psychological disturbance with secondary metabolic damages. Richardson (1939) described Simmonds' disease as rare. Of the six patients in his study, three were thought at one time to have Simmonds' disease or pituitary cachexia; all proved to have anorexia nervosa (Richardson, 1939, p. 27).

Berkman (1945) corrected the prevalent view that emaciation was a key symptom of pituitary disease and defined anorexia nervosa as a clinical entity. He wrote, "The clinical picture constitutes a clinical entity as satisfactorily as any other clinical entity in which we may be considered more familiar" (p. 679).

Finally, in 1949, Sheehan and Summers distinguished between anorexia nervosa and Simmonds' disease. The two shared symptoms of anorexia and hypopituitarism—amenorrhea and low basal metabolic rate—disappear with correction of the psychological disturbance and resumed adequate food intake. The authors concluded that "there is no justification in the present state of knowledge for postulating that the amenorrhea and low basal metabolic rate are due to functional hypopituitarism" (p. 356).

PSYCHOANALYTIC CONCEPTS OF ANOREXIA NERVOSA

That psychological factors figure prominently in the development of anorexia nervosa was a view supported by psychoanalytic concepts, which were assimilated into psychiatric theory and practice during the 1940s and 1950s (Strober, 1986, p. 236). In 1914, Freud commented on a neurosis occurring in girls around puberty that expresses aversion to sexuality by means of anorexia (Lucas, 1981, p. 257). Subsequently, psychoanalysts, upon examining anorexia nervosa patients, found evidence of fantasies linking eating and pregnancy (Dally, 1969, p. 10). Psychoanalysts focused on the disturbed eating function and attempted to "explain" anorexia nervosa with one psychodynamic formulation. Anorexia nervosa was conceptualized as an expression of repudiation of sexuality, and more specifically, the repudiation of oral impregnation fantasies (Bruch, 1973, p. 216). Thus, Waller, Kaufman, and Deutsch (1940) suggested that the main symptoms of anorexia nervosa—the reaction to food, constipation, and amenorrhea—represent "an elaborate and acting out in the somatic sphere of a specific type of fantasy" (p. 3). The authors defined anorexia nervosa in the following way: "The wish to be impregnated through the mouth which results, at times, in compulsive eating, and at other times, in guilt and consequent rejection of food, the constipation symbolizing the child in the abdomen and the amenorrhea as a direct psychological repercussion of pregnancy fantasies" (p. 15). Similarly, Moulton (1942) defined anorexia as a "psychosomatic entity, in which fantasies of oral impregnation are dramatized through starvation, vomiting, and amenorrhea" (p. 73).

Psychoanalysis brought about a new understanding of psychological factors in anorexia nervosa (Dally, 1969; Bruch, 1973). However, the view that anorexia nervosa represented a rejection of oral impregnation fantasies has been criticized. Russell (1970) questioned the "rather sweeping generalization of Waller, Kaufman, and Deutsch (1940) that anorexia nervosa is a defense against unconscious fantasies of oral insemination" (p. 1391). Dally (1969) stated that fears of sexuality are common in anorexia nervosa. However, he emphasized that pregnancy fantasies, which are widespread, rarely lead to anorexia nervosa. Also, oral impregnation fantasies do not exist in boys and men. Thus, Dally (1969) suggested that other factors must be involved. Bruch (1973) similarly stated that the type of sexual anxiety described as fears of oral impregnation are rarely found in primary anorexia nervosa. Disturbed attitudes toward sex and adulthood may be found, but these attitudes are manifestations of other developmental disturbances (p. 276).

MODERN CONCEPTS OF ANOREXIA NERVOSA

Bruch's Contributions

Bruch introduced a concept of anorexia nervosa that addressed these developmental disturbances, and in this concept, helped to make clear other sources of conceptual confusion resulting from the view held by some investigators that "there is no neurosis specific to anorexia nervosa and no specific anorexia nervosa" (Kay & Leigh, 1954, p. 428) and that anorexia nervosa is merely "a malnutrition due to deficient diet, in which the caloric restriction is entirely psychological (Bliss & Branch, 1960, p. 24). Bruch's concept included a primary anorexia nervosa syndrome—characterized by developmental disturbances in psychological functioning with relentless pursuit of thinness as a cardinal feature—that could be distinguished from other psychiatric illnesses that lead to malnutrition.

The Relentless Pursuit of Thinness

Bruch (1973) defined anorexia nervosa as a "desperate struggle for a self-respecting identity" (p. 251). The "relentless pursuit of thinness" (p. 555), described by Bruch as the key issue in anorexia nervosa, served as a "final step in this effort" (p. 557). The identification of the relentless pursuit of thinness as the cardinal feature of anorexia nervosa allowed it to be distinguished from other psychiatric illnesses that presented with weight loss (p. 555).

Other investigators used similar terminology in their definitions of anorexia nervosa. Russell (1970) described this feature as "a morbid fear of becoming fat" (p. 134). Theander (1970) noted the essential criterion of anorexia nervosa: The "changed attitude of the patient towards food, eating, and her own figure, which results in 'the pursuit of thinness' being a strong motivational force, dominating the patient's behavior" (p. 12). Selvini-Palazzoli (1974) viewed anorexia nervosa similarly, asserting that the anorexic patient exhibits "a deliberate wish to slim" (p. 24). She said the sole motive for the anorexic patient's behavior is "a desperate need to grow thinner" (p. 23). Sours (1974) defined anorexia nervosa through three primary symptoms; one of these was "pursuit of thinness as pleasure in itself" that "becomes paramount" (p. 568). Crisp (1977) defined anorexia nervosa as a "weight phobia" in which the central preoccupation of the anorexic focuses on "maintaining a low subpubertal body weight and of avoiding any weight gain" (p. 465). Investigators continued to describe this cardinal feature of anorexia nervosa. Casper et al. (1980) added the descriptive terms "willfull" and "covertly triumphant" to the cardinal feature of pursuit of thinness (p. 1030). Sholevar (1987) defined anorexia nervosa as "an illness characterized by pursuit of thinness and fear of gaining weight" (p. 31).

Primary Anorexia Nervosa

Those patients who exhibited a "relentless pursuit of thinness" and who exhibited disturbances in body image, interpretation of bodily stimuli, and an underlying sense of ineffectiveness represented, according to Bruch (1966), the true "anorexia nervosa syndrome" (p. 555) or primary anorexia nervosa. Primary anorexia nervosa represents a distinct entity as opposed to a secondary group of patients for whom no general picture can be drawn. In the primary anorexia nervosa group, "the main issue was recognized as a struggle for control, for a sense of identity and effectiveness, with relentless pursuit of thinness as a final step in this effort" (p. 557). Although this group developed bizarre food habits during the course of the illness, they were not primarily concerned with the eating function, in contrast to the secondary group whose "primary concern was with the eating function which was used in various symbolic ways" (p. 558). For the secondary group, the loss of weight, often complained about, proved incidental to another problem and was used only for its coercive effort (p. 558). The refusal to eat was related to neurotic or schizophrenic conflicts, and although often confused with patients with true anorexia nervosa, these patients "do not represent a special clinical entity" (p. 566). Bruch (1973) referred to this group as "atypical" anorexics.

Others similarly recognized a distinction between primary and secondary forms of anorexia nervosa. Thoma (1967) maintained that true or primary anorexia nervosa is a distinct psychiatric syndrome, distinguishable from anorexia secondary to schizophrenia, depression, or phobic anxiety. King (1963) subdivided anorexia nervosa into primary and secondary syndromes. In primary anorexia nervosa, food refusal was a source of pleasure and was continued, although it created difficulties. In the secondary variety, the avoidance of food "was a secondary product of a phobic dread or delusion, or was a manifestation of intense depression" (p. 470). The secondary variety represented a "mixed bag of cases with a secondary motivational type of anorexia" (p. 477), whereas the primary anorexia nervosa syndrome represented "an entity, separate from other psychiatric disorders, with its own psychophysical constraints" (p. 478). Theander (1970) recognized a primary anorexia nervosa syndrome, the essential criterion of which is "the changed attitude of the patient towards food, eating and her own figure, which results in 'the pursuit of thinness' being a strong motivational force, dominating the patient's behavior" (p. 187). (For a more in-depth review of the history of anorexia nervosa, please see chapter 1.)

DIAGNOSTIC CRITERIA FOR ANOREXIA NERVOSA

As noted earlier, Bruch (1973) based the diagnosis of anorexia nervosa on the drive for thinness along with the three psychopathological features: an underlying disturbance in body image, a disturbance in the recognition and interpretation of bodily stimuli, and an all-pervading sense of ineffectiveness. Although the drive for thinness is an important diagnostic feature recognized by many others, the three psychopathological features are hard to determine objectively and may not be present in all patients (Garfinkel & Kaplan, 1986, p. 277). Investigators before Bruch did not clearly define diagnostic criteria. For example, Nemiah (1950) based the diagnosis of anorexia nervosa on three criteria: "failure to eat, weight loss, and menstrual changes for which no evidence of gross disease had been found in a primary etiological role" (p. 227). Bliss and Branch (1960), while regarding weight loss as essential to the diagnosis of anorexia nervosa, arbitrarily accepted a 25-pound weight loss attributable to psychological causes as a suitable figure (p. 25). Theander (1970) set no strict limits regarding an age of onset or amount of weight lost; amenorrhea was not included as an essential criterion. The essential criterion for the diagnosis of anorexia nervosa was the patient's changed attitude toward food, eating, and body weight "which results in 'pursuit of thinness' being a strong motivational force, dominating the patient's behavior" (p. 187). This behavior, in turn, leads to weight loss.

Dally (1969) argued that in order for anorexia nervosa to be recognized as a specific syndrome, a precise definition is needed; thus, the importance of defining strict diagnostic criteria. Dally (1969) made one of the earliest attempts to establish operational criteria for the diagnosis of anorexia nervosa, and numerous other investigators followed a similar approach. Dally's (1969) criteria include: (a) active refusal to eat leading to weight loss of at least 10% of body weight; (b) amenorrhea of at least 3 months duration; (c) no evidence of schizophrenia, severe depression, or organic disease; and (d) age of onset between 11 and 35 years of age (pp. 5–6).

Feighner, Robbins, Guze, Woodruff, Winokur, and Munoz (1972) relied on an operational approach as well and established diagnostic criteria for use in research. As necessary conditions for the diagnosis of anorexia nervosa, Feighner and associates listed the following: (a) onset prior to age 25; (b) weight loss of at least 25% of original body weight; (c) a distorted attitude toward eating food or weight that overrides hunger, admonitions, reassurance, and threats; (d) anorexia and weight loss not accounted for by medical illness; (e) no evidence of psychiatric disorder, such as primary affective disorder, schizophrenia, or obsessive-compulsive neurosis; and (f) evidence of at least two of the following: amenorrhea, lanugo, bradycardia, periods of overactivity, and episodes of bulimia and vomiting (p. 61). These rather strict requirements have received criticism as excluding many individuals who should be diagnosed. However, it is worth noting that Feighner's criteria were intended to be strict so that investigators could be reasonably certain of the compatibility of patients in different studies (Garfinkel & Garner, 1982, p. 28).

The American Psychiatric Association continued the operational approach, and in 1980 anorexia nervosa became a diagnostic category as reflected in its listing as a mental disorder in the *Diagnostic and Statistical Manual of Mental Disorders (DSM-III)*. Anorexia nervosa was defined by its cardinal features that include the following: (a) intense fear of becoming obese, which does not diminish as weight loss progresses; (b) disturbance of body image, e.g., claiming to "feel fat" even when emaciated; (c) weight loss of at least 25% of original body weight or, if under 18 years of age, weight loss from original body weight plus projected weight gain expected from growth charts may be combined to make the 25%; (d) refusal to maintain body weight over a minimal normal weight for age and height; and (e) no known physical illness that would account for weight loss. These criteria include an age of onset. Also, the weight loss criterion took into account the growth of children.

In 1987, the American Psychiatric Association published a revised edition of the *Diagnostic and Statistical Manual of Mental Disorders (DSM-III-R)* and defined anorexia nervosa using the following criteria: (a) refusal to maintain body weight over a minimal weight for age and height, e.g., weight loss leading to maintenance of body weight 15% below that expected; or failure to make expected weight gain during period of growth, leading to body weight 15% below that expected; (b) intense fear of gaining weight or becoming fat, even though underweight; (c) disturbance in the way in which one's body weight, size, or shape is experienced, e.g., the person claims to "feel fat" even when emaciated, believes that one area of the body is "too fat" even when obviously underweight; and (d) in females, absence of at least three consecutive menstrual cycles when otherwise expected to occur. In this revised edition, the weight loss requirement was reduced, and amenorrhea was listed as an essential criterion, a criterion not listed in the 1980 edition.

The diagnostic criteria for anorexia nervosa in *DSM-III-R* would undergo yet other changes. The Eating Disorders Work Group of the American Psychiatric Association's Task Force on *DSM-IV* recommended that criterion C be rewritten to include two ways in which a body image disturbance is expressed. Criterion C would read: "Disturbance in the way in which one's body weight, size, or shape is experienced, e.g., denial of the seriousness of current low body weight, or undue influence of body shape and weight on self-evaluation" (Wilson & Walsh, 1991, pp. 362–363). Another prominent change would be in the addition of a sub-classification of anorexia nervosa.

Subtyping Within Anorexia Nervosa

The concept of anorexia nervosa as a heterogenous phenomenon composed of various subgroups has received considerable attention in the literature and has encouraged advancement in the diagnostic conceptualization of anorexia nervosa (Strober, 1986, p. 238).

Many investigators have noted evidence of binge eating and vomiting in their patients (Bliss & Branch, 1960; Bruch, 1973; Meyer & Weinroth, 1957; Sours, 1974). Similarly, Beumont, George, and Smart (1976) noted that although some anorexics induce weight loss through dieting, food refusal, and exercise, others induce weight loss using additional methods including self-induced vomiting and purgation. Beumont et al. (1976) labeled the former group dieters or abstainers and the latter group vomiters and purgers. These two subtypes are generally referred to as "restricting anorexics" or "restricters" and "bulimic anorexics."

Studies have suggested major differences between these two groups. Compared to restricters, bulimic anorexics have been found to show greater evidence of premorbid and familial history of obesity and to be more extroverted, more sexually active, and more emotionally labile (Beumont et al., 1976; Casper et al., 1980; Garfinkel, Moldofsky, & Garner, 1980; Russell, 1979; Strober, 1981). Some investigators have suggested that bulimic anorexics are characterized by a poorer long-term prognosis as compared to restricting anorexics (Beumont, et al., 1976; Casper et al., 1980; Garfinkel & Garner, 1982; Garfinkel, Moldofsky, & Garner, 1980; Hsu, 1988). However, Toner, Garfinkel, and Garner (1986) compared the long-term outcome of restricting and bulimic anorexic women and found that, in general, restricting and bulimic subtypes of anorexia nervosa have a similar long-term outcome. The only exception to this pattern was that the bulimic subgroup had a higher incidence of substance use disorders at follow-up than did restricting anorexics, which supports the suggestion of numerous investigators who maintain that bulimic anorexics have problems with impulse control (Casper et al., 1980; Crisp, Hsu, & Harding, 1980; Garfinkel, Moldofsky, & Garner, 1980; Strober, 1980; Woznica, 1990). Bulimic anorexics have been found to engage in impulsive behaviors including stealing, self-mutilation, suicide attempts, and use of alcohol and street drugs. Strober, Salkin, Burroughs, and Morrell (1982) found that personality trait disturbances in parents and a higher familial prevalence of affective and impulsive disorders distinguished the bulimic group, thus establishing the validity of a "typological differentiation of anorexia patients with bulimia from those normally defined as restricters" (p. 349).

DeCosta and Halmi (1992), members of the Eating Disorders Work Group of the American Psychiatric Association's Task Force on *DSM-IV,* examined the question of subtyping within anorexia nervosa for the patients who binge and purge and those who severely restrict food intake. Their literature review revealed consistent differences between restricting anorexics and bulimic anorexics as mentioned above; thus warranting a subclassification of anorexia nervosa into anorexia nervosa-bulimic type and anorexia nervosa-restricter type.

Anorexia Nervosa and Weight Preoccupation

Anorexia nervosa has struggled for recognition as a distinct clinical entity even after Gull (1874) and Lasegue (1873) recognized it as such in the late 19th century. Some who have questioned anorexia nervosa's status as a discrete syndrome have suggested that anorexia nervosa represents an extreme point on a continuum of dieting behaviors, fear of fatness/pursuit of thinness, and starvation effects (Garfinkel & Garner, 1982, p. 30). The view that anorexia nervosa represents an extreme point on a continuum of concern about weight results from the fact that many symptoms and behaviors of the anorexic occur as the result of dieting to lose weight. The question emerges, then, as to whether anorexia nervosa could be defined as dieting that has gotten out of hand. Hsu (1990) noted several reasons that seem to support such a definition. The population group showing the highest incidence of the disorder is also the most concerned with weight and dieting. Some individuals in nonclinical populations show a minor form of the disorder. The fact that amount of weight loss is used as a criterion for diagnosis suggests a continuity between dieting and anorexia nervosa. Many recovered anorexics are still preoccupied with dieting and weight, much like normal dieters. Also, the terms so often associated with anorexia nervosa—fear of fatness and pursuit of thinness—suggest a quantitative rather than a qualitative phenomenon (Hsu, 1990, p. 5).

Many investigators have suggested anorexia nervosa's existence along a continuum ranging from simple dieting to anorexia nervosa. Berkman (1948) suggested such a continuum exists in which the individual appears thin and exhibits mild symptoms to cases where severe symptoms result in emaciation, with "no sharp diagnostic line" separating the former from the latter (p. 237). Loeb (1964) shared a similar opinion. Defining anorexia nervosa as a symptom complex rather than as a disease entity, Loeb (1964) suggested that anorexia nervosa should be viewed as existing on a continuum ranging from near normal situations scarcely worthy of psychiatric notice to those cases resulting in hospitalization and eventually in death. Fries (1977) studied 21 patients with true anorexia and 17 women with a longstanding history of secondary amenorrhea and weight loss, yet who did not satisfy diagnostic criteria for anorexia nervosa. The latter group showed anorexic behavior scores and marked overestimations of body widths "not quantitatively different from those patients with 'true' anorexia nervosa" (p. 174). Fries (1977) concluded that the difference between the two groups "is more a matter of degree of illness . . . than a matter of diagnosis" (p. 174). Nylander (1971) found that 10% of female adolescents in Sweden had at least three anorexic symptoms related to weight loss. Labeling these cases as mild, Nylander suggested that prolonged dieting could lead to anorexia nervosa. A continuum of anorexic symptoms was suggested by Garner and Garfinkel's (1980) study of dancing students; 78% showed EAT (Eating Attitudes Test) scores in the anorexic range, yet only 7% met diagnostic criteria for anorexia nervosa. The dancing students with EAT scores in the anorexic range but who were not diagnosed with anorexia nervosa expressed concerns about weight and food that went beyond a typical dieter's. Their concerns were related to significant psychopathology, although they did not display the fully developed syndrome of anorexia nervosa.

Button and Whitehouse (1981) used the term *subclinical anorexia nervosa* to describe approximately 5% of postpubertal females who "experience the preoccupation with weight and the forms of behavior associated with anorexia nervosa without being extremely emaciated" (p. 514). Lowenkopf (1982), suggesting that "minor disorders do occur," proposed a new diagnostic category, pursuit of thinness, that would "provide a diagnostic home for a 'sick' population" (p. 239). In a study of 15-year-old school girls, Mann et al. (1983) placed girls into four categories, one of which was for those who showed a partial syndrome of anorexia nervosa. This group included girls who showed the essential psychopathological features of anorexia nervosa, but whose weight remained within normal limits and whose menstrual periods (though they may have been irregular) still persisted (pp. 574–575). Patton (1988) studied the spectrum of eating disorders in adolescence. In a prospective study of London schoolgirls, he found support for the view that adolescent dieting, which for the most part is unproblematic, serves as a precursor to more extreme methods of weight concerns and weight control in some instances. Being overweight and having depressive and neurotic symptoms best distinguished the elements of the eating disorders spectrum.

Others investigated the concept of a continuum, anchored at one end by anorexia nervosa. Garner, Olmstead, Polivy, and Garfinkel (1984) studied three groups of female subjects, including ballet students, college students, and anorexic patients. The college and ballet students were further divided into weight-preoccupied and non-weight-preoccupied subgroups on the basis of extreme scores on the Drive for Thinness subscale of the Eating Disorders Inventory (EDI). The authors found that the weight-preoccupied and anorexic groups were best differentiated by the Ineffectiveness, Interpersonal Distrust, and Lack of Interoceptive Awareness subscales. Using cluster analysis methods, the investigators further divided the weight-preoccupied group. Those in Cluster One scored as high or higher on all EDI subscales as the anorexic patients, indicating significant psychopathology comparable to that found in classic anorexia nervosa. Those in Cluster Two, who could be described as normal dieters, only showed elevated scores on Drive for Thinness, Perfectionism, and Body Dissatisfaction subscales. The authors concluded that "although there are some individuals within the extremely weight-preoccupied segment of the female population for whom concomitant psychological disturbances are quite similar to those found in anorexia nervosa (Cluster One), other weight-preoccupied women only superficially resemble patients suffering from eating disorders (Cluster Two)" (p. 264). Garner et al. (1984) maintained that presumed mild cases of anorexia nervosa should be evaluated not only in behavioral and dieting terms, but also in psychological terms "since the meaning or motivation behind the anorexic's dieting may be different in essential ways from that of the extreme dieter" (p. 264).

Crisp (1970, 1977) distinguished anorexia nervosa from other forms of dieting. He defined anorexia nervosa as a psychobiological regression to a prepubertal state, which he viewed as a functional avoidance response to adolescence and its demands for which the anorexic is unprepared. Also, Crisp emphasized the need for a weight loss that would force the individual below the menstrual weight threshold or "critical weight." Thompson and Schwartz (1982) noted qualitative distinctions between anorexia nervosa and those with anorexic like symptoms. More recently, Polivy and Herman (1987) reinforced earlier studies by concluding that eating-disordered patients possess several psychological attributes that differentiate them from weight-preoccupied dieters, including ego deficits and perceptual disturbances; more specifically, they have an underlying sense of ineffectiveness, lack of interoceptive awareness, interpersonal distrust, and maturity fears (p. 638).

Anorexia Nervosa and Other Psychiatric Illnesses

Anorexia nervosa's status as a distinct entity has also been questioned by those who view it as a variant of other psychiatric illnesses. More specifically, at times, anorexia nervosa has been considered a variant of schizophrenia, obsessive-compulsive disorder, hysteria (conversion disorder), and affective disorder.

Anorexia Nervosa and Schizophrenia   Nicolle (1938) and Brill (1939) shared the view that anorexia nervosa was a form of schizophrenia. In the famous case of Ellen West, Binswanger (1958) described in detail the case of a young woman with anorexia nervosa; however, Binswanger concluded the patient was schizophrenic.

Bruch (1966) stated that the psychological issues found in anorexia nervosa resembled those described as significant for schizophrenia. However, while schizophrenics may refuse to eat for a variety of reasons, they, unlike anorexics, do not do so "with the singular goal of achieving autonomy and effectiveness through the bizarre control over the body and its functions" (p. 565). Theander (1970) noted only superficial similarities between anorexia nervosa and schizophrenia. Furthermore, research has indicated that anorexics are not likely to develop schizophrenia later. Dally (1969) found that only 1 in 140 anorexics was schizophrenic at follow-up. Similarly, Theander (1970) found at follow-up that of 94 patients, none showed "unequivocal symptoms of schizophrenia" and only "one was regarded as a borderline case" (p. 188). Russell (1979) considered anorexia nervosa and schizophrenia to be distinct conditions. Garfinkel and Kaplan (1986) noted that "fundamental schizophrenic disturbances in affect, thought processes, and volition are not found in anorexia nervosa" (p. 274).

Recent cases have been reported in which patients met diagnostic criteria for both anorexia nervosa and schizophrenia (Ferguson & Damluji, 1988; Lyon & Silber, 1989; Sumners & Ghen, 1987). Although such cases of the concurrence of anorexia nervosa and schizophrenia have been reported, according to Hsu (1990), no one has recently suggested that anorexia nervosa is a form of schizophrenia.

Anorexia Nervosa and Obsessive-Compulsive Disorder   In addition to being considered a form of schizophrenia, anorexia nervosa has been linked to obsessive-compulsive disorder. Numerous authors have noted obsessional traits and symptoms in anorexic patients (Halmi, 1974, p. 22; Kay & Leigh, 1954, p. 428; Nemiah, 1958, p. 247; Warren, 1968, p. 35). Some investigators even labeled anorexia nervosa a form of obsessive-compulsion neurosis. Palmer and Jones (1939) labeled anorexia nervosa "a compulsion neurosis the pattern of which is fixed on anorexia and vomiting" (p. 857). Rahman, Richardson, and Ripley (1939) defined anorexia nervosa as "a neurosis with compulsive, obsessive, anxiety and depressive features" (p. 364). DuBois (1949) defined anorexia nervosa as a compulsion neurosis with cachexia (p. 115). Numerous investigators have continued to note obsessive-compulsive features in anorexic patients. Smart, Beumont, and George (1976) confirmed the "marked obsessional features" (p. 59) of a group of anorexic patients as compared to normal subjects. Similarly, Solyom, Miles, and O'Kane (1982) reported on the obsessive personality traits and obsessional symptoms in anorexic patients (p. 282). Waters, Beumont, Touyz, and Kennedy (1990) noted that when an individual developed anorexia nervosa, obsessive-compulsive features became evident. Similarly, Kerr, Skok, and McLaughlin (1991) suggested that females with anorexia nervosa are obsessive-compulsive in nature. Rothenberg (1986) concluded that anorexia nervosa, among women of Western culture, was the "modern obsessive-compulsive syndrome" (p. 45). Rothenberg (1990) reiterated this point in 1990, concluding that the "current eating disorders picture, therefore, appears to be a modern form of obsessive-compulsive illness" (p. 485).

Dally (1969) included an obsessional group in his categorization of anorexia nervosa patients, and he remarked that obsessive and compulsive traits factor strongly in the personality of anorexia nervosa patients. However, Dally (1969) did not accept that anorexia nervosa was a form of compulsive neurosis (p. 12). Garfinkel and Garner (1982) suggested that the obsessiveness displayed by anorexic patients when they are ill may be a product of the starvation state. Garfinkel and Kaplan (1986) agreed with Dally. While noting that obsessive symptomatology may be displayed by anorexic patients, they stated this "does not signify an obsessive-compulsive disorder" (p. 274). Even more recently, Hsu (1990) suggested that, although a link between anorexia nervosa and obsessive-compulsive disorder at the neurochemical level is possible, "it would be premature at this stage of our knowledge of the neurotransmitters to suggest that anorexia nervosa is a variant of obsessive-compulsive disorder" (p. 29). Holden (1990) compared the symptoms of obsessive-compulsive disorder (OCD) and anorexia nervosa and examined the genetic and epidemiological evidence linking them. He noted that "premorbid obsessional personality traits are over-represented in those with anorexia nervosa, and the illness process, especially starvation, seems to exacerbate these" (Holden, 1990, p. 4). Holden (1990) also noted "some overlap between the phenomenology of obsessional and anorectic symptoms" (p. 4). However, he concluded that "any further hypothesis about the relationship of anorexia nervosa and OCD remains highly speculative" (Holden, 1990, p. 4). Furthermore, Holden (1990) maintained that viewing anorexia nervosa as a distinct disease entity has relevance for the understanding, management, and prognosis of the disorder. Fahy (1991) failed to find evidence to support anorexia nervosa as a subtype of OCD.

Anorexia Nervosa and Hysteria   In addition to being labeled a form of schizophrenia and obsessive-compulsive disorder, anorexia nervosa has also been linked to hysteria. This link dates back to Lasegue's observations of anorexia nervosa in the late 19th century. Emphasizing the hysterical origin of anorexia nervosa, Lasegue (1873) labeled the disorder *hysterical anorexia.* Vandereycken and Beumont (1990) reported on Astles' 1882 case description of anorexia nervosa in which symptoms of hysteria were noted in one patient; however, Astles did not take a firm position on whether anorexia nervosa belonged to the hysterical disorders. Gilles de la Tourette (1895) viewed primary anorexia nervosa as a manifestation of hysteria, which had to be separated from *anorexie gastrique* or secondary anorexia nervosa. Janet (1919) described two subgroups of anorexia nervosa: obsessive and hysterical. According to Dally (1969), Janet (1919) was very clear about the existence of a hysterical form of anorexia nervosa that was "associated with loss of hunger, anesthesia, and queer tastes in the mouth, tongue, throat, and overactivity without a sense of fatigue" (p. 12). Hobhouse (1938) viewed anorexia nervosa as a form of conversion hysteria (p. 162).

However, other investigators distinguished between anorexia nervosa and hysteria. Bruch (1962) noted one important difference between anorexia nervosa and hysteria: Anorexic patients are unaware of their weakness, unlike noneaters of the hysterical variety who "are very much aware of their weakness" (p. 190). In their differentiation between anorexia nervosa and conversion disorder, Garfinkel,

Kaplan, Garner, and Darby (1983) noted that patients with conversion disorder, older at the onset of their illness, were less preoccupied with dieting, weight, and body size. Those with conversion disorder not only underestimated their body size, but they also had a larger ideal size and "displayed a stronger sense of self-control, less obsessive-compulsive behavior, and more consistent social relationships. They also had more medical illness and more illness requiring surgery in the past" (p. 1021). Garfinkel and Kaplan (1986) noted that some of the confusion regarding hysteria itself may have resulted in its unclear relationship to anorexia nervosa. Although hysterical personality disorder, somatization disorder, and conversion disorder have all been linked to hysterical phenomena, "anorexia nervosa does not clearly resemble any of these" (p. 275).

Anorexia Nervosa and Affective Disorder   Although anorexia nervosa has been considered a variant of schizophrenia, obsessive-compulsive disorder, and hysteria, the relationship between anorexia nervosa and affective disorder has perhaps received the most attention. According to Thoma (1967), Kraeplin diagnosed cases of anorexia nervosa as melancholia. Also, in 1948, Zutt defined anorexia nervosa as related to manic-depressive psychosis.

The link between anorexia nervosa and affective disorder is based on the following facts: many anorexic patients exhibit depressive symptoms; many anorexic patients show depressive symptomatology at the time of follow-up; depression occurs more frequently in family members of anorexics; and many anorexics may respond to antidepressant drugs.

Numerous investigators have noted depressive symptoms in anorexic patients (Blitzer, Rollins, & Blackwell, 1961; Eckert, 1985; Kay, 1953; Morgan & Russell, 1975; Nemiah, 1950; Rollins & Piazza, 1978; Warren, 1968). Sykes, Leuser, Melia, and Gross (1988) found a 50% prevalence rate of depression in 252 patients referred to a clinic for anorexia nervosa and bulimia, which is significantly higher than that found in the general population. Garfinkel and Kaplan (1986) observed shared features of anorexia nervosa and depression including sleep disturbance, weight loss, reduced libido, amenorrhea, cognitive disturbance, and a reduced self-esteem. However, they also noted that in anorexia nervosa, self-esteem is directly tied to weight loss and appearance, and that in anorexia "many of these signs and symptoms result from starvation" (p. 272).

Anorexia nervosa and affective disorder are linked by more than shared symptoms. Cantwell et al. (1977) found that many anorexic patients showed depressive symptomatology in the premorbid and postmorbid states as well as at the time of follow-up. Of the 26 patients followed for nearly 5 years, two thirds were given a psychiatric diagnosis; of these, one half met the criteria for affective disorder. Cantwell et al. (1977) then argued that in some cases, anorexia nervosa could be considered a variant of affective disorder (p. 1093). Toner, Garfinkel, and Garner's (1988) study described the incidence and onset of affective and anxiety disorders in women who were diagnosed with anorexia nervosa 5 to 14 years earlier. The investigators "found that regardless of clinical outcome anorexic groups had a higher lifetime prevalence of affective and anxiety disorders compared with a nonclinical comparison group" (p. 362). In a follow-up study of anorexia nervosa patients that focused on clinical symptomatology and psychosocial adjustment, Santonasto, Pantano, Panarotto, and Silvestri (1991) found that 40% showed major depression, atypical depression, or dysthmic disorder. However, Hsu (1988) maintained that anorexia nervosa does not "change" into depression (pp. 810–811); in 1990, he noted that the most common diagnosis of recovered anorexic patients is bulimia nervosa, not depression (p. 10).

Others have linked anorexia nervosa to affective disorder on the basis of findings of depression in the families of anorexic patients. Warren (1968) suggested that depression was a common feature in the families of anorexic patients (p. 33). Cantwell et al. (1977) discovered a family history of affective disorder in anorexic patients, especially in the mothers (p. 1093). Dally (1977) discovered that three fourths of the youngest of three anorexic groups studied (11 to 14 years of age) had a depressed mother (p. 471). Winokur, March, and Mendels (1980) discovered that 22% of the relatives of patients with anorexia nervosa had histories of affective disorder, whereas only 10% of relatives of control subjects exhibited such histories (p. 695). Sholevar (1987) cited studies which showed a greater-than-expected prevalence of primary affective disorder in relatives of anorexic patients (p. 35). Szmukler (1987) suggested the strongest evidence for a link between anorexia nervosa and eating disorders "comes from the significantly enhanced morbid risk for affective disorder in the relatives of anorexic probands, two-to three-fold compared with controls, demonstrated in a number of studies" (p. 182). Logue, Crow, and Bean (1989) conducted a family study to assess the association between affective illness and eating disorders. Using logistic regression analysis, the investigators' results supported previous findings of a familial association of eating disorders and affective illness. In particular, this study supported an association between eating disorders and major depression, with crude estimates of major depression of 13% for eating disorders and 5% for controls (p. 185).

On the other hand, Garfinkel, Moldofsky, and Garner (1980) did not find a significant number of parents of anorexic patients with affective disorder. Also, Altshuler and Weiner (1985) concluded the link between anorexia nervosa and affective disorder based on depression found in family members of anorexics to be unclear in suggesting that anorexia nervosa is a variant of affective disorder (p. 328).

Others have tied anorexia nervosa to affective disorder on the basis of the fact that anorexics may respond to antidepressant treatment. Winokur et al. (1980) reported that a subgroup of anorexics who displayed a mixed picture of anorexia nervosa and affective disorder may be "specifically responsive to treatment with tricyclic antidepressant drugs or lithium carbonate" (p. 697). However, to suggest that anorexia nervosa is a variant of affective disorder on the basis of the similar treatment of tricyclic antidepressants is weak on two counts. The efficacy of the anorexic patients' responsiveness to these drugs has not been established, and common response to medication is a weak basis on which to link two illnesses (Garfinkel & Garner, 1982, p. 22; Garfinkel & Kaplan, 1986, p. 272). Also, according to Szmukler (1987), Halmi et al.'s (1986) controlled trial showed little response to amitriptyline in terms of weight gain and none in terms of anorexic attitudes (p. 182).

Others have distinguished between anorexia nervosa and depression. Stonehill and Crisp (1977) noted that patients with anorexia nervosa report themselves as significantly less depressed than did a population of depressed females of comparable age, thus lending "support to the view that anorexia nervosa is not a simple variant of depressive illness" (p. 191). Ben-Tovim, Marilov, and Crisp (1979) reported that, although depression was the predominant symptom in a group of 21 anorexic patients, their "overall mental state was quite distinct from that of a published series of depressives" (p. 321). Although Carlson and Cantwell (1980) recognized a complex relationship between anorexia nervosa and affective disorder, they also found that anorexic adolescents' global ratings of depression were much less than those with primary affective disorder (p. 449). Eckert et al. (1982) found a range of depression in anorexic patients; however, "the group as a whole was only mildly to moderately depressed and did not show as high a level of depression as a normative group of primarily depressed neurotics" (p. 120). Garfinkel and Garner (1982) stated that the fundamental drive for thinness that dominates the anorexic's clinical picture warrants a separate classification of the illness (p. 22). Sholevar (1987) differentiated depressive illness and anorexia nervosa on the basis of symptoms such as depressed affect, psychomotor retardation, suicidal ideals, and the recognition of loss of appetite in patients with depressive disorders, which are not found in patients with anorexia nervosa (p. 35).

After examining observations that suggest a relationship between anorexia nervosa and affective disorder based on clinical phenomenology; family-genetic and biologic correlates; and course, outcome, and epidemiology of eating disorders and affective disorder, Strober and Katz (1987) determined that evidence points to greater divergence than overlap, thus arguing against the hypothesis that they share a common etiology. The authors concluded that, although depressive traits and affective disorder play an important role in predisposition to eating disorders, "a sharpened focus on the differentiating features of eating disorders still offers the greatest opportunity for uncovering clues to their etiology and more effective management" (p. 178). Walsh, Gladis, and Roose (1987) concluded that it would be premature to consider anorexia nervosa a variant of major depression. When biological disturbances characteristic of major depression occur in anorexia nervosa, their significance is blurred by serious weight loss. The meaning of an increased prevalence of major depression among relatives of anorexic patients is uncertain. Also, the fact that some patients with eating disorders respond to antidepressant medication does not show that eating disorders are a form of major depression (p. 235).

CONCLUSION

Most investigators today conceptualize anorexia nervosa as a distinct psychological syndrome with a core group of symptoms that allows for its diagnosis and its separation from other forms of dieting behavior and from other psychiatric illnesses. In other words, anorexia nervosa is viewed today as a distinct clinical entity. In 1970, Russell suggested that to discuss the identity of anorexia nervosa might appear to be an idle scholarly exercise "were it not for the danger that to dismiss it as a mere symptom of a variety of psychiatric illnesses might result in a loss of interest and a stifling of research" (p. 132). Twenty years later, Hsu (1990) reiterated a similar point. Discussion of the identity of eating disorders, such as anorexia nervosa, is not just academic. Investigators must agree on a definition so that anorexia nervosa can be distinguished from other forms of dieting behavior and other psychiatric illnesses. The study of anorexia nervosa as a distinct entity will aid further progress in scholarship and treatment of this life-threatening disorder.

DISCUSSION QUESTIONS

1 Discuss Gull and Lasegue's contributions to the modern concept of anorexia nervosa.

2 How did anorexia nervosa regain its status as a distinct psychological entity following Simmonds' (1914) report of anterior pituitary lesions and cachexia?

3 What was the "rather sweeping generalization" of Waller, Kaufman, and Deutsch (1940)?

4 Name the three areas of disturbed psychological functioning identified by Bruch.

5 Discuss the "relentless pursuit of thinness."

6 What do Dally's (1969) diagnostic criteria, Feighner et al.'s (1972) criteria, DSM-III, and DSM-III-R have in common?

7 Identify and explain the changes in DSM-IV.

8 Discuss the idea that anorexia nervosa represents an extreme point on a continuum ranging from simple dieting behaviors to anorexia nervosa.

9 Anorexia nervosa has been linked to four other psychiatric illnesses. What are they, and which connection has received the most attention?

REFERENCES

Altshuter, K. Z., & Weiner, M. (1985). Anorexia nervosa: A dissenting view. *American Journal of Psychiatry, 142,* 328–332.

American Psychiatric Association. (1980). *Diagnostic and statistical manual of mental disorders* (3rd ed.). Washington, DC: Author.

American Psychiatric Association. (1987). *Diagnostic and statistical manual of mental disorders* (3rd ed., rev.). Washington, DC: Author.

Ben-Tovim, D., Marilov, V., & Crisp, A. H. (1979). Personality and mental state (P.S.E.) in patients with anorexia nervosa. *Journal of Psychosomatic Research, 23,* 321–325.

Berkman, J. M. (1945). Anorexia nervosa: The diagnosis and treatment of inanition resulting from functional disorders. *Annals of Internal Medicine, 22,* 679–691.

Berkman, J. M. (1948). Anorexia nervosa, anterior-pituitary insufficiency, Simmonds' cachexia, and Sheehan's disease, including some observations on disturbances in water metabolism associated with starvation. *Postgraduate Medicine, 3,* 237–246.

Beumont, P. J. V., George, G. C. W., & Smart, D. E. (1976). 'Dieters' and 'vomiters and purgers' in anorexia nervosa. *Psychological Medicine, 6,* 617–622.

Binswanger, L. (1958). The case of Ellen West. In R. May, E. Angel, and H. Ellenberger (Eds.), *Existence* (pp. 237–264). New York: Basic Books.

Bliss, E. L., & Branch, C. H. H. (1960). *Anorexia nervosa: Its history, psychology, and biology.* New York: Paul B. Hoeber.

Blitzer, J. R., Rollins, N., & Blackwell, A. (1961). Children who starve themselves. *Psychosomatic Medicine, 23,* 370–386.

Brill, A. A. (1939). In discussion following: Pardoe I. Cachexia nervosa: A psychoneurotic Simmonds syndrome. *Archives of Neurology and Psychiatry, 41,* 842–843.

Bruch, H. (1962). Perceptual and conceptual disturbances in anorexia nervosa. *Psychosomatic Medicine, 24,* 187–194.

Bruch, H. (1966). Anorexia nervosa and its differential diagnosis. *Journal of Mental Disease, 141,* 555–566.

Bruch, H. (1973). *Eating disorders.* New York: Basic Books.

Button, E. J., & Whitehouse, A. (1981). Subclinical anorexia. *Psychological Medicine, 11,* 509–516.

Cantwell, D. P., Sturzenberger, S., Burroughs, J., Salkin, B., & Green, J. K. (1977). Anorexia nervosa: An affective disorder? *Archives of General Psychiatry, 34,* 1087–1093.

Carlson, G. A., & Cantwell, P. P. (1980). Unmasking masked depression in children and adolescents. *American Journal of Psychiatry, 37,* 445–449.

Casper, R. C., Eckert, E. D., Halmi, K. A., Goldberg, S. C., & Davis, J. M. (1980). Bulimia: Its incidence in patients with anorexia nervosa. *Archives of General Psychiatry, 37,* 1030–1034.

Crisp, A. H. (1970). Premorbid factors in adult disorders of weight with particular reference to primary anorexia nervosa (weight phobia): A literature review. *Journal of Psychosomatic Research, 9,* 67–78.

Crisp, A. H. (1977). Diagnosis and outcome of anorexia nervosa: The St. George's view. *Proceedings of the Royal Society of Medicine, 70,* 464–470.

Crisp, A. H., Hsu, L. K. G., & Harding, B. (1980). The starving hoarder and voracious spender: Stealing in anorexia nervosa. *Journal of Psychometric Research, 24,* 225–231.

Dally, P. J. (1969). *Anorexia nervosa.* New York: Grune and Stratton.

Dally, P. J. (1977). Anorexia nervosa: Do we need a scapegoat? *Proceedings of the Royal Society of Medicine, 70,* 470–480.

Dally, P., & Gomez, J. (1979). *Anorexia nervosa.* London: William Heinemann Medical Books Limited.

DeCosta, M., & Halmi, K. A. (1992). Classification of anorexia nervosa: Question of subtypes. *International Journal of Eating Disorders, 11,* 303–315.

DuBois, F. S. (1949). Compulsion neurosis with cachexia (anorexia nervosa). *American Journal of Psychiatry, 106,* 107–115.

Eckert, E. D. (1985). Characteristics of anorexia nervosa. In James E. Mitchell (Ed.), *Anorexia Nervosa and Bulimia: Diagnosis and Treatment* (pp. 3–26). Minneapolis, MN: University of Minnesota Press.

Eckert, E. D., Goldberg, S. C., Halmi, K. A., Casper, R. C., & Davis, J. M. (1982). Depression in anorexia nervosa. *Psychological Medicine, 12,* 115–122.

Fahy, T. A. (1991). Obsessive-compulsive symptoms in eating disorders. *Behaviour-Research and Therapy, 29,* 113–116.

Farquharson, R. F., & Hyland, H. H. (1936). Anorexia nervosa: A metabolic disorder of psychologic origin. In M. R. Kaufman & M. Heimann, (Eds.), *Evolution of Psychosomatic Concepts* (pp. 202–226). New York: International Universities Press.

Feighner, J. P., Robbins, E., Guze, S. B., Woodruff, R. A., Winokur, G., & Munoz, R. (1972). Diagnostic criteria for use in psychiatric research. *Archives of General Psychiatry, 26,* 57–63.

Ferguson, J. M., & Damluji, N. F. (1988). Anorexia nervosa and schizophrenia. *International Journal of Eating Disorders, 7,* 343–352.

Fries, H. (1977). Studies on secondary amenorrhea, anorectic behavior, and body image perception: Importance for the early recognition of anorexia nervosa. In R. G. Vigersky (Ed.), *Anorexia nervosa* (pp. 163–176). New York: Raven Press.

Garfinkel, P. E., & Garner, D. M. (1982). *Anorexia nervosa: A multidimensional perspective.* New York: Brunner/Mazel.

Garfinkel, P. E., & Kaplan, A. S. (1986). Anorexia nervosa: Diagnostic conceptualizations. In K. D. Brownell & J. P. Foreyt (Eds.), *Handbook of eating disorders* (pp. 262–282). New York: Basic Books.

Garfinkel, P. E., Kaplan, D. S., Garner, D. M., & Darby, P. L. (1983). The differentiation of vomiting and weight loss as a conversion disorder from anorexia nervosa. *American Journal of Psychiatry, 140,* 1019–1022.

Garfinkel, P. E., Moldofsky, H., & Garner, D. M. (1980). The heterogeneity of anorexia nervosa: Bulimia as a distinct subgroup. *Archives of General Psychiatry, 37,* 1036–1040.

Garner, D. M., & Garfinkel, P. E. (1980). Sociocultural factors in the development of anorexia nervosa. *Psychological Medicine, 10,* 647–656.

Garner, D. M., Olmstead, M. P., Polivy, J., & Garfinkel, P. E. (1984). Comparison between weight-preoccupied women and anorexia nervosa. *Psychosomatic Medicine, 46,* 255–266.

Gilles de la Tourette, G. A. E. B. (1895). *Traite clinique et therapeutique de l'Hysteria* [Clinical and Therapeutic Stages of Hysteria]. Paris: Plou, Nourit et Co.

Gull, W. W. (1868). The address in medicine delivered before the annual meeting of the British Medical Association at Oxford. *Lancet, 2,* 171–176.

Gull, W. W. (1874). Anorexia nervosa. *Transactions of Clinical Society* (London), *7,* 22–28.

Halmi, K. A. (1974). Anorexia nervosa: Demographic and clinical features of 94 cases. *Psychosomatic Medicine, 36,* 18–26.

Halmi, K. A., Eckert, E., LaDu, T. J., & Cohen, J. (1986). Anorexia nervosa: Treatment efficacy of cyroheptidine and amitriptyline. *Archives of General Psychiatry, 43,* 177–181.

Hobhouse, N. (1938). Discussion of paper by Grace Nicolle on prepsychotic anorexia. *Proceedings of the Royal Society of Medicine, 32,* 153–162.

Holden, N. L. (1990). Is anorexia nervosa an obsessive-compulsive disorder? *British Journal of Psychiatry, 157,* 1–5.

Hsu, L. K. G. (1988). The outcome of anorexia nervosa: A reappraisal. *Psychological Medicine, 18,* 807–812.

Hsu, L. K. G. (1990). *Eating disorders.* New York: The Guilford Press.

Hsu, L. K. G., Crisp, A. H., & Harding, B. (1979). Outcome of anorexia nervosa. *Lancet, 1,* 61–75.

Janet, P. (1919). *Les obsessions et la psychoasthenie* [Obsessions and Psychoses]. Paris: Felix Alcan.

Kay, D. W. K. (1953). Anorexia nervosa: A study in prognosis. *Proceedings of the Royal Society of Medicine, 46,* 669–674.

Kay, D. W. K., & Leigh, D. (1954). The natural history, treatment, and prognosis of anorexia nervosa, based on a study of 38 patients. *Journal of Mental Science, 100,* 411–439.

Kerr, J. K., Skok, R. L., & McLaughlin, T. F. (1991). Characteristics common to females who exhibit anorexic or bulimic behavior: A review. *Journal of Clinical Psychology, 47,* 846–853.

King, A. (1963). Primary and secondary anorexia nervosa syndromes. *British Journal of Psychiatry, 109,* 470–479.

Lasegue, C. (1873). On hysterical anorexia. *Medical Times Gazette, 2,* 265–266, 367–369.

Loeb, L. (1964). The clinical course of anorexia nervosa. *Psychosomatics, 5,* 345–347.

Logue, C. M., Crowe, R. R., Bean, J. A. (1989). A family study of anorexia nervosa and bulimia. *Comprehensive Psychiatry, 30,* 179–188.

Lowenkopf, E. L. (1982). Anorexia nervosa: Some nosological considerations. *Comparative Psychiatry, 23,* 233–240.

Lucas, A. R. (1981). Toward the understanding of anorexia nervosa as a disease entity. *Mayo Clinic Proceedings, 56,* 254–264.

Lyon, M. E., & Silber, T. J. (1989). Anorexia nervosa and schizophrenia in an adolescent female. *Journal of Adolescent Health Care, 10,* 419–420.

Mann, A. H., Wakeling, A., Wood, K., Monck, E., Dobbs, R., & Szmukler, G. (1983). Screening for abnormal eating attitudes and psychiatric morbidity in an unselected population of 15-year-old school girls. *Psychological Medicine, 13,* 573–580.

Meyer, B. C., & Weinroth, L. A. (1957). Observations on psychological aspects of anorexia nervosa. *Psychosomatic Medicine, 19,* 389–398.

Morgan, H. G., & Russell, G. F. M. (1975). Value of family background and clinical features as predictors of long-term outcome in anorexia nervosa: Four-year follow-up study of 41 patients. *Psychological Medicine, 5,* 355–371.

Morton, R. (1694). *Phthisiologica: Or a treatise of consumptions.* London: S. Smith & B. Walford.

Moulton, R. (1942). A psychosomatic study of anorexia including the use of vaginal smears. *Psychosomatic Medicine, 4,* 62–64.

Nemiah, J. C. (1950). Anorexia nervosa: A clinical psychiatric study. *Medicine, 29*, 225–268.

Nemiah, J. C. (1958). Anorexia nervosa: Fact and theory. *American Journal of Digestive Diseases, 33*, 249–274.

Nicolle, G. (1938). Prepsychotic anorexia. *Royal Society of Medicine, 32*, 153–162.

Nylander, I. (1971). The feeling of being fat and dieting in a school population: Epidemiologic interview investigation. *Acta Sociomedica Scandivica, 3*, 17–26.

Palmer, H. D., & Jones, M. S. (1939). Anorexia nervosa as a manifestation of compulsive neurosis. *Archives of Neurology and Psychiatry, 41*, 856–860.

Patton, G. C. (1988). The spectrum of eating disorders in adolescence. 31st Annual Conference for Psychosomatic Research. *Journal of Psychosomatic Research, 32*, 579–584.

Polivy, J., & Herman, C. P. (1987). Diagnosis and treatment of normal eating. *Journal of Consulting and Clinical Psychology, 55*, 635–644.

Rahman, L., Richardson, H. B., & Ripley, H. S. (1939). Anorexia nervosa with psychiatric observations. *Psychosomatic Medicine, 1*, 335–365.

Richardson, H. B. (1939). Simmonds' disease and anorexia nervosa. *Archives of Internal Medicine, 163*, 1–28.

Rollins, N., & Piazza, E. (1978). Diagnosis of anorexia nervosa: A critical reappraisal. *Journal of Child Psychiatry, 17*, 126–132.

Rothenberg, A. C. (1986). Eating disorders as a modern obsessive-compulsive syndrome. *Psychiatry, 49*, 49–52.

Rothenberg, A. C. (1990). Adolescence in eating disorders: The obsessive-compulsive syndrome. *Psychiatric Clinics of North America, 13*, 469–488.

Russell, G. F. M. (1970). Anorexia nervosa: Its identity as an illness and its treatment. In J. H. Price (Ed.), *Modern trends in psychological medicine: Vol. 2* (pp. 131–164). London: Butterworths.

Russell, G. F. M. (1979). Bulimia nervosa: An ominous variant of anorexia nervosa. *Psychological Medicine, 9*, 429–448.

Ryle, J. A. (1936). Anorexia nervosa. *Lancet, 2*, 893–899.

Santonasto, P., Pantano, M., Panarotto, L., Silvestri, A. (1991). A followup study on anorexia nervosa: Clinical features and diagnostic outcome. *European Psychiatry, 6*, 177–185.

Selvini-Palazzoli, M. P. (1974). *Self-starvation*. London: Chaucer.

Sheehan, H. L., & Summers, V. K. (1949). The syndrome of hypopituitarism. *Quarterly Journal of Medicine, 18*, 319–378.

Sholevar, G. P. (1987). Anorexia nervosa. In H. L. Field & B. B. Domangue, *Eating Disorders Throughout the Lifespan* (pp. 31–47). New York: Praeger Publishers.

Sibley, D. C., & Blinder, B. J. (1988). Anorexia nervosa. In B. J. Blinder, B. F. Chaitin, & R. Goldstein (Eds.), *The eating disorders* (pp. 247–259). New York: PMA Publishing Group.

Simmonds, M. (1914). Ueber embolische Prozesse in des Hypophysis [About Embolism Processing in the Pituitary Gland]. *Archives fur Pathologie und Anatomie, 217*, 226–239.

Smart, P. E., Beumont, P. J. V., & George, G. C. W. (1976). Some personality characteristics of patients with anorexia nervosa. *British Journal of Psychiatry, 128*, 57–60.

Solyom, L., Miles, J. E., & O'Kane, J. (1982). A comparative psychometric study of anorexia nervosa and obsessive neurosis. *Canadian Journal of Psychiatry, 27*, 282–286.

Sours, J. A. (1974). The anorexia nervosa syndrome. *International Journal of Eating Disorders, 55*, 567–576.

Stonehill, E., & Crisp, A. H. (1977). Psychoneurotic characteristics of patients with an-
orexia nervosa before and after treatment and at follow-up 4–7 years later. *Journal of Psychosomatic Research, 21,* 187–193.

Strober, M. B. (1981). The significance of bulimia in juvenile anorexia nervosa: An exploration of possible etiologic factors. *International Journal of Eating Disorders, 1,* 28–43.

Strober, M. B. (1986). Anorexia nervosa: History and psychological concepts. In K. D. Brownell & J. P. Foreyt (Eds.), *Handbook of eating disorders* (pp. 231–246). New York: Basic Books.

Strober, M. B., & Katz, J. (1987). Do eating disorders and affective disorder share a common etiology? A dissenting opinion. *International Journal of Eating Disorders, 6,* 171–180.

Strober, M., Salkin, B., Burroughs, J., & Morrell, W. (1982). Validity of the bulimia restricter distinction in anorexia nervosa: Parental personality characteristics and family psychiatric morbidity. *Journal of Nervous and Mental Disease, 170,* 345–351.

Sumners, D., & Cohen, R. I. (1987). Anorexia nervosa and schizophrenia: A case study. *International Journal of Eating Disorders, 6,* 435–438.

Sykes, D. K., Leuser, B., Melia, M., & Gross, M. (1988). A demographic analysis of 252 patients with anorexia nervosa and bulimia. [Special issue: Nutrition, Stress, and Aging]. *International Journal of Psychosomatics, 35,* 5–9.

Szmukler, G. I. (1987). Some comments on the link between anorexia nervosa and affective disorder. *International Journal of Eating Disorders, 6,* 181–189.

Theander, S. (1970). Anorexia nervosa: A psychiatric investigation of 94 female patients. *Acta Psychiatrica Scandivica. 214* (Suppl.), 1–94.

Thoma, H. (1967). *Anorexia nervosa.* New York: International University Press.

Thompson, M. G. & Schwartz, D. M. (1982). Life adjustment of women with anorexia nervosa and anorexic-like behavior. *International Journal of Eating Disorders, 1,* 47–60.

Toner, B. B., Garfinkel, P. E., & Garner, D. M. (1986). Long-term follow-up of anorexia nervosa. *Psychosomatic Medicine, 48,* 520–529.

Toner, B., Garfinkel, P. E., & Garner, D. M. (1988). Affective and anxiety disorders in the long-term follow-up of anorexia nervosa. *International Journal of Psychiatry in Medicine, 18,* 357–364.

Vandereycken, W., & Beumont, P. J. (1990). The first Australian case of anorexia nervosa. *Australian and New Zealand Journal of Psychiatry, 24,* 109–112.

Waller, J., Kaufman, M. R., & Deutsch, F. (1940). Anorexia nervosa: A psychosomatic study. *Psychosomatic Medicine, 2,* 3–16.

Walsh, T. B., Gladis, M., & Roose, S. P. (1987). Food intake and mood in anorexia nervosa and bulimia. *Annals of the New York Academy of Sciences, 499,* 231–238.

Warren, W. (1968). A study of anorexia nervosa in young girls. *Journal of Child Psychology and Psychiatry, 9,* 27–40.

Wilson, T. G., & Walsh, T. B. (1991). Eating disorders in the DSM-IV. Special issue: Diagnoses, dimensions, and DSM-IV: The science of classification. *Journal of Abnormal Psychology, 100,* 362–365.

Winokur, A., March, V., & Mendels, J. (1980). Primary affective disorder in relatives of patients with anorexia nervosa. *American Journal of Psychiatry, 137,* 695–698.

Woznica, J. C. (1990). Delay of gratification in bulimic and restricting anorexia nervosa patients. *Journal of Clinical Psychology, 46,* 706–713.

Chapter 6

Anorexia Nervosa:
Theories of Etiology

Russell D. Marx

It has been said that "many psychiatric disorders are multidetermined but probably none more so than anorexia nervosa" (Rakoff, 1982, p. vii). Much remains to be learned about the causes of anorexia nervosa. Current work includes contributions from wide-ranging fields including psychology, family studies, neurobiology, genetics, and social and cultural studies.

The earliest probable description of anorexia nervosa in Western literature is that of Richard Morton in 1694. He placed the immediate cause of this distemper "in the destruction of the tone of the nerves," and found causation in an 18-year-old girl from "a multitude of cares and passions of her mind" (Anderson, 1985, p. 11).

The first modern descriptions of anorexia nervosa are those of Gull in 1873 and Lasegue in 1873 (both reprinted in Andersen, 1985). Gull felt "the want of appetite is, I believe, due to a morbid mental state. I have not observed in these cases any gastric disorder to which the want of appetite could be referred. I believe, therefore, that its origin is central and not peripheral" (Gull, 1874). Lasegue also postulated a psychological causation for anorexia nervosa, believing it to be "one of the forms of hysteria of the gastric centre" (Lasègue, 1873).

In 1914, a new, but unfortunately incorrect, theory of causation was introduced for anorexia nervosa. Morris Simmonds, a German pathologist, provided anatomical evidence of atrophy of the anterior lobe of the pituitary gland in a patient with cachexia and for the next two decades the cause of anorexia nervosa was felt to be panhypopituitarism (Sours, 1980).

By 1939, this theory had been discredited by the work of Sheehan and others (Sours, 1980). For the next several decades, psychoanalytic thinking was preeminent in providing various theories of causation of anorexia nervosa. In the 1940s and 1950s, "anorexia nervosa was viewed as a form of conversion hysteria that symbolically expressed repudiation of sexuality, specifically of 'oral impregnation fantasies'" (Bruch, 1985, p. 8). Since that time, more complex models have been developed and theories of psychological causation of anorexia nervosa have incorporated advances in psychoanalysis such as work on object relations, separation-individuation, and self-psychology.

Modern thinking about the causation of anorexia nervosa looks at factors that predispose, precipitate, and perpetuate the disorder. Garfinkel and Garner (1982) have provided a thoughtful review of these different aspects of causation.

PREDISPOSING CAUSES

Social and cultural factors are among the first areas of predisposing causes to be examined. Garner, Rockert, Olmsted, Johnson, & Coscina (1985) have documented increasing cultural pressures for excessive thinness in women. Their studies have documented such trends as an increasing disparity between the actual weight of young women (which has been increasing in the past several decades) and the decreasing weight and shape of Western ideals of female beauty as exemplified in Playboy magazine centerfolds or Miss America Pageant contestants. Garner et al. (1985) have also documented an increasing cultural obsession with thinness by showing a 70% increase in diet articles in popular women's magazines in the 1970s compared to the previous decade.

This increasing cultural pressure for excessive thinness is likely to be a significant factor in the current increasing incidence of anorexia nervosa found in most epidemiological studies. Hsu (1990), summarizing recent screening surveys, finds a prevalence of anorexia nervosa between 0.2% and 0.8%, with a higher percentage in upper social classes. Furthermore, recent studies suggest there has been an increase in dieting behaviors among young females, and this seems to be a causative factor in the development of anorexia nervosa (Hsu, 1990).

Shifting from culture to biology, another area of predisposing factors that has been investigated involves genetic components. In a recent summary, Hsu (1990) pooled the data from several studies to yield 42 female twin pairs in which at least one twin has anorexia nervosa. A genetic predisposition to anorexia nervosa is strongly suggested by the contrast between the 50% concordance for anorexia nervosa among the 28 monozygotic twin pairs compared to the 7% concordance among the 14 dizygotic twin pairs.

Another area of research suggesting a genetic component to anorexia nervosa is family risk studies. In a recent study, Strober, Lampert, Morrell, Burroughs, & Jacobs (1990) found that anorexia nervosa was eight times as common among close relatives of anorexia nervosa patients as in the general population. Other studies have found a substantially higher lifetime prevalence of affective disorders among relatives of anorexic patients. These studies may be relevant both for patients who themselves have a preexisting vulnerability for depression as well as patients growing up in a family impacted by significant depression in one or more family members. Additionally, some studies, though not all, have found increased prevalence of alcohol and substance abuse among relatives of anorexic patients.

Turning from biology to psychology, one of the most important contributions to modern conceptualization of anorexia nervosa is the work of Hilde Bruch. In her last work she wrote the following:

> In my early formulations, I recognized three features as characteristic of the anorexic illness: the nearly delusional misperception of the body (disturbed body image), confusion about body sensations, and an all-pervasive sense of ineffectiveness. Now I am inclined to visualize these under a more general heading, namely, as an expression of defective self-concept, the fear of inner emptiness or badness, as something to be concealed under all circumstances. Anorexics are extraordinarily successful in this concealment because they are over compliant to the wishes of others. Perfectionistic behavior elicits approval from parents and teachers, who think of the potentially anorexic child as unusually good and competent. Some of the more serious conceptual disturbances can be traced to this pseudo success of being praised and recognized for fake good behavior. This praise reinforces the anorexic's fear of being spontaneous and natural, and interferes with her developing concepts, especially a vocabulary for her true feelings, or even the ability to identify feelings. (Bruch, 1988, p. 4)

This fake good behavior can develop into something analogous to Winnicott's false self. There is a vulnerability to a loss of cohesiveness of the self, which is then defended against by what has been termed *intrapsychic paranoia* (Selvini Palazzoli, 1974). In this state the body is experienced as "foreign" and needs to be rigorously controlled against the danger of becoming "fat" (Bruch, 1988, p. 4).

In her early object relations work, Selvini-Palazzoli felt that separation-individuation difficulties lead to incorporation of a bad, overcontrolling maternal introject. The anorexic's own body is identified with this bad maternal introject. Therefore, the demands of the body (such as hunger) are experienced as attempting to overpower and enslave the patient, and its demands must be resisted (Selvini-Palazzoli, 1974).

More recent advances have come from self-psychology. Goodsitt (1985) made a case for the inadequate internalization of "self-objects" by the anorexic resulting in deficiencies in self-regulatory structures to handle tension, self-esteem, and feelings of cohesiveness. Because of these deficiencies, anorexics are excessively dependent on external self-objects. The anorexia nervosa leads to feelings of strength and specialness, which counter underlying feelings of inadequacy, and the obsession with food and weight "narrows down her world to something she feels she can manage" (p. 62).

Another perspective comes from the work of Crisp (1980). He viewed the essential cause of anorexia nervosa as a phobic avoidance of mature body weight. He saw anorexia as providing a sense of relief to an overwhelming maturational crisis that occurs in a patient who is "not equipped to be a competent adult" (p. 00). Crisp saw the central mechanism as a "reversal of the pubertal process" resulting in a return to the patient experiencing herself as "being a child biologically and hence also in many ways psychologically and socially" (p. 79).

Empirical studies are only partially helpful in evaluating theories of psychological predisposing factors in the causation of anorexia nervosa because concepts such as maternal introject and self-object are difficult to quantify. It is useful, however, to look at studies of personality characteristics in anorexic patients. Strober (1985) found the following:

> Evidence from naturalistic clinical and psychometric studies suggests strongly that social insecurity, excessive dependency and compliancy, limited spontaneity of expression, and a relative lack of self-directed autonomy reflect early signs of disturbance in the premorbid personality and predispose to later disorder, whereas such phenomena as introversion, obsessionality, and depression are more transient reactions that arise from malnutrition and other state-dependent influences on functioning" (p. 137).

Attempts to empirically explore Bruch's concept of body image disturbance have been quite complex. Szmukler (1987), in a review of studies, found that they have "not produced consistent findings." Furthermore, a number of variables, not related to the eating disorder, may also produce overestimation of body size (e.g., younger age, obesity, pregnancy) (p. 34).

Shifting focus from individual psychology to family interaction, it has long been recognized that family interaction plays an important role in anorexia nervosa. In the 19th century, Lasegue and Charcot both recommended separation of the patient from the family (Vanderlinden & Vandereycken, 1989, p. 190). In modern times, the theories of Bruch on the negative parental impact on the development of the future anorexic have been discussed above. She saw these families as "enormously preoccupied with outer appearances" (Bruch, 1973, p. 82). Although these patients had a superficially congenial relationship to their parents, "actually it is too close, with too much involvement, without necessary separation and individuation" (Bruch, 1988, p. 7).

In the 1970s, both Selvini-Palazzoli and Minuchin independently developed family systems models for the causation of anorexia nervosa that had numerous similarities. Minuchin postulated five major characteristics of the interactions of families of anorexics: enmeshment, overprotectiveness, rigidity, lack of conflict resolution, and over-involvement of the anorexic child in parental conflicts. Inadequate boundaries were seen between the parental and child subsets of the family (Minuchin, Rosman, & Baker, 1978). Using different terms, Selvini-Palazzoli (1988) described marital dysfunction, unwillingness by family members to assume leadership, rejection of communication, poor ability to resolve conflicts, blame-shifting, secret alliances among family members, and rigidity.

Although these theories have had a substantial impact on the treatment of anorexia nervosa, they have yet to be empirically validated. Using a sophisticated methodology, Kog, Vandereycken, and Vertommen (1989) investigated Minuchin's model and found great variability in the interactions of families of anorexics rather than the characteristic features described by Minuchin.

Råstam and Gillberg (1991) recently completed the first controlled study of family background in a population-based anorexia nervosa group. Family characteristics were studied comparing the entire population of families of anorexics in Goteborg, Sweden, with a matched control group of families. Major family problems and the death of first-degree relatives were significantly more common in the anorexia nervosa group as was a tendency toward depression in the mothers. However, family characteristics in normal and anorexic groups were strikingly similar. Also, they found little support for Minuchin's concepts of greater enmeshment, rigidity, or overprotectiveness in families of anorexics.

Finally, Hsu (1990), summarizing studies on family interaction patterns, stated, "The findings all suggest that eating-disorder families have more disturbed interactions than normal families, but we lack evidence to indicate that such disturbances are the cause of the eating disorder. In summary, much more work needs to be done to clarify whether, in fact, anorexic families show a characteristic interaction pattern . . ." (p. 101).

PRECIPITATING CAUSES

Various studies have identified precipitating events in one third to virtually all patients studied. Some of this variability stems from differences in determining what constitutes a significant precipitating event.

Bruch felt that in her patients "most gave a fairly definite time of onset and also recalled the event that had made them feel 'too fat.'" However, she downplayed the importance of the event itself in her discussion of the "seeming triviality of the precipitating event." One pattern Bruch does discern is that anorexia nervosa sometimes begins when the patient is "confronted with new experiences such as going to camp or entering a new school" and she feels "embarrassed" or at a "disadvantage" (Bruch, 1973, p. 255).

Garfinkel and Garner (1982) summarized the results of a number of studies of the precipitants to the development of anorexia nervosa. A common feature to these precipitants is that "the individual perceives personal distress in the form of a threat of loss of self-control and/or a threat or actual loss of self-worth" (p. 204).

Five specific types of precipitants are distinguished by Garfinkel and Garner (1982). First, separation and losses are commonly seen, including deaths in the family, parental separation, and "events involving the patient leaving home." Second, "disruptions of family homeostasis" are seen, including such events as parental illness or infidelity. Third are "new environmental demands," such as a romantic relationship, which may bring out threatening issues of intimacy and sexuality. Fourth, a "direct threat of loss of self-esteem" may be a precipitant. This could take the form of fear of failure at school or elsewhere or may be a reaction to a successful accomplishment of a sibling. Finally, a physical illness may trigger the onset of anorexia, often with some initial weight loss resulting from the illness itself.

Categorizing these various types of precipitants may be helpful in understanding the genesis of individual cases of anorexia. However, Garfinkel and Garner (1982) doubt there is a great deal of specificity to these events. They stated, "Moreover, these precipitants do not differ from those reported to be significant initiators for other psychiatric illnesses" (p. 203).

PERPETUATING CAUSES

Various factors perpetuate or maintain anorexia nervosa. Many of the predisposing factors, such as cultural pressures for thinness, continue to operate during the course of the illness. Also, by reducing fears or by stabilizing a family situation, the anorexia nervosa is adaptive and therefore harder to overcome.

One important perpetuating factor comes from the direct effect of the starvation itself. In a classic experiment that is crucial for understanding anorexia nervosa, Keys worked with 36 young, healthy male volunteers. Food intake was reduced by 50% during a 6-month period, resulting in 25% loss of original body weight. The results of this experiment have been well summarized by Garner et al. (1985). The increasing starvation produced a "dramatic increase in preoccupation with food." Food became a principal topic of conversation and the men began reading cookbooks and collecting recipes. Dreaming about food increased and three men became chefs after the study ended (p. 523).

Many classic anorexic behaviors emerged in these men. For example, many subjects stretched out their meals for hours at a time and unusual concoctions were made by mixing foods together. Dramatic increases in coffee consumption and gum chewing were seen.

The emotional changes seen were even more striking. Because the selection procedure included psychological screening, this group was psychologically more healthy than a randomly selected control group would be. During the course of the experiment, depression, anger, irritability, and anxiety greatly increased. Social withdrawal became common and sexual interests were dramatically reduced.

Approximately 20% of these men "experienced extreme emotional deterioration that markedly interfered with their functioning." A weight loss of as little as 7% of original body weight could produce "gross personality changes." Two men developed "disturbances of 'psychotic' proportions." One man even "chopped off three fingers of one hand in response to stress" (Garner et al., 1985, p. 526).

The distress of these men did not stop once they were allowed to begin gaining weight. They found it difficult to control eating; they engaged in massive food binges, which disturbed them; and they frequently felt hungry even after a large meal. Some men had abnormal hunger and satiety responses and persisted in eating excessive amounts even 8 months after they had started to gain weight. This is certainly relevant to understanding the substantial proportion of anorexics who go on to develop bulimia.

In the 40 years since the Keys study, more has been learned about some of the specific physical factors that perpetuate anorexia nervosa. Szmukler (1992) recently reviewed gastric disorders in anorexia nervosa. Numerous studies show that gastric emptying is delayed in most patients with anorexia nervosa. This may "help to perpetuate the disorder in some patients by limiting the amount of food that can be comfortably eaten." Delayed gastric emptying may also increase "feeling fat" in anorexics by contributing to "a learning process in which normal sensory signals are interpreted as abnormal" (p. 5).

Another abnormality in anorexic patients involves disturbed cholecystokinin secretion. Cholecystokinin (CCK) is a hormone released from the intestine after eating that induces satiety and reduces food intake. Recently, Philipp, Pirke, Kellner, & Krieg (1991) demonstrated high CCK levels in anorexic patients, which they felt helped to perpetuate the anorexia nervosa. Other studies have shown CCK abnormalities in bulimia (Geracioti & Liddle, 1988).

Numerous other physical changes have been well documented in anorexia nervosa. Abnormalities have been seen in almost every endocrine system including thyroid, reproductive, and cortisol systems. In a recent review of studies on brain neurotransmitter disturbances in anorexia nervosa, Kaye, Ebert, & Lake (1988) found abnormalities both in low-weight and in weight-restored anorexics. These neurotransmitter abnormalities, including serotonin and norepinephrine systems, "could contribute to the disturbances of appetite, mood, motor activity, and metabolism" and thus serve as perpetuating factors in anorexia nervosa (p. 222).

Another major area of perpetuating factors lies in the psychological realm. Bruch has written about anorexic patients: "They continue to function with the morality and style of thinking of early childhood that Piaget has called the period of egocentricity, of preconceptual and concrete operations. They cling rigidly to early childhood concepts and interpret human relationships this way. The next step in conceptual development—that of formal operations, with the new ability to perform abstract thinking and evaluation, which is characteristic of adolescence—is deficient or completely absent in them" (Bruch, 1985, p. 11).

This leads to numerous cognitive distortions such as all or nothing thinking, personalization, and magical thinking. Distorted thoughts in anorexics, such as "If I start eating I won't be able to stop until I am fat," are very common and play a major perpetuating role in this illness.

Some of the psychological deficits discussed previously as predisposing factors also continue to operate as perpetuating factors. For example, the sense of ineffectiveness can be countered by feelings of competence, strength, and specialness that accompany the weight loss.

The need to avoid the maturational crisis described by Crisp (1980) can become even more compelling as the anorexic lags ever further behind her peers in psychosocial development. Furthermore, the withdrawal from social interactions that accompanies starvation further hampers the development of adequate social skills.

The impact of the anorexia on the patient's family can also serve as a perpetuating factor. In various ways, anorexia nervosa may be reinforced by the family if it helps to maintain the status quo in a family system threatened by the possibility of change.

One final area that is too often ignored in work on the etiology of anorexia involves male patients with anorexia nervosa. In a recent review, Andersen stated that "males, matrons, and minorities are three groups with eating disorders that are frequently misdiagnosed by being overlooked." He points out that current diagnostic criteria for anorexia are "gender biased" because "while a requirement of three months of amenorrhea is necessary to diagnose anorexia nervosa in females, there is no analogous criteria for males . . . abnormal reproductive hormone function in males can be well documented and should be a requirement for noting the diagnosis just as for females" (Andersen, 1993, p. 2). After research with more than 1,500 patients, Andersen found a 1:10 male to female ratio. This is consistent with recent Swedish and Danish population studies.

In addition to the clinical importance of correctly diagnosing eating disorders in male patients, it is also useful to examine eating disorders in males to learn more about the etiology of eating disorders. One important area of research is to compare clinical features of male and female patients with eating disorders. Crisp and Burns compared clinical characteristics and outcome of 27 male patients with anorexia nervosa with 100 female patients with anorexia nervosa. Their major finding was that "males and females afflicted with anorexia nervosa are similar in terms of both premorbid characteristics and illness features including prognosis" (Crisp & Burns, 1990, p. 92). Similarities included social class backgrounds and ages of onset of the anorexia. One difference between the male and female patients was that bulimia and vomiting to avoid weight gain were not associated with a poor prognosis in the males.

A comparison of 20 males who met DSM-III-R criteria for anorexia or bulimia with a matched female sample was done by Woodside, Garner, Rockert and Garfinkel. They also "generally found male patients to be no different from female patients either clinically or in terms of their responses to treatment, or in clinical course" (Woodside, Garner, Rockert, and Garfinkel, 1990, p. 110). One area of difference was that the male patients had significantly lower scores than females on the Dieting subscale of the Eating Attitudes Test (EAT-26). Consistent with this finding, the only significant difference between males and females on the Eating Disorders Inventory (EDI) was that the male patients had less pathological scores on the Drive for Thinness subscale. Woodside, Garner, Rockert, and Garfinkel speculate that these differences "could represent a culturally dependent difference between male and female attitudes toward dieting as a means of weight control" (Woodside, Garner, Rockert, and Garfinkel, p. 112).

Given the clinical similarities between male and female eating disorder patients, what factors are responsible for the vast majority of these patients being female? Andersen has pointed out some of the biological differences between males and females such as in the ratio of testosterone to estrogen, and in the way tryptophan is metabolized in the brain. He questions, however, whether these differences are significant in explaining the female preponderance of eating disorder patients (Andersen, 1993).

One likely cause of this gender difference is the greater cultural pressure for thinness among females compared with males. For example, a recent study by Andersen and DiDomenico showed that "the ratio of ads and articles promoting thinness in magazines most commonly read by women aged 18 to 24 versus ads in magazines read by males aged 18 to 24 was exactly 10:1" (Andersen, 1993, p. 3).

This gender difference has been described in male eating disorder patients by Woodside, Garner, Rockert, and Garfinkel. They point out that males concern about body shape seems to cluster more around looking "masculine" than around wishing to be thin. This is particularly true of the bulimic group. There is a group of restricting AN patients who simply want to be thin; this latter group is very similar to the female patients in this regard. (Woodside, Garner, Rockert, and Garfinkel, 1990, p. 119).

Andersen has described a similar observation. He points out that the terms males "use to express conflicts regarding body shape and size may differ from those commonly used by females. Men, for example, rarely complain about the number of pounds they weigh or the size of the clothes they wear. They are, instead, intensely worried about perceived abnormalities in body shape and form, and express intense desire to lose 'flab' and to achieve a more classical male definition of muscle groups. We have not observed in males anything comparable to the psychological trauma some women suffer in going from a size 3 to a size 5, for example, or in overinvestment in a certain number of pounds, like staying in the 'double digits' in weight, below 100 pounds" (Andersen, 1990, p. 137).

Since dieting is a significant risk factor for the development of an eating disorder, and since men are not subjected to the same degree of cultural pressures for thinness as are women, it is useful to look at some of the specific reasons why males diet to achieve thinness. Andersen has pointed out at least four different reasons for males, as compared to females, to diet (Andersen, 1993, p. 3).

First of all, males are more likely than females to actually be overweight prior to development of an eating disorder. For example, Edwin and Andersen, comparing male with female eating disorder patients at Johns Hopkins Hospital found that "males have often been medically overweight, while females have more often suffered from the perception of being overweight (means of 123% of ideal body weight for males, compared with 111% for women at maximum)" (p. 128). Furthermore, they state "overall, males choose a preferred body weight about 90% of the population mean, while the desired weights of females averaged about 80%. This is certainly consistent with the female tendency to report feeling 'obese' at lower weight levels" (Edwin and Andersen, 1990, p. 128–129).

A second reason raised by Andersen involves male dieting to improve sports performance or to avoid weight gain after sustaining a sports injury. He also points out that eating disorders are more common in sports where thinness is important, for example, among male wrestlers and jockeys.

A third reason observed by Andersen involves male dieting out of fears of the health risks of obesity, which he finds much less common among women.

A fourth reason cited by Andersen involves dieting by male homosexuals. He finds that about 20% of males with eating disorders are homosexual, which is a significantly greater percentage than the general population. Herzog, Norman, Gordon, and Pepose found in a study of anorexic and bulimic patients that 26% of the males were homosexual, versus only 4% of the females. (Herzog, Norman, Gordon, and Pepose, 1984). Herzog, Bradburn, and Newman state that "the finding that a non-clinical sample of homosexual men was underweight and considered a thin figure ideal supports the notion that "gay" male culture places greater value on men being slender than does "straight" culture. That the homosexual men were also more dissatisfied with their bodies than their heterosexual counterparts suggests a motivational factor for developing an eating disorder that may be different from, and place them at a higher risk than, other men" (Herzog, Bradburn, and Newman, 1990, p. 48).

Much remains to be learned about the causes of anorexia nervosa. Hopefully new research will give us better approaches to prevention and treatment. With greater awareness of current knowledge, lifesaving early detection and treatment of anorexia nervosa can become more widespread.

DISCUSSION QUESTIONS

1   Who wrote the earliest probable description of anorexia nervosa in Western literature?

2   Discuss research which demonstrates increasing cultural pressures for excessive thinness.

3 What is the prevalence of anorexia nervosa in our society, and is it related to social class?

4 Discuss evidence for genetic components of predisposing factors in anorexia nervosa.

5 Discuss the views of Crisp on the causation of anorexia nervosa.

6 What characteristics does Minuchin describe for anorexia nervosa families?

7 Have recent controlled studies confirmed Minuchin's family characteristics?

8 Discuss the importance of the Keys experiment for our understanding of anorexia nervosa.

9 What is the male to female ratio of eating disorder patients and what is a likely cause of this gender difference?

10 What are some of the specific reasons that males diet to achieve thinness?

REFERENCES

Andersen, A. (1985). *Practical comprehensive treatment of anorexia nervosa and bulimia.* Baltimore, MD: Johns Hopkins University Press.

Andersen, A. (1990). Diagnosis and treatment of males with eating disorders. In Andersen, A. (Ed.), *Males with Eating Disorders* (pp 133–162). New York: Brunner/Mazel.

Andersen, A. (1993). Males with eating disorders: An endangered species? An adverse risk factor? *Eating Disorders Review,* 4(5), 1–4.

Bruch, H. (1973). *Eating disorders: Obesity, anorexia nervosa and the person within.* New York: Basic Books.

Bruch, H. (1985). Four decades of eating disorders. In D. Garner & P. Garfinkel (Eds.), *Handbook of psychotherapy for anorexia nervosa and bulimia* (pp. 7–18). New York: The Guilford Press.

Bruch, H. (1988). *Conversations with anorexics.* New York: Basic Books.

Crisp, A. (1980). *Anorexia nervosa: Let me be.* London: Academic Press.

Crisp, A., & Burns, T. (1990). Primary anorexia nervosa in the male and female: a comparison of clinical features and prognosis. In Andersen, A. (Ed.), *Males with Eating Disorders* (pp 77–99). New York: Brunner/Mazel.

Edwin, D., & Andersen, A. (1990). Psychometric testing in 76 males with eating disorders. In Anderson, A. (Ed.), *Males with eating disorders* (pp 116–130). New York: Brunner/Mazel.

Garfinkel, P., & Garner, D. (1982). *Anorexia nervosa: A multidimensional perspective.* New York: Brunner/Mazel.

Garner, D., Rockert, W., Olmsted, M., Johnson, C., & Coscina, D. (1985). Psychoeducational principles in the treatment of bulimia and anorexia nervosa. In D. Garner & P. Garfinkel (Eds.), *Handbook of psychotherapy for anorexia nervosa and bulimia* (pp. 513–572). New York: Guilford Press.

Geracioti, T., & Liddle, R. (1988). Impaired cholecystokinin secretion in bulimia nervosa. *New England Journal of Medicine, 319,* 683–688.

Goodsitt, A. (1985). Self psychology and the treatment of anorexia nervosa. In D. Garner & P. Garfinkel (Eds.), *Handbook of psychotherapy for anorexia nervosa and bulimia* (pp. 55–82). New York: Guilford Press.

Gull, W. W. (1874). Anorexia nervosa (apepsia hysterica, anorexia hysterica). *Trans Clin Soc Lond, 7,* 22–28.

Herzog, D., Norman, D., Gordon, C. & Pepose, M. (1984). Sexual conflict and eating disorders in 27 males. *American Journal of Psychiatry,* 141, pp 989–990.

Herzog, D., Bradburn, I., & Newman, K. (1990). Sexuality in males with eating disorders. In Andersen, A. (Ed.), *Males with Eating Disorders* (pp 40–53). New York: Brunner/Mazel.

Hsu, L. K. G. (1990). *Eating disorders.* New York: Guilford Press.

Kaye, W., Ebert, M., & Lake, C. (1988). Disturbances in brain neurotransmitter systems in anorexia nervosa: A review of CSF studies. In B. Blinder, B. Chaitin, & R. Goldstein (Eds.), *The eating disorders* (pp. 215–225). New York: PMA Publishing.

Kog, E., Vandereycken, W., & Vertommen, H. (1989). Multimethod investigation of eating disorder families. In W. Vandereycken, E. Kog, & J. Vanderlinden (Eds.), *The family approach to eating disorders* (pp. 81–106). New York: PMA Publishing.

Lasègue. (1873). On hysterical anorexia.

Minuchin, S., Rosman, B., & Baker, L. (1978). *Psychosomatic families: Anorexia nervosa in context.* Cambridge, MA: Harvard University Press.

Philipp, E., Pirke, K., Kellner, M., & Krieg, J. (1991). Disturbed cholecystokinin secretion in patients with eating disorders. *Life Sciences, 48,* 2443–2450.

Rakoff, V. (1982). Foreword. In P. Garfinkel & D. Garner (Eds.), *Anorexia nervosa: A multidimensional perspective* (p. vii). New York: Brunner/Mazel.

Råstam, M., & Gillberg, C. (1991). The family background in anorexia nervosa: A population-based study. *Journal of The American Academy of Child and Adolescent Psychiatry, 30,* 283–289.

Selvini-Palazzoli, M. (1974). *Self starvation.* New York: Jason Aronson.

Selvini-Palazzoli, M. (1988). *The work of Mara Selvini-Palazzoli.* Northvale, NJ: Jason Aronson.

Sours, J. A. (1980). *Starving to death in a sea of objects: The anorexia nervosa syndrome.* New York, London: Jason Aronson.

Strober, M. (1985). *Pediatrician, 12,* 134–138.

Strober, M., Lampert, C., Morrell, W., Burroughs, J., & Jacobs, C. (1990). A controlled family study of anorexia nervosa: Evidence of familial aggregation and lack of shared transmission with affective disorders. *International Journal of Eating Disorders, 9,* 139–155.

Szmukler, G. (1987). *Anorexia nervosa: A clinical view.* In R. Boakes, D. Popplewell, & M. Burton (Eds.), *Eating habits: Food physiology and learned behaviour.* Chichester: John Wiley & Sons.

Szmukler, G. (1992). Combatting gastric disorders. *Eating Disorders Review, 3,* 5–6.

Vanderlinden, J., & Vandereycken, W. (1989). Overview of the family therapy literature. In W. Vandereycken, E. Kog, & J. Vanderlinden (Eds.), *The family approach to eating disorders.* New York: PMA Publishing.

Woodside, D., Garner, D., Rockert, W., & Garfinkel, P. (1990). Eating disorders in males: Insights from a clinical and psychometric comparison with female patients. In Anderson, A. (Ed.), *Males with Eating Disorders* (pp. 100–115). New York: Brunner/Mazel.

Chapter 7

Anorexia Nervosa:
Methods of Treatment

Elliot M. Goldner
C. Laird Birmingham

Anorexia nervosa can vary from a brief disorder to a chronic condition and from a relatively mild disturbance to a debilitating or mortal illness (Hsu, 1990). Although it primarily affects teenagers and young adults, it is encountered in children as young as 7 years of age (Fosson, Knibbs, Bryant-Waugh, & Lask, 1987) as well as adults in the later decades of life (Cosford & Arnold, 1992; Gowers & Crisp, 1990). Consequently, a treatment approach to anorexia nervosa must be sufficiently flexible to address a wide range of circumstances.

The best treatment approach to anorexia nervosa has not been determined. Nonetheless, researchers and clinicians agree on the importance of the following set of primary treatment components:

- medical stabilization
- establishment of therapeutic alliance
- weight restoration
- promotion of healthy eating attitudes, behaviors, and activity levels
- psychotherapeutic treatment
- family and community interventions

Each of these components is reviewed in this chapter and current controversies in treatment of anorexia nervosa are discussed. Additionally, information on treatment efficacy derived from clinical investigations is summarized.

PRIMARY TREATMENT COMPONENTS

Medical Stabilization

Optimally, profound weight loss and malnutrition can be prevented by early diagnosis and treatment. However, when rapid weight loss has occurred or when body weight is extremely low, medical instability and death can result. One pathophysiological mechanism resulting in the sudden death of anorexic patients is cardiac dysrhythmia (Isner, Roberts, Heymsfield, & Yager, 1985). Recurrent vomiting, misuse of laxatives (Mitchell & Boutacoff, 1986), enemas, diuretics, and ipecac (Palmer & Guay, 1986); and underuse of insulin in insulin-dependent diabetics (Yager & Young, 1992) can lead to volume depletion, electrolyte abnormalities, vitamin and mineral deficiencies, and organ dysfunction (Abdu, Garritano, & Culver, 1987; Brotman, Stern, & Brotman, 1986; Cuellar & Van Thiel, 1986).

Signs and symptoms that can signal medical instability and should prompt full medical assessment including laboratory testing are as follows:

- rapid weight loss (e.g. > 15 lbs [7 kg] in 4 weeks)
- syncopal episodes
- organic brain syndrome
- bradycardia (heart rate less than 50 bpm)
- frequent exercise-induced chest pain
- dysrhythmias
- renal dysfunction or low urine output (< 400 cc/day)
- volume depletion
- tetany
- rapidly diminishing exercise tolerance

If medical instability is suspected, the physical examination should include cardiorespiratory and neuromuscular assessment and measurement of postural blood pressure and pulse rate change. Chvostek's and Trousseau's signs[1] are usually due to hypomagnesemia in anorexia nervosa. Laboratory investigation should include measurement of sodium, potassium, chloride, bicarbonate, creatinine, BUN, ferritin, folate, B_{12}, zinc, and albumin levels. A complete blood count, urinalysis, and electrocardiogram should be obtained; other tests may be indicated.

---

[1]Chvostek's sign is the involuntary contraction of the facial muscles elicited by tapping over the seventh cranial nerve just anterior to the ear and Trousseau's sign is the involuntary contraction of the hand elicited by occlusion of the brachial artery by pressure from a blood pressure cuff.

If medical instability is present, stabilization is begun through bed rest, intravenous fluid and potassium repletion, and normalization of any deficiencies. Feeding may initially exacerbate deficiencies as a result of the movement of electrolytes, vitamins, and minerals into cells and between fluid spaces. Thus, volume, electrolyte, and mineral repletion must precede feeding. Reassessment of electrolyte levels, renal function, and phosphorus and magnesium levels should be routinely undertaken during initial refeeding (usually every 3 days). When required, the choice of intravenous fluids given should be assessed individually, but commonly 5% dextrose in 0.9% saline or 3.3% dextrose in 0.3% saline given at a rate of 100 to 150 cc per hour is used to provide some calories and volume expansion. If renal function is markedly impaired, potassium chloride should not be added until the patient has urinated to ensure that hyperkalemia does not occur.

The appearance of chest pain or cardiac dysrhythmia should prompt immediate investigation. If frequent ventricular premature beats, a prolonged QT interval, or mitral valve prolapse coexist with severe hypokalemia or hypomagnesemia, cardiac monitoring should be considered.

The nutritional repletion that follows initial stabilization should begin slowly and be monitored carefully. Methods of refeeding are discussed in the section entitled Weight Restoration. Usually, oral feeding is begun at 1,200 to 1,400 kcal/day, enteral feeding at 50 cc/hour of 1 kcal per cc strength solution undiluted. Total parenteral feeding is reserved for the rare patient in whom a significant reduction in the level of consciousness makes oral and enteral routes too dangerous.

The refeeding of the starved patient is also complicated by refeeding edema and muscle cramps due to the nutritional recovery syndrome. The patient should be warned that rapid weight gain due to edema and muscle aches may occur. The amount of edema is related to the extent of the initial volume depletion and can be minimized by preventing excess fluid and salt administration. Diuretics should not be given as they will only reduce the edema transiently and may lead to cyclic edema. Without treatment, edema usually clears in 5 to 14 days.

Even when laxative misuse has been extreme, it is generally safe to stop the use of all laxatives promptly and provide a diet containing bulk, added oral bran, and adequate fluid intake. The addition of a prokinetic agent such as cisapride 5 to 20 mg at mealtimes may be useful in promoting gastrointestinal motility. Although they occur infrequently, care must be taken to prevent obstipation and to treat impaction if it develops.

If possible, psychotropic agents should be avoided in the acutely ill anorexic patient as they may lower the threshold to seizures and cardiac dysrhythmias.

After medical stabilization occurs and as renutrition continues, a daily multivitamin may be given to lessen the likelihood of deficiencies developing as vitamin and mineral stores are depleted by their use in tissue formation. A cellular deficiency of zinc, which may be present despite a normal serum zinc level, alters serotonin metabolism and changes taste sensation and eating behavior. Routine addition of zinc gluconate 100 mg per day (14 mg of elemental zinc) for 2 months will improve the rate of weight gain (Birmingham, Goldner, & Bakan, 1994).

Osteoporosis is common in anorexic patients (Rigotti, Neer, Skates, Herzog, & Nussbaum, 1991). Normally, bone density achieves its zenith in adolescence and then diminishes with age. Because of protein-calorie malnutrition, diminished mineral intake, and amenorrhea, anorexic individuals are prone to osteoporosis and may not establish the adolescent peak in bone density. In such patients, the first priority in the treatment of osteoporosis is its prevention or minimization by early treatment of anorexia nervosa with promotion of adequate weight gain and nutrition. Intake of 400 International Units (IU) of vitamin D a day in the multivitamin preparation and a total intake of at least 1,000 to 1,500 mg of calcium per day should be prescribed. Whether estrogen or progesterone supplementation prevent or reverse osteoporosis in anorexia nervosa is uncertain. As they may be beneficial, their administration in the form of birth control pills should not be discouraged but assessed in light of their possible side effects and the effect of menstruation on anorexic patients with prolonged amenorrhea.

Dental care should be encouraged to prevent and treat gingivitis and erosion of enamel caused by poor nutrition, binge-eating, and purging.

Although anorexia nervosa results in amenorrhea and infertility (Stewart, Robinson, Goldbloom, & Wright, 1990), ovulation and pregnancy can occur, especially in the recovery stages. As ovulation can precede the return of menses, sexually active anorexic individuals should be encouraged to use contraception. Fetal development can be complicated by malnutrition, ketosis, or medications used in the treatment of anorexia nervosa. If pregnancy occurs, ongoing care should be coordinated with an obstetrician who follows high-risk pregnancies.

When diabetes mellitus coexists with anorexia nervosa, close monitoring of blood sugar levels is fundamental to prevent blindness, renal failure, or hypoglycemia. The frequent coexistence of bingeing with underuse of insulin may lead to a dangerous fluctuation of blood sugar levels (Fairburn & Steel, 1980; Yager & Young, 1992) that usually requires hospitalization and monitoring by a specialist in diabetology or an internist.

Rare complications of anorexia nervosa include the following: superior mesenteric artery syndrome in which bowel obstruction of the duodenum occurs in conjunction with severe weight loss, rupture of the stomach (Boerhave's syndrome) from severe vomiting, and central pontine myelinolysis from severe hyponatremia due to malnutrition.

Establishment of Therapeutic Alliance

A strong therapeutic alliance between the patient and treatment personnel is important in the treatment of anorexia nervosa. It provides a holding environment (Stern, 1986; Winnicott, 1965) and supplies a relatively safe and secure base from which the anorexic individual can undertake changes in behavior and identity.

In order to recover, anorexic individuals will have to confront those things they fear most and will have to surrender the feelings of accomplishment gained by weight control. A therapeutic alliance is needed to catalyze and nurture the anorexic individual's motivation for recovery.

For various reasons, the development of a therapeutic alliance may prove difficult. A morbid fear of weight gain often propels anorexic patients into antagonistic or defensive positions. Consequently, health professionals are often perceived as dangerous and threatening. Furthermore, the psychological characteristics of many anorexic individuals may dispose them toward a mistrust of interpersonal relationships (Garner, Olmsted, & Polivy 1983; Stern, 1991).

Clinicians have identified a worrisome punitive approach adopted by some health professionals toward anorexic patients (Brotman, Stern, & Herzog, 1984; Garner, 1985; Johnson, 1991; Morgan, 1977; Tinker & Ramer, 1983; Selvini-Palazzoli, 1978). Too frequently, feelings of frustration and helplessness experienced by staff result in pejorative labeling of patients (e.g., "manipulators," "liars," or "cheaters"). Some patients describe feeling they have been unjustly portrayed and treated as delinquent.

A more subtle manifestation of this phenomenon is the inappropriate labeling of the patient with the diagnosis of borderline personality disorder. This exemplifies Vaillant's (1992) assertion that "almost always the diagnosis 'borderline' is a reflection more of therapists' affective rather than their intellectual response" (p. 120). Research findings contradict the myth that anorexics most often have borderline personality disturbance (Gartner, Marcus, Halmi, & Loranger, 1989; Wonderlich & Swift, 1990; Wonderlich, Swift, Slotnick, & Goodman, 1990). The disturbed behaviors that are misconstrued as indicators of borderline personality disorder may be a consequence of acute starvation; such behavioral disturbance tends to resolve with renutrition (Bhanji & Mattingly, 1988). Substantial normalization of personality measures after short-term renutrition in anorexia nervosa patients has been demonstrated (Kennedy, McVey, & Katz, 1990).

In view of the negative feelings commonly engendered in health professionals working with anorexic patients, it is wise to heed the advice of colleagues who recommend a careful examination of transference and countertransference issues (Cohler, 1977; Johnson, 1991; Wooley, 1991).

Although there has been a tendency for health professionals to accentuate and misconstrue personality disturbance in anorexic patients, it is equally important that the presence of personality disturbance and developmental difficulties not be ignored. Psychometric studies indicate that anorexic patients' personality patterns are often characterized by compulsiveness, social avoidance, perfectionism, feelings of ineffectiveness, and restricted expressivity (Casper, Hedeker, & McClough, 1992; Garner, Olmstead, & Polivy, 1983). Even when weight is restored, anorexic individuals are significantly more self-doubting, submissive, deferential to authority, compliant with outside demands, and stimulus-avoidant than their peers (Strober, 1980).

The personality and developmental disturbances associated with anorexia nervosa are thought to affect treatment staff strongly. Stern (1986) suggested that anorexic individuals unconsciously test the treatment system in areas of control, tolerance of autonomy, initiative, aggression, and fostering of the true self. Additionally, Strober (1991) suggested that much of the interpersonal behavior of anorexic individuals is explained by hereditary influences on personality. Individuals who develop anorexia nervosa are predominately introverted and cautious in temperament. They may frustrate those therapists who expect affective responsiveness and easy interpersonal relations.

When providing treatment to children and young adolescents with eating disorders, treatment staff will more readily establish therapeutic relationships when a clear awareness of age-appropriate needs is maintained. The young patient does not expect to assume the responsibility for recovery. This is considered an adult concern. The adolescent anorexic characteristically ignores long-term implications of his or her behavior. As a result, the younger anorexic patient may benefit from a treatment approach that offers more protection and structure.

Essential skills and a level of comfort in working with the adolescent population must be developed. Adolescents tend to be labile in affect and ambivalent in their feelings about relationships with adults. Initial encounters may be met with stony silences or disdainful grimaces. A warm and active therapist who models healthy behavior will quickly break down the barriers and establish a positive relationship. Humor, sincerity, and a genuine interest in the adolescent's social world help to build an alliance.

The adult with anorexia nervosa will generally require more autonomy within the therapeutic alliance. Establishing trust with the members of the treatment team will generally be a precondition of effective treatment. Trust is best gained by an early acknowledgment by health professionals that they cannot and do not wish to force the patient to recover. Instead, treatment staff primarily provide assistance to the patient's movement toward recovery.

One approach that helps to build a therapeutic alliance with anorexic individuals at various developmental stages can be described as externalizing the problem, a component of narrative therapy (White & Epston, 1990). Within this conceptual framework, anorexia nervosa is viewed as an external problem that tricks its victims and encroaches on their quality of life. The therapist can then engage with the person who has been "taken by anorexia nervosa" and provide support in the battle against the problem. This approach builds a framework that avoids blame and preserves dignity.

Another method of strengthening the therapeutic alliance is described by Stern (1991) and is primarily derived from the interpersonal school of psychoanalysis:

[The therapist] meets the patient at a distance he or she is comfortable with, stays with what is preoccupying the patient, identifies and accepts the conflicting currents in the patient's efforts to master developmental problems, and suggests a path toward possible integration. (p. 96)

If a strong therapeutic alliance is developed, then the important components of weight restoration and normalization of eating behaviors may more easily be accomplished.

Weight Restoration

An essential component of recovery in anorexia nervosa is restoration of a healthy weight. Although an individual's target weight can roughly be estimated by the use of actuarial tables such as the Metropolitan Height and Weight Tables (Metropolitan Life Insurance Company, 1983), a slavish adherence to such methods ignores the large variability in weights at any height in healthy people. A more effective approach will take additional factors into consideration such as premorbid weight, extent and duration of weight loss, occupational and sociocultural considerations, and family weight patterns. If available, measurement of total body fat is preferable to weight because the range of body fat is much smaller and is not confounded by the large individual variation in lean body mass.

The target should be a range at which the physical and emotional effects of starvation are fully resolved, hormonal function is restored, and eating without dieting is possible (Fairburn & Cooper, 1989). The caloric requirements for weight gain vary considerably. Some anorexic individuals gain weight with as little as 1,400 kcal/day whereas others require more than 4,000 kcal/day. Determinant factors include variability in metabolic rate, activity levels, and purging behaviors (Kaye, Gwirtsman, Obarzanek, & George, 1988).

Various approaches to weight restoration are used. Most advocate the superiority of normal eating, i.e., a normal diet without the use of liquid supplements, enteral tube feeds, parenteral nutrition or other artificial methods (Williams, Touyz, & Beumont, 1985). In fact, some clinicians consider these other methods intrusive and antitherapeutic and warn against their use (Garner, 1985). In contrast are claims that the use of liquid supplements (e.g., Ensure, Boost, Enercal) and tube feeding allow easier weight recovery under certain circumstances (Kennedy & Abbas, 1993; Williams, 1958).

Anorexic individuals who require a large caloric intake to achieve weight restoration sometimes find it helpful to eat no more than a normal amount at meals and snacks and increase their caloric intake by regularly drinking liquid supplements. The supplement may be considered a medicine that can be discontinued when the individual's target weight has been reached (Fairburn & Cooper, 1989). This approach has the advantage of helping accustom the anorexic individual to a standard amount of food necessary for weight maintenance.

Occasionally, anorexic patients prefer exclusive nasoenteric tube feeds for weight restoration. Tube feeding may allow some anorexic individuals to distance themselves from a painful inner battle over actively eating and gaining weight. However, the treatment team should encourage establishment of normal eating behaviors at the earliest opportunity.

The following two methods are most commonly used to promote weight restoration: (a) encouragement and support, which are often provided by nursing staff in hospital programs and by trusted friends or family members in other settings; and (b) behavioral interventions such as operant reinforcement methods using privileges as positive reinforcers (Touyz, Beumont, Glaun, Phillips, & Cowie, 1984). The spirit in which weight restoration is promoted is of primary importance. While coercion and punishment should be scrupulously avoided, a persistent adherence to the goal of weight normalization should be maintained.

In general, weight gain should not proceed more quickly than 2 pounds (1 kg) per week in order to minimize refeeding edema, decrease the chance of medical complications of refeeding, and lessen conflict over body image dissatisfaction.

As weight increases, the anorexic individual may experience an overwhelming fear of surpassing firmly held weight barriers. Often, these are weights that had previously been set by the patient as ceilings, e.g., "I must keep my weight below 100 pounds." Treatment staff should anticipate such barriers and ceilings, and additional support and encouragement should be provided.

The treatment team should advise against the frequent use of weight scales and should de-emphasize discussions of weight. The anorexic individual may benefit from assistance in shifting attention to other areas of interest. Tight-fitting clothing will generally serve as an unwelcome reminder of changes in weight and body shape. Loose clothing may be preferable, and it is helpful for the anorexic individual to discard clothing that has become too small.

It is important to acknowledge the fear and distress most individuals with anorexia nervosa have concerning weight gain. Assistance with body image adjustment is valuable and can be facilitated by counseling, artwork, and mental and physical exercises (Thompson, 1990). It may be helpful for the anorexic individual to receive advance warning that body fat often seems maldistributed during initial weight restoration. Initially, the abdomen will seem disproportionately large due primarily to lax abdominal musculature and intestinal distention but will revert to normal as improved physical health is achieved.

Promotion of Healthy Eating Attitudes, Behaviors, and Activity Levels

Usually, individuals with anorexia nervosa experience distress in their attempts to adopt healthy eating patterns. Behaviors such as calorie restriction, avoidance of feared foods, purging behaviors, and binge eating may have become routine and resistant to change.

Cognitive-behavioral principles and practices can be usefully employed in restoring healthy eating (Davis & de Groot, 1993; Fairburn & Cooper, 1989;

Garner & Bemis, 1982). Underpinning this form of therapy is an acknowledgment of the potency of personal meaning systems and cognitive sets in influencing affect and behavior. Consequently, efforts are directed toward revising thoughts and behaviors in the present and future.

The treatment team can encourage the anorexic individual to shift behaviors and advance toward goals:

- increasing caloric intake
- expanding the range of foods
- eating discrete meals and snacks
- normalizing pace of eating
- elimination of purging
- elimination of binge eating
- avoidance of diet foods
- eating in company of others

In establishing normal eating patterns, it is generally advisable to focus initially on a limited number of goals. It is often best to focus first on the cessation or decrease of purging behaviors such as vomiting, emetic misuse, and laxative misuse if these are present. Diminution of these behaviors often markedly increases anxiety temporarily. In some instances, purging cessation may require an environment where intensive support can be provided, such as an inpatient hospital program or day treatment facility. Engagement in structured activities during time periods immediately following meals or snacks can assist in managing anxiety and in preventing purging behaviors.

The establishment of normal eating patterns may be facilitated by use of a daily eating diary. Figures 7-1 and 7-2 provide one example of such a diary

Time	Food eaten	Binge (Y?N)	Purge (Y?N)	Location	Context
4:00 p.m.	½ bran muffin 1 cup diet ginger ale			kitchen	
7:30 p.m.	8 cookies 1 cup skim milk	✓	✓	bedroom	feel fat and disgusting

Figure 7-1 Excerpt from a daily food diary early in the course of the treatment of an individual with anorexia nervosa.

Time	Food eaten	Binge (Y?N)	Purge (Y?N)	Location	Context
8:30 a.m.	1 slice of toast with peanut butter 1 cup regular milk			Kitchen	
11:00 a.m.	orange			classroom	
12:30	cheese sandwich carrot sticks 1 cup regular milk			lunch room at school	felt full and anxious eating in front of friends
3:30 pm	chocolate milk				
6:00 pm	chicken breast (piece) baked potato peas			dining room	
9:30 pm	chocolate milk			kitchen	

Figure 7-2 Excerpt from a daily food diary later in the course of treatment of the same patient as in Figure 7-1.

format. Various other types have been used successfully. The diary becomes a practice record and worksheet that the anorexic individual may use to receive assistance from the treatment team in changing behavior and challenging thoughts and attitudes.

Generally, the anorexic individual will find it difficult to increase caloric intake to adequate levels. With the help of the food diary, a regular meal and snack schedule can be designed so that anxiety is minimized. It is sensible to consider frequent meals and snacks with a maximum 3-hour gap during daytime.

It is often helpful to construct a hierarchy of feared foods for an anorexic individual and recommend a gradual desensitization plan. Foods that arouse little anxiety may be included first. As the individual feels ready, those foods that are particularly frightening can be introduced gradually. Most commonly, these are foods with a high fat content. It is best to avoid diet and low-calorie foods. It is also helpful to encourage the relinquishing of behaviors aimed at slowing or diminishing caloric intake, such as cutting food into minuscule pieces, pausing during eating, water-loading, and drinking large quantities of caffeinated drinks.

Many individuals with anorexia nervosa require substantial support to implement changes in eating behavior. Within intensive treatment programs such as day hospital or inpatient programs, a meal support program is often helpful. Generally, staff sit with patients during mealtimes and provide support and encouragement in advancing toward goals such as those mentioned earlier. When in outpatient settings, some anorexic individuals benefit from arrangements with friends or family members in which meal support and encouragement is provided. As always, the spirit in which the support is provided is a critical factor; a lighthearted and warm approach in which positive steps, no matter how small, are acknowledged is required.

Additionally, the anorexic individual often benefits from assistance in establishing healthy exercise and activity levels. As a feature of anorexia nervosa, sports, dance, and exercise activities have often become compulsively driven (Yates, 1991). Even those physical activities generally not considered exercise routines, e.g., walking and climbing stairs, have often been transformed into symptoms of the drive for thinness.

Clearly, it is important to gauge the anorexic individual's medical condition and need for energy conservation when considering an appropriate level of activity. As appropriate, the introduction of low exertion activities that help sustain muscle tone and minimize cardiovascular exertion may be of value. For example, slow strolls and gentle stretching exercises may prove helpful in allowing the anorexic individual learn to modify physical activity patterns.

In conjunction with changes in behaviors, thoughts and attitudes should be addressed. Initially, anorexic individuals interpret events and communications in relation to the effect on their drive for thinness. Thus, an invitation to a friend's home may induce fear due to the thought that food will be offered, and a comment from the friend such as "You look nice today" may be reinterpreted as "You've gained weight."

Cognitive interventions usually involve the Socratic method of dialogue, which challenges attitudes and beliefs by posing questions. In this way, the anorexic individual's cognitive sets are examined and challenged, leading to the adoption of healthier and more accurate replacements (Davis & deGroot, 1993; Garner & Bemis, 1982). Homework exercises are often given in which old beliefs and attitudes are identified and new thoughts are practiced. Ultimately, the goal is to facilitate a conversion to an alternative cognitive set in which the importance of thin body shape is diminished and the value attached to other aspirations is increased.

A recognition of the importance of promoting healthy eating attitudes and behavior in treatment of the eating disorders has prompted the development of group psychoeducation programs (Davis & Olmsted, 1992). Generally, such programs aim to promote the attitudinal and behavioral shifts described above by presentation of information through books, manuals, and didactic teaching sessions. In keeping with the principles described earlier in this section, recent psychoeducational materials promote a nondieting approach to eating and advocate acceptance of each individual's natural body weight set point (Davis, Dearing, Faulkner, Jasper, Olmstead, Rice, & Rockert, 1992). To date, the efficacy of psychoeducational programs has been evaluated only in treatment of individuals with bulimia nervosa (Davis, Olmsted, & Rockert, 1990; Olmsted, Davis, Rockert et al., 1991). The use of psychoeducation in the treatment of anorexia nervosa may constitute an efficient method of promoting change in eating attitudes and behaviors and an important adjunct to other treatment interventions.

Psychotherapeutic Treatment

The core psychological feature associated with anorexia nervosa is poor self-concept. Paradoxically, anorexia nervosa appears to develop in an attempt to mend self-esteem. At the onset of anorexia nervosa, common thoughts are as follows: "If I can only be slim, I will be less unattractive and will feel better about myself" and "If I control my eating in a way that others cannot, I will prove that I am not weak and ineffectual." Clinicians and theorists have described this quality in anorexia nervosa as a pervasive sense of ineffectiveness; they have further explained the ubiquitous perfectionism and the development of a false self as signals of a desperate drive to remodel one's self-concept (Bruch, 1973; Johnson, 1991). Moreover, Crisp (1980) described the anorexic individual's attempt at solving inner distress as a "psychobiological solution to an existential crisis." A central aim in psychotherapeutic treatment of anorexia nervosa is amelioration of self-concept.

Goals that might be included in a comprehensive psychotherapeutic approach to anorexia nervosa are:

- establishment of therapeutic alliance
- repudiation of anorexia nervosa as a solution
- amelioration of self-concept
- establishment of healthy attitudes toward shape and weight
- resolution of family conflict
- improved social and occupational function

Many of these goals are addressed elsewhere in this chapter. Here, we will focus on methods to ameliorate self-esteem in view of its centrality as a psychotherapeutic aim. While various psychotherapeutic approaches have been applied to the treatment of anorexia nervosa, all share the goal of bolstering self-esteem.

When psychodynamic psychotherapies are applied in treatment of anorexia nervosa, clinicians have recommended they be implemented in the following manner:

- relatively high level of therapist activity
- emphasis upon relational issues (as opposed to intrapsychic)
- incorporation of feminist principles

Bruch's (1973) study of psychodynamic psychotherapy in anorexia nervosa convinced her that the therapist should be active by providing structure, giving feedback, and maintaining the foci of the therapy. Steiger (1989) has found that incorporation of the more active techniques associated with brief therapies, particularly those of Davanloo (1980) and Sifneos (1979), are of particular value in the treatment of eating disorders, but a brief intervention is often an unrealistic goal in this population.

The extreme case of the overtalkative and intrusive therapist is, of course, not what is recommended here. However, it should be remembered that anorexic individuals often feel lost when first exploring the world of emotions and inner thoughts. They have usually not come to psychotherapy in order to solve some psychological concerns. Rather, the presence of distressing symptoms has generally propelled the individual into psychotherapy, an experience that is often foreign and threatening. This is likely to be accentuated in the younger patient who may feel uncomfortable in the adult world of psychotherapy. An active therapist can provide a healthy framework and setting in which psychotherapy can be undertaken. The anorexic individual can more comfortably follow the lead of a therapist who establishes a safe and open atmosphere in which trust can be rooted. In time, the anorexic individual can become more active in therapy. As this occurs, it will become important for the therapist to accommodate and support the patient's developing autonomy and competence.

In view of the intimate association between an individual's self-concept and his or her interpersonal relationships, psychodynamic psychotherapy in anorexia nervosa is best applied within a relational orientation. Therapists operating in a self-psychology framework view the relational disturbances associated with anorexia nervosa as manifestation of defects in the self (Geist, 1989; Goodsitt, 1985). Through the transference relationship, the therapist aims to assist the patient to develop the capacity to better regulate inner tensions.

The content of therapy sessions will often center on events typically encountered during adolescence and young adulthood including individuation from family, peer relationships, sexuality, and school or occupational challenges (Mogul, 1989). Initially, anorexic individuals will feel inept in aspects of their current relationships. The therapist can be most helpful by resisting the urge to instruct. Instead, the therapist should promote the patient's initiatives in revising his or her relationships. The ability to manage relations with family members, peers, and authority figures better will ultimately enhance self-concept.

Often, the symptoms of anorexia nervosa will have become entwined within unhealthy relationships. As relationships that can be salvaged become more healthy and as detrimental relationships are relinquished, the anorexic individual generally gains more freedom to disengage from anorexic symptomatology.

The transference relationship should be used to provide a safe setting in which the anorexic individual's relational skills can be further developed. A high level of therapist activity tends to diminish the intensity of the transference neurosis and provides a structure that is experienced as safe and secure. Again, it is helpful for the therapist to take the lead in demonstrating that it is safe and beneficial to discuss all aspects of the relationship arising between the therapist and the patient. Negative emotions, e.g., feelings of anger and rejection, may be particularly difficult for the patient to face. The experience of healthy resolution of conflict within the therapy relationship is of great value to the patient and can quickly generalize to settings outside the therapy room.

The vast majority of individuals with anorexia nervosa are female and the importance of attending to feminist principles in applying psychodynamic psychotherapy has been emphasized by a number of clinicians (Kearney-Cooke, 1991; Orbach, 1986; Robertson, 1992; Steiner-Adair, 1991). Due to the identity confusion inherent in anorexia nervosa, the gender basis and context in which psychotherapy is provided becomes an important therapeutic factor. Although many individuals struggle to integrate their adopted gender roles with the societal and cultural conflicts facing females, anorexic girls and women are particularly prone to such identity confusion. A feminist approach maintains attention to gender inequities and supports the development of esteem and respect for women. Such an approach further acknowledges the unique nature of female psychology and avoids imposing male-oriented biases (e.g., dependency in relationships is not viewed as weak or pathological).

The overarching goal of psychodynamic psychotherapy is to provide a safe structure in which anorexic individuals can feel free to explore their identity and to incorporate positive changes in self-concept and interpersonal behavior.

As discussed in the previous section of this chapter, cognitive-behavioral psychotherapy can be employed to promote healthy eating attitudes and behaviors, as well as to enhance the anorexic individual's self-concept (Davis & deGroot, 1993). Through monitoring thoughts and beliefs, dysfunctional thoughts are identified and are related to maladaptive emotions and behaviors. Faulty thinking patterns that typically occur in anorexia nervosa (Garner & Bemis, 1982) are listed in Table 7-1. Anorexic individuals are taught to examine evidence for the validity of thoughts related to their self-concept. The therapist then actively helps to correct distortions in thinking that maintain low self-esteem. Emphasis is placed

Table 7-1 Cognitive Distortions Commonly Encountered in Individuals with Anorexia Nervosa

Overgeneralization, or extracting a rule on the basis of one event and applying it to other dissimilar situations.

Personalization and self-reference, or egocentric interpretations of impersonal events or overinterpretation of events relating to the self.

Magnification, or overestimation of the significance of undesirable consequent events. Stimuli are embellished with surplus meaning not supported by an objective analysis.

Superstitious thinking, or believing in the cause-effect relationship of noncontingent events.

Selective abstraction, or basing a conclusion on isolated details while ignoring contradictory and more salient evidence.

Dichotomous reasoning, or thinking in extreme and absolute terms. Events can be only black or white, right or wrong, good or bad.

Note. From "A cognitive-behavioral approach to anorexia nervosa" by D. M. Garner and K. Bemis, 1982, *Cognitive Therapy and Research, 6,* p. 129. Copyright 1982 by Academic Press. Adapted by permission.

on self-validation through self-defined goals rather than external performance standards (Garner & Bemis, 1985). Behavioral assignments are used to help to anchor changes in experience.

Clinicians have described the integration of psychodynamic and cognitive-behavioral approaches into an effective framework in individual psychotherapeutic treatment of patients with eating disorders (Steiger, 1989; Tobin & Johnson, 1991).

Group psychotherapy has been used as a modality in the treatment of anorexia nervosa. Previously, group treatment occurred primarily as a component of inpatient hospitalization (Duncan & Kennedy, 1992). More recently, group psychotherapy of anorexia nervosa has been applied in outpatient settings such as day programs (Kaplan, Kerr & Maddocks, 1992). Potential advantages of group psychotherapy include the following: (a) mutual support to group members; (b) the provision of structured opportunity for interpersonal development; and (c) efficiency in treatment provision. To date there is an inadequate empirical basis for comparison of group and individual formats of therapy in anorexia nervosa.

Family and Community Interventions

Because the families of individuals who develop anorexia nervosa are not uniform in nature, sweeping generalizations in recommending an approach to family intervention should be avoided. The vast majority of families will wish to provide support and to assist the family member in his or her recovery from anorexia nervosa; however, a small minority of families will constitute a destructive environment contrary to the best interests of the anorexic individual.

When an individual develops anorexia nervosa, family members are generally profoundly affected. Parents, siblings, and partners commonly experience emotional responses that include desperation, anger, frustration, guilt, demoralization, and intense fear. Family members often blame themselves or others for the development of anorexia nervosa. Often, the first task of the treatment team is to defuse unproductive blaming and to redirect the family's efforts toward providing mutual support.

It is useful to discern two levels of family intervention. Family support and education refers to simple interventions aimed at improving the family support network of the individual with anorexia nervosa. Family therapy constitutes a psychotherapeutic intervention and aims to facilitate changes in family function that will assist the anorexic individual in recovery and concurrently improve the emotional health of other family members.

A group psychoeducational program for families and friends is an efficient means of delivering family support and education. Such programs generally are structured as a series of classroom-style lectures or discussions that run weekly for three or four sessions. Family members and friends are invited to attend and to bring their questions and concerns. The following topics may be emphasized:

- multidetermined nature of anorexia nervosa
- dispelling common myths
- providing appropriate support to an anorexic individual
- support for families and friends

Written materials that provide useful information on the above topics have been prepared specifically for the purpose of providing family support and education (Valette, 1988). Additionally, organizations such as the National Association of Anorexia Nervosa and Associated Disorders and the National Anorexic Aid Society can provide a strong network of support and education to all family members.

Our experience has been that family therapy is a powerful form of psychotherapy that can be of great value in advancing treatment in the younger age group. Initially, the therapist may encounter a reluctance by various family members to enter therapy. Often, the anorexic individual, because of feelings of shame or fear of coercion, wishes to avoid intensive discussions with family members. Family members may be hesitant to enter family therapy due to fear they will be blamed or that their personal lives will be exposed. The treatment team must effectively defuse blame and demonstrate a respectful approach that exhibits empathy for all family members. We generally remind the family that the development of anorexia nervosa is multidetermined and that it is unproductive to affix blame. Instead, it is important to improve family support and communication as this will buttress the anorexic individual's ability to make forward steps and will be helpful to other family members. Once the specter of blame is removed and a supportive philosophy is adopted, family members will experience greater freedom to express their concerns and resolve their problems.

Although some family therapists characteristically instruct parents of anorexic patients to take charge and compel their child to eat properly, most clinicians do not subscribe to this approach. Our approach is to suggest to the family that they can be most helpful to their family member with anorexia nervosa by strengthening their relationship outside of the arena of food and weight. We ask the family to consider giving responsibility for food and weight concerns to the anorexic individual and treatment team. We also inform the family that given the seriousness of anorexia nervosa, we cannot guarantee that food and weight problems will be completely fixed. Family members report that this approach defuses battles that have become entrenched and allows them to improve communication and closeness in a conflict-free zone.

In reviewing various forms of family therapy for eating disorders, DiNicola (1993) described three major approaches: (a) Insight-oriented family therapy (Stierlin & Weber, 1989); (b) Structural family therapy (Minuchin et al., 1978); and (c) Strategic-systemic family therapy (Selvini-Palazzoli, 1978). Dare and Szmukler (1991) have described an approach that has been shown to be effective for younger patients with relatively recent onset (Dare & Szmukler, 1991; Russel,

Szmukler, Dare, & Eisler, 1987). White and Epston (1990) report that narrative methods are particularly beneficial in treatment of anorexia nervosa.

CONTROVERSIES IN TREATMENT

Right to Refuse Treatment

Opposing opinions have been expressed as to the appropriate response to the individual with anorexia nervosa who is seriously ill and refusing to accept treatment (Dresser, 1984; Fost, 1984). Briefly, the majority opinion recommends that medical committal to involuntary treatment should generally be avoided and should be undertaken only when an anorexic individual is at immediate risk of death (Goldner, 1989; Hsu, 1990). In such instances, imposed treatment can be lifesaving.

Inpatient versus Outpatient Treatment

Crisp and his colleagues (Crisp, Norton, Gowers, Halek, Bowyer, Yeldham, Levett, & Bhat, 1991) found that inpatient hospitalization did not produce superior outcomes at 1-year follow-up when compared to outpatient treatment. However, the authors have noted that the methodological problems associated with randomizing patients with anorexia nervosa complicate interpretation of their findings.

Day hospital programs appear to be a viable alternative to inpatient hospitalization of certain patients with anorexia nervosa (Piran, Langdon, Kaplan, & Garfinkel, 1990).

Pharmacotherapy in Anorexia Nervosa

Most clinicians report that pharmacotherapy is of limited value in the treatment of anorexia nervosa. In the medically compromised anorexic patient, risks often outweigh benefits. A small number of controlled studies of medication use have been undertaken and indicate that cyproheptadine and amitriptyline are of some benefit to hospitalized anorexic patients (Halmi, Eckert, LaDu, & Cohen, 1986). Clomipramine (Lacey & Crisp, 1980), pimozide (Vandereycken & Pierloot, 1982), and lithium carbonate (Gross, Ebert, & Faden, 1981) have not been found to be effective. Uncontrolled trials of treatment with fluoxetine indicate some patients may benefit (Kaye, Weltzin, Hsu, & Bulik, in press; Gwirtsman, Guze, Yager, & Gainsley, 1991). Bhanji and Mattingly (1988) reported that the use of combined chlorpromazine and insulin aids in weight restoration of hospitalized anorexic patients, but controlled studies are lacking.

TREATMENT EFFICACY AND OUTCOME

In a review of outcome research in anorexia nervosa, Hsu (1991) concluded that the findings are quite uniform at a minimum of 4 years after onset. He estimated that approximately 75% of anorexic patients have improved, 5% have died, and the remainder have not improved. When reviewing studies that had followed patients for approximately 20 years, Hsu (1991) estimated that 14% of anorexic patients died from suicide or from complications of anorexia nervosa. Results of recent studies suggest that fewer anorexic patients are now dying during the first few years of the disorder and may indicate improved treatment and prognosis.

Few controlled studies of treatment outcome in anorexia nervosa have been undertaken. Crisp et al. (1991) concluded that all three treatment interventions tested in their randomized controlled trial—inpatient treatment, combined outpatient individual and family therapy, and outpatient group therapy—were effective.

Recommendations for the appropriate methodology in conducting outcome follow-up in anorexia nervosa have been suggested (Hsu, 1980). It is our hope that careful attention to treatment methods in anorexia nervosa will help to decrease the numbers of lives lost and will promote return to health for an increasing number of affected individuals.

DISCUSSION QUESTIONS

1   Why is it important to medically stablize an anorexic patient before refeeding is begun?

2   What is the treatment for osteoporosis caused by anorexia nervosa?

3   Why is it important to form a therapeutic alliance with an anorexic patient?

4   When should an anorexic patient be admitted to hospital?

5   What drug therapy is useful in treatment of anorexia nervosa?

6   Is nutritional therapy or psychotherapy alone sufficient in the treatment of anorexia nervosa?

REFERENCES

Abdu, R. A., Garritano, D., & Culver, O. (1987). Acute gastric necrosis in anorexia nervosa and bulimia. *Archives of Surgery, 122,* 830–832.

Bhanji, S., & Mattingly, D. (1988). *Medical aspects of anorexia nervosa.* London: Wright.

Birmingham, C. L., Goldner, E. M., & Bakan, R. (1994). A controlled trial of zinc in anorexia nervosa. *International Journal of Eating Disorders 15,* 251–255.

Brotman, A. W., Stern, T. A., & Brotman, D. L. (1986). Renal disease and dysfunction in two patients with anorexia nervosa. *Journal of Clinical Psychiatry, 47,* 433–434.

Brotman, A. W., Stern, T. A., & Herzog, D. B. (1984). Emotional reactions of house officers to patients with anorexia nervosa, diabetes and obesity. *International Journal of Eating Disorders, 3,* 71–77.

Bruch, H. (1973). *Eating disorders: obesity, anorexia nervosa, and the person within.* New York: Basic Books.

Casper, R. C., Hedeker, D., & McClough, J. F. (1992). Personality dimensions in eating disorder and their relevance for subtyping. *Journal of the American Academy of Child and Adolescent Psychiatry, 31,* 830–840.

Cohler, B. J. (1977). The significance of the therapist's feelings in the treatment of anorexia nervosa. In S. C. Feinstein & P. L. Giovacchini (Eds.), *Adolescent psychiatry* (pp. 352–384). New York: Jason Aronson.

Connors, M. E., & Morse, W. (1993). Sexual abuse and eating disorders: A review. *International Journal of Eating Disorders, 13,* 1–11.

Cosford, P., & Arnold, E. (1992). Eating disorders in later life: A review. *International Journal of Geriatric Psychiatry, 7,* 491–498.

Crisp, A. H. (1980). *Anorexia nervosa: Let me be.* London: Academic Press.

Crisp, A. H., Norton, K., Gowers, S., Halek, C., Bowyer, C., Yeldham, D., Levett, G., & Bhat, A. (1991). A controlled study of the effect of therapies aimed at adolescent and family psycopathology in anorexia nervosa. *British Journal of Psychiatry, 159,* 325–333.

Cuellar, R. E., & Van Thiel, D. H. (1986). Gastrointestinal complications of the eating disorders anorexia nervosa and bulimia nervosa. *American Journal of Gastroenterology 81,* 1113–1124.

Dare, C., & Szmukler, G. (1991). Family therapy of early-onset, short-history anorexia nervosa. In D. B. Woodside & L. Shekter-Wolfson (Eds.), *Family approaches in treatment of eating disorders* (pp. 23–47). Washington DC: American Psychiatric Press.

Davanloo, H. (1980). *Short-term dynamic psychotherapy.* New York: Jason Aronson.

Davis, R., Dearing, S., Faulkner, J., Jasper, K., Olmsted, M. P., Rice, C., & Rockert, W. (1992). The road to recovery: A manual for participants in the psychoeducation group for bulimia nervosa. In H. Harper-Giuffre & K. R. MacKenzie (Eds.), *Group psychotherapy for eating disorders* (pp. 273–342). Washington, DC: American Psychiatric Press.

Davis, R., & deGroot, J. (1993). Psychotherapy for the eating disorders. In S. H. Kennedy (Ed.), *University of Toronto handbook of eating disorders* (pp. 49–58). Toronto: University of Toronto Press.

Davis, R., & Olmsted, M. P. (1992). Cognitive-behavioral group treatment for bulimia nervosa: Integrating psychoeducation and psychotherapy. In H. Harper-Giuffre & K. R. MacKenzie (Eds.), *Group psychotherapy for eating disorders* (pp. 71–103). Washington, DC: American Psychiatric Press.

Davis, R., Olmsted, M. P., & Rockert, W. (1990). Brief group psychoeducation for bulimia nervosa: Assessing the clinical significance of change. *Journal of Clinical and Consulting Psychology, 58,* 882–885.

DiNicola, V. F. (1993, May). Family interventions and eating disorders. Paper presented at 4th Eating Disorders Symposium, Vancouver, Canada.

Dresser, R. (1984). Feeding the hunger artists: Legal issues in treating anorexia nervosa. *Wisconsin Law Review, 2,* 297–394.

Duncan, J., Kennedy, S. H. (1992). Inpatient group treatment. In H. Harper-Giuffre & K. R. MacKenzie (Eds.), *Group psychotherapy for eating disorders* (pp. 149–160). Washington, DC: American Psychiatric Press.

Fairburn, C. G., & Cooper, P. J. (1989). Eating disorders. In K. Hawton, P. M. Salkovskis, J. Kirk, & D. M. Clark (Eds.), *Cognitive behaviour therapy for psychiatric problems: A practical guide* (pp. 277–314). Oxford: Oxford University Press.

Fairburn, C. G., & Steel, J. M. (1980). Anorexia nervosa in diabetes mellitus. *British Medical Journal, 280,* 1167–1168.

Fosson, A., Knibbs, J., Bryant-Waugh, R., & Lask, B. (1987). Early onset anorexia nervosa. *Archives of Diseases of Childhood, 62,* 114–118.

Fost, N. (1984). Food for thought: Dresser on anorexia. *Wisconsin Law Review, 2,* 375–384.

Garner, D. M. (1985). Iatrogenesis in anorexia nervosa and bulimia nervosa. *International Journal of Eating Disorders, 4,* 701–726.

Garner, D. M., & Bemis, K. (1982). A cognitive-behavioral approach to anorexia nervosa. *Cognitive Therapy and Research, 6,* 123–150.

Garner, D. M., & Bemis, K. (1985). Cognitive therapy for anorexia nervosa. In D. M. Garner & P. E. Garfinkel (Eds.), *Handbook of psychotherapy for anorexia nervosa and bulimia* (pp. 107–146). New York: Guilford.

Garner, D. M., Olmsted, M. P., & Polivy, J. (1983). Development and validation of a multidimensional inventory for anorexia nervosa and bulimia. *International Journal of Eating Disorders, 2,* 15–34.

Gartner, A. F., Marcus, R. N., Halmi, K. A., & Loranger, A. W. (1989). DSM-III-R personality disorders in patients with eating disorders. *American Journal of Psychiatry, 146,* 1585–1591.

Geist, R. A. (1989). Self psychological reflections on the origins of the eating disorders. In J. R. Bemporad & D. B. Herzog (Eds.), *Psychoanalysis and Eating Disorders* (pp. 5–28). New York: Guilford Press.

Goldner, E. (1989). Treatment refusal in anorexia nervosa. *International Journal of Eating Disorders, 8,* 297–306.

Goodsitt, A. (1985). Self psychology and the treatment of anorexia nervosa. In D. M. Garner & P. E. Garfinkel (Eds.), *Handbook of psychotherapy of anorexia nervosa and bulimia* (pp. 55–82). New York: Guilford Press.

Gowers, S. G., & Crisp, A. H. (1990). Anorexia nervosa in an 80-year-old woman. *British Journal of Psychiatry, 157,* 754–757.

Gross, H. A., Ebert, M. H., Faden, V. V. (1981). A double-blind controlled study of lithium carbonate in primary anorexia nervosa. *Journal of Clinical Psychopharmacology, 1,* 376–381.

Gwirtsman, H. E., Guze, B. H., Yager, J., Gainsley, B. (1990). Fluoxetine treatment of anorexia nervosa: An open clinical trial. *Journal of Clinical Psychiatry, 51,* 378–382.

Halmi, K. A., Eckert, E., LaDu, T. J., Cohen, J. (1986). Anorexia nervosa: Treatment efficacy of cyproheptadine and amitriptyline. *Archives of General Psychiatry, 48,* 712–718.

Hsu, L. K. G. (1980). Outcome of anorexia nervosa: A review of the literature (1954–1978). *Archives of General Psychiatry, 37,* 1041–1046.

Hsu, L. K. G. (1990). *Eating disorders.* New York: Guilford Press.

Hsu, L. K. G. (1991). Outcome studies in patients with eating disorders. In S. M. Mirin, J. T. Gossett, & M. C. Grob (Eds.), *Psychiatric treatment advances in outcome research* (pp. 159–180). New York: American Psychiatric Press.

Isner, J. M., Roberts, W. C., Heymsfield, S. B., & Yager, J. (1985). Anorexia nervosa and sudden death. *Annals of Internal Medicine, 102,* 49–52.

Johnson, C. (1991). Treatment of eating disordered patients with borderline and false self/narcissistic disorders. In C. Johnson (Ed.), *Psychodynamic treatment of anorexia nervosa and bulimia* (pp. 165–193). New York: Guilford Press.

Kaplan, A. S., Kerr, A., Maddocks, S. E. (1992). Day hospital group treatment. In H. Harper-Giuffre & K. R. MacKenzie (Eds.), *Group psychotherapy for eating disorders* (pp. 161–180). Washington, DC: American Psychiatric Press.

Kaye, W. H., Gwirtsman, H. E., Obarzanek, E., & George, D. R. (1988). Relative importance of calorie intake needed to gain weight and level of physical activity in anorexia
nervosa. *American Journal of Clinical Nutrition, 47,* 989–994.

Kaye, W. H., Weltzin, T. W., Hsu, L. K. G., & Bulik, C. (1991). An open trial of fluoxetine
in patients with anorexia nervosa. *Journal of Clinical Psychiatry 57,* 464–471.

Kearney-Cooke, A. (1991). The role of the therapist in the treatment of eating disorders: A
feminist psychodynamic approach. *Psychodynamic treatment of anorexia nervosa and
bulimia* (pp. 295–320). New York: Guilford Press.

Kennedy, S. H., & Abbas, A. (1993). Inpatient treatment for anorexia nervosa and bulimia
nervosa. In S. H. Kennedy (Ed.), *University of Toronto handbook of eating disorders*
(pp. 30–36). Toronto: University of Toronto Press.

Kennedy, S. H., McVey, G., & Katz, R. (1990). Personality disorders in anorexia nervosa
and bulimia nervosa. *Journal of Psychiatric Research, 24,* 259–269.

Lacey, J. H., & Crisp, A. H. (1980). Hunger, food intake and weight: The impact of clomipramine on a refeeding anorexia nervosa population. *Postgraduate Medical Education
Journal, 56,* 79–85.

Metropolitan Life Insurance Company. (1983). *Statistics Bulletin, 64,* 2.

Minuchin, S., Rosman, B. L., & Baker, L. (1978). *Psychosomatic families: Anorexia
nervosa in context,* Cambridge: Harvard University Press.

Mitchell, J. A., & Boutacoff, L. I. (1986). Laxative abuse complicating bulimia:
Medical and treatment implications. *International Journal of Eating Disorders, 5,*
325–334.

Mogul, S. L. (1989). Sexuality, pregnancy, and parenting in anorexia. In J. R. Bemporad
& D. B. Herzog (Eds.), *Psychoanalysis and eating disorders,* (pp. 65–88). New York:
Guilford Press.

Morgan, H. G. (1977). Fasting girls and our attitudes to them. *British Medical Journal, Dec.
2* (6103), 1652–1655.

Olmsted, M. P., Davis, R., Rockert, W., Irvine, M. J., Eagle, M., & Garner, D. M. (1991).
Efficacy of a brief psychoeducational intervention for bulimia nervosa. *Behavioral
Research and Therapy, 29,* 71–83.

Orbach, S. (1986). *Hunger strike: The anorectic's struggle as a metaphor for our age.* New
York: Norton.

Palmer, E. P., & Guay, A. T. (1986). Reversible myopathy secondary to abuse of ipecac
in patients with major eating disorders. *New England Journal of Medicine, 313,*
1457–1459.

Piran, N., Langdon, L., Kaplan, A. S., & Garfinkel, P. E. (1990). Program evaluation. In N.
Piran & A. S. Kaplan (Eds.), *A day hospital group treatment program for anorexia
nervosa and bulimia nervosa* (pp. 139–150). New York: Brunner/Mazel.

Rigotti, N. A., Neer, R. M., Skates, S. J., Herzog, D. B., Nussbaum, S. R. (1991). The
clinical course of osteoporosis in anorexia nervosa: A longitudinal study of cortical
bone mass. *Journal of the American Medical Association, 265,* 1133–1138.

Robertson, M. (1992). *Starving in the silences: An exploration of anorexia nervosa.* New
York: New York University Press.

Russell, G. F., Szmukler, G. I., Dare, C., & Eisler, I. (1987). An evaluation of family
therapy in anorexia nervosa and bulimia nervosa. *Archives of General Psychiatry,
44,* 1047–1056.

Selvini-Palazzoli, M. (1978). *From individual to family therapy in the treatment of anorexia nervosa.* New York: Jason Aronson.

Sifneos, P. E. (1979). *Short-term dynamic psychotherapy: Evaluation and technique.* New York: Plenum Books.

Steiger, H. (1989). An integrated psychotherapy for eating disorder patients. *American Journal of Psychotherapy, 43,* 229–237.

Steiner-Adair, C. (1991). New maps of development, new models of therapy: The psychology of women and the treatment of eating disorders. In C. Johnson (Ed.), *Psychodynamic treatment of anorexia nervosa and bulimia* (pp. 225–244). New York: Guilford Press.

Stierlin, H., & Weber, G. (1989). *Unlocking the family door: A systemic approach to the understanding and treatment of anorexia nervosa.* New York: Brunner/Mazel.

Stern, S. (1986). The dynamics of clinical management in the treatment of anorexia nervosa and bulimia: An organizing theory. *International Journal of Eating Disorders, 5,* 233–254.

Stern, S. (1991). Managing opposing currents: An interpersonal psychoanalytic technique for the treatment of eating disorders. In C. Johnson (Ed.), *Psychodynamic treatment of anorexia nervosa and bulimia* (pp. 86–105). New York: Guilford Press.

Stewart, D. E., Robinson, G. E., Goldbloom, D. S., Wright, C. (1990). Infertility and eating disorders. *American Journal of Obstetrics and Gynecology, 163,* 1196–1199.

Strober, M. (1980). Personality and symptomatological features in young, nonchronic anorexia nervosa patients. *Journal of Psychosomatic Research, 24,* 353–359.

Strober, M. (1991). Disorders of the self in anorexia nervosa: An organismic-developmental paradigm. *Psychodynamic treatment of anorexia nervosa and bulimia* (pp. 354–373). New York: Guilford Press.

Thompson, J. K. (1990). *Body image disturbance: Assessment and treatment.* New York: Pergamon.

Tinker, D. E., & Ramer, J. C. (1983). Anorexia nervosa: Staff subversion of therapy. *Journal of Adolescent Health Care, 4,* 35–39.

Tobin, D. L., & Johnson, C. L. (1991). The integration of psychodynamic and behavior therapy in the treatment of eating disorders: Clinic issue versus theoretical mystique. *Psychodynamic treatment of anorexia nervosa and bulimia* (pp. 374–397). New York: Guilford Press.

Touyz, S. W., Beumont, P. J. V., Glaun, D., Phillips, T., & Cowie, I. (1984). A comparison of lenient and strict operant conditioning programmes in refeeding patients with anorexia nervosa. *British Journal of Psychiatry, 144,* 517–520.

Vaillant, G. E. (1992). The beginning of wisdom is never calling a patient a borderline; or, The clinical management of immature defenses in the treatment of individuals with personality disorders. *Journal of Psychotherapy Practice and Research, 1,* 117–134.

Valette, B. (1988). *A parent's guide to eating disorders: Prevention and treatment of anorexia nervosa and bulimia.* New York: Walker.

Vandereycker, W., & Pierloot, R. (1982). Pimozide combined with behavior therapy in the short-term treatment of anorexia nervosa: A double blind, placebo-controlled crossover study. *Acta Psychiatrica Scandinavica, 66,* 445–450.

White, M., & Epston, D. (1990). *Narrative means to therapeutic ends.* New York: Norton & Company.

Williams, E. (1958). Anorexia nervosa: A somatic disorder. *British Medical Journal, ii,* 190–194.

Williams, H., Touyz, S. W., Beumont, P. J. V. (1985). Nutritional counselling in anorexia nervosa. In S. W. Touyz & P. J. V. Beumont (Eds.), *Eating disorders: Prevalence and treatment* (pp. 23–31). Balgowlah: Williams & Wilkins.

Winnicott, D. W. (1965). *The maturational process and the facilitating environment: Studies in the theory of emotional development.* New York: International Universities Press.

Wonderlich, S. A., & Swift, W. J. (1990). Borderline versus other personality disorders in the eating disorders: Clinical description. *International Journal of Eating Disorders, 9,* 629–638.

Wonderlich, S. A., Swift, W. J., Slotnick, H. B., & Goodman, S. (1990). DSM-III-R personality disorders in eating-disorder subtypes. *International Journal of Eating Disorders, 9,* 607–616.

Wooley, S. C. (1991). Uses of countertransference in the treatment of eating disorders: A gender perspective. In C. Johnson (Ed.), *Psychodynamic treatment of anorexia nervosa and bulimia.* New York: Guilford Press.

Yager, J., & Young, R. T. (1992). Eating disorders and diabetes mellitus. In J. Yager, H. E. Gwirtsman, & C. K. Edelstein (Eds.), *Special problems in managing eating disorders.* Washington, DC: American Psychiatric Press.

Yates, A. (1991). *Compulsive exercise and the eating disorders: Toward an integrated theory of activity.* New York: Brunner/Mazel.

Part Three

Bulimia Nervosa

Unlike anorexia nervosa, bulimia was not identified as a separate syndrome until the 1960s and 1970s. Before this time, many considered bulimia to be an atypical form of anorexia nervosa. Throughout this period of time, the terms *dietary chaos syndrome, bulimarexia, dysorexia,* and *abnormal weight control syndrome* were used to describe the binge-eating syndrome in patients with near normal weight. In 1980, the *DSM-III* recognized bulimia as a syndrome separate from anorexia nervosa and listed the following diagnostic criteria:

1 Recurrent episodes of binge eating.
2 At least three of the following:
   (a) consumption of high-caloric, easily ingested food during a binge;
   (b) inconspicuous eating during a binge;
   (c) termination of such eating episodes by abdominal pain, sleep, social interruption, or self-induced vomiting;
   (d) repeated attempts to lose weight by severely restricted diets, self-induced vomiting, or the use of cathartics or diuretics;
   (e) frequent weight fluctuations due to alternating binges and fasts.

3 Awareness that the eating pattern is abnormal and fear of not being able to stop eating voluntarily.

4 Depressed mood and self-deprecating thoughts following eating binges.

In 1987, the term *bulimia* was changed to *bulimia nervosa* in *DSM-III-R,* and changes in the criteria were set forth, most notably in the specification of the frequency of binges; in the necessity of vomiting, purging, and/or exercise to be present for a diagnosis; and in the addition of "persistent overconcern with body size and weight" as a criterion. The criteria follow:

1 Recurrent episodes of binge eating.

2 A feeling of lack of control over eating behavior during eating binges.

3 The person regularly engages in either self-induced vomiting, use of laxatives or diuretics, strict dieting or fasting, or vigorous exercise in order to prevent weight gain.

4 A minimum average of two binge eating episodes a week for at least three months.

5 Persistent overconcern with body shape and weight.

As for anorexia nervosa, the *DSM-IV* will contain changes in the diagnostic criteria for bulimia nervosa.

Chapters in this part examine the definition of bulimia nervosa, describe the condition, discuss theories of etiology and medical complications, and assess methods of treatment.

Chapter 8

Bulimia Nervosa: Definition, Diagnostic Criteria, and Associated Psychological Problems

Lillie Weiss
Melanie Katzman
Sharlene Wolchik

This chapter is about understanding bulimia, also referred to as the binge-purge syndrome. Problems defining this disorder, as well as epidemiology, personality characteristics, psychological correlates and theories of etiology are discussed. We begin with a case description to illustrate this syndrome.

Corrine is a 26-year-old mother of two preschoolers. She is tall, attractive, and immaculately groomed. To all outward appearances she fits the image of the professional career woman she is. Corrine was recently promoted to manager of her section and is very proud of her outstanding record. She has a reputation for taking on and always following through on any responsibilities assigned to her. After working all day, usually staying overtime for some last minute meeting, she comes home and fixes dinner for her husband and children. Late into the night she irons, vacuums, and does the laundry. Corrine's husband runs his own business and has a demanding job as well. Consequently, he does very little around the house, leaving her with the majority of the work. Corrine's parents are getting old, and recently they have become more dependent on her. Corrine feels like she "doesn't have enough hands" to do all that is demanded of her. After clearing the dinner dishes, doing the rest of the housework, calling to check on her parents, and putting the children to bed, Corrine is exhausted. After her husband goes to bed, she goes to the refrigerator and takes out a cake. Not bothering to cut it or use utensils, she eats it with her fingers while standing up. Then she takes out a gallon of ice cream from the freezer. With a large spoon, she starts eating ice cream directly from the carton, barely tasting it. To her horror, it is all gone before she knows it. She looks inside the cabinets for more food. After devouring a bag of chocolate chip cookies, she starts on the box of crackers next to it. Her stomach starts to hurt, but she ignores the pain. She feels aghast at her binge and heads for the toilet. As she turns on the faucet to drown out any noise, she sticks her finger down her throat and throws up. Afterward, she feels weak and drained and is very angry at herself. When will she ever stop this terrible habit?

Corrine had been of average weight most of her life, but started to gain weight with each of her pregnancies. She became worried she would become obese like her older sister. She had gone on many diets and lost weight each time, only to gain it back. Each time she had gone on a diet, she had felt deprived. Each time she had stopped dieting, she rapidly regained the weight she had lost. A year ago, she overate when dining out. When she came home, she started feeling nauseous and went to the bathroom and made herself throw up. She was relieved to discover she felt much better. The next time Corrine ate too much, she forced herself to throw up again. Soon this became a habit; Corrine was bingeing and purging daily, sometimes two or more times a day if she was not working. After each binge and purge cycle, Corrine would feel depressed and vow to herself it would not happen again. She would promise herself she would be "good" the next day, and indeed she would—just as she had today. She had not put a morsel of food in her mouth in the morning, had worked right through lunch, had ignored the hunger pangs she felt, and had even not touched the hors d'oeuvres and drinks that were served at the late staff meeting. When she arrived home, she had watched her husband and children eat a hearty dinner, while she had only nibbled at her salad. Then after everyone had gone to bed, Corrine went on one of her worst eating binges.

DEFINITION

Corrine is one of the increasing number of women suffering from bulimia nervosa, an eating disorder commonly referred to as the binge-purge syndrome. *Bulimia* refers to regular episodes of eating very large quantities of food that are generally highly caloric and easily ingested, followed by vomiting, fasting, vigorous exercise, or using laxatives or diuretics in an attempt to get rid of food. The bingeing is generally done in private, as in Corrine's case, and this secret is kept from others. Like Corrine, bulimic women feel angry after a binge and suffer pangs of guilt, remorse, and shame.

Although bulimia was once considered a rare disorder, in the past decade it has begun to receive a great deal of attention in both the professional and popular literature. It was not until 1980 that bulimia was even listed as a separate disorder by the American Psychiatric Association in its *Diagnostic and Statistical Manual of Mental Disorders (DSM-III)* (American Psychiatric Association, 1980). In 1987, the diagnostic criteria for bulimia were further operationalized and the name of the disorder changed to *bulimia nervosa* to highlight the relation with anorexia nervosa. The *Diagnostic and Statistical Manual of Mental Disorders, Revised (DSM-III-R)* (APA, 1987) defined the disorder as recurrent episodes of binge eating; a feeling of lack of control during the eating binges; and engaging in either self-induced vomiting, use of laxatives or diuretics, strict dieting or fasting, or vigorous exercise in order to prevent weight gain. Two additional criteria for the diagnosis include a minimum of two binge eating episodes a week for at least 3 months and persistent overconcern with body shape and weight.

The use of the term *bulimia nervosa* has been confusing as it has been used to describe both a symptom (binge eating) and a syndrome. As a symptom, bulimia nervosa has been used to describe binge eating in subgroups of patients with anorexia nervosa and an eating pattern in patients who are overweight or obese. Consequently, when used as a symptom, the term *bulimia nervosa* has been applied to anorexics and obese and overweight persons as well as to binge eaters. Whether these groups of patients bear any clinical similarities to people with bulimia nervosa who are of normal weight has been a subject of much debate. As a syndrome, bulimia nervosa has been studied under many different names, which makes interpretation of the literature difficult. Some of the terms that have been used include thinfats (Bruch, 1973), bulimarexia or binge starvers (Boskind-Lodahl, 1976), bulimia nervosa (Russell, 1979), vomiters and purgers (Beumont, George, & Smart, 1976), and compulsive eaters (Green & Rau, 1974). When we use the term, we are referring primarily to women of average weight who are suffering from the *DSM-III-R*-defined syndrome bulimia nervosa.

Even the *DSM-III-R* criteria leave some ambiguity about the definition of bulimia nervosa. Although there is an attempt to operationalize the definition by adding the criterion of a minimum of two binge eating episodes per week for at least 3 months, there is no operationalized definition of what constitutes a binge and how to differentiate binges from large meals. For our purposes, we have defined a binge as consisting of at least 1,200 calories. In this definition, meals do not constitute binges.

In view of the inconsistency in definitions of bulimia nervosa, integration and comparison of the research findings on this disorder must be made with these methodological limitations in mind. Another difficulty is the bias of research samples that have focused primarily on college-age women or women seeking treatment rather than community-based, epidemiological samples. While a growing body of research has examined the adolescent with eating problems, less attention has been given to the mature bulimic in her 40s or 50s who may have struggled with the problem for more than a quarter of a decade. In spite of these methodological problems, however, there is a large body of literature on bulimia nervosa. Some of the characteristics of bulimics are reviewed in this chapter and

descriptions of the epidemiology, topography, personality and behavioral characteristics, physiological consequences, and theories of bulimia nervosa are given.

EPIDEMIOLOGY

Bulimia nervosa occurs most often in women; as a result, the focus of this chapter
will be on women with the disorder. It has been estimated that 5% to 10% of
persons with bulimia nervosa are men (Pyle et al., 1981). (For a recent review of
bulimia nervosa in men, see Carlot and Camargo [1991]). Although the average
bulimic can be characterized as a white, single, college-educated woman from an
upper- or middle-class family (Fairburn & Cooper, 1982), researchers have been
criticized for failing to survey cross-cultural and socioeconomic groups ade-
quately (Dolan, 1991). In fact, when researchers have examined minority college
students (Smith & Krejci, 1991), increased rates of disturbed eating have been
noted. The age of onset is usually in the late teens (Fairburn & Cooper, 1982;
Johnson & Berndt, 1983; Leon, Carroll, Chernyk, & Finn, 1985; Pyle, Mitchell, &
Eckert, 1981). Many women, however, do not seek treatment for 4 to 5 years after
the onset (Johnson, Stuckey, Lewis, & Schwartz, 1982; Leon et al, 1985; Russell,
1979) .

Estimates of the frequency of bulimia nervosa in college-age women range
from 3.8% to 19%, depending on how binge eating is defined (Halmi, Falk, &
Schwartz, 1981; Katzman, Wolchik, & Braver, 1984; Pyle, Mitchell, Eckert,
Halvorson, Neuman, & Goff, 1983; Stangler & Prinz, 1980). Bulimia is also
common among high school women, with prevalence rates ranging from 3% to
8.3% (Crowther, Post, & Zaynor, 1985; Johnson, Lewis, Love, Lewis, & Stuckey,
1984). Several authors note that their findings may underestimate prevalence due
to a reluctance to report eating disorders (Halmi, Falk, & Schwartz, 1981; Stangler
& Prinz, 1980). It is likely that more women than we know engage in bingeing and
purging. Like Corrine, many women binge in private and keep their behavior
secret. It has been our experience that most of our patients do not even report their
bulimia to their doctors, even when they have medical complications ensuing
from the disorder. Although the number of reports on bulimia nervosa has increased markedly in the last few years, we do not know whether this increase
reflects a true rise in frequency or whether bulimic patients are only now receiving
professional attention (Mitchell & Pyle, 1981).

In addition to prevalence studies on bulimia nervosa, studies on binge eating
have been reported. Prevalence rates for binge eating have ranged from 56% to
86% for college women (Halmi et al., 1981; Hawkins & Clement, 1984; Katzman,
Wolchik, & Braver, 1984; Ondercin, 1979). The definition of binge eating in most
studies has generally been a "yes" response to the question "Do you binge eat?" or
variations thereof. When a stricter definition of binge eating was employed (for
example, binge eating at least eight times in the past month), the prevalence
estimate dropped to 7.2% (Katzman et al., 1984). Although several researchers

have studied the personality and behavioral characteristics of binge eaters (Dunn & Ondercin, 1981; Hawkins & Clement, 1984), the similarity in symptomatology between binge eaters and bulimics is not clear and has only been addressed in one study (Katzman & Wolchik, 1984).

Although bulimic women are generally of normal weight (Abraham & Beumont, 1982; Johnson et al., 1982), many have a history of disordered eating. Johnson et al. (1982) reported that 50% of their sample had a history of being overweight, whereas other researchers (Katzman & Wolchik, 1984; Leon Carroll, Chernyk, & Finn, 1985; Russell, 1979) reported that at least a third of their samples had histories of extreme weight loss. In almost every case, the women were struggling to maintain a below-normal weight (Katzman & Wolchik, 1984; Pyle et al., 1981; Russell, 1979; Weiss & Ebert, 1983). Like Corrine, many bulimics use purging as a way to control their weight. There is some evidence that binge purging is learned, either by accident as in Corrine's case when she became nauseous after overeating and found that vomiting made her feel better or from friends or the media (Fairburn & Cooper, 1982; Katzman & Wolchik, 1984). Once a woman begins the binge-purge cycle, she becomes preoccupied with food, continually experiences hunger, and feels guilty when she binges (Katzman & Wolchik, 1983; Leon et al., 1985; Mizes, 1983; Russell, 1979).

TOPOGRAPHY OF BINGE EATING

The frequency of binge eating varies across studies. A number of researchers (Johnson et al., 1982; Leon et al., 1985) have reported that of the women in treatment they sampled, 50% binged on a daily basis. Mitchell, Pyle, and Eckert (1981), also using a clinical sample, reported a mean of 11.7 binges per month, with a range of 1 to 14. Using a nonclinical sample, Katzman and Wolchik (1982) noted a mean of 23 binges per month.

The caloric intake during binges has been reported to range from 1,200 (Mitchell et al; 1981) to 55,000 calories (Johnson et al., 1982). Katzman and Wolchik (1983a) and Leon et al. (1985) found an average consumption of 2,500 calories per binge. Women report spending an average of $8.30 per binge (Johnson et al., 1982), with some spending as much as $70.00 per binge (Wooley & Wooley, 1982).

Several researchers have provided descriptions of binge eating behavior (Johnson et al., 1982; Katzman & Wolchik, 1983a; Pyle et al., 1981). Across these reports, the average binge lasted an hour. Most women binged at home and alone, like Corrine who waited for everyone in the house to go to sleep before bingeing. Women generally ate late in the day or at night and ate foods that were highly caloric and required little preparation, such as ice cream or doughnuts. The binge often included items the women would not typically eat given their dieting concerns (Abraham & Beumont, 1982).

In addition to bingeing, bulimics show other disturbances in eating, frequently alternating between binge eating and periods of very low food consumption and fasting (Weiss & Ebert, 1983). Bulimics frequently do not eat for more than 24 hours after a binge and then find themselves very hungry, thereby prompting a binge and starting the bingeing-fasting cycle again. Very few bulimics eat three meals a day, even on those days they do eat (Leon et al., 1985; Mizes & Lohr, 1983).

Vomiting is the most frequent purging technique and was reported in 81% to 94% of women in studies (Fairburn & Cooper, 1982; Johnson et al., 1982; Pyle et al., 1981). Across these studies, approximately 50% of the women who vomited did so daily. About 50% of the women in these studies also abused laxatives. Of the women who used laxatives, roughly a quarter of those did so daily (Johnson et al., 1982). Diuretics, enemas, and appetite suppressants were also employed for weight control, although not as frequently.

Most binge-eating episodes occur together with negative emotional states such as anxiety or depression (Abraham & Beumont, 1982; Crowther et al., 1983; Katzman & Wolchik, 1983a; Ondercin, 1979). Both self-report and self-monitoring data gathered on normal-weight bulimics suggest that binge-eating episodes are precipitated by feelings of anxiety and negative emotional states, as well as hunger. As in Corrine's case, binge eating is often preceded by food-oriented thoughts accompanied by anxious or depressive affective states. Like Corrine who "didn't have enough hands" to do all that was required of her, many bulimics binge in response to stress, such as poor grades or exams (Katzman & Wolchik, 1983a). Unfortunately, the binge does not alleviate the negative feelings, except maybe temporarily. Most bulimics report feeling anger, disgust, and guilt after a binge (Johnson & Larson, 1982; Katzman & Wolchik, 1983a; Leon et al., 1985; Pyle et al., 1981). Similarly, Abraham and Beumont (1982) reported that whereas 100% of their sample ate to reduce tension, only 66% reported feeling less anxious after a binge.

PERSONALITY AND BEHAVIORAL CHARACTERISTICS

Research findings suggest that bulimics have many personality and behavioral characteristics that coexist with the disturbed eating pattern. Katzman and Wolchik (1984) compared the personality and behavioral characteristics of 30 women who met the DSM-III criteria for bulimia with those of 22 women who reported binge eating but did not fulfill these criteria and with those of 28 controls. In comparison with both binge eaters and controls, bulimics were more depressed and had lower self-esteem, poorer body image, higher self-expectations, higher need for approval, greater restraint, and higher binge scores. No significant differences occurred on measures of dating, assertion, or sex role orientation. Weiss and Ebert (1983) tested 15 normal weight *DSM-III* bulimics and 15 controls. In comparison with controls, bulimics reported themselves to have significantly more psychopathology on all nine symptom dimensions: somatization, obsession-compulsion, interpersonal sensitivity, depression, anxiety, anger, phobic anxiety, paranoid ideation, and psychotism. They also reported greater external locus of control, greater fear of fat, and more anxiety in situations related to eating than controls.

A great deal of research suggests that bulimia and depression are related (Pope & Hudson, 1985). Russell (1979) reported that after preoccupation with eating, dieting, and weight, depressive symptoms are most prominent. Using *DSM-III* criteria for depression, Herzog (1982) found that 75% of the bulimic women reported significant depressive symptoms. Other researchers have reported significant depression and psychological distress in bulimics (Hatsukami, Owen, Pyle, & Mitchell, 1982; Johnson & Larson, 1982; Pyle et al., 1981; Ross, Todt, & Rindflesh, 1983). In addition, studies of family history (Hudson, Laffer, & Pope, 1982; Pyle et al., 1981) and of response to the dexamethasone suppression test (Hudson et al., 1982) have demonstrated a similarity between patients with bulimia and patients with major depression.

The studies that have reported a decrease in bulimic symptoms using antidepressants (Pope, Hudson, Jonas, & Yergulun-Todd, 1983; Walsh, Stewart, Wright, Harrison, Roose, & Glassman, 1982) lend further support to the contention that bulimia and depression are related. However, whether bulimics are depressed because of their condition or because a depression is underlying or putting them at risk for bingeing and purging is unclear. Additional research in this area is warranted before any firm conclusions can be drawn.

Bulimics tend to set high self-expectations and tend to be perfectionistic (Johnson & Connors, 1987; Katzman & Wolchik, 1984). They tend to set unrealistic goals for themselves in both their personal lives and in how much they should weigh. Most feel they are never "thin enough," and many have high expectations in areas other than weight, e.g., getting straight A's, studying all the time, and so on (Root, Fallon, & Friedrich, 1986).

Although bulimics frequently report a desire to be thinner than their current weight (Katzman & Wolchik, 1984; Leon et al., 1985; Pyle et al., 1981; Russell, 1979), research conducted on the bulimics' perceived weight suggests they never see themselves as thin enough. Other research suggests that bulimics tend to overestimate their weight significantly more than controls and believe that they weigh more than they do (Halmi et al., 1981). In addition, they have poorer body image in comparison to normal subjects and binge eaters and are preoccupied with their weight and body size (Fairburn, 1980; Palmer, 1979; Russell, 1979; Wermuth, Davis, Hollister, & Stunkard, 1977).

The research findings on bulimics' identification with sex roles are mixed. Rost, Neuhaus, and Florin (1982) and Alderdisson, Florin, and Rost (1981) found that when compared with matched controls, women who reported eating binges and purges were significantly less liberated in both sex role attitudes and behavior. In addition, Minnesota Multiphasic Personality Inventory (MMPI) profiles of bulimics (Hatsukami et al., 1982; Leon et al., 1985; Pyle et al., 1981) are characterized by an overemphasis of the stereotypic female role. Binge purgers also indicated less enjoyment of sexual relationships, more difficulty expressing their sexual wishes, and more fear of not meeting their partners' sexual expectations. They also believed their enjoyment of sex would improve if they were slimmer and more attractive (Allerdisson et al., 1981). Other researchers (Katzman & Wolchik, 1984) did not find sex role differences between bulimics and controls. Differences in group definition and measures may account for the discrepancy. It may be that an attempt to combine many roles predisposes women to bulimia. Steiner-Adair (1991) reported that high school girls who attempted to combine traditional female expectations with increased possibilities of fulfilling male roles—in essence to be superwomen—were more prone to eating disorders than girls who acknowledged that superwoman expectations were not achievable.

Several researchers have suggested that bulimics have difficulty with impulse control because of self-reports of stealing (Leon et al., 1985; Pyle et al., 1981; Russell, 1979), alcohol use (Leon et al., 1985; Pyle et al., 1981) and drug use (Leon et al., 1985; Russell, 1979). When bulimics were compared with controls on use of alcohol and cigarettes, no significant differences were found (Johnson et al., 1982; Katzman & Wolchik, 1984). However, if the prevalence of eating disorders in women seeking treatment for substance abuse is examined, an increased rate of comorbidity is reported (Katzman, Marcus, & Greenberg, 1991).

Overall, the research suggests there are specific personality and behavioral deficits that characterize bulimics. It is generally agreed that bulimics suffer from anxiety and depression, have a high need for approval, set unrealistically high goals for themselves, and experience low self-esteem. Also, they are preoccupied with weight, have a poor body image, overemphasize physical appearance, and experience sex role difficulties.

Although these characteristics provide a summary of the "typical" bulimic, they do not go far enough in portraying a psychological picture for the student or clinician who wants to understand bulimia. In the next section, a more descriptive clinical picture will be painted in order to help the reader gain an understanding of the bulimic's world.

THE PSYCHOLOGICAL PICTURE

Psychological Consequences

The practical considerations and stresses in dealing day by day with bulimia are overwhelming and can only be deduced from the research findings. The binge-purge cycle is an all-encompassing symptom and pervades almost every aspect of the bulimic woman's daily existence. The habit interferes with her work, her social life, her family relationships, and her health. Although some women originally view bulimia as an easy way to eat and stay slim, they soon learn of its many psychological and physical consequences. Like Corrine, bulimics feel out of control, depressed, and guilty about their behavior.

The bulimic feels ashamed of her eating habits and is constantly afraid she will be found out. Feeling abnormal or different is common to most bulimics, and the shame associated with the behavior can be overwhelming. Since bingeing and purging are usually secretive behaviors, the feeling of hiding and of having to keep a large part of their lives under wraps is a significant source of stress. The bulimic feels she cannot confide in anyone lest she repel them with her aberrant behavior. She isolates herself from friends and family and then feels even more lonely. This isolation and withdrawal reinforce her feeling that she is "abnormal," "weird," or "different" and prevent her from getting the intimacy she craves.

Bingeing and purging are not circumscribed behaviors that only interfere peripherally with a woman's functioning. The bulimic is constantly thinking about food and planning her next binge. This preoccupation with food results in deliberate or inadvertent neglect of other areas. Because she binges in secret, she plans her day around the time when she can be alone so she can binge, thus neglecting friends and family. Her social and family relationships as well as her functioning at work or at school suffer. As several of our clients have said in one form or other, "It's hard to concentrate on anything else when you are always thinking about food."

It is not only the time spent in bingeing and planning the next binge that leads to the neglect of school, work, and friendship. The depression and the fatigue associated with this eating pattern result in limited energy to give to other activities. This point was poignantly brought home to us when one of our colleagues, an eating disorders therapist, became temporarily ill and was nauseated for several weeks. She said, "I just never realized how draining it can be to vomit all the time and how tired and depleted I feel." The feeling is not unlike having a constant hangover.

The financial considerations involved in this behavior are also tremendous. Many bulimic women have limited financial resources; some are students and have no steady income. Because they hide their habit from others, it is difficult to explain to their families where their money is going. They are frequently worried about the monetary aspect of their symptoms. Some women report stealing to support their bingeing and purging.

An additional source of stress lies in the nature of the habit. Because eating is a normal and daily part of living, the bulimic woman is reminded every day, at every meal, that her behavior is different from others. She cannot let her friends and family see how much she eats, so she avoids going out with them. Her hunger resulting from attempts to starve herself is also a constant reminder of her problem. The feelings of depression, shame, and isolation resulting from her secret are compounded by medical concerns.

The medical and physical problems associated with bulimia add to her stress. As well as feeling tired, drained, and hung over, she frequently has some serious health problems that result from the disorder. Although the bulimic may originally engage in this behavior to become attractive, this may result in some very unattractive physical changes such as rotting teeth caused by the wearing away of the enamel. In addition, she can have some serious medical complications such as electrolyte abnormalities, amenorrhea, and fatigue. As we can see, the time, energy, money, and health hazards involved with binge eating and purging make it more than just a daily nuisance and help us understand why depression and bulimia usually go hand in hand.

Thoughts, Feelings, and Behaviors Associated with Binge Eating

The typical bulimic seldom eats three meals a day. Usually she either starves herself all day or eats very limited portions. Like Corrine, most bulimics skip breakfast, ignore the hunger pangs they experience during the day, and are famished by evening. If they should eat lunch, it is usually a salad, a piece of fruit, or something low in calories. They deprive themselves all day long. Later on, the combination of excessive hunger and certain thoughts and feelings trigger an eating binge.

What kinds of thoughts and emotions go through the bulimic woman's mind before bingeing? Some common emotional triggers for binge eating are boredom, loneliness, anger, and anxiety. Many women, like Corrine, feel stressed all day and binge to deal with these negative feelings. We frequently hear comments from bulimics such as, "This was such a stressful day—I just wanted to relax" or "I came home and I was all alone and there was nothing else to do." Over and over we hear the words "I'm so nervous," "I'm so tired," "I have nothing else to do," or "I just wanted to stop thinking."

When we listen to the feelings underneath the words, we can see that women frequently use bingeing to cope with a variety of negative feelings. Sometimes women binge to calm down ("I just wanted to relax"; "I just needed something to comfort me"). At other times, they binge to escape or avoid difficult situations or to procrastinate ("I don't feel like working on that paper"; "I don't want to deal with my boss"). When the feelings are very intense or unpleasant, many women use food to numb these hurtful emotions ("This is so painful I can't let myself think about it"). Bingeing is frequently a response to boredom or used to fill an emptiness ("I feel lonely at nights so I go and eat").

In addition to the above thoughts, bulimic women "feed" themselves many other negative thoughts that encourage bingeing; for example, "I have discovered an easy way to diet" or "this is the only way I can lose weight." One very common thought that often leads to bingeing is "I am going to get rid of all this food anyway, so I might as well pig out."

Many of the negative cognitions are typical of the overgeneralization and all-or-nothing thinking that characterize perfectionists (Burns, 1980). Frequently, bulimics are either on or off a diet. When a bulimic woman is on a diet, she starves; when she's off, she binges. When she eats a cookie after starving herself all day, she may say, "Well, I blew it. I'm off my diet now. I might as well eat the whole bag." Many bulimics see eating in extremes—dieting or gorging—with no happy medium. The all-or-nothing thinking is also illustrated in their labeling their day, their food, and themselves as "good" or "bad" in relation to their eating habits. A good day or being good usually means not eating anything all day. Good food is generally limited to lettuce, celery, carrots, or cottage cheese. If the bulimic is bad, meaning she started the day off with a doughnut, then she may as well continue to be bad and binge. This all-or-nothing thinking not only frequently leads to binges but also to feeling depressed and guilty. Similar to all-or-nothing thinking is the overgeneralization from one situation to many. For example, a bulimic may tell herself: "If I gain one pound, I'll gain 5 or 10" or "I blew it today. I'll always blow it."

Another type of thinking that bulimics engage in is "should" statements. Bulimics tend to set impossible goals for what they should weigh (regardless of what is normal for their frames), how much food they should eat, and how fast they should lose weight. "I should be skinny," "I should lose 5 pounds this week," or "I should weigh 110 pounds" are thoughts that lead to starvation and bingeing when they do not meet these unrealistic goals.

Bulimics use should statements in areas other than weight and thinness. "I should study more . . . I should get straight A's. . . ." In short, they tell themselves "I should be perfect." Of course, that does not happen. When perfectionists make mistakes, rather than trying to learn from them, they punish themselves by other should statements: "I should not have done that" or "I should have known better." These statements lead to guilt, depression, and other general negative feelings that precede binges.

Other negative monologues that are common to bulimics have to do with their feelings about their bodies. For many women, regardless of their size and shape, their bodies tend to be a source of anxiety and hurt. Bulimics experience a great deal of emotional pain in their perceptions of their bodies. "I feel fat" is a common statement that leads to bingeing. More specifically, the bulimic tells herself "I have this gross bulge in by stomach" and then proceeds to purge herself after bingeing. Many bulimics feel depressed and are ashamed of their bodies. Many women report that their feelings about their bodies interfere with sexual enjoyment because they won't allow their partners to look at them closely. These negative thoughts about the body and about themselves lead some women to binge. Unfortunately, the binge eating further reinforces the negative feelings about the body.

THEORIES OF ETIOLOGY

Biological, psychological, and social factors have been hypothesized to play a role in the development of bulimia nervosa. Because of its complex nature, no simple explanations for the etiology of bulimia have been found. Researchers have stressed different causal aspects, but the differences among theories of etiology are more a matter of emphasis rather than the exclusion of other factors. Most theorists acknowledge the interaction of psychological and social factors, and many do not discount possible biological mechanisms. In this section, some of the common etiological models will be discussed.

Feminist Models

Boskind-Lodahl (1976) developed one of the first theories of etiology. On the basis of clinical observations of 36 female clients seen at a university mental health clinic, she hypothesized that an overacceptance of the feminine stereotype was causal in bulimia nervosa. She speculated that the pursuit of thinness reflects perfectionistic strivings to achieve an ideal of feminity through which the bulimic hopes to gain the approval of others and validate her own self-worth. In addition to striving to perfect their physical appearances, these women have a strong need for achievement in other areas. The binge-purge behavior, which begins as a means of dieting, generalizes into a release in the face of concerns about sexuality, dating, and achievement.

Certainly, no theory of etiology of bulimia nervosa can be separated from the backdrop of shifting sociocultural expectations in the socialization of women. Johnson and Connors (1987) identified two major cultural shifts that have emerged concomitantly with the food- and body-related symptoms we see today. The first has been an emphasis on thinness, with documentation over the last two decades of the ideal body type becoming progressively slimmer (Garner, Garfinkel, Schwartz, & Thompson, 1980). Another trend has been the antifat prejudice (Brown & Rothblum, 1989) that has become more pronounced. Against this cultural backdrop that encourages women to achieve like men and still remain feminine, thinness can be understood as a way to have the power, strength, and success of a man and to look beautiful and feminine (Meadow & Weiss, 1992; Striegel-Moore, Silberstein, & Rodin, 1986).

Numerous authors (Meadow & Weiss, 1992; Orbach, 1978; Root, Fallon, & Friedrich, 1986) have emphasized that eating disorders can best be understood within the wider context of the psychology of women and of their relationships to others. Women have been socialized to please other people and not pay attention to their own inner needs. They are socialized to deny their basic hungers and deprive themselves to be pleasing to others and to feel related. Steiner-Adair (1991) stated that women with eating disorders are experts in false relationships. Surrey (1991) noted that for women with eating disorders, pleasing others may become more important than learning to listen to oneself. The chronic dieting and push for slimness are seen as reflecting a critical loss of self. Meadow and Weiss (1992) described this dilemma: to meet their basic needs for love and connectedness, women have to deprive themselves of their more basic life-sustaining drives.

Other authors discussed the issue of power as central to the struggle with food and eating. Brown (1985) presented a feminist analysis of eating disorders and concluded that in a society in which men have maintained the prominent voice and power of decision, the pressure on women to be small reflects an attempt to deprive women of basic nourishment and to literally stop them from taking up space. For American women, to be comfortably larger would be akin to having permission to be a presence in our society.

Family Models

Although much has been written about the wider sociocultural environment of the bulimic, the more narrow cultural environment, her family, has received much less attention. Before the mid-1980s, much of the literature on families of women with eating disorders focused on families of anorexics. Dynamic conceptualizations of anorexia and bulimia often cited disturbances in the early mother-child relationship as predisposing the child to developing eating disorders in adolescence (e.g., Bruch, 1973; Goodstitt, 1983). However, clinical research shows that disturbed patterns in the family remain very much alive and powerful throughout the child's development and clearly involve both mother and father (Humphrey, 1991; Strober & Humphrey, 1987).

Systemic conceptualizations of bulimics' families have likened them to families in which there is a psychosomatic disorder (Minuchin, Rosman, & Baker, 1978) with enmeshment, overprotection, and conflict avoidance as major patterns. Selvini-Palazzoli (1978) emphasized the importance of self-sacrifice, filial loyalty, and preserving appearance in these families. Root et al. (1986) emphasized the family life cycle and patterns surrounding food and eating through the generations. They classified bulimic families into "perfect," "overprotective," and "chaotic" subgroups and developed a specific treatment approach for each.

A number of theorists have asserted that histories of sexual and physical abuse may be prominent in bulimics (Goldfarb, 1987; Oppenheimer, Howells, Palmer, & Chaloner, 1985; Root & Fallon, 1988; Smolak, Levine, & Sullins, 1990). While this suggestion has been supported by research studies that have found incest histories in a significant number of women seeking treatment for eating disorders (Root & Fallon, 1988), other studies have failed to confirm this hypothesis (e.g., Finn, Hartman, Leon, & Lawson, 1986).

Biological Models

Some researchers have hypothesized that biological and physiological factors underlie bulimia. Russell (1979) stated that pathophysiological mechanisms interact with psychological mechanisms in the development of bulimia. His model is based on 30 bulimic women, 24 of whom had a history of anorexia nervosa.

According to Russell (1979), some psychological disorder leads the woman to reject her healthy weight and to opt for a thinner ideal. Urges to eat result in emotional distress, and fear of weight gain leads to purging after overeating. Vomiting or laxative abuse keeps the weight at a reduced level, which may produce many physiological disturbances, most important of which are hypo-thalamic disturbances. Russell hypothesized that the hypothalamus responds to the suboptimal body weight by triggering bouts of overeating.

Pope and Hudson (1985) propose that bulimia is closely related to major affective disorder, which they view as having a biological basis. They state that about 80% of the bulimic patients they have studied have had major affective disorder at some point during their lifetime.

Stress-Coping Models

Hawkins and Clement (1984) have suggested that cultural expectations for weight consciousness are particularly salient for females and that compliance with these expectations causes a constant pursuit of slimness. Binge eating only results when there are also certain pathogenic predispositions. The coaction of these pathogenic predispositions and the psychosocial pressure result in a particular personality pattern. Within this context, Hawkins (1982) stated that the binge is best under-stood using a stress-coping framework. Hawkins suggested that daily stressors precipitate overeating, mediated by the bulimic's negative assessment of the event and a feeling of loss of control. Feeling helpless, the woman turns to food as a coping mechanism to help her feel better.

Mizes (1983) proposed a model of bulimia that draws heavily on the theories of Boskind-Lodahl (1976) and Hawkins and Clement (1984). In this model, irrational beliefs and self-control deficits play central roles. He views the bulimic as generally deficient in self-control coping strategies and sees her relying almost exclusively on bingeing as a coping skill.

Contrary to Hawkins and Clement (1984) and Mizes (1983) who stressed bingeing as a way of coping, Rosen and Leitenberg (1982) placed the emphasis on the vomiting. They suggested that eating causes tremendous anxiety about weight gain and that vomiting reduces the anxiety. Vomiting is seen as having an anxiety-reducing function similar to compulsive rituals such as handwashing and lock checking. This model focuses exclusively on the eating behavior and is restricted to women who vomit following a binge.

We have used previous research and theories (Beck, 1967; Boskind-Lodahl, 1976; Coyne, Aldwin, & Lazarus, 1981; Hawkins & Clement, 1984; Russell, 1979) to develop an empirically based model of bulimia. In this model (Weiss, Katzman, & Wolchik, 1985), two interacting, positive feedback loops contribute to the bulimic cycle. First is the extreme dieting behavior, subsequent binge eating, and purging. The second factor is the bulimic's ineffective use of both food and other ways of coping with stressful situations.

Certain personality characteristics such as poor body image, low self-esteem, high need for approval, high self-expectations, and depression predispose women to develop maladaptive methods of weight control when confronted with societal pressures to conform to a thin ideal. Initially, these women engage in highly restrictive dieting that ultimately results in binge eating and difficulty maintaining a low body weight. Purging starts as a way to counteract the weight gain, but when women view their eating habits as out of their control, depression and anxiety result. These negative mood states lead to more binge eating. The personality deficits mentioned earlier predispose women to cope with interpersonal, work, or academic stressors by binge eating and/or purging. In addition to binge eating, bulimics use many other coping behaviors, which they evaluate as ineffective. The inability to cope successfully exacerbates their low self-esteem, depression, and anxiety, and leads to further binge eating. Although binge eating provides tempo-rary distraction from anxiety, it causes additional tension. Our model suggests that bulimia nervosa occurs with personality and behavioral deficits and ineffective coping strategies, and that treatment programs need to address cognitive, affec-tive, and behavioral problems as well as dysfunctional eating patterns.

Two common themes are apparent in these theoretical models. First, each theory suggests that bulimics differ from controls in more than just their eating habits and that bulimia nervosa develops against a backdrop of personality de-ficits. Second, most theories suggest that the reduction of anxiety becomes an important factor in maintaining the eating behavior.

In summary, bulimia nervosa appears to be multidetermined, with cultural, psychological, and biological factors playing some role in the development and maintenance of this disorder. Clearly, more research is needed before the different models can be integrated into a comprehensive theory.

DISCUSSION QUESTIONS

1 What are some of the problems in defining bulimia nervosa? What implications do these problems have both for conducting research and for comparing findings on bulimia nervosa?

2 How would you characterize the average bulimic? In your opinion, what are some of the reasons for these demographic characteristics?

3 How prevalent is bulimia nervosa? What are some of the problems in assessing prevalence in bulimia nervosa and in binge eating?

4 Describe the eating behavior of a typical bulimic woman. What other eating disturbances occur in bulimic women besides the bingeing and purging? Provide a description of binge-eating behavior (e.g., number of calories con-sumed, how often, where, when, feelings during a binge, etc.).

5 What are the personality characteristics of bulimic women?

6 Why are most bulimic women generally depressed? What are some of the reasons why bulimia and depression usually go hand-in-hand?

7   What are some of the common triggers for binge eating?

8   True or false: Bulimia nervosa is a circumscribed eating disorder and relates primarily to disturbed eating. Discuss why this is or is not so. What implications does this have for treatment?

9   Discuss the relationship of all-or-nothing thinking to bulimia nervosa. What implications does this have for treating bulimics?

10   Describe and discuss the types of thinking that are common to bulimics. How does the thinking affect the binge-purge cycle?

11   What are some of the prevalent theories of etiology for bulimia? What factors play a role in the development and maintenance of this disorder? What implications does this have for research? What implications does this have for treatment?

REFERENCES

Abraham, S. F., & Beumont, P. J. V. (1982). How patients describe bulimia or binge eating. *Psychological Medicine, 12,* 625–635.

Alderdissen, R., Florin, I., & Rost, W. (1981). Psychological characteristics of women with bulimia nervosa (bulimarexia). *Behavioral Analysis and Modification, 4,* 314–317.

American Psychiatric Association. (1980). *Diagnostic and statistical manual of mental disorders* (3rd ed.). Washington, DC: Author.

American Psychiatric Association. (1987). *Diagnostic and statistical manual of mental disorders* (4th ed.). Washington, DC: Author.

Beck, A. T. (1967). *Depression: Causes and treatments.* Philadelphia, PA: University of Pennsylvania Press.

Beumont, P. J. V., George, G. C. W., & Smart, D. E. (1976). "Dieters" and "vomiters and purgers" in anorexia nervosa. *Psychological Medicine, 6,* 617–622.

Boskind-Lodahl, M. (1976). Cinderella's stepsisters: A feminist perspective on anorexia nervosa and bulimia. *Signs' Journal of Women in Culture and Society, 2,* 342–356.

Brown, L. S. (1985). Women, weight, and power: Feminist theoretical and therapeutic issues. *Women and Therapy, 4,* 61–71.

Brown, L. S., & Rothblum, E. D. (Eds.). (1989). *Overcoming fear of fat.* New York: Harrington.

Bruch, H. (1973). *Eating disorders: Obesity, anorexia nervosa and the person within.* New York: Basic Books.

Burns, D. (1980, November). The perfectionist's script for self-defeat. *Psychology Today,* pp. 34–52.

Carlot, D. J., & Camargo, C. A. (1991). Review of bulimia in males. *American Journal of Psychiatry, 148,* 831–843.

Coyne, J. C., Aldwin, C. A., & Lazarus, R. S. (1981). Depression and coping in stressful episodes. *Journal of Abnormal Psychology, 5,* 439–447.

Crowther, J. H., Lingswiler, V. M., & Stephens, M. P. (1983, November). *The typography of binge eating.* Paper presented at the 17th annual convention of the Association for the Advancement of Behavior Therapy, Washington, DC.

Crowther, J. H., Post, G., & Zaynor, L. (1985). The prevalence of bulimia and binge eating in adolescent girls. *International Journal of Eating Disorders, 4,* 29–42.

Dolan, B. (1991). Cross-cultural aspects of anorexia nervosa and bulimia: A review. *International Journal of Eating Disorders, 10,* 67–78.

Dunn, P. K., & Ondercin, P. (1981). Personality variables related to compulsive eating in college women. *Journal of Clinical Psychology, 37,* 43–49.

Fairburn, C. G. (1980). Self-induced vomiting. *Journal of Psychosomatic Research, 24,* 193–197.

Fairburn, C. G., & Cooper, P. J. (1982). Self-induced vomiting and bulimia nervosa: An undetected problem. *British Medical Journal, 284,* 1153–1155.

Finn, S. E., Hartman, M., Leon, G. R., & Lawson, L. (1986). Eating disorder and sexual abuse: Lack of confirmation for a clinical hypothesis. *International Journal of Eating Disorders, 5,* 1051–1060.

Garner, D. M., Garfinkel, P. E., Schwartz, D., & Thompson, M. (1980). Cultural expectations of thinness in women. *Psychological Reports, 47,* 483–491.

Goldfarb, L. (1987). Sexual abuse antecedent to anorexia, bulimia and compulsive eating: Three case reports. *International Journal of Eating Disorders, 6,* 675–680.

Goodstitt, A. (1983). Self-regulatory disturbances in eating disorders. *International Journal of Eating Disorders, 2,* 51–60.

Green, R. S., & Rau, J. H. (1974) Treatment of compulsive eating disturbance with anticonvulsant medications. *American Journal of Psychiatry, 131,* 428–432.

Halmi, K. A., Falk, J. R., & Schwartz, E. (1981). Binge eating and vomiting: A survey of a college population. *Psychological Medicine, 11,* 697–706.

Hatsukami, D., Owen, P., Pyle, R., & Mitchell, J. (1982). Similarities and differences on the MMPI between women with bulimia and women with alcohol or drug abuse problems. *Addictive Behaviors, 7,* 435–439.

Hawkins, R. C., II. (1982). *Binge eating as coping behavior: Theory and treatment implications.* Unpublished manuscript, University of Texas, Austin.

Hawkins, R. C., II, & Clement, P. F. (1984). Binge eating: Measurement problems and a conceptual model. In R. C. Hawkins, II, W. J. Fremouw, & P. F. Clement (Eds.), *The binge-purge syndrome* (pp. 229–251). New York: Springer.

Herzog, D. B. (1982). Bulimia: The secretive syndrome. *Psychosomatics, 23,* 481–483, 487.

Hudson, J. I., Laffer, P. S., & Pope, H. G. (1982). Bulimia related to affective disorder by family history and response to the dexamethasone suppression test. *American Journal of Psychiatry, 139,* 685–687.

Humphrey, L. (1991). Family object relations. In C. Johnson (Ed.), *Psychodynamic treatment of anorexia and bulimia.* New York: Guilford Press.

Johnson, C., & Berndt, D. J. (1983). Preliminary investigation of bulimia and life adjustment. *American Journal of Psychiatry, 140,* 774–777.

Johnson, C., & Connors, M. E. (1987). *The etiology and treatment of bulimia nervosa.* New York: Basic Books.

Johnson, C., & Larson, R. (1982). Bulimia: An analysis of moods and behavior. *Psychosomatic Medicine, 44,* 341–351.

Johnson, C. L., Lewis, C., Love, S., Lewis, L., & Stuckey, M. (1984). Incidence and correlates of bulimic behavior in a female high school population. *Journal of Youth and Adolescence, 13,* 15–26.

Johnson, C. L., Stuckey, M. K., Lewis, L. D., & Schwartz, D. M. (1982). Bulimia: A descriptive study of 316 cases. *International Journal of Eating Disorders, 2,* 3–16.

Katzman, M. A. (1982, November). *Bulimia and binge eating in college women: A comparison of eating patterns and personality characteristics*. Paper presented at the 16th annual convention of the Association for the Advancement of Behavior Therapy, Los Angeles, CA.

Katzman, M., Marcus, I., & Greenberg, A. (1991). Bulimia in female opiate addicts: A developmental cousin and relapse factor. *Journal of Substance Abuse Treatment, 8,* 2.

Katzman, M. A., & Wolchik, S. A. (1983a, April). *Behavioral and emotional antecedents and consequences of binge eating in bulimic and binge eating college women*. Paper presented at the Eastern Psychological Association, Philadelphia, PA.

Katzman, M. A., & Wolchik, S. A. (1984). Bulimia and binge eating in college women: A comparison of personality and behavioral characteristics. *Journal of Consulting and Clinical Psychology, 52,* 423–428.

Katzman, M. A., Wolchik, S. A., & Braver, S. L. (1984). The prevalence of frequent binge eating and bulimia in a nonclinical college sample. *International Journal of Eating Disorders, 3,* 53–62.

Leon, G. R., Carroll, K., Chernyk, B., & Finn, S. (1985). Binge eating and associated habit patterns within college student and identified bulimic populations. *International Journal of Eating Disorders, 4,* 43–47.

Meadow, R., & Weiss, L. (1992). *Women's conflicts about eating and sexuality: The relationship between food and sex*. Binghamton, NY: Haworth Press.

Minuchin, S., Rosman, B. L., & Baker, L. (1978). *Psychosomatic families: Anorexia nervosa in context*. Cambridge, MA: Harvard University Press.

Mitchell, J. E., & Pyle, R. L. (1981). The bulimic syndrome in normal weight individuals: A review. *International Journal of Eating Disorders, 1,* 61–73.

Mitchell, J. E., Pyle, R. L., & Eckert, E. D. (1981). Frequency and duration of binge-eating episodes in patients with bulimia. *American Journal of Psychiatry, 138,* 835–836.

Mizes, J. S. (1983). *Bulimia: A review of its symptomatology and treatment*. Unpublished manuscript, North Dakota State University, Fargo.

Mizes, J. S., & Lohr, J. M. (1983). The treatment of bulimia (binge-eating and self-induced vomiting): A quasiexperimental investigation of the effects of stimulus narrowing, self-reinforcement, and self-control relaxation. *International Journal of Eating Disorders, 2,* 59–63.

Ondercin, P. A. (1979). Compulsive eating in college women. *Journal of College Student Personnel, 20,* 153–157.

Oppenheimer, R., Howells, K., Palmer, R., & Chaloner, P. (1985). Adverse sexual experiences in childhood and clinical eating disorders: A preliminary description. *Journal of Psychiatric Research, 19,* 357–361.

Orbach, S. (1978). *Fat is a feminist issue*. New York: Paddington Press.

Palmer, R. L. (1979). The dietary chaos syndrome: A useful new term? *British Journal of Medical Psychology, 52,* 187–190.

Pope, H. G., & Hudson, J. I. (1985). *New hope for binge eaters*. New York: Harper & Row.

Pope, H. C., Hudson, J. I., Jonas, J. M., & Yurgelun-Todd, D. (1983). Bulimia treated with imipramine: A placebo-controlled, double-blind study. *American Journal of Psychiatry, 140,* 554–558.

Pyle, R. L., Mitchell, J. E., & Eckert, E. D. (1981). Bulimia: A report of 34 cases. *Journal of Clinical Psychiatry, 42,* 60–64.

Pyle, R. L., Mitchell, J. E., Eckert, E. D., Halvorson, P. A., Neuman, P. A., & Goff, G. M. (1983). The incidence of bulimia in college freshman students. *International Journal of Eating Disorders, 2,* 75–85.

Root, M., & Fallon, P. (1988). The incidence of victimization experiences in a bulimic sample. *Journal of Interpersonal Violence, 3,* 161–173.

Root, M. P., Fallon, P., & Friedrich, W. N. (1986). *Bulimia: A systems approach to treatment.* New York: Norton & Co.

Rosen, T. C., & Leitenberg, H. (1982). Bulimia nervosa: Treatment with exposure and response prevention. *Behavior Therapy, 13,* 117–124.

Ross, S. M., Todt, E. H., & Rindflesh, M. A. (1983, April). *Evidence for an anorexic/bulimic MMPI profile.* Paper presented at the annual convention of the Rocky Mountain Psychological Association, Salt Lake City, UT.

Rost, W., Neuhaus, M., & Florin, I. (1982). Bulimia nervosa: Sex role attitude, sex role behavior, and sex role related locus of control in bulimarexic women. *Journal of Psychosomatic Research, 26,* 403–408.

Russell, G. (1979). Bulimia nervosa: An ominous variant of anorexia nervosa. *Psychological Medicine, 9,* 429–448.

Selvini-Palazzoli, M. (1978). *Self-starvation: From individual to family therapy in the treatment of anorexia nervosa.* New York: Jason Aronson.

Smith, J. E., & Krejci, J. (1991). Minorities join the majority: Eating disturbances among Hispanic and Native American youth. *International Journal of Eating Disorders, 10,* 179–186.

Smolak, L., Levine, M., & Sullins, E. (1990). Are child sexual experiences related to eating disordered attitudes and behaviors in a college sample? *International Journal of Eating Disorders, 9,* 167–178.

Stangler, R. S., & Prinz, A. M. (1980). DSM-III: Psychiatric diagnosis in a university population. *American Journal of Psychiatry, 137,* 937–940.

Steiner-Adair, C. (1991). New maps of development, new models of therapy: The psychology of women and the treatment of eating disorders. In C. L. Johnson (Ed.), *Psychodynamic treatment of anorexia nervosa and bulimia* (pp. 225–244). New York: Guilford.

Striegel-Moore, R. H., Silberstein, L. R., & Rodin, J. (1986). Toward an understanding of risk factors of bulimia. *American Psychologist, 41,* 246–263.

Strober, M., & Humphrey, L. (1987). Familial contributions to the etiology and course of anorexia and bulimia. *Journal of Consulting and Clinical Psychology, 55,* 654–659.

Surrey, J. L. (1991). Eating patterns as a reflection of women's development. In J. V. Jordan, A. G. Kaplan, J. B. Miller, I. P. Stiver, & J. L. Surrey (Eds.), *Women's growth in connection: Writings from the Stone Center* (pp. 237–249). New York: Guilford.

Walsh, T., Stewart, J. W., Wright, L., Harrison, W., Roose, S., & Glassman, A. (1982). Treatment of bulimia with monoamine oxidase inhibitors. *American Journal of Psychiatry, 139,* 1629–1630.

Weiss, L., Katzman, M. A., & Wolchik, S. A. (1985). *Treating bulimia: A psychoeducational approach.* New York: Pergamon.

Weiss, L., Katzman, M. A., & Wolchik, S. A. (1986). *You can't have your cake and eat it too: A self-help program for controlling bulimia.* Saratoga, CA: R & E Publishers.

Weiss, S. R., & Ebert, M. H. (1983). Psychological and behavioral characteristics of normal-weight bulimics and normal-weight controls. *Psychomatic Medicine, 45,* 293–303.

Wermuth, B. M., Davis, K. L., Hollister, L. E., & Stunkard, A. J. (1977). Phenytoin treatment of the binge-eating syndrome. *American Journal of Psychiatry, 134,* 1249–1253.

Wooley, O. W., & Wooley, S. C. (1982). The Beverly Hills eating disorder: The mass marketing of anorexia nervosa. *International Journal of Eating Disorders, 1,* 57–69.

Chapter 9

Bulimia Nervosa: Medical Complications

Randy A. Sansone
Lori A. Sansone

A variety of medical complications are associated with eating disorders. Unlike the complications related to low body weight and starvation/malnutrition that are seen in anorexia nervosa, those in bulimia nervosa are usually secondary to binge eating and/or the method of compensation employed following a massive calorie ingestion. It is important to acknowledge that while these complications are discussed in the context of individuals with bulimia nervosa, they may also develop in everyday dieters who are experiencing episodes of overeating and/or employing episodic methods of weight control. Many of these complications have also been reviewed in several excellent overview articles (Russell, 1979; Sansone, 1984; Mitchell, Seim, Colon, & Pomeroy, 1987) that may be of particular interest to the reader.

MEDICAL COMPLICATIONS OF BINGE EATING

Although binge eating has never really been consistently defined (Habermas, 1991; Beglin & Fairburn, 1992), we arbitrarily define a clinical binge as the ingestion of 2,500 calories or more (i.e., $2\frac{1}{2}$ times a normal meal size) during a discrete time period, usually less than 2 hours. Eating binges are typically secretive, involve "forbidden foods" (i.e., off-diet foods such as high-calorie carbohydrates), and are followed by some type of counteractive behavior to compensate for the massive calorie ingestion (e.g., self-induced vomiting).

Significant medical complications due to binge eating are rare. Abdominal fullness, discomfort, and pain may occur with large ingestions of food. Case reports of acute gastric dilation as well as gastric rupture following binge eating are rare (Pyle, Mitchell, & Eckert, 1981). Gastric rupture is extremely dangerous and has a mortality rate of 80% (Harris, 1984). Starvation and/or calorie-deficit states may predispose to this dramatic complication (Harris, 1984). Cases of post-binge-eating pancreatitis (Gavish, Eisenberg, Berry, Kleinman, Witztum, Norman, & Leitersdorf, 1987) may be due to elevated blood lipids, a known cause of pancreatitis.

MEDICAL COMPLICATIONS OF WEIGHT CONTROL EFFORTS

Beyond restricting calories, a variety of weight control efforts may be undertaken by bulimic individuals, as well as others invested in regulating body weight. These may include self-induced vomiting; the use of laxatives, diuretics, and stimulants; and exercise. Each will be reviewed beginning with self-induced vomiting.

Self-Induced Vomiting

In an eating-disordered population, self-induced vomiting is second only to calorie restriction as a method of weight control (Mitchell, Hatsukami, Eckert, & Pyle, 1985). Vomiting may occur spontaneously or be induced by stimulating a gag reflex (i.e., deeply inserting into the throat a finger or other object such as a food utensil or toothbrush) (Russell, 1979). Vomiting is frequently facilitated by gastric distention, which may be achieved by ingesting large volumes of food and/or fluids (i.e., fluid loading). Vomiting may occur several times during as well as at the end of an eating episode. In reviewing the medical concerns associated with vomiting, we will begin with the complications that may occur at the entrance to the upper digestive system and proceed inward (see Figure 9-1).

Dental Erosion   During vomiting, the contact of the acidic gastric juices with the dental enamel causes erosion, a process called *perimylolysis*. The surfaces of the teeth that are most at risk for this complication are those that are exposed to the exiting stomach contents. These are: (1) the occlusal surfaces of the posterior teeth and (2) the posterior surfaces of the upper front teeth (maxillary incisors). The lower front teeth (mandibular incisors) are usually protected by the tongue as it protrudes and are generally unaffected (Stege, Visco-Dangler, & Rye, 1982; see Figure 9-2).

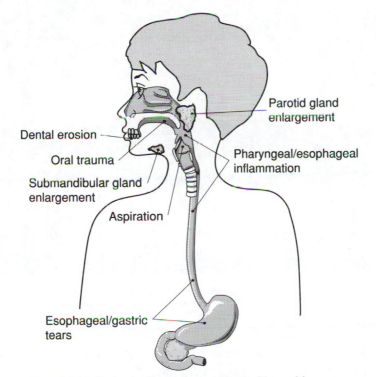

Figure 9-1 Potential medical complications associated with vomiting.

Perimylolysis causes a variety of signs and symptoms. The process initially results in the removal of stains from the teeth as the surface layers of enamel erode. As the dental erosion continues, the crisp sharp lines of the teeth become rounded and smooth (House, Grisius, Bliziotes, & Licht, 1981) (see Figure 9-3). Small gaps may appear between neighboring teeth. The tips of the teeth, where the enamel is the thinnest, may wear rapidly, resulting in shortened crown lengths (Stege et al., 1982). The erosion of enamel can result in the loss of the fillings (amalgams) that they support (see Figure 9-4). As the tooth pulps become exposed, discoloration of the teeth and sensitivity to temperature change (i.e., hot and cold foods) gradually increase (Wolcott, Yager, & Gordon, 1984) (see Figure 9-5).

The rate of perimylolysis probably varies depending on the frequency of vomiting, the hereditary constitution of the teeth, and the dental care/intervention provided. According to one authority, dental erosion will occur in most patients who are vomiting a minimum of three times per week for 4 years (Simmons, Grayden, & Mitchell, 1986). As expected, these complications have a significant cosmetic impact on the patient.

The treatment of dental erosion is primarily preventive as these changes are irreversible. The use of baking soda rinses following vomiting can help neutralize

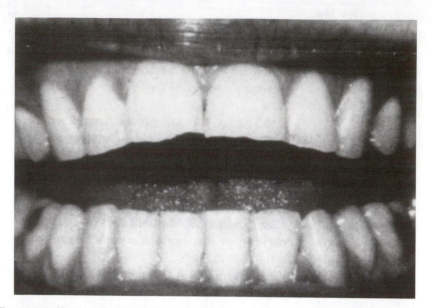

Figure 9-2 Perimylolysis: Eroding upper teeth, intact lower teeth. Reproduced from "Anorexia nervosa: Review including oral and dental manifestations" by P. Stege, L. Visco-Dangler, and L. Rye, 1982, *Journal of the American Dental Association, 104,* p. 651. Copyright 1982 by American Dental Association Publishers. Reprinted by permission.

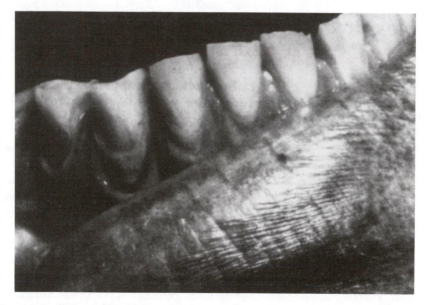

Figure 9-3 Perimylolysis: Scalloping, erosion of tips of teeth with small gaps between teeth. Reproduced from "Anorexia nervosa: Review including oral and dental manifestations" by P. Stege, L. Visco-Dangler, and L. Rye, 1982, *Journal of the American Dental Association, 104,* p. 651. Copyright 1982 by American Dental Association Publishers. Reprinted by permission.

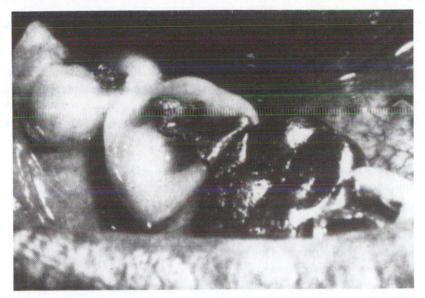

Figure 9-4 Perimylolysis: Erosion of teeth supporting fillings. Reproduced from "Anorexia nervosa: Review including oral and dental manifestations" by P. Stege, L. Visco-Dangler, and L. Rye, 1982, *Journal of the American Dental Association, 104,* p. 650. Copyright 1982 by American Dental Association Publishers. Reprinted by permission.

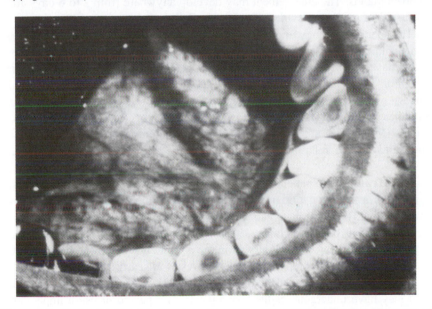

Figure 9-5 Perimylolysis: Advanced erosion with exposed dental pulps. Reproduced from "Anorexia nervosa: Review including oral and dental manifestations" by P. Stege, L. Visco-Dangler, and L. Rye, 1982, *Journal of the American Dental Association, 104,* p. 650. Copyright 1982 by American Dental Association Publishers. Reprinted by permission.

the acid and reduce erosion (Mitchell et al., 1987). Routine fluoride applications by the dentist are recommended as well as the regular use of toothpastes that contain fluoride (Hasler, 1982; Wolcott et al., 1984). Perhaps surprisingly, there is some controversy about brushing the teeth after vomiting. Some investigators believe brushing in the presence of the acid residue etches the surfaces of the teeth (Mitchell et al., 1987). In our experience, many patients have required extensive intervention with crown work to replace teeth that have been destroyed by perimylolysis.

Salivary Gland Enlargement   Salivary gland enlargement is a medical complication in some, but not all, vomiters. Jacobs and Schneider (1985) report that on physical examination, only 8% of bulimic patients in their study population demonstrated glandular enlargement. In our experience, the presence of salivary gland enlargement indicates frequent bouts of vomiting by the patient, usually several times per day. However, we have seen many patients who vomit at this frequency and never develop this finding.

Both the parotid and/or submandibular glands are involved (see Figures 9-1 and 9-6). They are usually smooth to the touch and may or may not be tender (Tylenda, Roberts, Elin, Li, & Altemus, 1991). In our experience, the involvement is usually bilateral. There are no local skin or temperature changes at or around the involved glands. The enlargement may develop anywhere from 2 to 6 days after an episode of purging (Levin, Falko, Dixon, Gallup, & Saunders, 1980).

The specific etiology and medical significance of these enlarged glands remains unknown (Riad, Barton, Wilson, Freeman, & Maran, 1991). Microscopic studies have shown some focal fibrosis of the glandular tissue along with minimal but chronic inflammation (Ahola, 1982). No medical sequelae from chronic salivary gland enlargement have been reported. There is no known treatment. With the cessation of vomiting, the glands recede, a process that may take several months (Mitchell et al., 1987). For recovering patients who originally demonstrated this finding, relapse may be signaled by the reappearance of these glands.

Oral Trauma   In patients who require a gag reflex to stimulate vomiting, the insertion of a finger or foreign object deep into the mouth and throat can cause local trauma. These traumata can include lacerations and bleeding (e.g., hematomas) as well as bruising (Harris, 1983). If a finger or hand is used to induce the gag reflex, either may suffer injury from the abrupt and forceful impact with the upper front teeth. When repetitive, this may result in scarring, particularly in the area of the knuckles (Mitchell et al., 1987). In addition, some areas of skin on the hand may have undergone callus formation from repeated pressure impact and trauma (Crisp, 1967; Russell, 1979; see Figure 9-7). Treatment for these injuries is typically symptomatic (i.e., treatment that focuses on alleviating symptoms rather than on the underlying cause).

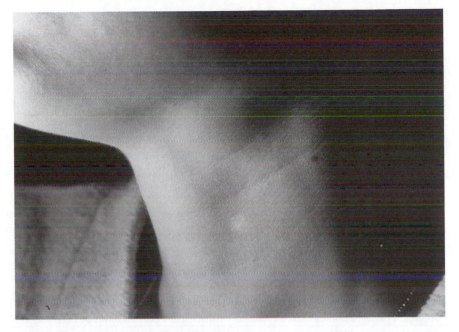

Figure 9-6 Submandibular gland enlargement.

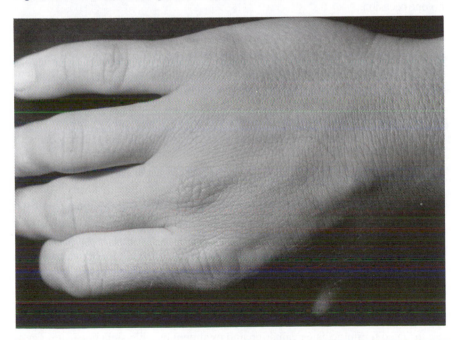

Figure 9-7 Callused, scarred area on hand due to impact trauma from teeth during self-induced vomiting.

Pharyngeal/Esophageal Inflammation   The contact of the acidic gastric contents with the esophagus and pharynx results in irritation (Cuellar & Van Thiel, 1986). The epithelium (surface tissue) in these two areas has no protective features for accommodating the passage of digestive enzymes. The result is at minimum a mild irritation. Patients with this complication may report heartburn and/or sore throats. The general treatment for pharyngeal/esophageal irritation is symptomatic (e.g., antacids, gargles, throat lozenges).

Two cases of adenocarcinoma of the esophagus in bulimic women have been reported, presumably related to acquired epithelial changes in the esophagus from the repeated reflux of gastric digestive juices (Mullai, Sivarajan, & Shiomoto, 1991). This relationship has been theorized about in the past and warrants further investigation.

Aspiration   Aspiration, the entry of digestive system contents into the trachea (see Figure 9-1), is a rare complication in bulimic individuals. However, it can potentially occur with any episode of vomiting regardless of the cause (Harris, 1983). The result of this unusual physiologic circumstance is an inflammation of the lungs (i.e., chemical pneumonitis) induced by the pH and particulate matter of the inhaled contents. The pneumonitis can be extremely difficult to treat and requires consultation with and management by a pulmonary specialist. We have only seen this complication on one occasion.

Esophageal/Gastric Tears   During vomiting, the upper digestive system undergoes significant stress and strain. These abrupt and intense pressure changes can result in superficial tears of the mucosal lining of the digestive tract, particularly in the esophagus. Indeed, a significant minority of bulimic patients report the vomiting of blood on at least one occasion (Cuellar & Van Theil, 1986). These superficial tears appear to be self-healing, although a medical evaluation is indicated to eliminate other causes of upper digestive system bleeding in patients with eating disorders (see below).

Three specific syndromes have been reported as acute complications of self-induced vomiting due to tears or perforations in the upper digestive tract. Mallory-Weiss syndrome is a mucosal tear that occurs specifically at the juncture of the esophagus and stomach. It has been associated with the use of Syrup of Ipecac (Tandberg, Liechty, & Fishbein, 1981). The second syndrome, Boerhaave's syndrome, is the rupture of the esophagus, muscular layer and all. It is extremely rare, but has been reported in eating-disordered patients (Mitchell et al., 1987); the mortality rate is 25% (Larsen, Skov Jensen, & Axelsen, 1983). The third syndrome is the rupture of the stomach (Breslow, Yates, & Shisslak, 1986). The latter two complications are typically accompanied by the abrupt onset of pain, thus signaling the need for immediate evaluation and treatment by a physician in an emergency setting.

Syrup of Ipecac   Syrup of Ipecac is a bottled syrup that is commercially available in most drugstores. It is used to emergently induce vomiting following the ingestion of dangerous substances, particularly certain types of drugs. Therefore, Ipecac is commonly encountered in the offices of school nurses, in the supplies of emergency squad personnel, in hospital emergency rooms, and in households with small children. The emetic effects are pronounced and may continue well after the stomach is emptied (i.e., dry heaves).

Syrup of Ipecac is available, without prescription, in bottles containing one fluid ounce. The active emetic ingredient, emetine, has a relatively long half-life, indicating that its elimination from the body is somewhat slow. For example, in mammal studies, 35% of the drug was still present after 35 days (Tandberg et al., 1981). With repeated use, emetine accumulates and may become toxic to the heart. The explicit mechanism underlying this toxicity is unknown. The associated clinical findings are an accelerated heart rate, shortness of breath, dizziness, and chest pain (Friedman, 1984). These signs and symptoms are accompanied by abnormalities on the electrocardiogram (EKG), including life-threatening arrhythmias. The precise amount of Syrup of Ipecac that will result in death is unknown, although there is a case report of a fatal cardiac arrest following the ingestion of 3 to 4 bottles per day for 3 months (i.e., an accumulated dose of 1.25 grams of emetine) (Adler, Walinsky, Krall, & Cho, 1980).

A second complication of repetitive Syrup of Ipecac ingestion is neuromuscular dysfunction, which is characterized by weakness, aching, tenderness, and stiffness of the skeletal muscles. There may also be sensory disturbances (Palmer & Guay, 1985). Again, this is a rare phenomenon we have seen in only one patient. Symptoms recede with the discontinuation of Ipecac.

While drug screens can detect the presence of Syrup of Ipecac in the body, no methods for determining the exact amount that is present in serum (i.e., there are no available serum levels) or tissues are currently available. There is no specific treatment for emetine toxicity other than supportive measures. As is apparent, the use of this substance for weight control should be absolutely discouraged.

Metabolic Complications   Vomiting can result in a variety of metabolic complications. The loss of hydrogen chloride and potassium in the vomitus can lead to hypochloremia (i.e., low serum chloride), elevated bicarbonate levels (i.e., metabolic alkalosis), and hypokalemia (i.e., low serum potassium; Oster, 1987). Bulimic patients may also experience hypomagnesemia (i.e., low serum magnesium; Hall, Hoffman, Beresford, Wooley, Tice, & Hall, 1988), a metabolic situation that can complicate the treatment of hypokalemia.

Hypokalemia is typically the metabolic issue of primary urgency. The signs, symptoms, and treatment of hypokalemia are discussed under the section Diuretics because diuretics are more efficient than vomiting and laxatives in eliminating potassium from the body. When evaluating and resolving metabolic complications, consultation with a physician is indicated.

Elevated serum amylase levels without associated clinical symptoms have been reported in bulimic patients (Blinder & Hagman, 1986; Walsh, Wong, Pesce, Hadigan, & Bodourian, 1990). Amylase is an enzyme found in salivary gland fluid and digestive (pancreatic) juices. While the cause of the elevation remains unknown, it seems to correlate with the frequency of binging/purging (Gwirtsman, Kaye, George, Carosella, Greene, & Jimerson, 1989), but not necessarily with parotid gland enlargement. There is no specific treatment for elevated serum amylase levels.

Elevated amylase levels in bulimic patients may be accompanied by abdominal pain and vomiting secondary to pancreatitis (i.e., pancreatic inflammation; Gavish et al., 1987). As mentioned previously, pancreatitis may be precipitated by high serum levels of lipids following binge eating and can lead to death. When pancreatitis is present, the treatment is supportive and directed toward resolving the underlying cause.

Laxatives

Eating-disordered patients may resort to using laxatives as an adjunct to weight control. Mitchell et al. (1985) reported that while 60% of bulimic individuals used laxatives at some time for weight control, only 20% did so on a daily basis. Although a variety of laxative types are available (e.g., stimulant, osmotic, lubricant, bulk), patients with eating disorders almost exclusively use stimulant laxatives (Oster, Materson, & Rogers, 1980). These include a variety of over-the-counter products such as Correctol, Ex-Lax, Evacugen, and others that have various irritating ingredients (see Table 9-1). The abused amounts vary widely, but laxative abusers in an eating-disordered population may typically use anywhere from 5 to 30 units at a time. We have had three patients who reported using 150 Ex-Lax tablets per day. The medical complications of laxatives may be divided into acute-use digestive system complications versus chronic-use digestive system complications.

Acute-Use Digestive System Complications   While hardly life-threatening, the acute use/abuse of laxatives, particularly large laxative loads, tends to cause a variety of very uncomfortable nonspecific abdominal complaints. These include constipation, diarrhea, abdominal cramping and/or pain, nausea and vomiting, distension, and bloating (Oster et al., 1980). These are temporary symptoms that resolve with the discontinuation of the laxatives.

Chronic-Use Digestive System Complications   Chronic laxative use/abuse has been associated with a variety of medical complications. Perhaps the most common is laxative dependence, which is the need to continue to use laxatives to obtain the same cathartic effect. Chronic use can also result in the poor absorption of certain nutrients with the loss of fat in the stool (steatorrhea) and the loss of protein (protein-losing enteropathy) (Mitchell & Boutacoff, 1986). The treatment of these conditions includes laxative weaning (see below).

Table 9.1 Over-the-Counter Irritant Laxatives

Laxative brand	Active ingredient(s)	mg/unit
Carter's Little Pills Laxative	Bisacodyl	5.0 mg
Correctol	Yellow phenolphthalein	65.0 mg
	Docusate sodium	100.0 mg
Doxidan	Yellow phenolphthalein	65.0 mg
	Docusate sodium	60.0 mg
Dulcolax Laxative Suppositories	Bisacodyl	10.0 mg
Dulcolax Tablets	Bisacodyl	5.0 mg
Ex-Lax Chocolate Laxative	Yellow phenolphthalein	90.0 mg
Ex-Lax Laxative Pills	Yellow phenolphthalein	90.0 mg
Feen-a-mint Laxative Gum	Yellow phenolphthalein	97.2 mg
Feen-a-mint Laxative Plus Softener	Yellow phenolphthalein	65.0 mg
	Docusate sodium	100.0 mg
Modan	Phenolphthalein	130.0 mg
Nature's Remedy	Cascara sagrada	150.0 mg
Senokot Tablets	Sennocides	8.6 mg

Chronic laxative use/abuse may also result in cathartic colon, a serious medical condition in which the colon no longer properly functions. Cathartic colon is physiologically characterized by thinning of the mucosal and muscular layers of the colon, dilation of the colon, loss of colonic propulsion, and mucosal inflammation (Oster et al., 1980). The diagnosis is confirmed by barium enema examination (Cuellar & Van Theil, 1986). The treatment is the weaning of laxatives (see below). However, reversibility may be limited in some cases and the removal of the colon may be indicated. Fortunately, this is an uncommon complication, perhaps because of the age range of the patients who are currently suffering from eating disorders (i.e., they may not have had sufficient exposure time for cathartic colon to develop).

Another lower digestive system complication is melanosis coli, a brownish-black discoloration of the mucosal membranes of the lower colon and rectum that is due to the abuse of anthracene laxatives (i.e., laxatives that contain senna, cascara, and danthron) (Oster et al., 1980). This dramatic pigmentation change develops over a 4 to 12-month period of regular laxative use; likewise, it disappears over a 4 to 12-month period after the discontinuation of the laxative. The cause of the pigmentation is unknown. Melanosis coli is diagnosed by sigmoidoscopy, which enables the visualization of the mucosal discoloration (see Figure 9-8) and thus reveals the abuse of laxatives of this type (Cuellar & Van Theil, 1986). This complication is medically benign as there is no structural damage or impairment that occurs from it.

Fixed Drug Eruption   An interesting, but rare, complication of laxative usage is a *fixed drug eruption* (Sarner, 1976). This complication occurs when physiologically sensitive individuals take laxatives that contain phenolphthalein.

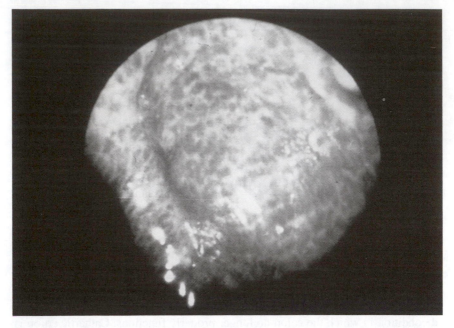

Figure 9-8   Melanosis coli: Mottled discoloration of rectal mucosa as seen through sigmoidoscope. Reprinted by permission.

The exposure results in a generalized or localized skin rash that recurs at the same site with reexposure to phenolphthalein (hence, the term *fixed*). A variety of skin disturbances have been described during the initial inflammatory phase of the rash (Fitzpatrick, Polano, & Suurmond, 1983). As the reaction subsides, there is a residual area of brownish-gray hyperpigmentation. The treatment of the rash is symptomatic. The laxative should be discontinued and the patient advised to avoid phenolphthalein-containing products in the future.

Metabolic Complications   Laxative abuse may cause a variety of metabolic abnormalities (e.g., hypokalemia, hypocalcemia, hyperchloremia, metabolic acidosis) (Oster, 1987). In conjunction with these metabolic abnormalities, the hypokalemia, if longstanding, may result in damage to the kidneys (i.e., hypokalemic nephropathy) (Oster et al., 1980). Hypokalemic nephropathy results in the inability of the kidneys to concentrate urine and is accompanied by thirst and frequent urination. First described by Schwartz and Relman (1953), this condition may be alleviated by potassium replacement (Wright & Du Val, 1987). However, advanced damage may require kidney dialysis or transplantation. The symptoms and treatment of hypokalemia are discussed under the section entitled Diuretics. As noted previously, potential electrolyte abnormalities need to be monitored by a physician and, when present, treated as indicated.

As a final metabolic complication, the abuse of laxatives can result in the formation of kidney stones that contain ammonium urate. This is an unusual composition for kidney stones and is highly suggestive of laxative abuse (Dick, Lingeman, & Preminger, 1990).

Treatment of Uncomplicated Laxative Abuse   The presence of laxatives can be detected by testing stool (Wright & Du Val, 1987) or urine (de Wolff, de Haas, & Verweij, 1981; Oster, 1987). If the history, stool/urine testing, and/or symptoms suggest abuse, laxative weaning is undertaken. The abrupt cessation of laxatives following chronic use is discouraged as it can result in severe constipation. Prior to weaning, patients should be counseled that they may experience fluid retention resulting in weight gain (Mitchell et al., 1987). This is due to the chronic dehydration induced by the laxatives and the body's ongoing adaptive response of retaining fluid. For weaning, we recommend: (1) the gradual reduction of the laxatives over several weeks, (2) the concurrent intake of sufficient fluids, and (3) the gradual increase of fiber in the diet (consultation with a dietitian may be beneficial). If a laxative is required in the future, we suggest an osmotic (e.g., Milk of Magnesia) or bulk (e.g., Perdiem, Metamucil) type.

Diuretics

Diuretics, also known as water pills, can be obtained by prescription as well as over the counter (see Table 9-2). They may contain a variety of ingredients and function to eliminate water from the body. The dehydration that results from the use of diuretics may be confused by the patient with the perception of weight loss.

Diuretics tend to be more popular with adult patients. Indeed, we have encountered a small group of adult patients who appear to be addicted to diuretics.

Table 9-2   Over-the-Counter Diuretics

Diuretic brand	Active ingredients
Aqua Ban Diuretic Water Pill	Ammonium chloride Caffeine (100 mg)
Diūrex Long-Acting Water Capsules	Acetaminophen Potassium salicylate Extract of Bucher Uva Ursi
Diūrex Water Pills	Potassium salicylate Caffeine Extract Uva Ursi Salicylamide Methylene blue Extract of Bucher Junniper P. E.

They demonstrate dysmorphophobic-like features (i.e., the distortion or mis-perception of body/appearance) that they feel are corrected by the abuse of diuretics. In our experience, these individuals tend to be very compulsive and highly resistant to treatment.

Dehydration   The most predominant feature of diuretic use/abuse is de-hydration. This condition is characterized by thirst, dry mucous membranes, rapid heart beat, fatigue, poor skin turgor, and dizziness. Pronounced cognitive changes may also occur, including concentration difficulties, confusion, and at its worst, delirium. If the dehydration is significant, kidney damage can occur (i.e., acute tubular necrosis).

Metabolic Complications   The most frequently encountered electrolyte dis-turbance with diuretic abuse is hypokalemia. Early symptoms include fatigue, lassitude, and weakness (Oster, 1987). On occasion, the patient may develop pa-resthesias, tetany, and seizures, particularly when other metabolic disturbances are present (metabolic alkalosis). Severe hypokalemia, particularly in association with hypomagnesemia, can precipitate heart arrhythmias and lead to death (Reyes & Leary, 1984). As mentioned previously, hypokalemia from the use of laxatives and vomiting can result in similar complications.

Treatment of Diuretic Abuse   Diuretic abuse can be diagnosed by the pa-tient's self-disclosure, the presence of suspicious symptoms, and/or urine testing. The treatment includes fluid replacement, by intravenous means if necessary. Electrolytes, especially the serum potassium, should be monitored by a physician and replaced, when indicated, either orally or intravenously. It should be noted that the serum potassium level is not always an adequate indication of the total body stores of potassium, which may be depleted despite a low but unremarkable laboratory result. High-risk patients may require periodic laboratory evaluation as well as potassium and fluid replacement (oral or intravenous), particularly when suspicious symptoms occur.

Stimulants

Stimulants for weight control tend to fall into several categories: (1) over-the-counter products, (2) prescription stimulants, and (3) caffeine. Drugs in the first two categories stimulate the body's metabolism and/or suppress appetite, resulting in weight loss (Williams, 1990). Caffeine provides stimulation; however, its efficacy regarding weight loss is in question. Each category will be reviewed separately.

Over-the-Counter Weight Loss Products   A variety of over-the-counter weight loss products are available to consumers (see Table 9-3). Until recently, the majority of these products contained either caffeine and/or phenylpropanolamine.

Table 9-3   Over-the-Counter Weight-Loss Pills

Diet pill brand	Active ingredients	mg/unit
Acutrim Late Day Strength	Phenylpropanolamine HCl	75 mg
Acutrim 16 Hour Steady Control	Phenylpropanolamine HCl	75 mg
Acutrim II Maximum Strength	Phenylpropanolamine HCl	75 mg
Maximum Strength Appedrine	Phenylpropanolamine HCl	25 mg
Maximum Strength Dexatrim	Phenylpropanolamine HCl	75 mg
Maximum Strength Permathene-12	Phenylpropanolamine HCl	75 mg

Due to government intervention, these products no longer contain caffeine and several are now marketed as caffeine-free. The current active ingredient is phenylpropanolamine.

Phenylpropanolamine is a nonamphetamine stimulant that suppresses appetite (Altschuler, Conte, Sebok, Marlin, & Winick, 1982; Lasagna, 1988). It is readily absorbed from the gastrointestinal tract, reaches peak serum levels in 1 to 2 hours, and has a half-life of 3 to 4 hours. The usual amounts in over-the-counter preparations are 25 to 75 mg per unit.

Phenylpropanolamine can cause typical stimulatory effects such as nervousness, restlessness, headache, insomnia, palpitations, increased heart rate, and elevation in blood pressure (Williams, 1990). In addition, psychotic reactions including hallucinations (Schaffer & Pauli, 1980) as well as seizures have been reported (Bernstein & Diskant, 1982; Howrie & Wolfson, 1983). Finally, phenylpropanolamine has been reported to cause cerebral hemorrhage and death (Forman, Levin, Stewart, Patel, & Feinstein, 1989).

Prescription stimulants   A variety of amphetamine and nonamphetamine products are available by prescription for weight control (see Table 9-4). Despite their long history of popularity, the use of prescription stimulants has only resulted in a 1/2 pound per week greater weight loss when compared to placebo (Shaban & Galizia, 1989). Compared to the amphetamine prescription stimulants, the nonamphetamines are associated with a lower potential for abuse and dependence. However, concerns about the risk-benefit ratio of these drugs is significant. Therefore, the prescribing of amphetamines for weight control has been controversial and is now regulated by each state.

As expected, prescription stimulants can cause overstimulation. They may also cause dizziness, hypervigilence, euphoria, fatigue, insomnia, motor tics, dry mouth, nausea, and abdominal discomfort. Cardiac effects can include hypertension, palpitations, and arrhythmias (Shaban & Galizia, 1989). Initial cognitive vigilance and increased ideation may be followed by poor concentration and a poverty of ideation. Headache, tremor, and confusion may occur. Finally, psychosis with grandiose and paranoid features can occur with use (Renner, 1987).

Table 9-4   Prescription Stimulants

Trade name	Generic name	Schedule	Amphetamine
Biphetamine	Dextroamphetamine	II	+
Desoxyn	Methamphetamine	II	+
Didrex	Benzphetamine	III	−
Fastin/Ionamin	Phentermine	IV	−
Plegine/Trimstat	Phendimetrazine	III	−
Pondimin	Fenfluramine	IV	−
Preludin	Phenmetrazine	II	−
Sanorex/Mazanor	Mazindol	IV	−
Tepanil/Tenuate	Diethylpropion	IV	−

Note: Schedule refers to the Federal Controlled Substances Act of 1970, which places drugs into categories. Schedule II drugs have a high likelihood of abuse, whereas schedule IV drugs have much less risk.

Source: Adapted from Shaban and Galizia (1989) and the *American Hospital Formulary Service Drug Information 92* (American Society of Hospital Pharmacists, Inc., 1992).

Amphetamine discontinuation may precipitate a withdrawal syndrome that is characterized by fatigue and somnolence (the "amphetamine crash"). In healthy individuals, amphetamine withdrawal is not a medical threat.

Caffeine   Caffeine is a stimulant that is commonly abused by eating-disordered patients, most often in the form of diet beverages, coffee, and/or tea (Sours, 1983). Carbonated diet beverages are particularly attractive to the dieter because of the stimulant effects, abdominal fullness created by the carbonation, sweet taste, and absence of significant calories.

Caffeine has a half-life in the body of about 4 hours. It is readily absorbed by the gastrointestinal tract and peak serum levels occur 30 to 60 minutes after ingestion. Perhaps surprisingly, caffeine can be lethal in doses of 3 to 10 grams (Wrenn & Oscher, 1989).

We routinely take caffeine histories on all of our patients using the following estimates (Goldfrank, Lewin, Melinek, Weisman, & Bluestone, 1981):

Substance	Milligrams of caffeine/serving
Cocoa	50
Coffee	100–150
Cola	45
Tea	100–150

Although many individuals are sensitive to caffeine in doses as low as 250 mg per day, most experience effects at doses of 600 mg or more per day (Pilette, 1983).

Caffeine can cause restlessness, nervousness, excitement, insomnia, flushing, urination, stomach irritation, muscle twitches, rambling thoughts/speech, heart arrhythmias, agitation, and depression (Benowitz,.1990). With abrupt cessation of routine doses, users may experience a caffeine withdrawal headache (van Dusseldorp & Katan, 1990) that usually develops 18 hours after the last dose. The headache begins with a sensation of head fullness and progresses to a diffuse throbbing headache (Greden, Victor, Fontaine, & Lubetsky, 1980). Caffeine withdrawal may also be accompanied by fatigue, irritability, anxiety, muscle tension, and concentration problems (Smith, 1987). Affected individuals typically report regular ingestions of 500 mg or more of caffeine per day.

Recommendations Regarding Stimulant Use   We routinely discourage the use of all over-the-counter and prescription stimulants whether or not abuse is occurring. The risks hardly justify the benefits in patients with eating disorders. We may or may not recommend the absolute discontinuation of caffeine use. This is usually determined by the patient's history as well as any predisposition to caffeine abuse. For example, we may recommend eliminating all caffeine use in chronic abusers with obvious signs of caffeinism. However, for mild users, we may encourage moderation to amounts less than 250 mg per day. Weaning of caffeine may reduce the possibility of the withdrawal headache, but in reality, the exact intake amounts can be difficult to determine, making symptom-free withdrawal difficult to guarantee.

Exercise

At times, bulimic individuals may use strenuous exercise to compensate for extensive calorie ingestions. This level of exercise can have effects both on menstruation and the musculoskeletal system. Regarding menstruation, intensive exercise may result in amenorrhea (i.e., the absence of menstrual periods), oligomenorrhea (i.e., fewer menstrual periods than normal), or even menorrhagia (i.e., heavier menstrual flow than normal). Amenorrhea is related to a variety of factors including exercise intensity, type and duration of exercise, subnormal body weight, physical and emotional stress, nutritional factors, age, and body composition (Agostini, 1988). A secondary complication of amenorrhea is osteoporosis, or diminished bone mass, due to low estrogen levels. Indeed, female athletes demonstrate decreased estrogen levels as well as a decreased bone mineral density (Drinkwater, Nilson, Chestnut, Bremner, Shainholtz, & Southworth, 1984).

Overexercise may cause a variety of musculoskeletal problems. These may include muscular soreness and cramping, overuse injuries (particularly to the knee), and/or microscopic muscular tears. Another musculoskeletal problem in female athletes is patellofemoral pain (i.e., pain located beneath the kneecap) that is due to the misalignment of the kneecap in predisposed individuals. A final problem is stress fractures, which are minute fractures in bone that have been weakened by long-term microtrauma (Agostini, 1988). These usually occur during increased performance demands placed upon weight-bearing bones, such as a runner suddenly increasing mileage (Mercier, 1991). Estrogen deficiency may be an underlying risk factor for stress fractures (Olson, 1989; De Souza & Metzger, 1991).

Treatment for menstrual dysfunction may include decreasing exercise, increasing body weight, and/or undergoing estrogen replacement therapy. Calcium supplementation will help prevent osteoporosis (Olson, 1989). Musculoskeletal injuries are treated with rest, reduction of exercise, and anti-inflammatory medication.

CLOSING REMARKS

This chapter has provided an organized review of the many potential medical complications encountered in patients with bulimia nervosa. As is evident, all patients with eating disorders need to be medically evaluated (i.e., intervention with these patients needs to be undertaken in consultation with a physician). Treatment of medical complications facilitates the therapist's psychological access to the patient as well as good health, enabling the rigorous psychological treatments that will promote recovery.

DISCUSSION QUESTIONS

1 What is the clinical definition of a binge?
2 Describe five clinical features of perimylolysis or dental erosion.
3 Describe three clinical features of salivary gland enlargement, including the identification of which glands are involved.
4 What is the medical danger of using Syrup of Ipecac to induce vomiting?
5 What is laxative dependence?
6 Describe three features of cathartic colon.
7 What is a fixed drug eruption?
8 What is the most significant medical danger of diuretics (i.e., water pills)?
9 What is the active ingredient in the over-the-counter diet pills?
10 A patient reports the following history: "I drink two cups of coffee per day, six colas, and sometimes a glass of tea. I stay away from cocoa because of the calories." What amount of caffeine per day is this patient ingesting? Is this amount likely to cause symptoms?

REFERENCES

Adler, A. G., Walinsky, P., Krall, R. A., & Cho, S. Y. (1980). Death resulting from ipecac syrup poisoning. *Journal of the American Medical Association, 243,* 1927–1928.

Agostini, R. (1988). The athletic woman. In M. Mellion (Ed.), *Office management of sports injuries and athletic problems* (pp. 76–88). Philadelphia: Haney & Belfus.

Ahola, S. J. (1982). Unexplained parotid enlargement: A clue to occult bulimia. *Connecticut Medicine, 46,* 185–186.

Altschuler, S., Conte, A., Sebok, M., Marlin, R. L., & Winick, C. (1982). Three controlled trials of weight loss with phenylpropanolamine. *International Journal of Obesity, 6,* 549–556.

American Society of Hospital Pharmacists, Inc. (1992). *American hospital formulary service drug information 92* (pp. 1297–1313). Bethesda: Author.

Beglin, S. J., & Fairburn, C. G. (1992). What is meant by the term "binge"? *American Journal of Psychiatry, 149,* 123–124.

Benowitz, N. L. (1990). Clinical pharmacology of caffeine. *Annual Review of Medicine, 41,* 277–288.

Bernstein, E., & Diskant, B. M. (1982). Phenylpropanolamine: A potentially hazardous drug. *Annals of Emergency Medicine, 11,* 311–315.

Blinder, B. J., & Hagman, J. (1986). Serum salivary isoamylase levels in patients with anorexia nervosa, bulimia, or bulimia nervosa. *Hillside Journal of Clinical Psychiatry, 8,* 152–163.

Breslow, M., Yates, A., & Shisslak, C. (1986). Spontaneous rupture of the stomach: A complication of bulimia. *International Journal of Eating Disorders, 5,* 137–142.

Crisp, A. H. (1967). Clinical features in anorexia nervosa. *Hospital Medicine, 1,* 713.

Cuellar, R. E., & Van Thiel, D. H. (1986). Gastrointestinal consequences of the eating disorders: Anorexia nervosa and bulimia. *American Journal of Gastroenterology, 81,* 1113–1124.

De Souza, M. J., & Metzger, D. A. (1991). Reproductive dysfunction in amenorrheic athletes and anorexic patients: A review. *Medicine and Science in Sports and Exercise, 23,* 995–1007.

de Wolff, F. A., de Haas, E. J., & Verweij, M. (1981). A screening method for establishing laxative abuse. *Clinical Chemistry, 27,* 914–917.

Dick, W. H., Lingeman, J. E., & Preminger, G. M. (1990). Laxative abuse as a cause for ammonium urate renal calculi. *Journal of Urology, 143,* 244–247.

Drinkwater, B. L., Nilson, K., Chestnut, C. H., Bremner, W. J., Shainholtz, S., & Southworth, M. B. (1984). Bone mineral content of amenorrheic and eumenorrheic athletes. *New England Journal of Medicine, 311,* 277–281.

Fitzpatrick, T. B., Polano, M. K., & Suurmond, D. (1983). *Color atlas and synopsis of clinical dermatology.* New York: McGraw-Hill.

Forman, H. P., Levin, S., Stewart, B., Patel, M., & Feinstein, S. (1989). Cerebral vasculitis and hemorrhage in an adolescent taking diet pills containing phenylpropanolamine: Case report and review of the literature. *Pediatrics, 83,* 737–741.

Friedman, E. J. (1984). Death from ipecac intoxication in a patient with anorexia nervosa. *American Journal of Psychiatry, 141,* 702–703.

Gavish, D., Eisenberg, S., Berry, E. M., Kleinman, Y., Witztum, E., Norman, J., & Leitersdorf, E. (1987). Bulimia. An underlying behavioral disorder in hyperlipidemic pancreatitis: A prospective multidisciplinary approach. *Archives of Internal Medicine, 147,* 705–708.

Goldfrank, L., Lewin, N., Melinek, M., Weisman, R. S., & Bluestone, H. (1981). Caffeine. *Hospital Physician, 17,* 42–59.

Greden, J. F., Victor, B. S., Fontaine, P., & Lubetsky, M. (1980). Caffeine-withdrawal headache: A clinical profile. *Psychosomatics, 21,* 411–418.

Gwirtsman, H. E., Kaye, W. H., George, D. T., Carosella, N. W., Greene, R. C., & Jimerson, D. C. (1989). Hyperamylasemia and its relationship to binge-purge episodes: Development of a clinically relevant laboratory test. *Journal of Clinical Psychiatry, 50,* 196–204.

Habermas, T. (1991). Meaning of the term "bulimia" [Letter to the editor]. *American Journal of Psychiatry, 148,* 1274.

Hall, R. C., Hoffman, R. S., Beresford, T. P., Wooley, B., Tice, L., & Hall, A. K. (1988). Refractory hypokalemia secondary to hypomagnesemia in eating-disorder patients. *Psychosomatics, 29,* 435–438.

Harris, R. T. (1983). Bulimarexia and related serious eating disorders with medical complications. *Annals of Internal Medicine, 99,* 800–807.

Harris, R. T. (1984). The perils of gorging and purging. *Acute Care Medicine,* April, *1,* 15–27.

Hasler, J. F. (1982). Parotid enlargement: A presenting sign in anorexia nervosa. *Oral Surgery, Oral Medicine, Oral Pathology, 53,* 567–573.

House, R. C., Grisius, R., Bliziotes, M. M., & Licht, J. H. (1981). Perimylolysis: Unveiling the surreptitious vomiter. *Oral Surgery, Oral Medicine, Oral Pathology, 51,* 152–155.

Howrie, D. L. & Wolfson, J. H. (1983). Phenylpropanolamine-induced hypertensive seizures. *Journal of Pediatrics, 102,* 143–145.

Jacobs, M. B., & Schneider, J. A. (1985). Medical complications of bulimia: A prospective evaluation. *Quarterly Journal of Medicine, 54,* 177–182.

Larsen, K., Skov Jensen, B., & Axelsen, F. (1983). Perforation and rupture of the esophagus. *Scandinavian Journal of Thoracic and Cardiovascular Surgery, 17,* 311–316.

Lasagna, L. (Ed.). (1988). *Phenylpropanolamine: A review.* New York: John Wiley & Sons.

Levin, P. A., Falko, J. M., Dixon, K., Gallup, E. M., & Saunders, W. (1980). Benign parotid enlargement in bulimia. *Annals of Internal Medicine, 93,* 827–829.

Mercier, L. (1991). *Practical orthopedics* (3rd ed.). St. Louis: Mosby Yearbook.

Mitchell, J. E., & Boutacoff, L. I. (1986). Laxative abuse complicating bulimia: Medical and treatment implications. *International Journal of Eating Disorders, 5,* 325–334.

Mitchell, J. E., Hatsukami, D., Eckert, E. D., & Pyle, R. L. (1985). Characteristics of 275 patients with bulimia. *American Journal of Psychiatry, 142,* 482–485.

Mitchell, J. E., Seim, H. C., Colon, E., & Pomeroy, C. (1987). Medical complications and medical management of bulimia. *Annals of Internal Medicine, 107,* 71–77.

Mullai, N., Sivarajan, K. M., & Shiomoto, G. (1991). Barrett esophagus [Letter to the Editor]. *Annals of Internal Medicine, 114,* 913.

Olson, B. R. (1989) Exercise-induced amenorrhea. *American Family Physician, 39,* 213–221.

Oster, J. R. (1987). The binge-purge syndrome: A common albeit unappreciated cause of acid-base and fluid-electrolyte disturbances. *Southern Medical Journal, 80,* 58–67.

Oster, J. R., Materson, B. J., & Rogers, A. I. (1980). Laxative abuse syndrome. *American Journal of Gastroenterology, 74,* 451–458.

Palmer, E. P., & Guay, A. T. (1985). Reversible myopathy secondary to abuse of ipecac in patients with major eating disorders. *New England Journal of Medicine, 313,* 1457–1459.

Pilette, W. L. (1983). Caffeine: Psychiatric grounds for concern. *Journal of Psychosocial Nursing and Mental Health Services, 21,* 19–24.

Pyle, R. L., Mitchell, J. E., & Eckert, E. D. (1981). Bulimia: A report of 34 cases. *Journal of Clinical Psychiatry, 42,* 60–64.

Renner, J. A. (1987). Drug addiction. In T. P. Hackett and N. H. Cassem (Eds.), *Massachusetts general hospital handbook of general hospital psychiatry* (pp. 29–41). Littleton, MA: PSG Publishing.

Reyes, A. J., & Leary, W. P. (1984). Cardiovascular toxicity of diuretics related to magnesium depletion. *Human Toxicology, 3,* 351–371.

Riad, M., Barton, J. R., Wilson, J. A., Freeman, C. P., & Maran, A. G. (1991). Parotid salivary secretory pattern in bulimia nervosa. *Acta Oto-Laryngologica, 111,* 392–395.

Russell, G. (1979). Bulimia nervosa: An ominous variant of anorexia nervosa. *Psychological Medicine, 9,* 429–448.

Sansone, R. A. (1984). Complications of hazardous weight-loss methods. *American Family Physician, 30,* 141–146.

Sarner, M. (1976). Problems caused by laxatives. *Practitioner, 216,* 661–664.

Schaffer, C. B., & Pauli, M. W. (1980). Psychotic reaction caused by proprietary oral diet agent. *American Journal of Psychiatry, 137,* 1256–1257.

Schwartz, W. B., & Relman, A. S. (1953). Metabolic and renal studies in chronic potassium depletion resulting from the overuse of laxatives. *Journal of Clinical Investigation, 32,* 258–271.

Shaban, H. M., & Galizia, V. J. (1989). Obesity: Drug treatment (Part II). *Journal of Practical Nursing, 39,* 51–59.

Simmons, M. S., Grayden, S. K., & Mitchell, J. E. (1986). The need for psychiatric-dental liaison in the treatment of bulimia. *American Journal of Psychiatry, 143,* 783–784.

Smith, R. (1987). Caffeine withdrawal headache. *Journal of Clinical Pharmacy and Therapeutics, 12,* 53–57.

Sours, J. A. (1983). Case reports of anorexia nervosa and caffeinism. *American Journal of Psychiatry, 140,* 235–236.

Stege, P., Visco-Dangler, L., & Rye, L. (1982). Anorexia nervosa: Review including oral and dental manifestations. *Journal of the American Dental Association, 104,* 648–652.

Tandberg, D., Liechty, E. J., & Fishbein, D. (1981). Mallory-Weiss syndrome: An unusual complication of ipecac-induced emesis. *Annals of Emergency Medicine, 10,* 521–523.

Tylenda, C. A., Roberts, M. W., Elin, R. J., Li, S. H., & Altemus, M. (1991). Bulimia nervosa. Its effect on salivary chemistry. *Journal of the American Dental Association, 122,* 37–41.

van Dusseldorp, M., & Katan, M. B. (1990). Headache caused by caffeine withdrawal among moderate coffee drinkers switched from ordinary to decaffeinated coffee: A 12 week double blind trial. *British Medical Journal, 300,* 1558–1559.

Walsh, B. T., Wong, L. M., Pesce, M. A., Hadigan, C. M., & Bodourian, S. H. (1990). Hyperamylasemia in bulimia nervosa. *Journal of Clinical Psychiatry, 51,* 373–377.

Williams, D. M. (1990). Phenylpropanolamine hydrochloride. *American Pharmacy, NS30,* 47–50.

Wolcott, R. B., Yager, J., & Gordon, G. (1984). Dental sequelae to the binge-purge syndrome (bulimia): Report of cases. *Journal of the American Dental Association, 109,* 723–725.

Wrenn, K. D., & Oscher, I. (1989). Rhabdomyolysis induced by a caffeine overdose. *Annals of Emergency Medicine, 18,* 94–97.

Wright, L. F., & Du Val, J. W. (1987). Renal injury associated with laxative abuse. *Southern Medical Journal, 80,* 1304–1306.

Chapter 10

Bulimia Nervosa: Methods of Treatment

Scott J. Crow
James E. Mitchell

Over the last 15 years, the literature on treatment of bulimia nervosa has focused on two general treatment strategies. The first of these is psychotherapy. Beginning with the first report of psychotherapeutic treatment by Boskind-Lodahl and White (1978), a variety of types of psychotherapy have been reported in descriptive and/or controlled treatment trials including cognitive behavioral, nondirective psychodynamic, focal, behavioral, psychoeducational, and interpersonal. Methods employed have included individual, group, and combinations of group and individual treatments.

The second approach to management of bulimia nervosa has involved the use of medications. The first systematic report of medication management of bulimia nervosa appeared when Green and Rau (1974) hypothesized that the eating problems displayed by a series of their patients (many of whom probably would have satisfied DSM-III-R criteria for bulimia nervosa) represented an underlying seizure disorder. On that basis, they tried phenytoin as a therapeutic agent. Since that time, a wide variety of other medications have been tried, with the great majority of the studies being antidepressant trials.

In this chapter the current status of both psychopharmacologic and psychotherapeutic interventions for bulimia is reviewed and the limited attempts to date to compare the relative efficacies of these two types of treatments are examined. We will then offer some practical guidelines concerning the clinical management of these patients, focusing on the outpatient setting where most patients can be successfully treated.

BASIC PRINCIPLES OF MANAGEMENT

The initial evaluation of the bulimic patient should include a medical evaluation, whether medication treatment or psychotherapy is planned. As described elsewhere in this book, numerous medical complications of bulimia nervosa can occur. Among the most common of these are electrolyte disturbances. On occasion, emergency replacement of fluid or electrolytes may be required. If the bulimic behaviors persist during treatment, repeated monitoring for electrolyte imbalance is indicated. A full physical examination is usually indicated at the time the patient enters treatment.

All controlled treatment studies to date, save one, have involved outpatients. It appears that most patients can be treated outside of the hospital. Hospital treatment is much more expensive, and it can be stigmatizing. The hospital environment is also quite different from the setting in which the behaviors occur, and it is often more beneficial for the patients to learn new skills, coping mechanisms, and eating behaviors in their own social environment. In some instances treatment must be initiated in the hospital. One such instance is when there are severe medical complications such as dangerous fluid or electrolyte imbalances. In addition, some patients are unable to gain control of their bingeing or purging as outpatients. Comorbid conditions, such as poorly controlled substance abuse or severe depression with active suicidal thinking, may also necessitate admission.

PSYCHOTHERAPEUTIC APPROACHES

Since the initial report on the use of group psychotherapy by Boskind-Lodahl and White (1978), there have been a total of 20 controlled or comparative trials of psychotherapy in bulimic patients. Of these, 5 have involved individual treatment (Fairburn, Kirk, O'Connor, & Cooper, 1986; Fairburn, Jones, Peveler, Carr, Solomon, O'Connor, Burton, & Hope, 1991; Garner, Rockert, Davis, Garner, Olmsted, & Eagle, 1993; Ordman & Kirschenbaum, 1985; Wilson, Eldredge, Smith, & Niles, 1991) and 12, group treatment (Agras, Rossiter, Arnow, Schneider, Telch, Raeburn, Bruce, Perl, & Koran, 1992; Agras, Schneider, Arnow, Raeburn, & Telch, 1989; Connors, Johnson, & Stuckey, 1984; Hoage & Gray, 1990; Kirkely, Schneider, Agras, & Bachman, 1985; Laessle, Beumont, Butow, Lennerts, O'Connor, Pirke, Touyz, & Waadt, 1991; Laessle, Waadt, & Pirke, 1987; Lee & Rush, 1986; Leitenberg, Rosen, Gross, Nudelman, & Vara, 1988; Mitchell, Pyle, Eckert, Hatsukami, Pomeroy, & Zimmerman, 1990; Wilson, Rossiter, Kleifeld, & Lindholm, 1986; Yates & Sambrailo, 1984), while 3 have combined these two approaches (Freeman, Barry, Dunkeld-Turnbull, & Henderson, 1988; Lacey, 1983; Wolchik, Weiss, & Katzman, 1986). The literature involves a mixture of trials comparing two or three active treatments and trials comparing an active treatment with a waiting list or minimal intervention control group.

As described here and in Tables 10-1, 10-2, and 10-3, numerous forms of psychotherapy have been employed. The most commonly used treatment has been cognitive behavioral therapy (CBT). Other techniques that also have been investigated include psychoeducational, focal, nondirective, interpersonal, and exposure with response prevention. A few trials have attempted to dismantle individual treatments into their component parts in order to determine the critical elements.

While the specific treatment approaches vary from trial to trial, most published studies have shared certain elements. All studies have employed patient self-monitoring, the results of which provide important outcome data. Nutritional interventions are a component of nearly every treatment condition, although these are administered in various forms; however, patients typically receive instruction on modifying their eating patterns. Many programs also include meal planning. A major focus in many programs is the need to replace binge eating with more stable, consistent eating patterns. Less commonly, the reintroduction of feared foods is stressed.

Other behavioral techniques have been investigated. One such technique is exposure and response prevention. In this model, the patient is exposed to the stimulus that normally would evoke the pathologic response. This could be done by having the patient eat an amount or type of food that would usually be followed by purging, but in a controlled therapy environment. The usual purging response is prevented, leading to an increase in patient anxiety, which gradually diminishes after repeated exposure. In this sense the technique is analogous to a common form of treatment for obsessive-compulsive disorder. Exposure and response prevention can be used in both individual and group settings. An example of the latter condition would be group studies in which group members eat meals together, after which they remain together and vomiting is prevented.

Additional behavioral treatments described include a focus on the use of alternative behaviors and cue restriction to avoid binge eating. In the first of these, patients attempt to engage in other behaviors when confronted with the urge to binge eat, such as to contact a friend. Cue restriction involves identifying and avoiding situations that usually provoke the urge to binge eat. Another approach is to delay the vomiting response after binge eating to allow time for anxiety to diminish and to provide the time to reconsider whether or not to vomit.

Cognitive behavioral therapy has played a prominent role in treatment studies for bulimia nervosa since it was first adapted for use in eating disorders. Whether it is used in group or individual settings, the basic elements have been the same. The initial phase of treatment focuses on the interruption of the bulimic behavior. Sessions may occur several times each week to provide extra support during this

Table 10-1 Controlled Psychotherapy Trials in Bulimia

Group	Active treatment(s)	Control	N	Duration in weeks	Dropout rate (%)	% Decrease in binge eating	% Cessation
Connors et al., 1984	Psychoed	Waiting list	26	10	23	70	NR
Yates & Sambrailo, 1984	CBT & BT	—	24	6	33	NR	13
	CBT	—		6		NR	0
Kirkley et al., 1985	CBT	—	14	16	7	97	NR
	Nondirective	—	14	16	36	64	NR
Lee & Rush, 1986	CBT	Waiting list	15	6	27	70	29
Wilson et al., 1986	CR & ERP	—	9	16	33	82	71
	CR	—	8	16	25	51	33
Laessle et al., 1987	BT	Waiting list	8	16	0	82	38
Leitenberg et al., 1988	CBT & ERP (SS)	Waiting list	13	14	15	73	36
	CBT & ERP (MS)		13	14	8	67	42
	CBT		12	14	0	40	0
Agras et al., 1989	CBT	Waiting list	22	16	22.7	75	56
	CBT & ERP		17	16	5.7	52	31
	Self-monitor		19	16	15.8	63	24
Mitchell et al., 1990	CBT & placebo	Placebo	34	12	15	89	45
	CBT & IMI		52	12		92	56
	IMI		54	12	34	49	16
Hoage & Gray, 1990	ERP & CR	Waiting list	8	6	0	70	NR
Agras et al., 1992	CBT	—	23	16	4.3	82	50
	CBT & DMI		12	16	NR	83	65
	CBT & DMI		12	24	NR	75	70
	DMI		12	16	15	39	35
	DMI		12	24	17	54	42
Laessle et al., 1992	NM	—	27	12	18.5	70	50
	SM	—	28	12	7.1	70	26.9

Note: BT = behavioral therapy, CBT = cognitive behavioral therapy, Psychoed = psychoeducational group, CR = cognitive restructuring, IMI = imipramine, DMI = desipramine, ERP = exposure & response prevention, NM = nutritional management, SM = stress management.

206

Table 10-2 Controlled Psychotherapy Trials in Bulimia

Individual	Active treatment(s)	Control	N	Duration in weeks	Dropout rate (%)	% Decrease in binge eating	% Cessation
Ordman & Kirschenbaum, 1985	Full	—	10	Varied	0	79	20
	Brief	—	10	Varied	0	29	20
Fairburn et al., 1986	CBT	—	12	18	8	87	27
	Focal	—	12	18	8	82	36
Fairburn et al., 1991	CBT	—	25	18	16	97	—
	BT		25	18	24	91	62
	IPT		25	18	12	89	62
Wilson et al., 1991	CBT	—	25	20	18.2	94.5	63.6
	CBT/ERP	—	25	20	27.3	91.4	54.6
Garner et al., 1993	CBT	—	30	16	16.6	73	36
	SE	—	30	16	16.6	69.1	12

Note: BT = behavioral therapy, CBT = cognitive behavioral therapy, Psychoed = psychoeducational group, CR = cognitive restructuring, IMI = imipramine, DMI = desipramine, IPT = interpersonal therapy, ERP = exposure & response prevention, SE = support-expressive therapy.

Table 10-3 Controlled Psychotherapy Trials in Bulimia

Group and individual	Active treatment(s)	Control	N	Duration in weeks	Dropout rate (%)	% Decrease in binge eating	% Cessation
Lacey, 1983	Group and individual	Waiting list	30	10	0	95	80
Wolchik et al., 1986	Psychoed	Waiting list	13	7	15	68	9
Freeman et al., 1988	CBT (individual)	Waiting list	32	15	34	79	77
	BT (individual)		30	15	17	87	
	Group		30	15	34	87	

Note: BT = behavioral therapy, CBT = cognitive behavioral therapy, Psychoed = psychoeducational group, CR = cognitive restructioning, IMI = imipramine, DMI = desipramine.

period. Treatment may begin with an explanation of the relationship between cognitions and eating behaviors. Eating patterns that lead to binge eating, such as dietary restriction, are examined as the patient learns what cues trigger bulimic behavior. Nutritional education is also an important part of early treatment. Self-monitoring of eating behavior is usually instituted with an emphasis on helping the patient to consistently eat three to four times per day. Thus, the early focus is on helping the patient regain some control over eating. Each session may end with goal setting and the following session may begin with a review of what has been accomplished and what problems occurred since the last session.

As some degree of control over eating develops, the frequency of visits then diminishes in many programs. Patients are asked to further examine the cues that trigger behavior and their responses (both pathologic responses and more healthy alternatives) that follow the cues. The consequences, both positive and negative, of bulimic behavior are also reviewed. As these sequences of cues, thoughts, and consequences are exposed, the erroneous or irrational thoughts that are articulated can be examined and challenged.

As treatment progresses, the focus may shift to relapse prevention. Situations that provide a high risk for recurrence of symptoms or relapse are identified. Patients are encouraged to develop plans for dealing with these, such as through the use of high-risk exposure, during the latter phases of treatment. Both high-risk situations and high-risk foods that were identified during the treatment can be included.

Controlled Psychotherapy Trials

The controlled or comparative trials of psychotherapy for bulimia nervosa are reviewed in Tables 10-1, 10-2, and 10-3. The primary outcome measures for most studies were the amount of change in binge eating frequency and absence of bulimic symptoms at the end of treatment. As the tables show, the decrease in binge-eating behavior in subjects treated with psychotherapy has ranged from 51% to 97%, with most studies finding results in the range of 70% to 90%. Rates of post-treatment abstinence of behavior are more variable, ranging from 0% to 80%. Unfortunately, the abstinence rates are 50% or greater in only about half the studies.

Several other generalizations are apparent. Neither group, individual, nor combined treatment has a clear numerical advantage. The study of Agras et al. (1989) demonstrated that simple self-monitoring procedures had some therapeutic benefit. That study, as well as three others (Leitenberg et al., 1988; Wilson et al., 1991; Wilson et al., 1986), examined the effects of adding exposure and response prevention (ERP) to CBT on outcome. One study yielded positive (Wilson et al., 1986) and one study yielded negative results on outcome (Agras et al., 1989); two others (Leitenberg et al., 1988; Wilson et al., 1991) demonstrated no effects of ERP on outcome. Attempts to define the relative efficacy of CBT and behavioral therapy have also been made. Freeman et al. (1988) found no significant difference between CBT and behavioral therapy, suggesting that the behavioral component of CBT is most important. In an earlier study, Yates and Sambrailo (1984) suggested that the full CBT treatment was more effective than the behavioral component alone. In a more recent study, Fairburn et al. (1991) suggested that CBT was superior to behavioral therapy on the psychopathological variables associated with bulimia nervosa.

PSYCHOPHARMACOLOGIC APPROACHES

The first report of a drug trial for bulimia-like problems was that of Green and Rau (1974) and their collaborators. Since they reported their investigations using phenytoin, most of the pharmacologic research has focused on antidepressant therapy. The initial impetus for using antidepressants grew out of the observation that affective disorders frequently coexisted with eating disorders. This led some to hypothesize that bulimia was in fact an affective disorder variant. Although that hypothesis no longer appears tenable, the major emphasis has remained on the antidepressants, which have been investigated in a total of 16 double-blind, placebo-controlled studies (see Table 10-4).

Tricyclic Antidepressants

The first double-blind, placebo-controlled study of a tricyclic antidepressant was conducted by Pope, Hudson, Jonas, & Yurgelun-Todd (1983) using imipramine. In that study, the medication was superior to placebo in reducing the frequency of bulimic behaviors. Mitchell and Groat (1984) reported a controlled trial of amitriptyline in which the drug was not more effective than placebo for treatment of bulimic symptoms. Two further trials of imipramine were reported (Agras, Dorian, Kirkley, Arrow, & Bachman, 1987; Mitchell et al., 1990) following that of Pope, Hudson, Jonas, & Yurgelun-Todd (1983), both finding the medication more effective than placebo. Desipramine has been investigated in four controlled trials (Barlow, Blouin, Blouin, & Perez, 1988; Blouin, Blouin, Perez, Bushnik, Zuro, & Mulder, 1988; Hughes, Wells, Cunningham, & Ilstrup, 1986; Walsh, Hadigan, Devlin, Gladis, & Roose, 1991), three comparing with placebo and one (Blouin et al., 1988) comparing with fenfluramine and placebo. Each trial found the medication superior to placebo.

Other Antidepressants

Sabine, Yonace, Farrington, Barratt, & Wakeling (1983) reported a trial of the tetracyclic mianserin wherein the drug was not superior to placebo. Walsh, Gladis, Roose, Stewart, Stetner, & Glassman (1988) later reported a double-blind, placebo-controlled trial of phenelzine, which, despite frequently expressed concerns about dietary noncompliance, was quite well tolerated without hypertensive

Table 10-4 Controlled Trial of Antidepressants for Bulimia

Study	Drug	N	Duration in weeks	Dropout rate (%)		Maximum dosage (mg)	% Decrease in binge eating	% Cessation
				D	P			
Pope et al., 1983	Imipramine	36	8	18	9	200	70	35
Sabine et al., 1983	Mianserin	19	6	30	27	60	NS	NS
Mitchell & Groat, 194	Amitriptyline	32	8	24	6	150	NS	NS
Hughes et al., 1986	Desipramine	22	6	30	25	200	91	68
Agras et al., 1987	Imipramine	22	16	0	17	avg = 167	72	30
Walsh et al., 1988	Phenelzine	50	6	26	13	69–90	64	35
Barlow et al., 1988	Desipramine	24	6	49	—	150	47	4
Blouin et al., 1988	Desipramine	10	6	41	10	150	40	10
Horne et al., 1988	Bupropion	81	8	33	54	450	67	30
Pope et al., 1989	Trazodone	42	6	13	4	400	31	10
Mitchell et al., 1990	Imipramine	74	10	34	15	300	49	16
Walsh et al., 1991	Desipramine	78	6	23	16	300	47	13
Wheadon et al., 1991	Fluoxetine	390	16	11	6	60	50	NR
Freeman et al., 1991	Fluoxetine	40	6	0	0		51.4	
Fichter et al., 1991	Fluoxetine	40	5	31	39	60	67	NR
FBNC Study Group, 1992	Fluoxetine	387	8	24	—	20	45	NR

Note: NS = not significantly different from placebo.

reactions. In a report by Horne, Ferguson, Pope, Hudson, Lineberry, Ascher, & Cato (1988), bupropion proved superior to placebo in efficacy in treating bulimia nervosa, but a 5.7% incidence of seizure in the active treatment group was seen, leading to a recommendation that bupropion not be used in patients with eating disorders. Trazodone was reported superior to placebo in a report by Pope, Keck, McElroy, & Hudson (1989). More recently, two larger multicenter studies (Walsh, 1991; Fluoxetine Bulimia Nervosa Collaborative Study Group, 1992) involving by far the largest number of subjects studied with any medication showed high-dose fluoxetine (60 mg) to be superior to placebo.

As noted, most controlled trials of antidepressants for bulimia nervosa have found the active treatment superior to placebo; only the Mitchell and Groat (1984) study using amitriptyline and Sabine et al.'s (1983) study using mianserin failed to convincingly demonstrate superiority. Among the most common outcome measures examined in the studies have been the reduction in frequency of binge eating from baseline to the end of treatment and the percentage of abstinence of bulimic behaviors at the end of the treatment trial. The decrease in frequency of binge eating has ranged from 64% to 90%, with most studies in the range of a 65 to 75% decrease. Abstinence at the end of treatment has been observed in approximately 10% to 35% of subjects in the various studies.

Most of the studies of antidepressants have included both depressed and nondepressed subjects, although a few (e.g., Hughes et al., 1986; Horne et al., 1988, and Freeman, Davies, Morris et al., in press) have excluded patients with a current affective disorder in an attempt to determine if the drugs were working through their traditional antidepressant effects. However, the studies that excluded depressed subjects also found positive results, suggesting that the medications may have a separate action on binge eating or on some underlying element of the pathophysiology of the disorder. Some of the studies that have included depressed patients have described a correlation between treatment effects on depression and eating behavior, while other studies have not found this.

The results of these studies are summarized in Table 10-3. Most of these studies were of short duration, usually 6 to 10 weeks. The only long-term studies to date are those of Pope et al. (1985), who followed 20 subjects with bulimia nervosa for up to 2 years (although the follow-up was nonblind), and the maintenance study of Walsh et al. (1991). In the Pope et al. (1985) study, 50% of those subjects achieved complete remission of symptoms and 95% had some degree of improvement. During the follow-up period of up to 2 years, only four subjects (20%) received a single drug; the remainder had two to five medication trials, suggesting difficulty maintaining patients on a single drug. In their maintenance study, Walsh et al. (1991) used desipramine in a design combining an 8-week acute treatment phase with 16-week maintenance and 6-month discontinuation phases. Desipramine was clearly superior to placebo in the initial 8 weeks; however, only 36% of the initial subjects met criteria for inclusion in the maintenance phase. Twenty-nine percent of those patients relapsed during the 16-week maintenance phase. Insufficient numbers of subjects remained to analyze the discontinuation phase.

Other Medications

Several uncontrolled reports of the use of anticonvulsants (phenytoin and carbamazepine) have been published. A double-blind, placebo-controlled crossover study of phenytoin was reported by Wermuth, Davis, Hollister, & Stunkard (1977; see Table 10-5). The drug was effective, but an order effect was observed that made the results difficult to interpret. Fenfluramine has been examined in two controlled studies. Russell, Checkley, Feldman, & Eisler (1988) found the drug not superior to placebo, while Blouin et al. (1988) compared a higher dose of fenfluramine to both desipramine and placebo. In this study, both active treatments were superior to placebo, and fenfluramine was more effective than desipramine on bulimic behaviors. Hsu (1984) reported an open trial of lithium, finding the medication to be highly effective. This was followed by the recent publication of a randomized, controlled trial of lithium (Hsu, Clement, Santhouse, & Ju, 1991) in which the medication was not significantly more effective than placebo. Two placebo-controlled trials have investigated the effects of opiate antagonists on bulimia nervosa. Mitchell, Laine, Morley, & Levine (1986) treated bulimic subjects on a controlled research ward with the short-acting narcotic antagonist naloxone and observed binge-eating behavior. In that study, a single dose of naloxone significantly diminished bulimic behavior. In the same subjects, CCK-8 had no effect. Igoin-Apfelbaum and Apfelbaum (1987) reported a double-blind, placebo-controlled crossover trial of the long-acting opiate antagonist naltrexone in bulimic subjects. Analyzed as a whole, there was no significant effect on bulimic behavior. However, a significant order effect was observed. Subjects who received the active drug first had significant decreases in bulimic behavior that were largely preserved during the subsequent placebo phase and did not drop out. Subjects receiving placebo first had a high noncompletion rate and did not display significant decreases in bulimic behavior. Krohn and Mitchell found L-tryprophon to be ineffective in a placebo-controlled trial (1985). Methylamphetamine (Ong, Checkley, & Russell, 1983) and alprazolam (Opler and Mickley, 1986) have been reported effective in individual case studies or in small open label trials but have not been studied using controlled designs.

COMBINED TREATMENT TRIALS

Three trials to date have combined and compared the effects of psychopharmacologic and psychotherapeutic treatments. The first of these was reported by our group (Mitchell et al. 1990). Imipramine, placebo, intensive group therapy plus placebo, or group therapy plus imipramine were compared. In this study, subjects receiving group therapy had better outcomes than those who did not receive group therapy on most major outcome measures. Imipramine was more effective than

Table 10-5 Controlled Trials of Other Psychopharmacologic Agents in Bulimia

Study	Drug	N	Duration in weeks	Dropout Rate (%)		Maximum dosage	% Decrease in binge eating	% Cessation
				D	P			
Wermuth et al., 1977	Phenytoin	19	12	5	—	Varies	8/19 with moderate or marked improvement	NR
Krahn & Mitchell, 1985	L-Tryptophan	13	6	0	0	3 gm	NS	NR
Blouin et al., 1988	Fenfluramine	12	6	37		60 mg	NR	25%
Russell et al., 1988	Fenfluramine	42	12	38	42	30 mg	NS	NR
Hsu et al., 1991	Lithium	68	8	19	32	1,200 mg	NS	18%
Mitchell et al., 1986	Naloxone	5	—	—	—	18 mg	229	—
	CCK					20 ng/kg	NS	—
Igoin-Apfelbaum & Apfelbaum, 1987	Naltrexone	10	8	0	80*	120 mg	NS*	NR

Note. NR = not reported, D = drug, P = placebo.
*Double-blind, placebo-controlled crossover trial in which significant order effect was apparent.

placebo on many measures including self-ratings of eating behavior, total Eating Disorder Inventory (EDI) score, and scales measuring anxiety and depression. Addition of imipramine to group therapy did not significantly improve outcome, except in regard to anxiety and depression.

The second comparison trial was that of Agras, Rossiter, Arnow, Schneider, Telch, Raeburn, Bruce, Perl, & Koran (1992). These investigators compared three treatment strategies and five conditions: CBT alone, desipramine alone for either 16 or 24 weeks, and CBT plus desipramine for either 16 or 24 weeks. After 16 weeks the CBT and combined treatment groups were superior to medication alone. On longer term follow-up at 32 weeks, only the combined treatment with 24 weeks of drug therapy was superior to medication alone given for 16 weeks. The authors concluded that combined treatment was most efficacious; their data also suggested that the CBT component was particularly helpful in relapse prevention.

A third study, by Fichter, Leibl, Rief, Brunner, Schmidt-Auberger, & Engel (1991), did not directly compare psychotherapy and medication, but instead compared fluoxetine and placebo in bulimic inpatients receiving concurrent intensive psychotherapy. Both groups showed significant improvement over the 5 weeks of treatment, but fluoxetine did not add significantly more benefit than did placebo.

These three studies differ in regard to their findings as to whether or not medication management with an active drug augments psychotherapy. All three further support the importance of using some psychotherapeutic treatment. It is also of note that when reviewing the results of controlled trials of both medications and psychotherapy, the rates of abstinence from bulimic behavior following treatment are typically higher in psychotherapy treatment than in medication trials.

CONCLUSION

The treatment of bulimia nervosa begins with a thorough medical evaluation. Medications and psychotherapy have both been used to treat this disorder. Antidepressants have been used most commonly and typically yield a 65% to 75% decrease in binge-eating frequency with 10% to 35% of patients in remission after a short course of treatment. Group and individual psychotherapies are effective in the treatment of bulimia nervosa with abstinence rates often near 50% and overall decreases in binge-eating behavior of 70% to 90%. A few studies have compared the relative efficacies of pharmacologic and psychotherapeutic interventions, and although some of the results are conflicting, psychotherapy appears to exert a stronger effect, at least on a short-term basis.

DISCUSSION QUESTIONS

1 Describe the advantages and limitations of initiating treatment for bulimia nervosa as an outpatient.

2 What are some common behavioral techniques used to treat bulimia nervosa?

3 What are the limitations of current psychopharmacologic studies of bulimia nervosa treatment?

4 What are the effects of combining psychopharmacologic and psychotherapeutic treatments for bulimia nervosa?

5 How do psychotherapeutic and psychopharmacologic treatments compare with respect to efficacy, remission rates and compliance?

REFERENCES

Agras, W. S., Dorian, B., Kirkley, B. G., Arnow, B., & Bachman, J. (1987). Imipramine in the study of bulimia: A double blind, controlled study. *International Journal of Eating Disorders, 6,* 29–38.

Agras, W. S., Rossiter, E. M., Arnow, B., Schneider, J. A., Telch, C. F., Raeburn, S. D., Bruce, B., Perl, M., & Koran, L. M. (1992). Pharmacologic and cognitive-behavioral treatment for bulimia nervosa: A controlled clinical comparison. *American Journal of Psychiatry, 149,* 82–87.

Agras, W. S., Schneider, J. A., Arnow, B., Raeburn, S. D., & Telch, C. F. (1989). Cognitive behavioral and response prevention treatments for bulimia nervosa. *Journal of Consulting and Clinical Psychology, 57,* 215–221.

Barlow, J., Blouin, J., Blouin, A., & Perez, E. (1988). Treatment of bulimia with desipramine: A double blind, crossover study. *Canadian Journal of Psychiatry, 33,* 129–133.

Blouin, A. G., Blouin, J. H., Perez, E. L., Bushnik, T., Zuro, C., & Mulder, E. (1988). Treatment of bulimia with fenfluramine and desipramine. *Journal of Clinical Psychopharmacology, 8,* 261–269.

Boskind-Lodahl, M., & White, W. C. (1978). The definition and treatment of bulimarexia in college women—a pilot study. *Journal of American College Health, 27,* 84–97.

Connors, M. E., Johnson, C. L., & Stuckey, M. K. (1984). Treatment of bulimia with brief psychoeducational group therapy. *American Journal of Psychiatry, 141,* 1512–1516.

Fairburn, C. G., Kirk, J., O'Connor, M., & Cooper, P. J. (1986). A comparison of two psychological treatments for bulimia nervosa. *Behavior Research and Therapy, 24,* 629–643.

Fairburn, C. G., Jones, R. T., Peveler, R. C., Carr S. J., Solomon, R. A., O'Connor, M. E., Burton, J., & Hope, R. A. (1991). Three psychological treatments for bulimia nervosa. *Archives of General Psychiatry, 48,* 463–469.

Fichter, M. M., Leibl, K., Rief, W., Brunner, E., Schmidt-Auberger, S., & Engel, R. R. (1991). Fluoxetine versus placebo: A double-blind study with bulimic inpatients undergoing intensive psychotherapy. *Pharmacopsychiatry, 24,* 1–7.

Fluoxetine Bulimia Nervosa Collaborative Study Group. (1992). Fluoxetine in the treatment of bulimia nervosa. *Archives of General Psychiatry, 49,* 139–147.

Freeman, C. P. L., Barry, F., Dunkeld-Turnbull, J., & Henderson, A. (1988). Controlled trial of psychotherapy for bulimia nervosa. *British Medical Journal, 296,* 521–525.

Freeman, C. P. L., Davies, F., Morris, J., et al. (in press). A double-blind, controlled trial of fluoxetine versus placebo for bulimia nervosa. *British Journal of Psychiatry.*

Garner, D. M., Rockert, W., Davis, R., Garner, M. V., Olmsted, M. P., & Eagle, M. (1993). Comparison of cognitive-behavioral and supportive-expressive therapy for bulimia nervosa. *American Journal of Psychiatry, 150,* 37–46.

Green, R. S., & Rau, J. H. (1974). Treatment of compulsive eating disturbances with anticonvulsant medications. *American Journal of Psychiatry, 131,* 428–432.

Hoage, C. M., & Gray, J. J. (1990). Bulimia: Group behavior therapy with exposure and response prevention. *Psychological Reports, 66,* 667–674.

Horne, R. L., Ferguson, J. M., Pope, H. G., Hudson, J. I., Lineberry, C. G., Ascher, J., & Cato, A. (1988). Treatment of bulimia with bupropion: A multicenter, controlled trial. *Journal of Clinical Psychiatry, 49,* 262–266.

Hsu, L. K. G. Treatment of bulimia with lithium. (1984). *American Journal of Psychiatry, 141,* 1260–1262.

Hsu, L. K. G., Clement, L., Santhouse, R., & Ju, E. S. Y. (1991). Treatment of bulimia nervosa with lithium carbonate: A controlled study. *Journal of Nervous Mental Disorders, 179,* 351–355.

Hughes, P. L., Wells, L. A., Cunningham, C. J., & Ilstrup, D. M. (1986). Treating bulimia with desipramine. *Archives of General Psychiatry, 43,* 182–186.

Igoin-Apfelbaum, L., & Apfelbaum, M. (1987). Naltrexone and bulimic symptoms [Letter to the editor]. *Lancet, 2*(8567), 1087–1088.

Kirkely, G. B., Schneider, J. A., Agras, W. S., & Bachman, J. A. (1985). Comparison of two group treatments for bulimia. *Journal of Consulting and Clinical Psychology, 53,* 43–48.

Krahn, D., & Mitchell, J. E. (1985). Use of L-tryptophan in treating bulimia [Letter to the editor]. *American Journal of Psychiatry, 142,* 1130.

Lacey, J. H. (1983). An outpatient treatment program for bulimia nervosa. *International Journal of Eating Disorders, 286,* 1609–1613.

Laessle, R. G., Beumont, P. J. V., Butow, P., Lennerts, W., O'Connor, M., Pirke, K. N., Touyz, S. W., & Waadt, S. (1991). A comparison of nutritional management with stress management in the treatment of bulimia nervosa. *British Journal of Psychiatry, 159,* 250–261.

Laessle, R. G., Waadt, S., & Pirke, K. M. (1987). A structured, behaviorally oriented group treatment for bulimia nervosa. *Psychotherapy and Psychosomatics, 48,* 141–145.

Lee, N. F., & Rush, A. J. (1986). Cognitive-behavioral group therapy for bulimia. *International Journal of Eating Disorders, 5,* 599–615.

Leitenberg, H., Rosen, J. C., Gross, J., Nudelman, S., & Vara, L. S. (1988). Exposure plus response-prevention treatment of bulimia nervosa. *Journal of Consulting and Clinical Psychology, 56,* 535–541.

Mitchell, J. E., & Groat, R. (1984). A placebo-controlled, double-blind trial of amitriptyline in bulimia. *Journal of Clinical Psychopharmacology, 4,* 186–193.

Mitchell, J. E., Laine, D. E., Morley, J. E., & Levine, A. S. (1986). Naloxone but not CCK-8 may attenuate binge-eating behavior in patients with the bulimia syndrome. *Biological Psychiatry, 21,* 1399–1406.

Mitchell, J. E., Pyle, R. L., Eckert, E. D., Hatsukami, D., Pomeroy, C., & Zimmerman, R. (1990). A comparison study of antidepressants and structured intensive group psychotherapy in the treatment of bulimia nervosa. *Archives of General Psychiatry, 47,* 149–157.

Ong, Y. L., Checkley, S. A., & Russell, G. F. M. (1983). Suppression of bulimic symptoms with methylamphetamine. *British Journal of Psychiatry, 143,* 288–293.

Opler, L. A., & Mickley, D. (1986). Alprazolam in the treatment of bulimia [Letter to the editor]. *Journal of Clinical Psychiatry, 47,* 49.

Ordman, A. M., & Kirschenbaum, D. S. (1985). Cognitive behavioral therapy for bulimia: An initial outcome study. *Journal of Consulting and Clinical Psychology, 53,* 305–313.

Pope, H. G. Jr, Hudson, J. I., Jonas, J. M., & Yurgelun-Todd, D. (1983). Bulimia treated with imipramine: A placebo-controlled, double-blind study. *American Journal of Psychiatry, 140,* 554–558.

Pope, H. G., Hudson, J. I., Jonas, J. M., & Yurgelun-Todd, D. (1985). Antidepressant treatment of bulimia: A two year followup study. *Journal of Clinical Psychopharmacology, 5,* 320–327.

Pope, H. G., Keck, P. E., McElroy, S. L., & Hudson, J. I. (1989). A placebo-controlled study of trazodone in bulimia nervosa. *Journal of Clinical Psychopharmacology, 9,* 254–259.

Russell, G. F. M., Checkley, S. A., Feldman, J., & Eisler, I. (1988). A controlled trial of *d*-fenfluramine in bulimia nervosa. *Clinical Neuropharmacology, 11,* S146–S159.

Sabine, E. J., Yonace, A., Farrington, A. J., Barratt, K. H., & Wakeling, A. (1983). Bulimia nervosa: A placebo controlled double blind therapeutic trial of mianserin. *British Journal of Clinical Pharmacology, 15,* 195s–202s.

Walsh, B. T. Psychopharmacologic treatment of bulimia nervosa. (1991). *Journal of Clinical Psychiatry, 52*(Suppl.), 34–38.

Walsh, B. T., Gladis, M., Roose, S. P., Stewart J. W., Stetner, F., & Glassman, A. H. (1988). Phenelzine vs. placebo in 50 patients with bulimia. *Archives of General Psychiatry, 45,* 471–475.

Walsh, B. T., Hadigan, C. M., Devlin, M. J., Gladis, M., & Roose, S. P. (1991). Long term outcome of antidepressant treatment for bulimia nervosa. *American Journal of Psychiatry, 148,* 1206–1212.

Wermuth, B. M., Davis, K. L., Hollister, L. E., & Stunkard, A. J. (1977). Phenytoin treatment of the binge-eating syndrome. *American Journal of Psychiatry, 134,* 1249–1253.

Wilson, G. T., Eldredge, K. L., Smith, D., & Niles, B. (1991). Cognitive-behavioral treatment with and without response prevention for bulimia. *Behavior Research and Therapy, 29,* 575–583.

Wilson, G. T., Rossiter, E., Kleifeld, E. I., & Lindholm, L. (1986). Cognitive behavioral treatment of bulimia nervosa: A controlled evaluation. *Behavior Research and Therapy, 24,* 227–238.

Wolchik, S. A., Weiss, L., & Katzman, M. A. (1986). An empirically validated, short term psychoeducational group treatment program for bulimia. *International Journal of Eating Disorders, 5,* 21–34.

Yates, A. J., & Sambrailo, F. (1984). Bulimia nervosa: A descriptive and therapeutic study. *Behavioral Research and Therapy, 5,* 503–517.

Part Four

Obesity

The 1980 *Diagnostic and Statistical Manual of Mental Disorders* (*DSM-III*) identified the following eating disorders: anorexia nervosa, bulimia, pica, rumination disorder of infancy, and atypical eating disorder. Obesity is not listed as an eating disorder, but rather as a physical condition in *International Classification of Diseases,* 9th edition (*ICD-9CM*). The 1987 revised version of this manual (*DSM-III-R*) included revisions in the diagnostic criteria for anorexia nervosa and bulimia, and most important, the term *bulimia nervosa* was adopted to describe the "binge-purge syndrome." *DSM-III-R* recognized three eating disorders: anorexia nervosa, bulimia nervosa, and eating disorder not otherwise specified. Still, obesity is not listed as an eating disorder in *DSM-III-R.* Neither is *compulsive overeating,* a term used in connection with obesity and often viewed as a kind of eating disorder along with obesity.

What, then, is the relationship between compulsive overeating and obesity, and what role do they play in the eating disorders? Compulsive overeating is the name given to a pattern whereby typically overweight patients binge but do not purge. Compulsive overeaters engage in a pattern of overeating, sometimes daily over a prolonged period of time. However, they do not attempt to lose weight by vomiting or through the use of laxatives, diuretics, or exercise. Compulsive overeaters may diet or fast in an effort to lose weight. However, it is rare that they succeed; instead they regain any lost weight. This pattern results in obesity, defined as excessive adipose tissue. While not all binge eaters are overweight, the degrees of overweight and binge eating are positively correlated. The incidence of binge eating increases as the severity of obesity increases. Approximately 30% of obese patients in treatment have a bingeing history. Also, an association exists between binge eating in obese patients and increased psychopathology. In addition, obese patients who binge tend not to do as well in treatment. There is, then, a significant relationship between binge eating and obesity. However, it is worth noting that not all cases of obesity are the result of compulsive overeating. Several nonpsychological causes of obesity are known, including endocrine disorders and genetic illnesses.

People with overeating disturbances who binge but do not purge may represent a readily identifiable syndrome separate from bulimia nervosa. The Eating Disorders Work Group of the American Psychiatric Association's Task Force on *DSM-IV* is currently considering whether data would suggest adding a category to the *DSM-IV* to address people who have a significant problem with binge eating but who do not meet criteria for bulimia nervosa. Such a category would be labeled *binge eating disorder.* Tentative diagnostic criteria have been set up; the work group has recommended inclusion of the criteria for binge eating disorder in the appendix of *DSM-IV* as a diagnostic category meriting further study.

In this volume, we have included obesity as a category of eating disorders along with anorexia nervosa and bulimia nervosa. The arguments for including obesity in discussions of eating disorders are important. Numerous investigators have noted very positive results gained by researchers and clinicians in the areas of anorexia nervosa and bulimia nervosa sharing information and working together. Those in favor of adding obesity to discussions of eating disorders suggest that, while obesity is not considered to be an eating disorder per se, much can be gained by including obesity when considering the eating disorders. Research and clinical work in one area could benefit all three.

In this part, obesity is discussed in terms of its definition, diagnostic criteria, and health risks; treatment methods are outlined as well. Consequences of being obese in a society where thinness is equated with attractiveness, particularly in women are also explored here.

Chapter 11

Obesity: Definition, Diagnostic Criteria, and Associated Health Problems

Colleen S. W. Rand

The relationship between eating disorders and obesity is complex. In general, eating disorders develop in the context of avoiding obesity. Both the definition of what constitutes obesity and the prevalence of obesity influences the development of eating disorders. The prevalence of eating disorders will increase if either the threshold for defining obesity decreases or the prevalence of obesity increases. This chapter focuses on obesity: its prevalence and consequences of remaining rather than avoiding obesity.

The term *obesity* is used to describe excess body fat. People with enormous amounts of body fat are easily identified as being obese. However, the point where "normal" becomes "excessive" depends on why obesity is being identified; how obesity is being measured; and the particular index, formula, or number used to define obesity.

Obesity is usually identified for either medical or cultural purposes. Epidemiologists examine the demographic distribution and environmental/genetic causes of obesity, providing both information on the natural history of obesity and data relevant to preventive medicine (Hunt, 1972).

Medically significant obesity can be defined as a deposition of fat tissues that is sufficiently large to impair health. Enlargement of central, abdominal fat tissues is associated with increased risk of ischemic heart disease, stroke, and non-insulin-dependent diabetes (Bjorntorp, 1987, 1990). Enlargement of fat tissues in the buttocks and thighs is less medically serious, carrying an increased risk for varicose veins, joint problems, and possibly diabetes. Bjorntorp (1990) speculated that one reason Pima Indians and Polynesian populations have dramatically increased health risks associated with obesity is because these groups have a propensity to accumulate excess fat abdominally.

Culturally defined obesity identifies the degree of body fat compatible with social standards of physical attractiveness and, in certain professions, employment or competition criteria. Medical and cultural assessments of desirable fatness are rarely the same (e.g., Rand & Kuldau, 1990). Among contemporary Western industrialized societies, thinness is associated with feminine beauty while masculine attractiveness appears to be compatible with a fairly wide range of fatness. Among more traditional, non-Western agricultural societies, fatness for both men and women is often associated with prosperity, longevity, fertility, and, by extrapolation, physical attractiveness (Nasser, 1988; Sobal & Stunkard, 1989).

Industries, influenced by both economics and prevailing social standards, have formal height-weight standards for some personnel. In the United States, industries that use weight criteria include insurance agencies, airlines, some hospitals, and the military. Jockeys, boxers, wrestlers, dancers, and models have strict professional weight criteria. Excessive weight can result in dismissal or financial penalties.

The personal evaluation of being obese is usually based on cultural rather than medical criteria (Dawson, 1988; Rand & Kuldau, 1990). The prevalence of eating disorders, which is closely associated with desires to prevent obesity, follows the culturally defined standards of admissible fat associated with physical beauty (Connors & Johnson, 1987; Hamilton, Brooks-Gunn, & Warren, 1985; Rand & Kuldau, 1992).

The remainder of this chapter focuses on medically significant obesity.

HOW IS OBESITY MEASURED?

The only direct method of determining body composition is analysis of cadavers. Body fat is measured directly by dissection and ether extraction. Only eight cadavers have been analyzed in this way (Bray, 1976; Martin & Drinkwater, 1991). Measured body fat ranged from 4.5% to 27.9% of body weight.

Indirect estimates of body fat derive from equations that divide the body into fat and fat-free mass components. Unfortunately, the resulting estimates of total body fat are only crude approximations. This is because some of the parameters assumed to be constant in the equations actually have large variability (e.g., bone density; Martin & Drinkwater, 1991).

Measurement of body density has been the traditional laboratory "gold standard" for indirectly estimating total body fat. Body weight is determined in air and underwater, corrected for lung volume, and divided into fat and fat-free components. Formulae for estimating total body fat requires modification when estimating total body fat of children, lean athletes, and the elderly (Gray, 1989; Bray, 1990). Computed tomography scans will probably become the "gold standard" for validating other techniques for estimating distribution of body fat (Sjostrom, 1992).

Epidemiological studies have relied on anthropomorphic measurements to provide indirect estimates of body fat. (Laboratory methods are too cumbersome and expensive for epidemiological surveys.) Most recent studies derive estimates of total body fat from measurements of height and weight (Bray and Gray, 1988).

Weight alone is not a good measure of body fat because of its strong correlation with height. Height-weight tables and height-weight indexes largely correct for this correlation. All estimates of obesity that derive from height-weight measures are limited because overweight due to excess fat is not distinguished from overweight due to excess muscle (Segal et al., 1987).

Height-weight tables provide weight distributions for given heights. They are derived from observed heights and weights of selected populations. Obesity is defined as a weight above a given range for each height or a percentile above a given distribution of weights for each height. *Relative overweight* describes weight above a given standard; it is defined by dividing actual weight by the desirable weight for a given height.

The most commonly used American height-weight tables for adults are those that were published by actuaries of the Metropolitan Life Insurance Company in 1959 and revised in 1983 (Metropolitan Life Insurance Company, 1959; 1983). The desirable weights-for-height listed in the tables are based on the lowest mortality associated with a given height (for the population of insured policy holders). Changes between 1959 and 1983 reflect changes in the actuarial data. In general, weight limits are higher in the 1983 tables compared to the 1959 tables. This means that adults considered overweight by 1959 standards may be within the normal range by 1983 standards.

The body mass index (BMI) is the most common height-weight index used for adults. It has the advantage of having a single standard for all adults. The general equation for BMI is weight (in kilograms) divided by height (in meters) to the power P, where P is determined by the coefficient giving the lowest correlation of weight to height. Out of convenience, the value of 2 is now used for both men and women. This weight-height index is also called Quetelet's index. Comparisons of surveys using different values of "P" can be done by transforming data into percentiles of weight for a given height, and specifying the percentiles defining moderate and severe obesity (Appendix, Kumanyika, 1987).

A relative weight greater than 120% of desirable weight (Metropolitan Life Insurance Company, 1983) is approximately equivalent to a BMI of 27. Many epidemiological studies define overweight as a BMI of 27 and obesity as a BMI greater than or equal to 30 (Bray, 1976, 1980).

The Broca normal weight was used extensively in the past to define obesity in European epidemiological studies (Kluthe & Schubert, 1985), but is rarely used now. Normal weight (in kilograms) is defined as height (in centimeters) minus 100; obese is defined as more than 20% greater than the normal weight. A comparison of the Broca normal weight and BMI greater than or equal to 30 definitions of obesity shows there is agreement for the upper (180 cm or taller), but not for the shorter (160 to 179 cm) height range. Broca normal weight identifies more short people as obese than the BMI greater than or equal to 30 criteria. Since more women than men are short, prevalence of obesity among women is increased relative to men when Broca normal weight standards are used.

The different methods of estimating body fat and different standards for obesity have resulted in a quagmire of conflicting literature on measuring and defining obesity. A person whose relative weight is excessive may not be considered obese by measurement of skinfold thicknesses or by estimating the percentage of body fat by underwater weighing. The correspondence among measures is better in identifying extremely fat and thin people (Himes, Bouchard, & Pheley, 1991). For an epidemiologist, this means that conclusions about health risks associated with obesity depend on how obesity has been measured and defined.

PREVALENCE OF OBESITY

Regardless of how obesity is measured, obesity cannot exist without adequate calorie consumption. Many people do not have the option of becoming obese. *Peters Atlas of the World* (1990) describes the following countries as being "overnourished" (defined as an average daily caloric consumption ≥3,500): United States of America, Greenland, Ireland, France, Netherlands, Denmark, Italy, Greece, the former German Democratic Republic, the former Czechoslovakia, Hungary, the former Yugoslavia, Bulgaria, Libya, the United Arab Emirates, and New Zealand (pp. 138–139). Two atlas maps suggest possible causal relationships with overnourishment. First, the absolute number of calories derived from fat is greater in overnourished than in other countries. Second, all of the countries considered overnourished are also highly urbanized, with more than 75% of their population living in cities (pp. 160–161). (The reverse is not true; many urbanized countries are not considered overnourished, e.g., Australia, Japan, Argentina.)

War and weather are two forces that can quickly change the prevalence overnourished to "insufficient nourishment." The studies describing prevalence of obesity are valid only as long as the political climate and weather remain stable. For example, Somalia is described as badly nourished (2,000 to 2,500 calories daily) in the 1990 atlas. In 1992, it would be described as undernourished (less than 2,000 calories daily) since a third of its population is expected to starve to death. Similarly, it is likely that the 1992 civil war in the former Yugoslavia will effectively reduce the caloric consumption of its population, no longer permitting an overnourished status.

During the last several decades, epidemiologists have described prevalence of obesity in different parts of the world. The large variety of studies reflect actuarial, medical, and sociocultural interests. Appendix 11-A presents examples of prevalence data from many countries.

A few broad generalizations can be drawn from the data in Appendix 11-A. The prevalence of obesity is usually greater among women than men. The prevalence of obesity is greater today than in past decades. Also, although there are substantial ethnic variations, each race or ethnic group has subgroups where the prevalence of obesity is 20% or more.

Many of the studies in Appendix 11-A present clinical laboratory values that relate degree of obesity to the risk of acquiring specific diseases. For example, in the study on prevalence of obesity among urban Thais, the following biochemical assessments were made: serum total cholesterol, high-density lipoprotein cholesterol, triglyceride, uric acid, fasting blood glucose, and 2-hour blood glucose (Appendix 11-A; Tanphaichitr, Kulapongse, Pakpeankitvatana, Leelahagul, Tamwiwat, & Lochaya, 1990). Values were presented according to sex and BMI, but not age. The authors' conclusion, based on the distribution of laboratory values, was that obese subjects, especially obese men, have an increased risk of coronary heart disease and diabetes mellitus.

Because of the variety of clinical laboratory measurements, diseases, and diverse methodological specifications of the studies in Appendix 11-A, further enumeration of health data is unwieldy. The conclusions and controversies arising from these studies and from several large prospective studies regarding the relationship between obesity, morbidity, and mortality are discussed below.

MORBIDITY AND MORTALITY

The conclusion of the 1985 National Institutes of Health Consensus Development Conference was: "The evidence is now overwhelming that obesity . . . has adverse effects on health and longevity" (p. 1077). In contrast, in a more recent review evaluating treatments for obesity, Garner and Wooley (1991) stated with equal conviction: "There are conflicting opinions on the mortality and morbidity risks associated with obesity; the conclusion that obesity is dangerous represents a selective review of the data" (p. 751).

Most reviews consider obesity to be an important factor predisposing to some cancers, cardiovascular disease, type II diabetes (also called adult-onset diabetes and non-insulin-dependent diabetes), osteoarthritis, and gallbladder disease (e.g., Bray, 1985). However, the research data on morbidity associated with obesity is complicated and inconsistent. (Compare the relationship between coronary artery disease and obesity as reviewed in Barrett-Connor [1985] to the report of the 26-year follow-up of participants in the Framingham heart study by Hubert, Feinleib, McNamara, & Castelli [1983]; see also Kissebah, Freedman, & Peiris, 1989; Garner & Wooley, 1991; and Rimm, 1990.) Although studies vary in their scientific rigor, high-quality studies obtain contradictory findings. Differences in populations studied (e.g., self-selected insured policy holders versus an entire community or only men versus men and women; Sarlie, Gordon, & Kannel, 1980), measurement of obesity (e.g., relative overweight versus waist-to-hip ratio), type of study (e.g., cross-sectional versus longitudinal), duration of follow-up, sample size, outcome measures (e.g., differences in laboratory assessments and diseases selected), and impact of smoking (e.g., whether or not smoking and its health impact are considered) further complicate the task of evaluating health risks.

Perhaps because of the strong belief in the adverse health consequences of obesity, health benefits associated with obesity are usually ignored. Among these benefits are decreases in prevalence of osteoporosis, mitral valve prolapse, anemia, overall fatalities from infectious diseases, and overall cancer morbidity and mortality (Ernsberger & Haskew, 1987). Regarding cancer, many articles report the higher rates of some cancers found among obese women (biliary duct, endometrial, gallbladder, postmenopausal breast, and cervical cancer) and obese men (colon and prostate cancer). Few articles also mention the lower death rates from specific cancers for obese women (premenopausal breast, lung, stomach, and colon cancer) and for obese men (lung and stomach cancer). (Garner & Wooley, 1991).

The complexities in evaluating health impairments also apply to mortality data. Desirable weight or BMI associated with minimum mortality depends on age, sex, and possibly ethnicity (Gray, 1989; Andres et al., 1985). Some prospective studies have found that obesity shortens the life span, others have found decreasing mortality with moderate increases in weight, and still other studies have found no relationship between obesity and life span (see reviews in Andres, 1980, 1985; Barrett-Connor, 1985; Ernsberger & Haskew, 1987; Harrison, 1985; Keys, 1980, 1989). When mortality studies find that "desirable" weights (as defined by height-weight tables) are not associated with the lowest mortality, the desirability of the desirable weights can be questioned (Andres, 1985). Among Pima Indians, for example, lowest mortality is associated with a BMI between 35 and 40, equivalent to 167% to 190% of desirable weight for women and 145% to 176% of desirable weight for men (1959 Metropolitan Life Insurance tables; Pettitt, Lisse, Knowler, & Bennett, 1982). Frequently, only the extremes of weight have been found to be related to increased mortality (Ernsberger & Haskew, 1987). For example, the Framingham study found the mortality rate for women 5'3" to 5'6" to be the same within the weight range of 115 to 194 pounds. Increased mortality was observed in the lowest and highest quintiles of weight distribution for women and in the lowest quintile for men (Sorlie, Gordon, & Kannel, 1980).

Even when a positive relationship is documented between obesity and mortality, the way obesity is defined can unintentionally bias interpretation. The influential Society of Actuaries' build and blood pressure study (1960) documented a linear relationship between an overweight of 10%, 20%, and 30% and excess mortality of some 5 million policy holders. Overweight was determined by referring to the average weight of the insured population, not the ideal or desirable weight as defined by the 1959 Metropolitan Life Insurance Tables. According to Andres (1980) 10% over the average weight of the insured population translates into 25% over the desirable weight defined by the height-weight tables for men and 31% over for women.

Morbidity and mortality associated with medically significant obesity (defined as 100 pounds over ideal weight, 100% over ideal weight, or BMI $\geq$ 40) are less controversial. Diabetes, arthritis, hypertension, cardiovascular disease, sleep apnea, varicose veins, ulcers, gout, gallbladder disease, asthma, and menstrual abnormalities are some of the diseases either exacerbated or caused by extreme overweight (Brolin, 1987; Drenick, Bale, Seltzer, & Johnson, 1980; Kral, 1985). Excess mortality appears to be principally caused by cardiovascular disease and diabetes mellitus. In the obesity surgical literature, outcome studies of successful maintained weight loss are associated with amelioration of diabetes, arthropathy, hypertension, and asthma (Hall, Watts, O'Brien, Dustan, Walsh, Slavotinek, & Elmslie, 1989).

Fat Distribution

How body fat is distributed appears to be a better predictor of morbidity than obesity per se (Stunkard, 1988; Garner & Wooley, 1991; Sjostrom, 1992). Abdominal fat (also called upper body fat, android fat, apple-shaped fat, and belly fat) is associated with elevated rates of diabetes, hypertension, breast cancer, and coronary heart disease (e.g., Björntorp, 1985a,b; Donahue, Abbott, Bloom, Reed, & Yano, 1987; Lapidus, Bengtsson, Hallstrom, & Bjorntorp, 1989; Schapira, Kumar, Lyman & Cox, 1990; Shelgikar, Hockaday, & Yajnik, 1991). More specifically, visceral fat (accumulations in the abdominal cavity) rather than subcutaneous fat (accumulations mainly in the subcutis) seems to be connected with impaired glucose and lipid metabolism (Fujioka, Matsuzawa, Tokunaga, & Tarui, 1987; Rebuffe-Scrive, 1990). Excess fat deposited on buttocks and thighs (also called lower body fat, gynoid fat, and pear-shaped fat) has more limited negative health consequences, potentially exacerbating joint problems, varicose veins, and skin ulcers and rashes.

Evidence for both genetic and environmental influences on regional fat distribution has been found. Striking similarities exist between identical twins in the ease of weight gain and in visceral storage when they are experimentally overfed (Bouchard, 1990). Path analyses of measurements of skinfolds and circumferences of Canadians yielded heritability estimates for trunk and abdominal skinfolds ranging from 35% to 50% (Bouchard, 1990).

One environmental influence on regional fat distribution is cigarette smoking (Shimokata, Muller & Andres, 1989; Lapidus, Bengtsson, Hallstrom, & Bjorntorp, 1989). Smokers weigh less but have relatively more abdominal fat than nonsmokers, and there is a graded dose-response relationship between number of cigarettes smoked and relative amount of abdominal fat. Cessation of smoking leads to weight gain but relatively less abdominal fat, while starting smoking leads to relatively greater abdominal fat despite weight loss.

Diabetes: An Obesity Morbidity Case Study

The epidemiological and prospective studies of obesity suggest that both genetics and environment influence the morbidity associated with obesity. Factors "loading" on the genetic component include family history of a particular disease and pattern of fat deposition (Bjorntorp, 1987). Exercise, nutrient consumption (quantity and quality), and smoking can be considered to "load" on the environmental contribution. The link between obesity and diabetes provides an excellent example of how inconsistences and complexities within the literature on obesity related morbidity and mortality are being investigated.

Genetic Component   Second-generation Japanese-American (Nisei) men have a prevalence of diabetes two to four times higher than Japanese men in Japan or white American men (Fujimoto, Leonetti, Newell-Morris, Shuman, & Wahl, 1991). Because there is no reliable genetic marker for type II diabetes, family history for diabetes has been used to indicate hereditary susceptibility.

Among Nisei men who had a positive family history of diabetes, no relationships were found between obesity, fat distribution, and presence of diabetes. Among men with no family history of diabetes, however, a strong positive relationship was found between current BMI, lifetime maximum BMI, truncal fat distribution, and diabetes. Family history data were not presented for Nisei women, but those with diabetes had more intra-abdominal fat; a greater ratio of intra-abdominal to abdominal subcutaneous fat and were heavier than normal subjects (Fujimoto, Newell-Morris, Grote, Bergstrom, & Shuman, 1991). Similar findings on the impact of obesity on diabetes relative to family history of diabetes have been reported from studies in Germany, Japan, and the United States (cited in Fujimoto et al., 1991); when there is no family history of diabetes, the presence of obesity is related to the presence of diabetes.

Environment Component   Several studies have described a reduced occurrence of type II diabetes among physically active adults (e.g., Helmrich, Ragland, Leung, Paffenbarger, 1991; the role of muscle insulin sensitivity and other possible mechanisms are discussed in Bjorntorp, 1987). Exercise also appears to be of benefit to large adults. For example, in Japan, professional Sumo wrestling is a popular national sport. Sumo wrestlers are, without exception, very heavy and extremely highly muscled; many have large amounts of subcutaneous fat accumulation. Normal plasma glucose and normal lipidaemia are maintained by most active sumo wrestlers. Upon retiring, however, the incidence of diabetes among former sumo wrestlers increases markedly (Tarui, Tokunaga, Fujioka, & Matsuzawa, 1991).

Exercise—or lack thereof—also appears to contribute to the high rate of type 2 diabetes among adults whose BMI is greater than or equal to 40 (e.g., Pories, Caro, Flickinger, Meelheim, & Swanson, 1987). In a study designed to examine the effect of exercise on glucose intolerance, five morbidly obese white women and two morbidly obese white men were restricted to their hospital rooms for 4 days. Compared to baseline measures, both glucose intolerance and hyperinsulinemia worsened. Following a week of moderate exercise (a daily 5 to 7 km walk), however, patients showed marked improvements in glucose intolerance, hyperinsulinaemia, and triglyceridaemia (Misbin, 1983).

Both exercise and food composition may influence differences in obesity-related morbidity between black-American and black-African women: Like most other Americans, black-American women can be characterized as being relatively physically inactive and having a high-fat diet (about 40% of calories). They also have disproportionately high prevalence rates of obesity, diabetes, and hypertension (Kumanyika, 1987). In contrast, heavy black women (BMI ≥ 30) living in a rural area of Eastern Transvaal, South Africa, are very physically active with a low-fat diet (21% of calories; Walker, Walker, Walker, & Vorster, 1989). Very little morbidity was found among 40 women evaluated for obesity-related disorders; 35 (88%) had normal values for blood glucose, blood pressure, serum cholesterol, and triglycerides.

Exercise, food composition, and obesity are implicated in differences between traditional and Westernized Australian Aborigines. Traditional Aborigines were physically active nomadic hunter-gatherers with a low-fat diet. Adults were extremely lean (BMI ≤ 20), with no evidence of type II diabetes, hypertension, hyperlipidemia, or coronary heart disease (O'Dea & Hopper, 1990). With westernization, adults become sedentary, gain weight, and change their diet. About 50% of middle-aged adults develop diabetes or have impaired glucose tolerance. However, when diabetic adults resume a traditional lifestyle, their physical activity increases, intake of dietary fat decreases, weight decreases, and all the metabolic abnormalities associated with type II diabetes improve (cited in O'Dea & Hopper, 1990).

CONCLUSION

Epidemiological studies of obesity indicate a substantial proportion of adults in many parts of the world are obese. Prevalence rates are affected by how obesity is measured and defined. Morbidity and mortality associated with obesity are also affected by how obesity is measured and defined. Severe obesity (BMI ≥ 40) is associated with medically increased morbidity and mortality. The combined evidence from both epidemiological and prospective studies, however, suggest medical health risks for the mild and moderately obese may be relatively less serious than the psychosocial consequences.

Obesity is medically important because of the assumption that obesity has a negative influence on health and longevity. Many of the studies demonstrating a positive relationship between obesity and morbidity and mortality are excellent. At the same time, equally fine studies obtain negative results, weak associations, or no associations. It is clear that the relationships between obesity and health are complex, involving genetic and environmental/behavioral characteristics of the populations studied. Current research is now focusing on these factors.

Height-weight tables present guidelines for weights approved by many health professionals and insurance companies. The simplicity of height-weight tables will ensure their continued usage despite the considerable discrepancies in data on obesity-related morbidity and mortality. It is, however, reasonable to question the validity of using the tables to identify people as having health risks simply because they have body weights above the recommended range.

An adult whose genetics, fat distribution, degree of obesity, smoking history, food choices, age, and sedentary lifestyle load positively for an obesity-related disease probably is risking fate. The continued opinion that mild and moderate obesity are uniformly deleterious reflects the importance and impact of cultural attitudes in the evaluation of medical health risks.

DISCUSSION QUESTIONS

   1   What is the difference between medically significant obesity and culturally significant obesity?
   2   Body weight is not a good measure of obesity. Why?
   3   Body density provides a better estimate of body fat than anthropomorphic measurements. Why do epidemiological surveys rely on anthropomorphic measurements?
   4   Why is measurement of obesity a concern to epidemiologists?
   5   How is caloric consumption related to obesity?
   6   Describe negative and positive health consequences associated with obesity.
   7   How is fat distribution related to health?
   8   How does type 2 diabetes appear to be related to obesity and exercise?
   9   Examine 11-A. Compare prevalence rates and make some general conclusions based on the data presented. Dimensions to consider are country, age, sex, percentage of obese subjects, and average BMI.

REFERENCES

al Awade F., & Amine, E. K. (1989). Overweight and obesity in Kuwait. *Journal of Research in Social Health, 109,* 105–107.

Andres, R. (1980). Effect of obesity on total mortality. *International Journal of Obesity, 4,* 381–386.

Andres, R. (1985). Mortality and obesity: The rationale for age-specific height-weight tables. In R. Andres, E. L. Bierman, & W. R. Hazzard (Eds.), *Principles of Geriatric Medicine* (pp. 311–318). New York: McGraw-Hill.

Andres, R., Elahi, D., Tobin, J. D., Muller, D. C., & Brant, L. (1985). Impact of age on weight goals. *Annals of Internal Medicine, 103,* 1030–1033.

Barrett-Connor, E. L. (1985). Obesity, atherosclerosis, and coronary artery disease. *Annals of Internal Medicine, 103,* 1010–1019.

Björntorp, P. (1985a). Regional patterns of fat distribution. *Annals of Internal Medicine, 103,* 994–995.

Björntorp, P. (1985b). Obesity and the risk of cardiovascular disease. *Annals of Clinical Research, 17,* 3–9.

Björntorp, P. (1987). Classification of obese patients and complications related to the distribution of surplus fat. *American Journal of Clinical Nutrition, 45,* 1120–1125.

Björntorp, P. (1990). Editorial: How should obesity be defined? *Journal of Internal Medicine, 227,* 147–149.

Bouchard, C. (1990). Genetic and environmental influences on regional fat distribution. In Y. Oomura, S. Tarui, S. Inoue, & T. Sjimazu (Eds.), *Progress in Obesity Research 1990* (pp. 303–308). London: John Libbey.

Bray, G. A. (1976). *The obese patient.* Philadelphia: W. B. Saunders Company.

Bray, G. A. (Ed.). (1980). *Obesity in America.* NIH Publication No. 80-395. Washington, DC: U. S. Government Printing Office.

Bray, G. A. (1985). Obesity: Definition, diagnosis and disadvantages. *The Medical Journal of Australia, 142,*(Suppl.), 52–58.

Bray, G. A. (1990). Epidemiology of obesity. In Y. Oomura, S. Tarui, S. Inoue, & T. Shimazu (Eds.), *Progress in obesity research 1990* (pp. 639–643). London: John Libbey.

Bray, G. A., & Gray, D. S. (1988). Obesity. Part I—Pathogenesis. *Western Journal of Medicine, 4,* 429–441.

Brolin, R. E. (1987). Results of obesity surgery. *Gastroenterology Clinics of North America, 16,* 317–338.

Broussard, B. A., Johnson, A., Himas, J. H., Story, M., Fichtner, R., Hauck, F., Bachmanc, K., Hayes, J., Frohlich, K., & Gray, N. (1991). Prevalence of obesity in American Indians and Alaska natives. *American Journal of Clinical Nutrition, 53,* 1535–1542.

Dawson, D. A. (1988). Ethnic differences in female overweight: Data from the 1985 National Health Interview Survey. *American Journal of Public Health, 78,* 1326–1439.

Dhurandhar, N. V., & Kulkarni, P. R. (1992). Prevalence of obesity in Bombay. *International Journal of Obesity, 16,* 367–375.

Donahue, R. P., Abbott, R. D., Bloom, E., Reed, D. M., & Yano, K. (1987). Central obesity and coronary heart disease in men. *The Lancet, 1*(8537), 821–824.

Drenick, E. J., Bale, G. S., Seltzer, F., & Johnson, D. G. (1980). Excessive mortality and causes of death in morbidly obese men. *JAMA, 243,* 443–445.

Ernsberger, P., & Haskew, P. (1987). Health implications of obesity: An alternative view. *The Journal of Weight Regulation, 6,* 68–137.

Fujimoto, W. Y., Leonetti, D. L., Newell-Morris, L., Shuman, W. P., & Wahl, P. W. (1991). Relationship of absence or presence of a family history of diabetes to body weight and body fat distribution in type 2 diabetes. *International Journal of Obesity, 15,* 111–120.

Fujimoto, W. Y., Newell-Morris, M., Grote, R. W., Bergstrom, R. W., & Shuman, W. P. (1990). Visceral fat obesity and morbidity: NIDDM and atherogenic risk in Japanese American men and women. *International Journal of Obesity, 15,* 41–44.

Fujioka, S., Matsuzawa, Y., Tokunaga, K., & Tarui, S. (1987). Contribution of intra-abdominal fat accumulation to the impairment of glucose and lipid metabolism in human obesity. *Metabolism, 36,* 54–59.

Garner, D. M., & Wooley, S. C. (1991). Confronting the failure of bahavioral and dietary treatments for obesity. *Clinical Psychology Review, 11,* 729–780.

Gray, D. S. (1989). Diagnosis and prevalence of obesity. *Medical Clinics of North America, 73,* 1–13.

Gurney, M., & Gorstein, J. (1988). The global prevalence of obesity—An initial overview of available data. *World Health Statistical Quarterly, 41,* 251–254.

Hall, J. C., Watts, J. M., O'Brien, P. E., Dustan, R. E., Walsh, J. F., Slavotinek, A. H., & Elmslie, R. G. (1989). Gastric surgery for morbid obesity. *Annals of Surgery, 211,* 419–427.

Hamilton, L. H., Brooks-Gunn, J., & Warren, M. P. (1985). Sociocultural influences on eating disorders in professional female ballet dancers. *International Journal of Eating Disorders, 4,* 465–477.

Harrison, G. G. (1985). Height-weight tables. *Annals of Internal Medicine, 103,* 989–994.

Helmrich, S. P., Ragland, D. R., Leung, A. B., & Paffenbarger, R. S. (1991). Physical activity and reduced occurrence of non-insulin-dependent diabetes mellitus. *The New England Journal of Medicine, 325,* 147–152.

Himes, J. H., Bouchard, C., & Pheley, A. M. (1991). Lack of correspondence among measures identifying the obese. *American Journal of Preventative Medicine, 7,* 107–111.

Horibe, H. (1990). Trend of average height, weight and skinfolds in the Japanese. *Diabetes Research and Clinical Practice, 10,* S113–118.

Hubert, H. B., Feinleib, M., McNamara, P. M., & Castelli, W. P. (1983). Obesity as an independent risk factor for cardiovascular disease: A 26-year follow-up of participants in the Framingham heart study. *Circulation, 5,* 968–977.

Hunt, E. E., Jr. (1972). Epidemiologic considerations. *Advances in Psychosomatic Medicine, 7,* 148–172.

Jooste, P. L., Steenkamp, H. J., Benade, A. J., & Rossouw, J. E. (1988). Prevalence of overweight and obesity and its relation to coronary heart disease in the CORIS study. *South African Medical Journal, 74,* 101–104.

Kadyrova, R. K., & Salkhanov, B. A. (1990). The prevalence of obesity among the adult population of Kazakhstan. *Voprosy Pitania (Moskva),* Jan-Feb (1), 30–33.

Keys, A. (1980). Overweight, obesity, coronary heart disease and mortality. *Nutrition Reviews, 38,* 297–307.

Keys, A. (1989). Longevity of man: Relative weight and fatness in middle age. *Annals of Medicine, 21,* 163–168.

Kissebah, A. H., Freedman, D. S., & Peiris, A. N. (1989). Health risks of obesity. *Medical Clinics of North America, 73,* 111–138.

Kluthe, R., & Schubert, A. (1985). Obesity in Europe. *Annals of Internal Medicine, 103,* 1037–1042.

Kral, J. G. (1985). Morbid obesity and related health risks. *Annals of Internal Medicine, 103,* 1043–1047.

Kumanyika, S. (1987). Obesity in Black women. *Epidemiologic Reviews, 9,* 31–50.

Kuskowska-Wolk, A., & Rossner, S. (1990). Prevalence of obesity in Sweden: Cross-sectional study of a representative adult population. *Journal of Internal Medicine, 227,* 241–246.

Lapidus, L., Bengtsson, C., Hallstrom, T., & Bjorntorp, P. (1989). Obesity, adipose tissue distribution and health in women: Results from a population study in Gothenburg, Sweden. *Appetite, 12,* 25–35.

Lehtovirta, E., & Pyorala, K. (1974). Prevalence and natural history of obesity in Helsinki policemen. In A. Howard (Ed.), *Recent Advances in Obesity Research: 1* (pp. 39–41). Westport, CT: Technomic Publishing.

Martin, A. D., & Drinkwater, D. T. (1991). Variability in the measures of body fat—Assumptions or technique? *Sports Medicine, 11,* 277–288.

Martin, A. D., Ross, W. D., Drinkwater, D. T., & Clarys, J. P. (1985). Prediction of body fat by skinfold caliper: Assumptions and cadaver evidence. *International Journal of Obesity, 9*(Suppl. 1), 31–39.

McGarvey, S. T. (1991). Obesity in Samoans and a perspective on its etiology in Polynesians. *American Journal of Clinical Nutrition, 53,* 1586S–1594S.

Metropolitan Life Insurance Company. (1983). New weight standards for men and women. *Statistical Bulletin, 40,* 1–3.

Metropolitan Life Insurance Company. (1983). 1983 Metropolitan height and weight tables. *Statistical Bulletin, 64,* 2.

Misbin, R. I. (1983). Beneficial effects of a mild exercise programme on hypertriglyceridaemia, glucose tolerance and hyperinsulinaemia in obese patients. *Diabetologia, 25,* 375.

Modan, M., Lubin, F., Lusky, A., Chetrit, A., Fuchs, Z., & Halkin, H. (1987). Inter-relationships of obesity, habitual diet, physical activity and glucose intolerance in the four main Jewish ethnic groups. In E. B. Berry, S. H. Blondheim, H. E. Eliahou, & E. Shafrir (Eds.), *Recent advances in obesity research: V* (pp. 46–53). London: John Libbey.

Nasser, M. (1988). Culture and weight consciousness. *Journal of Psychosomatic Research, 32,* 573–577.

National Institutes of Health Consesus Development Panel (1985). Health implications of obesity. *Annals of Internal Medicine, 103,* 1073–1077.

O'Dea, K., & Hopper, J. (1990). Obesity and non-insulin-dependent diabetes in Australian Aborigines. In Oomura, Y., Tarui, S., Onoue, S., Shimazu, T. (Eds.), *Progress in Obesity Research 1990* (pp. 645–648). London: John Libbey.

Osancova, K. (1974). Trends of dietary intake and prevalence of obesity in Czechoslovakia. In A. Howard (Ed.), *Recent Advances in Obesity Research: 1* (pp. 42–44). Westport, CT: Technomic Publishing.

Pagano, R., Godi, L., & Cairella, M. (1988). Obesity in Italy. *Public Health, 102,* 555–563.

Peters Atlas of the World (1990). New York: Harper & Row.

Pettitt, D. J., Lisse, J. R., Knowler, W. C., & Bennett, P. H. (1982). Mortality as a function of obesity and diabetes mellitus. *American Journal of Epidemiology, 115,* 359–366.

Pories, W. J., Caro, J. F., Flickinger, E. G., Meelheim, H. D., & Swanson, M. S. (1987). The control of diabetes mellitus in the morbidly obese with the Greenville gastric bypass. *Annals of Surgery, 206,* 316–323.

Rand, C. S. W., & Kuldau, J. M. (1990). The epidemiology of obesity and self-defined weight problem in the general population: Gender, race, age, and social class. *International Journal of Eating Disorders, 9,* 329–343.

Rand, C. S. W., & Kuldau, J. M. (1992). The epidemiology of bulimia and symptoms in a general population: Sex, age, race, and socioeconomic status. *International Journal of Eating Disorders, 11,* 37–44.

Rebuffe-Scrive, M. (1990). Regional differences in visceral adipose tissue metabolism. In Y. Oomura, S. Tarui, S. Inoe, & T. Shimazu (Eds.), *Progress in Obesity Research 1990* (pp. 313–316). London: John Libbey.

Rimm, A. A. (1990). A reveal-conceal test for manuscript review: Its application in the obesity and mortality study. *Journal of Clinical Epidemiology, 8,* 753–754.

Schapira, D. V., Kumar, N. B., Lyman, G. H., & Cox, C. E. (1990). Abdominal obesity and breast cancer risk. *Annals of Internal Medicine, 113,* 182–186.

Schwarz, B., Bischof, H. P., & Kunze, M. (1991). Overweight and coronary risk factors results from a western Australian survey. *Sozial-und Praventivmedizin (Solothurn), 36,* 322–326.

Segal, K. R., Dunaif, A., Gutin, B., Albu, T., Nyman, A., & Pi-Sunger, F. X. (1987). Body composition, not body weight, is related to cardiovascular disease risk factors and sex hormone levels in men. *Journal of Clinical Investigation, 80,* 1050–1055.

Shelgikar, K. M., Hockaday, T. D. R., & Yajnik, C. S. (1991). Central rather than generalized obesity is related to hyperglycaemia in Asian Indian subjects. *Diabetes Medicine, 8,* 712–717.

Shimokata, H., Muller, D. C., & Andres, R. (1989). Studies in the distribution of body fat. III. Effects of cigarette smoking. *Journal of the American Medical Association, 261,* 1169–1174.

Sicree, R. A., Zimmet, P. Z., King, H., & Coventry, J. S. (1987). Weight change amongst Nauruans over 6.5 years: extent, and association with glucose intolerance. *Diabetes Research and Clinical Practice, 3,* 327–336.

Sjostrom, L. V. (1992). Morbidity of severely obese subjects. *American Journal of Clinical Nutrition, 55,* 508S–525S.

Sobal, J., & Stunkard, A. J. (1989). Socioeconomic status and obesity: A review of the literature. *Psychological Bulletin, 105,* 260–275.

Sorlie, P., Gordon, T., & Kannel, W. B. (1980). Body build and mortality: The Framingham study. *Journal of the American Medical Association, 243,* 845–848.

Steyn, K., Fourie, J., Rossouw, J. E., Langenhoven, M. L., Joubert, G., & Chalton, D. O. (1990). Anthropometric profile of the colored population of the Cape Peninsula. *South African Medical Journal, 78,* 68–72.

Stunkard, A. J. (1988). Obesity: Risk factors, consequences and control. *The Medical Journal of Australia, 148,* S21–28.

Tanner, J. M., & Whitehouse, R. H. (1962). Standards for subcutaneous fat in British children. *British Medical Journal, 1,* 446–450.

Tanphaichitr, V., Kulapongse, S., Pakpeankitvatana, R., Leelahagul, P., Tamwiwat, C., & Lochaya, S. (1990). Prevalence of obesity and its associated risks in urban Thais. In Y. Oomura, S. Tarui, S. Inoue, & T. Shimazu (Eds.), *Progress in Obesity Research 1990,* (pp. 649–653). London: John Libbey.

Tarui, S., Tokunaga, K., Fujioka, S., & Matsuzawa, Y. (1991). Visceral fat obesity: Anthropological and pathophysiological aspects. *International Journal of Obesity, 15,* 1–8.

Van Itallie, T. B. (1985). Health implications of overweight and obesity. *Annals of Internal Medicine, 103,* 983–988.

Walker, A. R., Walker, B. F., Walker, A. J., & Vorster, H. H. (1989). Low frequency of adverse sequelae of obesity in South African rural black women. *International Journal of Vitamin Nutrition Research, 59,* 224–228.

Appendix 11-A   Prevalence of Obesity*

Country	Age	Number	Obesity index	% of subjects or average BMI			
Micronesia				BMI Men			
Nauruans				1975/6		1982	
	20–29	47 M	Average BMI	32.3		37.1	
	30–39	29 M		33.1		34.1	
	40–49	35 M		31.6		33.1	
	50–59	17 M		30.2		30.5	
				BMI Women			
	20–29	66 W		34.4		38.3	
	30–39	31 W		35.6		38.2	
	40–49	35 W		35.7		36.7	
	50–59	23 W		33.8		35.2	
						(Sicree, 1987)	

Country	Age	Number	Obesity index	% Men		% Women	
Samoans	20–74	—		OW	O	OW	O
			OW = BMI				
Western Samoa	—	78 M	≥ 27.8 M	33	11.5	46	19.1
	—	89 W	≥ 27.3 W				
American Samoa: Manu	—	137 M	O = BMI	56	25.5	77	50.0
	—	238 W	≥ 31.1 M				
Tutuila	—	624 M	≥ 32.2 W	62	36.1	79	51.5
	—	848 W					
Oahu, Hawaii	—	222 M		75	44.6	80	54.5
	—	290 W				(McGarvey, 1991)	

Country	Age	Number	Obesity index	BMI men			
Japan, national nutrition survey			Average BMI	1947	1967	1987	
	30–39	—		21.5	21.9	23.1	
	40–49	—		21.5	22.1	23.2	
	50–59	—		21.1	22.1	23.1	
				BMI women			
	30–39	—		22.2	22.1	21.9	
	40–49	—		22.1	22.8	22.9	
	50–59	—		21.4	22.9	23.5	
						(Horibe, 1990)	

Country	Age	Number	Obesity index	% Men	% Women
Thailand, urban officials		2703 M 792 W			
	35–39	—	BMI 25–29	18.5	14.9
	40–44	—		22.8	12.7
	45–49	—		25.4	32.7
	50–54	—		30.7	22.9

(*continued on next page*)

Appendix 11-A   Prevalence of Obesity (*Continued*)

Country	Age	Number	Obesity Index	% of subjects or average BMI	
Thailand continued				% Men	% Women
	35–39	—	BMI ≥ 30	1.5	2.5
	40–44	—		1.8	1.9
	45–49	—		2.5	3.0
	50–54	—		3.9	12.5
				(Tanphaichitr et al., 1990)	
Bombay, India		791 M			
		993 W		% Men	% Women
	15–30	—	BMI 25–29	18.2	19.5
	31–50	—		40.6	45.7
	51–76	—		35.1	37.6
			BMI ≥ 30		
	15–30	—		0.3	3.1
	31–50	—		6.5	9.6
	51–76	—		8.1	9.8
				(Dhurandhar & Kulkarni, 1992)	
Kuwait	Adults	2999 W		—	% Women
			10–20% above reference standard		52.5
			>20%		42.0
					(al Awadi et al., 1989)
				% Men	% Women
Voralberg, Western Australia	25–64	635 M 693 W	BMI 25–29 BMI ≥ 30 (age standardized)	42.8 8.6	23.0 13.3
					(Schwartz et al., 1991)
				% Men	% Women
U.S.A.	20–74	—	BMI 25–30	31	24
Canada	20–69	—		40	28
Great Britain	16–65	—		34	24
Netherlands	20+	—		34	24
Australia	25–64	—		34	24
U.S.A.	20–74	—	BMI > 30	12	12
Canada	20–69	—		9	12
Great Britain	16–65	—		6	8
Netherlands	20+	—		4	6
Australia	25–64	—		7	7
					(Bray, 1990)

Appendix 11-A   Prevalence of Obesity (*Continued*)

Country	Age	Number	Obesity index	% of subjects or average BMI	
				% >120%	% >130%
Finland Helsinki policemen	30–34	222	Relative body weight (Finnish Life Insurance	5.8	1.4
	35–39	146		9.6	3.4
	40–44	296		8.4	1.4
	45–49	331		11.2	3.3
	50–54	194		16.0	6.7
	55–59	104		12.5	1.91
					(Lehtovirta & Pyorala, 1974)
				% Men	% Women
Sweden	16–84	14,549	Overweight (BMI not stated)	34.5	31.2
			BMI ≥ 30	6.6	13.1
				(Kuskowska-Wolk & Rossner, 1990)	
Czechoslovakia	20–50+	—	% ≥ 125% Desirable weight local standards	1956	
				% Men	% Women
				7.6	24.3
				1971	
				9.0	33.7
					(Osancova, 1974)
Kazakhstan, U.S.S.R.	15–65+	25,107	BMI = 0 (cutoff not specified)		% Both M & W
					23.7
					(Kadyrova, 1990)
West Germany			Brocca		% Both M & W
1955 Life Insurance	—	—	≥ 40%		8.0
				% Men	% Women
2 cities	30–60	4,709 M	> 20%	14.0	—
East Germany			Brocca		
Rural	—	1,918	> 20%	16.0	41.0
Rural & town	—	30,516	> 20%	27.0	52.0
Town & rural	—	79,708	> 20%	14.0	32.0
			> 20%	23.0	49.0
Great Britain national sample	20–26	5,362	> 20%	5–12	6–11
Netherlands Ede	19–31	3,857	BMI 25–29	22	12
			BMI ≥ 30	2	2

(*continued on next page*)

Appendix 11-A   Prevalence of Obesity (*Continued*)

Country	Age	Number	Obesity index	% of subjects or average BMI	
				% Men	% Women
Norway					
20 Oslo physician offices	40–49	3,751 M	Brocca 15–25%	14.1	—
Rumania	15–65	100,428	MLI over-		
town	—	—	weight	25.4	32.3
rural	—	—	> 20%	22.2	40.9
Switzerland	25–34	149 M	BMI ≥ 26.4	14.5	—
Basil industry	35–44	721 M		27.5	—
employees	45–54	1,187 M		35.5	—
	55–64	934 M		44.0	—
	65	339 M		43.0	—
					(Kluthe & Schubert, 1985)

Italy, regions:	Age	Number	Obesity index	% Men		% Women	
	15–	41,557 M		OW	O	OW	O
	80+	43,952 W					
Northwest	—	—	OW= BMI	28	3.0	14	4.4
Northeast	—	—	25–29.9	32	3.6	16	4.6
Center	—	—	O = BMI	32	4.1	18	5.3
South	—	—	≥ 30	31	3.1	18	5.0

(Pagano, Godi, & Cairella, 1988)

Israel, Jews	Age	Number	Obesity index	% Men	% Women
		2,783 M		1969–1972	
		2,928W			
first	30–39	—	BMI ≥ 27.0	23.3	16.0
assessment	40–49	—		25.3	31.4
	50+	—		28.9	37.3
				1977–1982	
second	40–49	—		33.3	27.9
assessment	50–59	—		30.3	44.3
	60+	—		34.5	48.4
					(Modan, 1987)

South Africa,	Age	Number	Obesity index	—	% Women
Eastern Transvaal Black rural	25–45	210 W	BMI ≥ 30		19.0
					(Walker et al., 1989)

Cape Peninsula, Black	Age	Number	Obesity index	% Men	% Women
		478 M			
		498 W			
	15–24	—	BMI 25–30	5.3	24.3
	25–34	—		19.8	41.5
	35–44	—		29.2	46.5

Appendix 11-A   Prevalence of Obesity (*Continued*)

Country	Age	Number	Obesity index	% of subjects or average BMI	
				% Men	% Women
	45–54	—		35.0	40.4
	55–64	—		26.6	34.7
	15–24	—	BMI ≥ 30	2.1	6.8
	25–34	—		1.0	17.0
	35–44	—		5.8	20.5
	45–54	—		6.3	42.6
	55–64	—		15.6	45.3
					(Steyn et al., 1990)
South Africa, White	15–64	7,188	BMI	% Men	% Women
			Overweight	41.9	38.8
			Obese	14.7	18.0
					(Jooste et al., 1988)
United States			Severe OW = 95th percentile weight/ height index of women 20–29 (NHANES I)	—	% Women
NHANES I 1971–1974	20–74	>10,000 W			1971–1974
White				—	7.3
Black				—	18.3
NHANES II 1976–1980	20–74	>10,000 W			1976–1980
White				—	7.9
Black				—	16.6
					(Kumanyika, 1987)
United States		>10,000		% Men	% Women
NHANES II 1976–1980	20–24	—	BMI	12.7	9.6
White	25–34	—	≥ 27.8 M	20.9	17.9
	35–44	—	≥ 27.3 W	28.2	24.8
	45–54	—		30.5	29.9
	55–64	—		28.6	34.8
	65–74	—		25.8	36.5
Black	20–24	—		5.5	23.7
	25–34	—		17.5	33.5
	35–44	—		40.9	40.8
	45–54	—		41.4	61.2
	55–64	—		26.0	59.4
	65–74	—		26.4	60.8
					(Van Itallie, 1985)

(*continued on next page*)

Appendix 11-A   Prevalence of Obesity (*Continued*)

Country	Age	Number	Obesity index	% of subjects or average BMI			

Country	Age	Number	Obesity index	% Men		% Women	
North American Indians		3,200					
	18–24	—	BMI≥	21.5		25.2	
	25–34	—	27.8 M	31.8		45.1	
	35–44	—	27.3 W	37.8		48.5	
	45–54	—		49.1		54.0	
	55–64	—		45.4		45.6	
	65+	—		25.2		45.6	
	total 18–65+		BMI≥ 31.1 M 32.3 W	9.1		8.2	

(Broussard et al., 1991)

				% Men		% Women	
U.S. Hispanic:	18–60+		OW = BMI≥ 85th percentile	OW	O	OW	O
Mexican American		1,694 M 2,137 W	NHANES II O = BMI	33.5	10.6	42.3	15.1
Puerto Rican		562 M 929 W	≥95th percentile	31.4	9.6	40.7	7.8
Cuban		423 M 423 W	NHAMES II	34.0	9.0	38.2	15.0

(Pawson, 1991)

Cental America				% Men	% Women
Costa Rica	20–25	61 M 106 W	BMI > 30	0.0	2.8
	40–45	52 M 83 W		5.7	14.4
El Salvador	20–25	51 M 77 W		0.0	1.3
	40–45	38 M 68 W		0.0	1.5
Guatemala	20–25	81 M 119 W		0.0	0.0
	40–45	48 M 89 W		0.0	5.6

Appendix 11-A   Prevalence of Obesity (*Continued*)

Country	Age	Number	Obesity index	% of subjects or average BMI	
				% Men	% Women
Honduras	20–25	43 M		0.0	1.0
		105 W			
	40–45	36 M		2.8	6.0
		67 W			
Nicaragua	20–25	43 M		2.3	3.0
		100 W			
	40–45	32 M		3.1	16.4
		67 W			
Panama	20–25	43 M		0.0	0.0
		71 W			
	40–45	44 M		2.3	1.7
		58 W			
Trinidad	40	—		—	32.0
(urban)	74	—		—	27.0
					(Gurney & Gorotein, 1988)

*Note: M = men; W = women; BMI = body mass index (kg/meters squared); MLI = Metropolitan Life Insturance tables; Brocca = Brocca normal weight; NHANES = National Health and Nutrition Examination Survey, 1976–1980 standards. Overweight = BMI ≥ 27.8 m, 27.3 f; severely overweight = BMI ≥ 31.1 m, 32.2 f. OW = overweight; O = Obese, severely overweight.

— Indicates that no information was available.

Chapter 12

Obesity: Sociocultural Perspectives

Harold E. Yuker
David B. Allison

Much has been written about attitudes toward and beliefs about obesity and obese persons. Research studies have been done and discussions have been held of the attitudes of nonobese people, obese people, children, educators, employers, professionals, and so forth. The purpose of this chapter is to summarize and interpret this research, with an emphasis on variables correlated with these attitudes and beliefs. Although we will briefly offer and evaluate some putative explanations for ethnic and social class differences in obesity rates, that material was covered in more detail by Rand in chapter 11.

ATTITUDES AND BELIEFS ABOUT OBESE PEOPLE

It is often stated that attitudes of nonobese children and adults toward those who are obese are negative and discriminatory (Allon, 1982; Goodman, Richardson, Dornbusch, & Hastorf, 1963; Horan, 1981; Matthews & Westie, 1966; Richard-

We gratefully acknowledge Angelique Fournier and Rebecca Amaru for their efforts in the technical preparation of this chapter and Meryl Allison for her helpful comments on an earlier draft.

son, Goodman, Dornbusch, & Hastorf, 1961). As discussed later in this chapter, other studies have documented negative attitudes among various groups including educators, employers, and helping professionals. A review by Wooley, Wooley, and Dyrenforth (1979) revealed that children who are overweight tend to be rejected by their peers. In their investigations of the attitudes of children, Richardson and colleagues (Richardson et al., 1961) concluded that obese children were consistently rated more poorly than those with other types of disabilities. Harris, Harris, and Bochner (1982) stated that the negative perception of obesity is so powerful that other characteristics such as gender or wearing glasses have no additional negative effects on person perception. In fact, Hiller (1981) and Dehger and Hughes (1991) assigned obesity the status of a "master identity," implying that it nullifies the usual effects of other attributes.

Several studies have compared attitudes toward obese persons with attitudes toward members of other stigmatized groups. Richardson and colleagues (see Richardson, 1983) concluded that obese children were consistently rated lower than those with other disabilities, e.g., a child on crutches, in a wheelchair, with a missing hand, or with a disfigured face. Yuker (1983), however, challenged the generality of Richardson's findings, pointing out the presence of group differences.

An early study by Wolfgang and Wolfgang (1971) measured preferred interpersonal distance among college students and military personnel. Using stick figures representing both "normal" persons and members of several "marginal" groups, they obtained data indicating the following preference hierarchy: normal, marijuana users, drug users, obese persons, homosexual persons. In contrast, with respect to the obese persons' attitude toward their own obesity, Harris, Waschull, & Walters (1990) reported that overweight people preferred being overweight to having a different stigmatizing disability.

Data indicate that negative attitudes toward obese persons may have profound deleterious consequences such as discrimination. Obese persons attend college at lower rates (Canning & Mayer, 1966) despite equal qualifications (Canning & Mayer, 1967). They are discriminated against in the job market (Kennedy & Homant, 1984; Larkin & Pines, 1979; Rothblum, Miller, & Garbutt, 1988) and in the search for housing (Karris, 1977). People are less compliant with the requests of obese persons (Rodin & Slochower, 1974; Steinberg & Birk, 1983). It has also been argued that obese persons experience emotional distress as the result of the negative attitudes directed toward them (Allon, 1982; Monello & Mayer, 1963).

It has even been suggested that some of the physiological aberrations associated with obesity (e.g., hypertension) are the result of the chronic derogation heaped upon obese persons (Mayer, 1983). This hypothesis is not entirely untenable. The mechanism behind the obesity-hypertension link is not fully understood (Dustan, 1991). Black persons, who face discrimination as well, also have an elevated incidence of hypertension. Moreover, blood pressure has been shown to be negatively correlated with the degree to which people are perceived as attractive (Hansell, Sparacino, & Ronchi, 1982) and positively correlated with the degree that people perceive themselves as receiving love (Sisca, Walsh, & Walsh, 1985). These relationships exist even after controlling for weight. Finally, suppressed anger, a likely outcome among persecuted groups, has been shown to be a consistent correlate of blood pressure (Johnson, Spielberger, Worden, & Jacobs, 1987). To our knowledge, no study has assessed the relationship between relative weight and blood pressure after controlling for "degree of derogation" experienced.

ANTIOBESE BIAS AS A WOMEN'S ISSUE

Several writers have begun to address the social and psychological concerns particular to obese women. Orbach (1978) termed fat a "feminist issue" and discussed the many meanings fat can have for obese women. *Shadow on a Tightrope* (Schoenfielder & Wieser, 1983) is a powerful collection of essays and poems in which women describe their experiences of society's condemnation of fat women. Spitzack (1987) goes so far as to state that "The discourse of weight reduction provides an archetype for contemporary domination strategies" (p. 366). In 1989, a special issue of *Women and Therapy* (Brown & Rothblum, 1989) addressed the role of "fat oppression" in psychotherapy from a feminist perspective. These expository works are supported by more data-based works in their contention that women are at particular risk for stigmatization due to obesity.

Obesity is stigmatized among men, but to a greater extent among women. Social norms tend to equate thinness and attractiveness in women. Oswalt and Davis (1990) found that during the past 80 years, pictures of young girls in children's readers have become progressively thinner while no consistent trend was evident for young boys. Numerous investigators (e.g., Rodin, Silberstein, & Striegel-Moore, 1985) have concluded that obesity is strongly stigmatized and that the sanctions are more severe for women. In the United States, both self-imposed and other-imposed norms of thinness seem to apply more to women than to men (Hesse-Biber, Clayton-Matthews, & Downey, 1987; Stake & Lauer, 1987; Sherman, 1981). Data indicate more women than men seek weight reduction treatments (Ashwell & Etchell, 1974; Gordon & Tobias, 1984; Horm & Anderson, 1992; Serdula, 1992) and the discrimination against obese persons seems to be stronger for women than men (Bellizzi et al., 1989; Harris, Walters, & Waschull, 1991; Hiller, 1981; Jasper & Klassen, 1990a, 1990b). These data are consistent with the finding that men are more concerned than women about the weight and physical appearance of the people they date (Davis, 1990; Harris et al., 1991; Smith, Waldorf, & Trembath, 1990).

In general, this is consistent with data showing that physical appearance is more central to self-esteem for females than for males (Musa & Roach, 1973; Lerner, Orlos, & Knapp, 1976; Secord & Jourard, 1953). Interestingly, in a recent study, Thornton and Ryckman (1991) did *not* find that physical attractiveness was differentially related to self-esteem for adolescent males versus females and suggested that this might be due to "changes occurring in sex-role expectations and socialization" (p. 85).

SOCIAL PSYCHOLOGY OF ATTITUDES TOWARD OBESE PERSONS

Only a few investigators have gone beyond mere description of attitudes toward obese persons and tried to understand the social-psychological processes giving rise to these attitudes. Attitudes toward people who are obese may be considered part of an *attitude constellation.* That is, they are related to other attitudes that have similar components. Thus, they can be related to attitudes toward stigmatized groups such as those with physical or mental disabilities or members of minority groups.

Authoritarianism

Crandall and Biernat (1990) presented evidence demonstrating that persons who are "antifat" (as measured by a five-item scale with a reliability of .65) share an ideologically conservative outlook on life. They found that such persons tend to be "politically conservative, racist, in favor of capital punishment, and less support-ive of nontraditional marriages" (p. 227), although the correlation coefficients were all low, ranging from .06 to .24. The correlations would presumably have been higher if the measures used were more reliable.

In a second study, Crandall and Biernat (1990) reported a correlation of .41 between antifat attitudes and *authoritarianism,* a result that corresponds to conver-gent data indicating that negative attitudes toward persons who are disabled tend to be correlated with both authoritarianism and negative attitudes toward members of minority groups and people who are "different" (Yuker & Block, 1986). Thus, negative attitudes toward obese persons do not occur in isolation but appear to be part of a constellation of generally authoritarian, oppressive, and bigoted attitudes.

Responsibility

Many obese persons blame themselves for being overweight (Harris et al., 1990). About 60% of overweight children believe obesity is the fault of the individual (Harris & Smith, 1982). Studies of attitudes toward disabled persons often indi-cate that those who are perceived as being responsible for their disability frequent-ly are viewed more negatively than those not responsible (Shurka, 1983; Wright, 1983). This has been demonstrated for obese persons as well (DeJong, 1980). When obesity is viewed as self-inflicted, the obese person is evaluated more negatively (Weiss, 1980). Recently we (Allison, Basile, & Yucker, 1991) reported correlations ranging from .40 to .45 between the belief that obesity is within the obese person's control and more negative attitudes toward obese persons.

According to Allon (1979), those who viewed being overweight as both their own responsibility and as an illness that required their efforts and those of professional experts were more successful in losing weight than those who focused on only their own responsibility. Related to this are the findings of Uzark, Becker, Dielman, Rocchini, and Katch (1988). They reported that successful weight loss was positively correlated with perceptions that the individuals had personal control over their health and that obesity was attributable to medical problems. This raises an interesting question. Should health professionals attempt to dispute obese persons' beliefs in their ability to control their body shapes and thereby raise self-esteem as some (e.g., Ciliska, 1990) have suggested, or should they try to instill in obese persons the notion that they can control their body shapes and thereby increase the probability of successful weight control?

DEMOGRAPHIC CORRELATES

Data indicate that obesity is not a unitary syndrome (Allison & Heshka, 1991, 1992; Leon & Roth, 1977), and its prevalence varies as a function of demographic characteristics such as age, gender, ethnicity, and socioeconomic status (Rand & Kuldau, 1990). In addition, these variables interact with one another. For example, slightly more young white men are overweight than young black men, but substantially more black than white women are overweight (Kumanyika, 1987; Rand & Kuldau, 1990). In view of these data, attitude differences related to these variables could be postulated. Although correlations are not in and of themselves mechanisms of action, they may provide clues as to the social-psychological mechanisms underlying attitudes toward obese persons. Therefore, demographic correlates of attitudes toward obese persons are reviewed here.

Age

Data indicate that the negative attitudes toward obesity prevalent in the United States are even found in young children (Goodman et al., 1963; Lerner & Gellert, 1969; Staffieri, 1967), usually becoming apparent prior to age 7 (Feldman, Feldman, & Goodman, 1988). Harris and Smith (1982) reported that adults were less likely than children to consider obese people responsible for their condition, suggesting more positive attitudes toward obese persons with age. Harris and Hopwood (1983) reported that persons over age 30 held less prejudiced and more sympathetic attitudes toward obese persons than did persons under 30. Similarly, Young and Powell (1985) reported that older mental health workers had less negative attitudes toward obese patients than did younger mental health workers. Harris and Furukawa (1986) observed that the attitudes of elderly persons were less negative than those of young adults, which they said might be due to a diminished emphasis on personal appearance among older persons.

Discrepant results were reported by Chetwynd, Stewart, and Powell (1974) and Allison et al. (1991). Among their adult samples, age was unrelated to attitudes toward obese persons. Also, Bagley et al. (1989) reported that the attitudes of older nurses were less positive than those of younger ones.

These discrepancies underscore the fact that the answer to the question "What is the relationship between age and attitudes toward obese persons?" is probably "It depends." For example, Rand & Kuldau (1990) reported interactions between age, ethnicity, and gender. Thinness was prized most by white women, particularly those 18 to 34 years old. Whereas average weight was considered acceptable by young white men, being 6 to 10 pounds overweight was acceptable to white men aged 45 to 75. The majority of black women aged 55 to 74 who averaged 17 to 20 pounds overweight asserted they had no weight problem.

Gender

Given that the discrimination against obese persons appears to be more severe for women, one might expect that women themselves would be less prejudiced toward obese persons. However, the data pertaining to gender differences in attitudes toward obese persons are mixed. Four studies reported no gender differences in attitudes (Harris, Harris, & Bochner, 1982; Harris & Hopwood, 1983; Larkin & Pines, 1979; Ryckman, Robbins, Kaczor, & Gold, 1989), six reported that men have less negative attitudes (Allison et al., 1991; Crandall & Biernat, 1990; Hiller, 1981; Tiggeman & Rothblum, 1988; Worsley, 1981; Young & Powell, 1985), one reported that women have less negative attitudes (Chetwynd et al. 1974), and one reported that young girls had less negative attitudes than young boys (LeBow, 1988).

Ethnicity

In the United States, the prevalence of obesity among black women is approximately twice that among white women, although no substantial differences exists between black and white men (Kumanyika, 1987; Rand & Kuldau, 1990; Sobal, 1991). Similar trends exist among Hispanic women (Pawson, Martorell, & Mendoza, 1991). These ethnic differences appear to persist even after controlling for socioeconomic status (Dawson, 1988; Kumanyika, 1987; Rand & Kuldau, 1990). Obesity rates are higher still among American Indians, Alaskan Natives, and Native Hawaiians (Aluli, 1991; Broussard et al., 1991). Among Japanese Americans, obesity is less prevalent than among Whites and other ethnic groups (Curb & Marcus, 1991). According to Curb and Marcus (1991), there are insufficient data on body weight among Asian Americans other than Japanese Americans to draw firm conclusions.

There is little controlled data on any ethnic groups besides White, Black, and Hispanic Americans with respect to sociocultural aspects of obesity. For this reason, with few exceptions, the following discussion will be confined to these groups.

Some studies have suggested positive associations, lack of stigmatization, or less stigmatization of obesity among some African Americans (Sims, 1979; Styles, 1980), Mexican Americans (Lerner & Pool, 1972; Ritenbaugh, 1982; Ross & Mirowsky, 1983), and Puerto Ricans living in the United States (Massara, 1979, 1980; Massara & Stunkard, 1979). Stereotypes and anecdotal evidence suggesting greater desired body weight among minority groups, particularly African Americans, abound. For example, in an old blues tune, Ida Cox (a woman who was "plump" at most) sang "I'm a big fat mamma got some meat shakin' on my bones and every time I shake some skinny girl loses her home." In a recent music video, a rapper, "Sir Mixalot," verbally and visually extols the virtues of women with large bottoms.

However, we can find equally powerful anecdotal evidence suggesting the contrary. Rosemary Bray wrote an article in *Essence,* a popular magazine targeted toward black women. She stated:

> . . . imagine what it is like then to be a fat Black woman—to be, all at once, three of the worst things you can be in contemporary American culture . . . Big Black women are the caricature of excess. We are just *too* much to be tolerated, so excessive that we should be hidden, kept from view, trotted out only to be laughed at (1992, p. 90).

Although some data indicate that self-defined weight standards for blacks in the United States may be slightly higher than those for whites (Desmond, Price, Hallinan, & Smith, 1989; Rand & Kuldau, 1990), when it comes to ethnicity and attitudes toward obesity and obese persons, things are not simple. In 1963, Goodman et al. reported that Jewish children in the United States were less rejecting of an obese child than were most other groups. They had hypothesized this also would be true of Italian children, but their data failed to confirm this.

Harris et al. (1991) reported that among college students, blacks, particularly black women, were more satisfied with their body shape even though they were heavier than whites. Although compared to white men, black men viewed overweight women as somewhat less "unattractive, less sexless," and "less sloppy," in no case did they see overweight women as better than neutral with respect to these characteristics, and they also saw obese women as somewhat more pathetic. Hall, Cousins, & Power (1991) studied the body figure perceptions of Mexican-American mothers and their 7- to 12-year-old daughters and observed a linear relationship indicating that increasing relative weight was associated with decreasing attractiveness ratings. We recently completed two studies that specifically investigated ethnic differences in the women's body shapes men find attractive. We failed to find evidence of substantial ethnic differences in this regard (Allison, 1992; Hoy, Allison, & Heymsfield, 1992). In addition, Allan, Mayo, & Michel (1992) generally found no significant differences between black and white women in terms of the body shapes they preferred.

Harris and Smith (1982) reported that Native Americans, blacks, and Hispanics have negative attitudes toward individuals who are obese. Harris and Harris (1992) also found no ethnic differences in the body shapes viewed as desirable among Hispanic, Native-American, and white American men and women, and all groups preferred rather slim figures. Young (1985) found no significant differences among four ethnic groups (blacks, whites, Filipinos, East Indians) on attitudes toward obese persons, although the power of the statistical analysis was rather low. In a much larger sample with superior statistical methods, Sims (1979) found that black women had better attitudes toward obese persons than did white or Native-American women. However, it is difficult to invoke this as a straightforward explanation for ethnic differences in obesity since the Native-American women were heavier than the black women but had less positive attitudes toward obesity. Moreover, although black women had more positive attitudes toward obesity than did Native-American women, Native-American women desired higher body mass indices (BMIs). Finally, it should be noted that, on the average, none of the groups desired BMIs above 23.5, which is clearly not in the obese or even overweight range.

Thus, it is our belief that the notion that American minorities, particularly blacks, value obesity and view it as attractive is based more on anecdote and stereotype than on a consistently supportive body of data. What seems more probable is that members of certain minority groups may have modestly higher (though still normal) desired body weights and slightly less negative (though still not positive) attitudes toward obese persons.

Socioeconomic Status

In the world as a whole, the extent of obesity is usually positively related to social class, but the relationship tends to be negative in affluent societies (Brown & Konner, 1987). After an extensive review of 144 published studies dealing with the relationship between socioeconomic status (SES) and obesity, Sobal and Stunkard (1989) concluded there are differences between developing and developed societies.

The positive correlation between SES and fatness in developing societies is relatively easy to explain. Presumably because of insufficient food and high energy expenditure, particularly among lower SES persons, "Obesity is rare in unacculturated primitive populations, but the prevalence often increases rapidly during modernization" (Brown & Konner, 1987, p. 30). Although obesity is stigmatized in mainstream U.S. culture, most other societies perceive fatness as a sign of wealth and prosperity (Brown & Konner, 1987). Brown and Konner (1987) tabulated data from the Human Relations Area Files and reported that 31 (81%) of 38 societies preferred women who were plump or moderately fat to those who were thin, although none were reported to prefer obese women. Interestingly, 9 (50%) of 18 societies preferred women with large or long breasts, while the other 50% favored those with small breasts.

This suggests the preference for fatness of the lower body is more universal than is the preference for upper body fatness. This follows from an evolutionary point of view since upper body obesity poses a greater health risk than does lower body obesity (Bjorntorp, 1987). It is also consistent with observations by Tarui, Takunaga, Fukioka, & Matsuzawa (1991), who used figures depicted in art dating from prehistory to the present to argue that lower body fat as opposed to fatness per se is desired.

In more affluent societies, where even the poorest people often have sufficient access to food to become obese, the correlation between SES and fatness is negative for women and essentially zero for men. Sobel and Stunkard (1989) noted, "The way SES acts as a moderator variable is far less clear in developed than in developing societies" (p. 267). Several possibilities exist to explain the relationships. These include but are not limited to: (a) different cultural standards for body weight (Sobal, 1991); (b) downward social mobility among obese persons (Sonne-Holm & Sorensen, 1986); (c) cross-assortative mating between fatness and SES (Buss, 1985); (d) differential rates of parity among social classes (Kumanyika, 1987); (e) racial/genetic differences (Kumanyika, 1987); and (f) differential financial access to slimming foods and opportunities for exercise (Sobal, 1991). See chapter 11 for more details.

GROUP PERCEPTIONS AND ATTITUDES

Family Perceptions

When Kinston, Loader, and Miller (1987, 1988) examined the attitudes and emotional health of families with an obese child, the data were not always consistent. They reported that compared to families of an obese child recruited from a school, families of a child recruited from an obesity clinic had more negative attitudes toward obesity, felt greater stigma, and tried harder to lose weight. It is interesting that these studies, like those that examined siblings of children with physical disabilities, focused on the effect of the obese or disabled child on the family and seldom discussed the reaction of family to the child's obesity or the effect of that reaction on the child's feelings and behavior. This is of concern given that Sherman (1981) showed that prospective parents prefer not to have an obese child and ascribe negative characteristics to obese children.

Education

Schroer (1985) found that in-service and pre-service teachers rated photographs of obese children as having a lower energy level, less leadership ability, lower self-esteem, less ability to be socially outgoing, and less attractiveness. More than half of a group of elementary school principals believed that childhood obesity results from psychological problems or a lack of self-control (Price, Desmond, &

Stelzer, 1987). Ledoux (1981) found that college freshman essays received lower evaluations when the reader believed they were written by an obese student.

At the university level, a peculiar negative bias has been demonstrated. Canning and Mayer (1966) found that obese persons were underrepresented at some of the more prestigious universities. They later showed this was not a function of poorer academic qualifications (Canning & Meyer, 1967) and speculated that college admissions personnel might be discriminating against obese applicants. However, Pargman (1969) found that the obese were also underrepresented at a school that did not rely on face-to-face interviews. This raises the question of how admissions personnel knew which applicants were obese. A resolution to this quandary was recently offered by Crandall (1991) who found that the parents of fatter students were less likely to financially support their children's education than were parents of thinner students. This relationship held even after socioeconomic status was controlled. Thus, the obese may be underrepresented at some universities because they are insufficiently financially supported by their families and perhaps not because admissions personnel actively discriminate against them. This lack of financial support is consistent with data showing that prospective parents rate pictures of obese children as more "lazy," "stupid," "dirty," "immature," and less "likable" than thin or medium children (Sherman, 1981).

Employment

Weight loss has been reported to be accompanied by an increase in the percentage of obese persons who are employed (Drenick, 1973). Obese persons often are perceived negatively when they apply for work (Jasper & Klassen, 1990b; Kennedy & Homant, 1984; Klesges et al., 1990; Larkin & Pines, 1979; Laslett & Warren, 1975; Pingitore, Dugoni, & Tindale, 1992; Rothblum, Brand, Miller, & Oetjen, 1990; Rothblum, Miller, & Garbutt, 1988). Litigation over obese persons being dismissed from employment because of their obesity has been reported (Matusewitch, 1983). Discrimination in promotion (Brink, 1988) and work assignments (Bellizzi, Klassen, & Belonax, 1989) has also occurred. In addition, some research indicates the obese receive lower wages (Frieze, Olson, & Good, 1990; Register & Williams, 1990), although other data indicate obesity has no effect on the earnings of men who work full time (McLean & Moon, 1980). In a study by Jasper and Klassen (1990a), undergraduate students rated obese salespersons as less effective and less desirable as co-workers than nonobese salespersons. Surprisingly, Roe and Eickwort (1976) found that employers perceive obesity as worse than alcoholism (though not as bad as mental illness) in terms of employability. Even more strikingly, Kennedy and Homant (1984; Homant & Kennedy, 1982) found that, in terms of employment, undergraduate and graduate students rated obese persons as less desirable than ex-mental patients and ex-criminal offenders.

Health Personnel

Convergent data indicate individuals in health occupations often have negative attitudes toward their clients (e.g., Geskie & Salasek, 1988). Negative attitudes toward obese persons have been reported in helping professionals (Kaplan, 1981; Young & Powell, 1985), nurses (Bagley et al., 1989; Carson, 1987; Peternelj-Taylor, 1989; Price, Desmond, Ruppert, & Steltzer, 1987), physicians and medical students (Blumberg & Mellis, 1980; Breytspraak et al., 1977; Klein, Najman, Kohrman, & Munroe, 1982; Maddox, Bach, & Liederman, 1968; Maiman, Wang, Becker, Finlay, & Simonson, 1979; Price et al., 1987), psychologists (Agell & Rothblum, 1991), public health administrators (Benson, Severs, Tagenhorst, & Loddengaard, 1980), and graduate rehabilitation counseling students (Kaplan, 1984). It is ironic that, under some conditions, overweight counselors are also seen as less expert and trustworthy by their clients (McKee & Smouse, 1983).

It is important to realize that the negative attitudes of health professionals do not occur in a vacuum but have been shown to influence clinical decision making (Breytspraak et al., 1977) and diagnostic judgments (Young & Powell, 1985). Regarding psychoanalysis, Ingram (1978) maintained "inevitably the analyst's participation in a culture which [sic] so strictly defines the limits of body fatness must impair his [sic] ability to determine how much his own inner fantasies and associations are stimulated either by the transference on the one hand, or by the wash of cultural influences on the other" (p. 158).

The reason behind this derogation of obese persons by health professionals may hinge on perceptions of responsibility. As stated earlier, Perloff and Bohachick (1988) showed that health care professionals were more likely to view obesity as the result of dispositional attributes of obese patients than were the obese patients.

On the more positive (or perhaps less negative) side, Young (1985) found that the attitudes of nurses toward obese persons were neither particularly positive or negative, and we (Allison et al., 1991) found that the attitudes of graduate psychology students were not significantly different than those of members of the National Association to Advance Fat Acceptance. Peternelj-Taylor (1989) found that despite negative attitudes, nurses did not hold obese patients responsible for transgressions or withdraw from these patients.

Even though physicians advise patients about weight reduction, a study in Great Britain indicated that 27% of the physicians are overweight and 3% are obese (Cade & O'Connell, 1991). There are no data indicating how successful overweight physicians are in getting their patients to lose weight compared to physicians who are not overweight. A study of nurses indicated that those who were dissatisfied with their own weight tended to have negative attitudes toward obese persons (Bagley et al., 1989).

Interestingly, 58% of physicians who were overweight agreed they should be role models and maintain normal weight. The same study indicated that many of the physicians had little knowledge of obesity. Allon (1982) cited research indicating that physicians with negative attitudes often fail to consider medical causes for excess weight. Despite all of this, some data indicate that overweight professionals have less negative attitudes than other people (Young & Powell, 1985). Harris and Furukawa (1986) reported that elderly persons perceived physicians as exhibiting only a little discrimination against obese patients. The National Association to Advance Fat Acceptance recently prepared several pamphlets for health professionals describing appropriate and sensitive treatment of obese persons (see Appendix for address).

As is the case with other groups disliked by health workers (e.g., cancer patients, unclean patients; Klein et al., 1982), few studies examine the relationship between attitudes and professional competence. One such study reported a positive correlation between the attitudes of registered nurses (RNs) and the amount of professional education they had attained (Bagley et al., 1989). More research is clearly needed on the effects that negative attitudes toward obese persons have on patient care and outcome.

Everyday Life

Discrimination against the obese is not restricted to special settings. Data indicate that overweight persons sometimes are discriminated against in the search for housing (Karris, 1977). They pay more for goods and services (Petit, 1974, cited in Dehger & Hughes, 1991), are assisted less quickly by salespersons (Pauley, 1989), are perceived as less attractive (Clayson & Klassen, 1989), and find other people are less compliant with their requests (Rodin & Slochower, 1974; Steinberg & Birk, 1983). Obese persons have been removed from airplanes or charged for two seats because they would "encroach on the space of the person who would sit next to them," even on flights that were not full (NAAFA, 1992, p. 1). Finally, this discrimination extends from everyday life to everyday death as some cemeteries begin charging more for oversize patrons (Anonymous, 1987).

ATTITUDES OF OBESE PERSONS

Perhaps surprisingly, data indicate many obese persons share at least some of the common negative attitudes toward individuals who are obese (Allon, 1979; Crandall & Biernat, 1990; Harris et al., 1991; Young, 1985). Many severely overweight persons are aware of the negative feelings of others, internalize those feelings, and accept discrimination against obese individuals as appropriate (Allon, 1979; Degher & Hughes, 1991). It is important to appreciate and understand this process of internalization since research has shown that self-perceptions of overweight and attractiveness are stronger correlates of self-esteem and social anxiety than actual overweight or perceptions of attractiveness by others (Cash & Hicks, 1990; Haemmerlie, Montgomery, & Melchers, 1988; Kenealy, Gleeson, Frude, & Shaw, 1991).

Intrapersonal Effects of Negative Attitudes

It has been asserted that obese persons experience emotional distress and poor self-concepts as the result of the negative attitudes directed toward them (Allon, 1982; Crandall & Biernat, 1990; Degher & Hughes, 1991; Maddox et al., 1968; Monello & Mayer, 1963). Several studies indicate that obese persons have lower self-esteem than those who are not obese (Davis, Wheeler, & Willy, 1987; Martin et al., 1988; Mendelson & White, 1985; Stein, 1987), although some studies with children (e.g., Mendelson & White, 1982; Wadden, Foster, Brownell, & Finley, 1984) have failed to replicate these results.

Evidence also indicates that obese women experience more loneliness than those who are not obese, although there appears to be no difference in the degree of loneliness experienced between obese and nonobese men (Schumaker, Krejci, Small, & Sargent, 1985). Kuskowska-Wolk and Rossner (1990) found that obese persons had significantly less social contact than nonobese persons. Interestingly, Miller, Rothblum, Barbour, Brand, and Felicio (1990) found that during telephone conversations (used to eliminate visual cues about body size), obese women were rated as less socially skilled than nonobese women. Whether such differences in social skill are the cause or effect of diminished social contact or if reciprocal causation is at work remains unknown.

Counterculture

Although their numbers are small, a growing group of "fat activists" has organized. In part spurred by Louderback's (1970) *Fat Power,* several books and magazines have sprung up that deliver messages such as "Fat can be beautiful" and "People are worthy of respect regardless of size" (e.g., Wegeleben, 1986).

Organizations such as The National Association to Advance Fat Acceptance and the Council on Size & Weight Discrimination seek to battle the negative perceptions of obese persons and to help obese persons develop positive self-images. The Association for the Health Enhancement of Large Persons (AHELP) is an organization of professionals dedicated to enhancing the lives of obese persons without necessarily requiring weight loss.

We applaud the efforts of these organizations and believe it is incumbent upon health professionals and scientists interested in obesity to share their expertise with these groups and work toward the common goal of healthier and happier lives for obese persons. Addresses for the organizations can be found in the Appendix.

INFORMATION AND ATTITUDE CHANGE

A close relationship between information and attitude change is often assumed. Every year, hundreds of studies attempt to change attitudes by providing information. Although most of these attempts are not successful, researchers continue the attempts year after year, apparently not discouraged by the high percentage of failures (Shaver, Curtis, Jesunathodas, & Strong, 1989). For example, a survey of the effects of a 12-page British nutritional education leaflet distributed to a sample of more than 500 persons concluded that "mass distribution of this leaflet is not an effective method of health education" (Nichols, Waters, Woolaway, & Hamilton-Smith, 1988, p. 233). Physicians in Great Britain believe doctors are less effective than either family members or the media in persuading obese patients to lose weight (Cade & O'Connell, 1991).

Few studies have correlated knowledge and attitudes. When Stern, Pugh, Gaskill, and Hazuda (1982) correlated a person's relative weight and knowledge of obesity, only 2 of 24 correlations were significant, which could have occurred by chance. Harris (1983) reported a positive correlation of .18 between knowledge of obesity and attitudes. The low correlation was attributed to the low reliability of the knowledge measure. Dash and Brown (1977) found that successful dieters had more knowledge about weight loss than those who were unsuccessful. Overweight persons are not very knowledgeable about obesity (Harris et al., 1990). Women tend to be more knowledgeable than men, and thin persons tend to be more knowledgeable than those who are overweight.

As indicated earlier, many studies indicate that persons with negative attitudes tend to attribute negative characteristics to obese persons. Obese persons are often perceived as awkward, having emotional problems, insecure, lazy, sad, self-indulgent, ugly, unkempt, and lacking willpower and self-control (Maddox et al., 1968; Maiman et al., 1979; Price et al., 1987; Weiss, 1980).

Attitude and Behavior Change

We are aware of only two studies assessing attitude changes in response to some experience. Blumberg and Mellis (1980) found that among medical students who completed a psychiatry rotation working with obese persons, no change in attitudes was found as a result of the patient contact. In contrast, Wiese, Wilson, Jones, and Neises (1992) found that an educational intervention grounded in a social psychological theory of persuasion significantly improved the attitudes of medical students.

A major reason for the different results seems to have been that Wiese et al. (in press) did not rely on assumptions about what should be successful in attitude change (particularly regarding contact) and instead focused on literature reviews and theory that indicated what can be and has been successful. Future investigators of attitude change would do well to consider social psychological theory and data when designing their interventions.

For example, in discussing his theory of planned behavior, Ajzen stated that since behavior is based on both attitude toward the behavior and perceived behavioral control, attitude change is only likely when both of these factors are considered (Ajzen & Timko, 1986).

Contact

Although there have been many studies of the effects of contact on attitudes toward members of minority groups (Amir, 1969) and persons with various disabilities (Yuker, 1988), there seem to be few dealing with contact and attitudes toward obese individuals. This could be due to the fact that obese individuals are so ubiquitous in most modern societies that measures of the amount of contact may have low variability and thus this variable may not have a major influence on attitudes. Our own research (Allison et al., 1991) suggested that the number of obese friends and family members one had was essentially unrelated to attitudes toward persons. Despite this, there is a clear need for research comparing the attitudes of persons with extensive contact with obese persons to the attitudes of persons with minimal contact. Contact should be examined in the context of specific role interactions. In other words, one must examine not only the amount but also the type of contact that occurs.

METHODOLOGICAL ISSUES

Some authors have pointed out methodological problems with studies documenting prejudiced attitudes and behaviors toward obese persons. Harris and Hopwood (1983) stated that the data indicating prejudice toward obese persons is weak since much of it is anecdotal or based on ratings of drawings, photographs, or descriptions. Similarly, after a comprehensive review of the literature, Jarvie, Lahey, Graziano, and Framer (1983) pointed out problems with procedures such as forced choice techniques and claimed that even if attitudes are negative, the data fail to demonstrate conclusively that obese children are treated differently by their peers. Furthermore, some studies (LeBow, 1988; LeBow, Ness, Makarenko, & Lam, 1989) have reported attitudes that were not extremely negative. LeBow et al. (1989) stated, "Our results say that few who are fat are glad about it, and no one who is not fat wants to become so, but fatness is not derogated all that much" (p. 62).

Some research has dealt with body attitudes rather than attitudes toward obese persons. Staffieri (1967) reported on children's reactions to silhouettes of three body types: mesomorphs (muscular), ectomorphs (thin), and endomorphs (fat). The data indicated that children reacted positively to mesomorphs, but negatively to ectomorphs and endomorphs. In contrast, Jarvie et al. (1983) stated that while data showed that children have positive stereotypes of mesomorphs, studies have not revealed negative stereotypes of endomorphs. Ben-Tovim and Walker (1991) were very critical of the techniques used to measure women's attitudes toward their bodies and stated that studies indicating a strong link between a woman's satisfaction with her hips and thighs and her self-esteem may be an artifact resulting from the type of research done and the measuring instruments used. Similarly, in an insightful article titled "Hype & Weight," Nichter and Nichter

(1991) advise caution in interpreting results of surveys that show vast body dissatisfaction or extreme weight loss methods to be common among adolescent girls and young women. Through a large ethnographic study of adolescent girls, they found that many reports of extreme behavior (e.g., self-induced vomiting) were descriptions of one-time trials.

> The point to be stressed is that although most girls talk about being overweight and their desire to be slimmer, our ethnographic data indicates that discourse about dieting practices (behavior) must be viewed critically. Media coverage of teen dieting behavior focuses on anorexics and bulimics whose stories make good press. Normal eating behavior as well as dieting behavior among the vast majority of adolescent girls remains unstudied. Survey reports regarding dieting, while misrepresenting actual behavior patterns, may reveal much about cultural values . . . girls often claim to be on diets because they think they should be (Nichter & Nichter, 1991, p. 265).

Assuming that every adolescent who reports occasional dieting and has tried self-induced vomiting has an eating disorder is akin to assuming that every adolescent who reports having tried marijuana is a drug addict.

Another methodological issue concerns the definition of obesity used. Many studies do not provide a definition of obesity to persons responding to the attitude measures; when descriptions based on weight are given, they vary widely. Thus, it is somewhat difficult to compare results across studies.

Another problem can arise from the failure to distinguish between statistically significant differences and substantively meaningful differences. For example, Collins (1991) reported that black children preferred fatter figures than did white children but report no measure of effect size and do not even state the means for the two ethnic groups. Thus, the reader is unable to determine the importance of this "significant difference." Some differences that are statistically significant may be so small that they are not meaningful.

Measures

Many studies of attitudes toward obese persons have used data obtained from interviews (Allon, 1979; Cahnman, 1968), survey questions (Ashwell & Etchell, 1974; Harris & Furukawa, 1986), ratings (Strauss et al., 1985), rankings (Counts, Jones, Frame, Jarvie, & Strauss, 1986; Lerner & Korn, 1972; Richardson et al., 1961), attribution of characteristics to obese persons (Chetwynd et al., 1974), or sociometric techniques (Strauss et al., 1985) rather than from attitude scales. Most of these studies failed to present information pertaining to the reliability or validity of the data. Price, Desmond, and Hallinan (1987) pointed out that the way questions are worded can influence the specific response that is given, particularly to questions about weight.

The studies used various stimuli to evoke the attitudinal responses and different words to describe obese individuals. Some studies asked direct questions about obese or overweight people (Allon, 1979), and others used line drawings or pictures (Chetwynd et al., 1974; Counts et al., 1986; Galper & Weiss, 1976; Harris & Smith, 1982; Richardson et al., 1961; Staffieri, 1967) or sentence completion items (Canning & Mayer, 1967). The type of stimulus used could have influenced the responses. As Counts et al. (1986) pointed out, negative stereotypes of obese persons may be dominant when the only cue is information about body type; however, stereotypes can be influenced by other personality and social characteristics. The importance of standardized wording was indicated in a study by Price, Desmond, and Hallinan (1987), who reported that the terms *heavy, obese,* and *overweight* can lead to significantly different data.

Ben-Tovim and Walker (1991) reviewed four categories of instruments for measuring women's satisfaction with their bodies: self-reports, projective tests, silhouette choices, and interview assessments. They emphasized the need for better measuring instruments since most current measures were technically inadequate and measured a restricted range of attitudes.

Attitude Scales   Some studies have used *attitude scales*. An early scale was developed in a doctoral thesis by Bray (1972) and was revised in a thesis by Sims (1979). The Bray Obesity Attitude Scale consisted of 47 statements, while the Sims (1979) revision used only 24 items. Maiman et al. (1979) developed a 22-item scale in a six-category Likert format, but did not cite reliability and validity data. Young (1985) used this scale (it is included in her appendix) and obtained a coefficient alpha of only .58. Harris and Furukawa (1986) developed a 10-item obesity attitude scale using a 5-category Likert format, with alpha reliability of .66, which is still somewhat low. Bagley et al. (1989) developed semantic differential measures of nurses' attitudes. Recently we (Allison et al., 1991) developed a 20-item Likert scale with alpha reliability that ranges from .80 to .84. Our measure has been shown to be related to beliefs about obesity, which constitutes one indication of validity.

Knowledge Scales   Although there have been some studies of knowledge and/or beliefs about obesity (e.g., Harris & Smith, 1982), it is only recently that standardized measures have been developed. These are particularly important in view of the close relationship of beliefs and attitudes and the data indicating that attitudes toward obese persons are influenced by the extent to which the obesity is perceived as being controllable by the individual. Harris (1983) developed an eight-item true-false scale to measure knowledge of obesity. However, it was not at all reliable (r = .11), which Harris attributed to guessing, and only correlated .18 with positive attitudes.

A 12-item test was developed by Price, O'Connell, and Kukulka (1985) to measure general information, knowledge of etiology, weight loss techniques, and diseases related to obesity. They compared four different response formats, obtaining low to moderate reliability. The highest K-R 20 coefficient was .40 and the highest two-day test-retest reliability was .75. They did not report on the relationship between knowledge and attitudes. Price et al. (1985) studied the influence of format by comparing two true-false formats with a five-category Likert format and a multiple choice format in a 12-item scale measuring knowledge of obesity. All of the reliabilities were low. As in the other scales described above, this probably was due to the small number of items, but might have resulted from random guessing by the college students. Allison et al. (1991) developed an eight-item measure of beliefs about obese persons with alpha reliability that ranges from .65 to .82.

Self-Reports   An extensive literature deals with the accuracy of self-reports. In a recent review of their use in obesity research, Cameron and Evers (1990) pointed out that self-report data may result in overestimates of self-cure rates and the effects of treatment programs, but there was no discussion of attitudes. Regarding self-reported attitudes in general, an extensive literature has developed on the effects of factors such as anonymity (Tyson & Kaplowitz, 1977), self-awareness (Vaccarella, 1989), self-attention (Gibbons, 1983) and response sets (Paulhus, 1991). Unfortunately, this research seems to be largely ignored in investigations of attitudes toward obesity and obese persons.

Getting the Constructs Straight

An additional issue concerns the conflation of conceptually distinct constructs. It is not uncommon for "attitudes toward obesity" to be used interchangeably with "attitudes toward obese persons." Obviously, it is possible to dislike obesity for its health consequences and simultaneously respect obese persons.

As we pointed out earlier, where there is an affective neutral point, "less negative" is not quite the same as "more positive." Similarly, in the area of attraction, preferences for particular physiques need to be distinguished from the degree to which obtaining that physique (either in one's self or another) is important. Other things being equal, our investigations are informative to the extent that we specify *exactly* what we mean by any particular construct.

Biases of Researchers

Although hard data are lacking, it should be noted that at least some of the persons doing research on obesity attitudes may have attitudes and biases that sometimes result in statements not justified by the data. Similarly, data are lacking concerning the effect of experimenter appearance on research results. On the basis of research with black and disabled persons, it would be reasonable to hypothesize that some experimental subjects might respond differently to questionnaires administered by experimenters of differing relative weights.

Hall, S. K., Cousins, J. H., & Power, T. G. (1991). Self-concept and perceptions of attractiveness and body size among Mexican-American mothers and daughters. *International Journal of Obesity, 15*, 567–575.

Hansell, S., Sparacino, J., & Ronchi, D. (1982). Physical attractiveness and blood pressure: Sex and age differences. *Personality and Social Psychology Bulletin, 8*, 113–121.

Harris, M. B. (1983). Eating habits, restraint, knowledge, and attitudes toward obesity. *International Journal of Obesity, 7*, 271–286.

Harris, M. B., & Furukawa, C. (1986). Attitudes toward obesity in an elderly sample. *Journal of Obesity & Weight Regulation, 5*, 5–16.

Harris, M. B., & Harris, R. J. (1992). Responses to pictures of varying body weight by rural southwestern groups. *Journal of Nutrition Education, 24*, 37–40.

Harris, M. B., Harris, R. J., & Bochner, S. (1982). Fat, four-eyed, and female: Stereotypes of obesity, glasses, and gender. *Journal of Applied Social Psychology, 12*, 503–516.

Harris, M. B., & Hopwood, J. (1983). Attitudes toward the obese in Australia. *Journal of Obesity & Weight Regulation, 2*, 107–120.

Harris, M. B., & Smith, S. D. (1982). Beliefs about obesity: Effects of age, ethnicity, sex, and weight. *Psychological Reports, 51*, 1047–1055.

Harris, M. B., Walters, L. C., & Waschull, S. (1991). Gender and ethnic differences in obesity-related behaviors and attitudes in a college sample. *Journal of Applied Social Psychology, 21*, 1545–1566.

Harris, M. B., Waschull, S., & Walters, L. (1990). Feeling fat: Motivations, knowledge, and attitudes of overweight women and men. *Psychological Reports, 67*, 1191–1202.

Hesse-Biber, S., Clayton-Matthews, A., & Downey, J. A. (1987). The differential importance of weight and body image among college men and women. *Genetic, Social, and General Psychology Monographs, 113*, 509–528.

Hiller, D. V. (1981). The salience of overweight in personality characterization. *Journal of Psychology, 108*, 233–240.

Homant, R. J., & Kennedy, D. B. (1982). Attitudes toward ex-offenders: A comparison of social stigmas. *Journal of Criminal Justice, 10*, 383–391.

Horan, D. B. (1981). Attitudes of nondisabled preschool and kindergarten students toward visibly disabled and obese children and an investigation of an intervention to modify those attitudes: An empirical study. Unpublished doctoral dissertation, University of Iowa, Iowa City.

Horm, J., & Anderson, K. (1992). Who in America is trying to lose weight: National Health Interview Survey. In *Methods for voluntary weight loss and control.* An NIH Technology Assessment Conference. Bethesda, MD: National Institutes of Health.

Hoy, K., Allison, D. B., & Heymsfield, S. B. (1992, September). *Cultural preferences for body shape among New York males.* Paper presented to the North American Association for the Study of Obesity. Atlanta, GA.

Ingram, D. H. (1978). Cultural countertransference in the analytic treatment of the obese woman. *American Journal of Psychoanalysis, 38*, 155–161.

Jarvie, G. J., Lahey, B., Graziano, W., & Framer, E. (1983). Childhood obesity and social stigma: What we know and what we don't know. *Developmental Review, 3*, 237–273.

Jasper, C. R., & Klassen, M. L. (1990a). Perceptions of salespersons' appearance and evaluation of job performance. *Perceptual and Motor Skills, 71*, 563–566.

SUMMARY AND CONCLUSIONS

In sum, ample evidence now exists that in most Western societies obesity is greatly devalued and that attitudes toward obese persons are quite negative in general, especially for women. Negative attitudes toward obese persons appear to be strongly influenced by two factors: authoritarianism and belief in the controllability of obesity. These negative attitudes appear to lead to both discrimination and lower self-esteem among obese persons.

It is our opinion that researchers investigating attitudes should begin to move beyond this descriptive level and the mere documentation of negative attitudes. Future research might investigate moderators of the effects of these attitudes, both interpersonal interactions and intrapersonal self-evaluations, and the efficacy of theory-based interventions to improve attitudes toward obese persons and the self-esteem of obese persons.

DISCUSSION QUESTIONS

1 Using social psychological theory and knowledge regarding attitude change, how might we advise advocacy groups like the Council on Size Discrimination?

2 Using theory and knowledge from clinical psychology, how might we advise groups with support functions, such as the National Association to Advance Fat Acceptance, to maximize their ability to help people achieve increased self-esteem?

3 Do the negative attitudes of health professionals affect the way they treat obese patients? How can we study this?

4 In terms of increasing self-esteem of women with real or perceived weight problems, what are the relative advantages of the messages "fat can be beautiful" versus "self-worth should not be based on superficial beauty"?

5 Some obese people appear to incorporate negative societal attitudes and develop low self-esteem. Others do not. What determines the extent of this "incorporation" and its consequences?

6 Are there key developmental periods for the incorporation of negative attitudes and the development of lower self-esteem?

7 What kind of studies could test the hypotheses that some of the physical aberrations associated with obesity are at least partially the result of experiencing social discrimination?

REFERENCES

Agell, G., & Rothblum, E. D. (1991). Effects of clients' obesity and gender on the therapy judgments of psychologists. *Professional Psychology: Research & Practice, 22*, 223–229.

Ajzen, I., & Timko, C. (1986). Correspondence between health attitudes and behavior. *Basic and Applied Social Psychology, 7*, 259–276.

Allan, J. D., Mayo, K., & Michel, Y. (1992). *A naturalistic study of body size values among white and black Americans.* Manuscript submitted for publication.

Allison, D. B. (1992). Ethnic differences in perceptions of attractiveness of women's body shapes. *International Journal of Obesity, 16 (Suppl. 1),* 21.

Allison, D. B., Basile, V. C., & Yuker, H. E. (1991). The measurement of attitudes toward and beliefs about obese persons. *International Journal of Eating Disorders, 10,* 599–607.

Allison, D. B., & Heshka, S. (1991). Toward an empirically derived typology of obese persons. *International Journal of Obesity, 15,* 741–754.

Allison, D. B., & Heshka, S. (1992). Toward an empirically derived typology of obese persons: Derivation in a nonpatient population. *International Journal of Eating Disorders, 13,* 93–108.

Allon, N. (1979). Self-perceptions of the stigma of overweight in relationship to weight-losing patients. *American Journal of Nutrition, 32,* 470–480.

Allon, N. (1982). The stigma of overweight in everyday life. In B. B. Wolman (Ed.), *Psychological aspects of obesity: A handbook* (pp. 130–174). New York: Van Nostrand.

Aluli, N. E. (1991). Prevalence of obesity in a native Hawaiian population. *American Journal of Clinical Nutrition, 53,* 1556S-1560S.

Amir, Y. (1969). Contact hypothesis in ethnic relations. *Psychological Bulletin, 71,* 319–342.

Anonymous. (1987). A British town's cemeteries begin charging extra for oversize clients, and the plot thickens. *People Weekly, 27(May 18),* 129.

Ashwell, M., & Etchell, L. (1974). Attitude of the individual to his own body weight. In A. Howard (Ed.), *Recent advances in obesity research: I.* Westport CT: Technomic.

Bagley, C. R., Conklin, D. N., Isherwood, R. T., Pechiulis, D. R., & Watson, L. A. (1989). Attitudes of nurses toward obesity and obese patients. *Perceptual and Motor Skills, 68,* 954.

Bellizzi, J. A., Klassen, M. L., & Belonax, J. J. (1989). Stereotypical beliefs about overweight and smoking and decision-making in assignments to sales territories. *Perceptual & Motor Skills, 69,* 419–429.

Ben-Tovim, D. I., & Walker, M. K. (1991). Women's body attitudes: A review of measurement techniques. *International Journal of Eating Disorders, 10,* 155–167.

Benson, P. L., Severs, D., Tagenhorst, J., & Lodeengaard, N. (1980). The social costs of obesity: A non-reactive field study. *Social Behavior & Personality, 8,* 91–96.

Bjorntorp, P. (1987). The association between obesity, adipose tissue distribution and disease. *Acta Medica Scandinavica, 723*(Suppl.), 121–134.

Blumberg, P., & Mellis, L. P. (1980). Medical students' attitudes toward the obese and the morbidly obese. *International Journal of Obesity, 4,* 169–175.

Bray, C. (1972). *The development of an instrument to measure attitudes toward obesity.* Unpublished manuscript. University of Mississippi, University.

Bray, R. L. (1992, January). Heavy burden. *Essence, 52,* 54, 90–91.

Breytspraak, L. M., McGee, J., Conger, J. C., Whatley, J. L., & Moore, J. T. (1977). Sensitizing medical students to impression formation processes in the patient interview. *Journal of Medical Education, 52,* 47–54.

Brink, T. L. (1988). Obesity and job discrimination: Mediation via personality stereotypes. *Perceptual & Motor Skills, 66,* 494.

Brown, P. J., & Konner, M. (1987). An anthropological perspective on preadolescent children. *International Journal of Eating Disorders, 10,* 199–208.

Canning, H., & Mayer, J. (1966). Obesity—Its possible effects on college admissions. *New England Journal of Medicine, 275,* 1172–1174.

Canning, H., & Mayer, J. (1967). Obesity: An influence on high school performance? *American Journal of Clinical Nutrition, 20,* 352–354.

Counts, C. R., Jones, C., Frame, C. L., Jarvie, G. T., & Strauss, C. C. (1986). The perception of obesity by normal-weight versus obese school-age children. *Child Psychiatry and Human Development, 17,* 113–120.

Crandall, C. S. (1991). Do heavy-weight students have more difficulty paying for college? *Personality and Social Psychology Bulletin, 17,* 606–611.

Crandall, C. S., & Biernat, M. (1990). The ideology of anti-fat attitudes. *Journal of Applied Social Psychology, 20,* 227–243.

Curb, J. D., & Marcus, E. B. (1991). Body fat and obesity in Japanese Americans. *American Journal of Clinical Nutrition, 53,* 1552S-1555S.

Dash, J. D., & Brown, R. A. (1977). The development of a rating scale for prediction of success in weight reduction. *Journal of Clinical Psychology, 33,* 48–52.

Davis, J. M., Wheeler, R. W., & Willy, E. (1987). Cognitive correlates of obesity in a nonclinical population. *Psychological Reports, 60,* 1151–1156.

Davis, S. (1990). Men as success objects and women as sex objects: A study of personal advertisements. *Sex Roles, 23,* 43–50.

Dawson, D. A. (1988). Ethnic differences in female overweight. Data from the 1985 National Health Interview Survey. *American Journal of Public Health, 78,* 1326–1329.

Degher, D., & Hughes, G. (1991). The identity change process: A field study of obesity. *Deviant Behavior, 12,* 385–401.

DeJong, W. (1980). The stigma of obesity: The consequences of naive assumptions concerning the causes of physical deviance. *Journal of Health & Social Behavior, 21,* 75–87.

Desmond, S. M., Price, J. H., Hallinan, C., & Smith, D. (1989). Black and white adolescents' perceptions of their weight. *Journal of School Health, 59,* 353–358.

Drenick, E. J. (1973). Weight reduction by prolonged fasting. In G. A. Bray (Ed.), *Obesity in perspective,* (pp. 341–360). Washington, D.C.: U.S. Government Printing Office.

Dustan, H. P. (1991). Hypertension and obesity. *Primary Care, 18,* 495–507.

Feldman, W., Feldman, E., & Goodman, J. T. (1988). Culture versus biology: Children's attitudes toward thinness and fatness. *Pediatrics, 81,* 190–194.

Frieze, I. H., Olson, J. E., & Good, D. C. (1990). Perceived and actual discrimination in the salaries of male and female managers. *Journal of Applied Social Psychology, 20,* 46–67.

Galper, R. E., & Weiss, E. (1976). Attributions of behavioral intentions to obese and normal-weight stimulus persons. *European Journal of Social Psychology, 5,* 425–440.

Geskie, M. A., & Salasek, J. L. (1988). Attitudes of health care personnel toward persons with disabilities. In H. E. Yuker (Ed.), *Attitudes toward persons with disabilities.* New York: Springer.

Gibbons, F. X. (1983). Self-attention and self-report: The "veridicality" hypothesis. *Journal of Personality, 51,* 517–542.

Goodman, N., Richardson, S. A., Dornbusch, S. M., & Hastorf, A. H. (1963). Variant reactions to physical disabilities. *American Psychological Review, 28,* 429–435.

Gordon, J. B., & Tobias, A. (1984). Fat, female and the life course: The developmental years. *Marriage and Family Review, 7,* 65–92.

Haemmerlie, F. M., Montgomery, R. L., & Melchers, J. (1988). Social support, perceptions of attractiveness, weight, and the CPI in socially anxious males and females. *Journal of Clinical Psychology, 44,* 435–441.

Jasper, C. R., & Klassen, M. L. (1990b). Stereotypical beliefs about appearance: Implications for retailing and consumer issues. *Perceptual and Motor Skills, 71,* 519–528.

Johnson, E. H., Spielberger, C. D., Worden, T. J., & Jacobs, G. A. (1987). Emotional and familial determinants of elevated blood pressure in black and white adolescent males. *Journal of Psychosomatic Research, 31,* 287–300.

Kaplan, S. P. (1981). Rehabilitation counseling students' perceptions of obese male and female clients. *Dissertation Abstract International, 42,* 214.

Kaplan, S. P. (1984). Rehabilitation counseling students' perceptions of obese male and female clients. *Rehabilitation Counseling Bulletin, 27,* 172–181.

Karris, L. (1977). Prejudice against obese renters. *Journal of Social Psychology, 101,* 159–160.

Kenealy, P., Gleeson, K., Frude, N., & Shaw, W. (1991). The importance of the individual in the "causal" relationship between attractiveness and self-esteem. *Journal of Community and Applied Social Psychology, 1,* 45–56.

Kennedy, D. B., & Homant, R. J. (1984). Personnel managers and the stigmatized employee. *Journal of Employment Counseling, 21,* 89–94.

Kinston, W., Loader, P., & Miller, M. (1987). Emotional health of families and their members where a child is obese. *Journal of Psychosomatic Research, 31,* 583–599.

Kinston, W., Loader, P., & Miller, L. (1988). Talking to families about obesity: A controlled study. *International Journal of Eating Disorders, 7,* 261–275.

Klein, D., Najman, J., Kohrman, A. F., & Munroe, C. (1982). Patient characteristics that elicit negative responses from family physicians. *Journal of Family Practice, 14,* 881–888.

Klesges, R. V., Klem, M. L., Hanson, C. L., Eck, L. H., Ernest, J., O'Laughlin, D., Garrott, A., Rife, R. (1990). The effects of applicant's health status and qualifications on simulated hiring decisions. *International Journal of Obesity, 14,* 525–535.

Kumanyika, S. (1987). Obesity in black women. *Epidemiologic Reviews, 9,* 31–50.

Kuskowska-Wolk, A., & Rössner, S. (1990). Decreased social activity in obese adults. *Diabetes Research and Clinical Practice, 10,* S265–S269.

Larkin, J. C., & Pines, H. A. (1979). No fat persons need apply: Experimental studies of the overweight stereotype and hiring preference. *Sociology of Work and Occupations, 6,* 312–327.

Laslett, B., & Warren, C. A. B. (1975). Losing Weight: The organizational promotion of behavior change. *Social Problems, 23,* 69–80.

LeBow, M. D. (1988). Attitudes, perceptions, and practices of Canadian school children toward obesity. *Journal of Obesity and Weight Regulation, 7,* 43–55.

LeBow, M. D., Ness, D., Makarenko, P., & Lam, T. (1989). Attitudes, perceptions and practices of Canadian teenagers towards obesity. *Journal of Obesity and Weight Regulation, 8,* 53–65.

Ledoux, N. D. (1981). *Weight as a factor in the evaluation of college freshman essays.* Unpublished doctoral dissertation, Marquette University, Milwaukee, WI.

Leon, G. R., & Roth, L. (1977). Obesity: Psychological causes, correlations, and speculations. *Psychological Bulletin, 84,* 117–139.

Lerner, R. M., & Gellert, E. (1969). Body build identification, preference, and aversion in children. Developmental Psychology, 5, 456–462.

Lerner, R. M., & Korn, S. J. (1972). The development of body-build stereotypes in males. *Child Development, 43,* 908–920.

Lerner, R. M., Orlos, J. B., & Knapp, J. R. (1976). Physical attractiveness, physical effectiveness and self concept in late adolescents. *Adolescence, 11,* 313–326.

Lerner, R. M., & Pool, K. B. (1972). Body build stereotypes: A cross-cultural comparison. *Psychological Reports, 31,* 527.

Louderback, L. (1970). *Fat power.* New York: Hawthorn Books.

Maddox, G. L., Bach, K., & Liederman, V. R. (1968). Overweight as social deviance and disability. *Journal of Health & Social Behavior, 9,* 287–298.

Maiman, L. A., Wang, L. W., Becker, M. H., Finlay, J., & Simonson, M. (1979). Attitudes toward obesity and the obese among professionals. *Research, 74,* 331–336.

Martin, S., Housley, K., McCoy, H., Greenhouse, P., Stigger, F., Kenney, M. A., Shoffner, S., Fu, V., Korslund, M., Ercanli-Huffman, F. G., Carter, E., Choplin, L., Hegsted, M., Clark, A. J., Disney, G., Moak, S., Wakefield, T., & Stallings, S. (1988). Self-esteem of adolescent girls as related to weight. *Perceptual and Motor Skills, 67,* 879–884.

Massara, E. B. (1979). *Que gordita! A study of weight among women in a Puerto Rican community.* Unpublished doctoral dissertation. Bryn Mawr College, Philadelphia, PA.

Massara, E. B. (1980). Obesity and cultural weight variations. *Appetite, 1,* 291–298.

Massara, E. B., & Stunkard, A. J. (1979). A method of quantifying cultural ideals of beauty and the obese. *International Journal of Obesity, 3,* 149–152.

Matthews, V., & Westie, C. (1966). A preferred method for obtaining rankings: Reactions to physical handicaps. *American Sociological Review, 31,* 851–854.

Matusewitch, E. (1983). Employment discrimination against the obese. *Personnel Journal, 62,* 446–450.

Mayer, V. F. (1983). Foreword. In L. Schoenfielder & B. Wieser (Eds.). (1983). *Shadow on a tightrope. Writings by women on fat oppression.* San Francisco: Aunt Lute Book Company.

McKee, K., & Smouse, A. D. (1983). Clients' perceptions of counselor expertness, attractiveness, and trustworthiness: Initial impact of counselor status and weight. *Journal of Counseling Psychology, 30,* 332–338.

McLean, R. A., & Moon, M. (1980). Health, obesity, and earnings. *American Journal of Public Health, 70,* 1006–1009.

Mendelson, B. K., & White, D. R. (1982). Relation between body-esteem and self-esteem of obese and normal children. *Perceptual and Motor Skills, 54,* 899–905.

Mendelson, B. K., & White, D. R. (1985). Development of self-body-esteem of overweight youngsters. *Developmental Psychology, 21,* 90–96.

Miller, C. T., Rothblum, E. D., Barbour, L., Brand, P. A., & Felicio, D. (1990). Social interactions of obese and nonobese women. *Journal of Personality, 58,* 365–380.

Monello, L. F., & Mayer, J. (1963). Obese adolescent girls: An unrecognized "minority" group? *American Journal of Clinical Nutrition, 13,* 35–39.

Musa, K. E., & Roach, M. E. (1973). Adolescent appearance and self-concept. *Adolescence, 8,* 385–394.

National Association to Advance Fat Acceptance. Southwest protest: NAAFAns demonstrate in five cities. (1992). *NAAFA Newsletter, 22(4),* 1–2.

Nichols, S., Waters, W. E., Woolaway, M., & Hamilton-Smith, M. B. (1988). Evaluation of the effectiveness of a nutritional health education leaflet in changing public knowledge and attitudes about eating and health. *Journal of Human Nutrition & Dietetics, 1,* 233–238.

Nichter, M., & Nichter, M. (1991). Hype and weight. *Medical Anthropology, 13,* 249–284.

Orbach, S. (1978). *Fat is a Feminist Issue.* New York: Paddington Press.

Oswalt, R., & Davis, J. (1990, April). Societal influences on a thinner body size in children. *Proceedings and Abstracts of the Annual Meeting of the Eastern Psychological Association*. Philadelphia, PA.

Pargman, D. (1969). The incidence of obesity among college students. *Journal of School Health, 39,* 621–627.

Pauley, L. L. (1989). Customer weight as a variable in salespersons' response time. *Journal of Social Psychology, 129,* 713–714.

Paulhus, D. L. (1991). Measurement and control of response bias. In J. P. Robinson, P. R. Shaver, & L. S. Wrightsman (Eds.). *Measures of personality and social psychological attitudes* (pp. 17–59). New York: Academic Press.

Pawson, I. G., Martorell, R., & Mendoza, F. E. (1991). Prevalence of overweight and obesity in U.S. Hispanic populations. *American Journal of Clinical Nutrition, 53,* 1522S–1528S.

Perloff, E., & Bohachick, P. (1988). Actor-observer attributions for failure to control physical conditions. *Canadian Journal of Nursing Research, 20,* 53–63.

Peternelj-Taylor, C. A. (1989). The effects of patient weight and sex on nurses' perceptions: A proposed model of nurse withdrawal. *Journal of Advanced Nursing, 14,* 744–754.

Pingitore, R., Dugoni, B. L., & Tindale, R. S. (1992, March). *Selection bias against the employment of obese adults: The effects of body schema, gender, and job type.* Paper presented at the annual meeting of the Society of Behavorial Medicine, New York, NY.

Price, J. H., Desmond, S. M., & Hallinan, C. J. (1987). The importance of questionnaire wording: Assessments of weights as an example. *Health Education Quarterly, 18,* 40–43.

Price, J. H., Desmond, S. M., Kroll, R. A., Snyder, F. F., & O'Connell, J. K. (1987). Family practice physicians beliefs, attitudes, and practices regarding obesity. *American Journal of Preventive Medicine, 3,* 339–345.

Price, J. H., Desmond, S. M., Ruppert, E. S., & Stelzer, C. M. (1987). School nurses' perceptions of childhood obesity, *Journal of School Health, 57,* 332–336.

Price, J. H., Desmond, S. M., & Stelzer, C. M. (1987). Elementary school principals' perceptions of childhood obesity. *Journal of School Health, 57,* 367–370.

Price, J. H., O'Connell, J. K., & Kukulka, G. (1985). Development of a short obesity knowledge scale using four different response formats. *Journal of School Health, 55,* 382–384.

Rand, C. S. W., & Kuldau, J. M. (1990). The epidemiology of obesity and self-defined weight problem in the general population: Gender, race, age, and social class. *International Journal of Eating Disorders, 9,* 329–343.

Register, C. A., & Williams, D. R. (1990). Wage effects of obesity among young workers. *Social Science Quarterly, 71,* 130–141.

Richardson, S. A., Hastorf, A. H., Goodman, N., & Dornbusch, S. M. (1961). Cultural uniformity in reaction to physical disabilities. *American Sociological Review, 26,* 241.

Richardson, S. A. (1983). Children's values in regard to disabilities: A reply to Yuker. *Rehabilitation Psychology, 28,* 131–140.

Ritenbaugh, C. (1982). Obesity as a culture-bound syndrome. *Culture, Medicine & Psychiatry, 6,* 347–361.

Rodin, J., Silberstein, L. R., & Striegel-Moore, R. H. (1985). Women and weight: A normative discontent. In T. B. Sonderegger (Ed.), *Psychology and Gender. Nebraska Symposium on Gender, 1984* (pp. 267–307). Lincoln: University of Nebraska Press.

Rodin, J., & Slochower, J. (1974). Fat chance for a favor: Obese-normal differences in compliance and incidental learning. *Journal of Personality & Social Psychology, 29,* 557–565.

Roe, D. A., & Eickwort, W. R. (1976). Relationships between obesity and associated health factors with unemployment among low income women. *Journal of American Medicine Women's Association, 31,* 193–204.

Ross, C. E., & Mirowsky, J. (1983). Social epidemiology or overweight: A substantive and methodological investigation. *Journal of Health & Social Behavior, 24,* 288–298.

Rothblum, E. D., Brand, P. A. Miller, C. T., & Oetjen, H. A. (1990). The relationship between obesity, employment discrimination, and employment-related victimization. *Journal of Vocational Behavior, 37,* 251–266.

Rothblum, E. D., Miller, C. T., & Garbutt, E. D. (1988). Stereotypes of obese female job applicants. *International Journal of Eating Disorders, 7,* 277–283.

Ryckman, R. M., Robbins, M. A., Kaczor, L. M., & Gold, J. A. (1989). Male and female raters' stereotyping of male and female physiques. *Personality and Social Psychology Bulletin, 15,* 244–251.

Schoenfielder, L., & Wieser, B. (Eds.). (1983). *Shadow on a tightrope. Writings by women on fat oppression.* San Francisco: Aunt Lute Book Company.

Schroer, N. A. (1985). *Perceptions of in-service teachers and pre-service teachers toward obese and normal-weight children.* Unpublished doctoral dissertation, Texas A&M University, College Station.

Schumaker, J. F., Krejci, R. C., Small, L., & Sargent, R. G. (1985). Experience of loneliness by obese individuals. *Psychological Reports, 57,* 1147–1154.

Secord, P. F., & Jourard, S. M. (1953). The appraisal of body-cathexis: Body-cathexis and the self. *Journal of Consulting Psychology, 17,* 343–347.

Serdula, M. (1992). Weight control practices in U. S. adolescents and adults: Youth risk behavior survey and behavioral risk factor surveillance system. In *Methods for voluntary weight loss and control.* An NIH Technology Assessment Conference. Bethesda, MD: National Institutes of Health.

Shaver, J. P., Curtis, C. K., Jesunathadas, J., & Strong, C. J. (1989). The modification of attitudes toward persons with disabilities: Is there a best way? *International Journal of Special Education, 4,* 33–57.

Sherman, A. A. (1981). *Obesity and sexism: Parental child preferences and attitudes toward obesity.* Unpublished masters thesis. University of Cincinnati.

Shurka, E. (1983). Attitudes of Israeli Arabs toward the mentally ill. *International Journal of Social Psychiatry, 29,* 101–110.

Sims, H. J. (1979). *A study to identify and evaluate the attitudes toward obesity among three ethnic groups of women in Oklahoma: Black, white, and Indian.* Unpublished doctoral dissertation, University of Oklahoma, Oklahoma City.

Sisca, S. S., Walsh, A., & Walsh, P. A. (1985). Love deprivation and blood pressure levels among a college population: A preliminary investigation. *Psychology, A Quarterly Journal of Human Behavior, 22,* 63–70.

Smith, J. E., Waldorf, V. A., & Trembath, D. L. (1990). "Single white male looking for thin, very attractive . . ." *Sex Roles, 23,* 675–685.

Sobal, J. (1991). Obesity and socioeconomic status: A framework for examining relationships between physical and social variables. *Medical Anthropology, 13,* 231–247.

Sobal, J., & Stunkard, A. J. (1989). Socioeconomic status and obesity: A review. *Psychological Bulletin, 105,* 260–275.

Sonne-Holm, S., & Sørensen, T. I. A. (1986). Prospective study of attainment of social class of severely obese subjects in relation to parental social class, intelligence, and education. *British Medical Journal, 292,* 586–589.

Spitzack, C. (1987). Confession and signification: The systematic inscription of body consciousness. *Journal of Medicine and Philosophy, 12,* 357–369.

Staffieri, J. R. (1967). A study of social stereotype of body image in children. *Journal of Psychology & Social Personality, 7,* 101, 104.

Stake, J., & Lauer, M. L. (1987). The consequences of being overweight: A controlled study of gender differences. *Sex Roles, 17,* 31–47.

Stein, R. F. (1987). Comparison of self-concept of nonobese and obese university junior female nursing students. *Adolescence, 22,* 77–90.

Steinberg, C. L., & Birk, J. M. (1983). Weight and compliance: Male-female differences. *Journal of General Psychology, 109,* 95–102.

Stern, M. P., Pugh, J., Gaskill, S., & Hazuda, H. (1982). Knowledge, attitudes, and behavior related to obesity and dieting in Mexican Americans and Anglos: The San Antonio Heart study. *American Journal of Epidemiology, 115,* 917–928.

Strauss, C. C., Smith, K., Frame, C., & Forehand, R. (1985). Personal and interpersonal characteristics associated with childhood obesity. *Journal of Pediatric Psychology, 10,* 337–343.

Styles, M. H. (1980). Soul, black women and food. In J. R. Kaplan (Ed.), *A woman's conflict: The special relationship between women and food.* Englewood Cliffs, NJ. Prentice Hall.

Tarui, S., Tokunaga, K., Fujioka, S., & Matsuzawa, Y. (1991). Visceral fat obesity: Anthropological and pathophysiological aspects. *International Journal of Obesity, 15,* 1–8.

Thornton, B., & Ryckman, R. M. (1991). Relationship between physical attractiveness, physical effectiveness, and self-esteem: A cross-sectional analysis among adolescents. *Journal of Adolescence, 14,* 85–98.

Tiggeman, M., & Rothblum, E. D. (1988). Gender differences in social consequences of perceived overweight in the United States and Australia. *Sex Roles, 18,* 75–86.

Tyson, H. L., & Kaplowitz, S. A. (1977). Attitudinal conformity and anonymity. *Public Opinion Quarterly, 41,* 226–234.

Uzark, K. C., Becker, M. H., Dielman, T. T., Rocchini, A. P., & Katch, V. (1988). Perceptions held by obese children and their parents: Implications for weight control intervention. *Health Education Quarterly, 15,* 185–198.

Vaccarella, G. (1989). Self-report validity as a function of self-awareness and self-schemata. *Perceptual and Motor Skills, 69,* 963–974.

Wadden, T. A., Foster, G. D., Brownell, K. D., & Finley, E. (1984). Self-concept in obese and normal-weight children. *Journal of Consulting and Clinical Psychology, 52,* 1104–1105.

Wegeleben, E. (1986). *Just the weigh you are.* Renton, WA: Author.

Weise, H. J. C., Wilson, J. F., Jones, R. A., & Neises, M. (1992). Obesity stigma reduction in medical students. *International Journal of Obesity, 16,* 859–868.

Weiss, E. (1980). Perceived self-infliction and evaluation of obese and handicapped persons. *Perceptual and Motor Skills, 50,* 1268.

Wolfgang, A., & Wolfgang, J. (1971). Exploration of attitudes via physical interpersonal distance toward the obese, drug users, homosexuals, police, and other marginal figures. *Journal of Clinical Psychology, 27,* 510–515.

Wooley, O. K., Wooley, S. C., & Dyrenforth, S. R. (1979). Obesity and women II: A neglected topic. *Women's Studies International Quarterly, 2,* 81–92.

Worsley, A. (1979). Adolescents' views of obesity. *Food and Nutrition Australian. Notes and Reviews, 36,* 57–63.

Worsley, A. (1981). In the eye of the beholder: Social and personal characteristics of teenagers and their impressions of themselves and fat and slim people. *British Journal of Medical Psychology, 54,* 231–242.

Worsley, A. (1981). Teenagers' perceptions of fat and slim people. *International Journal of Obesity, 5,* 15–24.

Wright, B. A. (1983). *Physical disability: A psychosocial approach.* New York: Harper & Row.

Wright, E. J., & Whitehead, T. L. (1987). Perceptions of body size and obesity: A selected review of the literature. *Journal of Community Health, 12,* 117–129.

Young, J. A. (1985). *Differences in attitudes toward obesity between obese and non-obese nurses.* Unpublished master's thesis, Texas Women's University, Denton.

Young, L. M., & Powell, B. (1985). The effects of obesity on the clinical judgments of mental health professionals. *Journal of Health & Social Behavior, 26,* 233–246.

Yuker, H. E. (1983). The lack of a stable order of preference for disabilities: A response to Richardson and Ronald. *Rehabilitation Psychology, 28,* 93–103.

Yuker, H. E. (1988). *Attitudes toward persons with disabilities.* New York: Springer.

Yuker, H. E., & Block, J. R. (1986). *Research with the attitudes towards disabled persons scale (ATTP) 1960–1985.* Hempstead, NY: Hofstra University, Center for the Study of Attitudes Toward Persons with Disabilities.

APPENDIX

Association for the Health Enhancement of Large Persons
c/o Dr. Joseph McVoy
Eating Disorders Clinic
St. Alban's Hospital
Radford, VA 24143

Council on Size and Weight Discrimination, Inc.
P. O. Box 238
Columbia, MD 21045

National Association to Advance Fat Acceptance
P. O. Box 188620
Sacramento, CA 95818
Phone: 916-443-0303

Chapter 13

Obesity: Methods of Treatment

Sarah C. Sitton

For those who are significantly above ideal body weight, a major motivation for weight loss is the increased risk of disease associated with obesity. In a study of more than 750,000 people, Lew and Garfinkel (1979) found that as weight increased so did the overall mortality rate, an effect due primarily to increased cardiovascular disease, although diabetes and cancer rates also increased with weight. Other research has extended the association between obesity and disease to digestive disorders, bone and joint problems, and pulmonary disorders (Van Itallie, 1985; Bray, 1986). For severely overweight persons, health issues provide a compelling reason to lose weight, and many begin weight loss programs following medical advice to reduce.

In our culture obesity also carries a certain stigma, with obese individuals experiencing discrimination both in social and work settings. Certainly, the ideal feminine form has gotten thinner in recent years. (Garner, 1980; Wiseman, Gray, Mosimann, & Aherns, 1992).

Negative societal stereotypes about the obese begin to affect the individual during childhood and continue throughout the life span, almost certainly limiting the individual's prospects for employment as well as for social mobility (Wadden

& Stunkard, 1985; Bray, 1986). Children consistently selected a drawing of an obese child as the least liked among children with various disabilities (Richardson, Hastorf, Goodman, & Dornbusch, 1961). Similarly, college students stated a preference for drug addicts and former prisoners over the obese as future marriage partners. This type of discrimination also affects the college admission process. Canning and Mayer (1966) showed that obese women were less likely to be admitted to Ivy League colleges than slimmer counterparts with identical backgrounds.

In the workplace, the negative stereotype depicts the obese as lazier, more indecisive, and less successful than co-workers (Larkin & Pines, 1979). These stereotypes may ultimately be reflected in lower salaries for overweight employees (McClean & Moon, 1980). Recent measures of attitudes toward the obese reveal expectancies that they have different personalities, more social difficulties, and lower self-esteem than slimmer persons (Allison, Basile, & Yuker, 1991). Such negative attitudes toward the obese even appear in psychotherapeutic settings, with therapists expressing lowered expectancies of successful outcomes for overweight clients (Agell & Rothblum, 1991). The evidence is quite clear. Cultural expectancies for failure confront overweight individuals in all areas of life.

Given the widespread discrimination experienced by the obese, it is not surprising that they, too, hold some of these negative attitudes, and as a consequence often have lowered self esteem (Harris, Waschull, & Walters, 1990) and higher levels of depression (Lecke, 1967). For many obese persons, these personal and psychological problems are at least as important as the medical reasons for weight loss and provide a powerful impetus to reduce.

ASSESSMENT

The simplest criterion for obesity is the Metropolitan Life Insurance Company's height and weight table, which identifies an average weight range for various heights for men and women (see also Chapter 11). Obesity is defined as the condition of weighing more than 20% above the upper limit for height. A more sophisticated measure is the percentage of body fat or the body mass index (BMI), with obesity characterized by more than 25% body fat for men and 30% for women (Bray, 1986). Morbid obesity is defined as being more than 100 pounds over ideal body weight. The level of obesity—mild, moderate, or severe—helps to determine the choice of treatment, with mild obesity responding to self-help approaches and commercial weight loss programs and severe obesity usually requiring medical supervision.

During the initial visit, it is important to obtain the patient's family history regarding obesity as well as to determine the age at onset of the obesity. Research indicates a strong genetic predisposition for obesity (Stunkard, Stinnett, & Smoller, 1986), which when coupled with early onset, may dictate the selection of a goal weight considerably higher than that on the Metropolitan tables.

While the diagnosis of obesity is relatively simple, it must be differentiated from other types of eating disorders in order to determine appropriate treatment. Structured clinical interviews and self-report inventories are widely used for this (Williamson, 1990). For example, the Interview for Diagnosis of Eating Disorders differentiates among bulimia nervosa, anorexia nervosa, compulsive overeating, and obesity (Williamson, 1990). Similarly, a self-report inventory, the Eating Disorder Inventory (Garner & Olmstead, 1984), elicits information regarding behavioral patterns consistent with bulimia and anorexia. Abrams (1991) used data from the Eating Disorder Inventory to forecast treatment outcomes. Successful treatment for obese clients depends on the absence of evidence of purging, night bingeing, severe body image disturbance, or other forms of psychopathology associated with bulimia nervosa. If these symptoms are present, they should be addressed directly in treatment.

Secondary psychopathology can also be assessed by objective tests such as the Minnesota Multiphasic Personality Inventory. While an overview of data suggests that in general obese persons are as well adjusted as normal weight individuals (Streigel-Moore & Rodin, 1986), Scott and Baroffio (1986) found that bulimics, anorexics, and the morbidly obese all showed elevated scores on the scales measuring hypochondriasis, depression, and psychopathic deviation. Similarly, research by Prather and Williamson (1988) suggests a continuum of psychopathology with the binge-purgers showing the highest levels followed in diminishing order by obese binge eaters, the morbidly obese, the obese, and nonobese controls. Once again, these issues should be addressed if treatment for obesity is to be successful.

One area of psychopathology that has been suggested as relevant to obesity is the obsessive-compulsive personality disorder. Binge eating often exhibits elements of ritualistic behavior found in compulsive acts, with the types of foods, the location, and the manner of consumption following a rigid pattern. However, whereas evidence suggests that morbidly obese persons may indeed be obsessed with food, as a rule they have no general obsessive-compulsive personality characteristics (Hart, 1991).

On the other hand, those obese persons who did score high on obsessive-compulsive eating tendencies maintained weight loss significantly better following treatment that emphasized exposure and response prevention rather than simple stimulus control (Mount, Neziroglu, & Taylor, 1990). Stimulus control techniques such as the removal of high-risk foods from the home characterizes the behavioral approach to weight control. Conversely, response prevention in the presence of the target stimulus has been used successfully to treat compulsive behaviors. For this reason, assessing obsessive-compulsive eating tendencies prior to treatment is advisable.

In general, atypical eating patterns, especially binge eating, are widely associated with failure to complete weight loss programs successfully. A binge is defined by the following characteristics: (1) eating when not hungry, (2) eating until physically uncomfortable, (3) rapid consumption of large amounts of food, (4) feelings of being out of control, and (5) feelings of shame or disgust following a binge. The incidence of binge eating increases as the severity of obesity increases (Telch, Agras, & Rossiter, 1988). Spitzer (1992) found that as many as 30% of patients in a hospital-based weight reduction program had histories of bingeing.

A recent review of the literature confirmed the existence of a binge-eating disorder in the absence of bulimia nervosa (Devlin, Walsh, Spitzer, & Hasin, 1992). Typically, the type and quantity of food consumed by obese binge eaters resembles that of bulimics (Marcus & Wing, 1987). Unlike bulimics, however, they do not purge following a binge, gaining weight as a result of the extra calories.

Not surprisingly, obese binge eaters often have difficulty completing a weight loss program. Even a history of carbohydrate craving (simple carbohydrates are the food of choice for most binge eaters) correlated with a tendency to drop out of a medically supervised weight loss program during the first month of treatment (Sitton, 1991). Treatment for persons with a history of binge eating needs to focus on identifying and avoiding situations that trigger binges and on cultivating regular eating patterns. Also, cognitive restructuring, which trains patients to identify and avoid negative self-statements concerning binge eating, was more effective in controlling binge eating in a laboratory setting than simple self-monitoring (Pecsok & Fremouw, 1988).

Broad spectrum psychotherapy may be advisable as well for this group, since obese binge eaters show higher levels of psychopathology than non-binge eaters. This includes more depression (Marcus, Wing & Hopkins, 1988) and higher scores on the psychasthenia scale of the Minnesota Multiphasic Personality Inventory (MMPI; Kolotkin, Revis, Kirkley, & Janick, 1987; Prather & Williamson, 1988).

Perhaps the most common form of psychopathology associated with obesity is depression. Obesity has even been characterized as a defense against depression, with food serving as a kind of self-medication. While, as Wadden and Stunkard (1985) suggest, depression may be a rational reaction to the types of discrimination that beset the obese, severely depressed persons are less likely to succeed at weight loss programs (Castillo et al., 1989). Thus, persons scoring in the depressed range on the Beck Depression Inventory (Beck, 1978) would not normally be considered good candidates for traditional weight loss programs. If there are compelling medical reasons for rapid weight loss, simultaneous treatment for depression is advisable.

PREDICTING SUCCESSFUL TREATMENT

In addition to formal assessment criteria, other client characteristics may predict treatment outcome. For example, knowledge of nutrition and a history of exercise may correlate with successful weight control. Pretreatment eating style, especially the rate of eating, has been suggested as an important factor in obesity. However, although the obese tend to eat faster at the beginning of a meal than normal weight persons, studies have generally failed to find consistent differences in eating rates (Streigel-Moore & Rodin, 1986). It is even difficult to verify that the obese eat more than the nonobese. In laboratory settings both groups consume the same amount, an effect that may be due to being observed. However, slowing the rate of eating results in consumption of less food for all diners (Epstein, Parker, McCoy, & McGee, 1976).

Frequently, the meal patterns of the obese do not conform to the traditional norm of three meals per day. Some report snacking or "grazing" throughout the day. Many skip breakfast and lunch, consuming most of their calories in the late afternoon and evening. These pretreatment eating patterns correlate with unsuccessful treatment. Obese persons who ate three meals per day prior to treatment with a very low-calorie diet were more successful in completing the program than those who skipped breakfast (Sitton & Miller, 1991).

Another factor associated with successful weight loss is the level of family and social support available to the dieter. In fact, for some dieters the presence of others who encourage adherence to the weight loss program may be a deciding factor in its success. Certainly, having to resist the temptation of highly desirable foods offered by former "eating buddies" creates added strain for the dieter. Often the realization that a family member or friend may attempt to sabotage one's efforts at weight loss leads to the creation of specific plans to deal with this situation. Role playing the refusal of food can be effective in this instance. In extreme cases, such as the case of a mother who physically stuffed cookies into the mouth of her adult son after he refused them, avoiding the person for the duration of the diet may be the best solution (Sitton, 1983). If assessment reveals a pattern of dysfunctional social or family relationships, interpersonal therapy may be recommended.

Other environmental issues to be explored during assessment include stress levels. Individuals experiencing high levels of personal or job-related stress usually have difficulty adhering to a weight loss program. Even successful dieters frequently revert to previous eating patterns during periods of unusual stress.

An important client characteristic that influences successful weight loss is level of self-efficacy. Self efficacy refers to a belief in one's ability to perform a behavior and that, once performed, the behavior will produce certain outcomes (Bandura, 1977, Bandura & Schunk, 1981). Research indicates that a belief that one can adhere to a weight loss program and a belief that this adherence will result in weight loss is an important determinant in dieting success (Desmond & Price, 1988). The Weight Efficacy Life-Style Questionnaire (Clark et al., 1991) segments self-efficacy with regard to weight loss into five factors: negative emotions, availability, social pressure, physical discomfort, and positive activities. Successful treatment builds feelings of efficacy in all of these areas.

TYPES OF TREATMENT FOR OBESITY

At least as many types of treatments for obesity exist as there are theories for its cause. Ideally, following a thorough assessment of the client's needs and abilities, an individualized weight loss program is developed. This avoids mismatches that can contribute to unsuccessful treatment outcomes, such as placing a shy introvert in an exuberant group setting (Sitton & Weber, 1987).

Treatment ranges from simply advising the patient to eat less to intensive psychotherapy to discover and work through the causes of obesity. At one end of this continuum of treatment, the psychodynamic approach to obesity focuses on problems in personality development associated with fixation at the pregenital developmental level (Ihanus, Keltinkangas-Jarcinwen, & Mustajoki, 1986). These include passivity, dependence, and poor coping abilities (McReynolds, 1982). Psychodynamic therapy for obesity focuses on working through these problems and on the emotional distress associated with them. It is often a lengthy process and is not widely used for the treatment of obesity.

Behavioral Therapy

Most current therapies do not concentrate on identifying and treating underlying causes for obesity, focusing instead on eating behavior. These behavioral approaches to the treatment of obesity have become increasingly popular in recent years. They emphasize breaking old habits regarding eating and exercise and replacing them with patterns more consistent with normal weight. Wadden and Bell (1989) reported that more than 150 studies have demonstrated the effectiveness of behavioral programs in comparison to other approaches.

The hallmark of behavior therapy is the identification of the antecedents to overeating by self-monitoring. Clients keep records of the types and amounts of food eaten daily and the situations in which the food is eaten. They may also record emotions associated with eating. Self-monitoring creates an awareness of the patterns of behavior surrounding overeating that allows the substitution of other behaviors. For example, if late afternoon snacking is the main source of unneeded calories, changing behavior to eliminate the possibility of eating at this time may eliminate the problem.

Another aspect of behavioral therapy for obesity involves stimulus control. This reduces the number of stimuli associated with overeating by keeping certain foods out of the house or stored out of sight; by reducing the number of times, places, or circumstances associated with eating; and by active planning to deal with dangerous situations such as social occasions. By limiting eating to certain times and places, the association between the stimuli of other times and locations to the response of eating gradually weakens. Even Pavlov's dogs eventually stopped salivating to the bell when it was no longer paired with meat. The average weight loss for these behavioral programs is about one pound per week (Brownell & Wadden, 1986).

The behavioral technique has been combined with many other approaches. For example, studies have found behavior therapy to be a useful adjunct to gastric surgery (Carmody & Brischetto, 1986) and to protein-sparing fasts (Brownell, 1984). (Protein-sparing fasts are very low calorie diets that are high in protein.)

Current behavioral approaches to weight loss also emphasize the importance of increased exercise, social support, and cognitive restructuring (Brownell & Wadden, 1986; Perpina, 1989). To assess the importance of social support, Clifford, Tan, and Gorsuch (1991) compared the effects of behavioral treatment coupled with three types of support: group and professional therapist, group and peers, and group only. All three conditions were superior to control groups but did not differ significantly among themselves.

Involving the family in the treatment has been suggested as a means of improving long-term treatment outcomes. A study by Murphy, Bruce, and Williamson (1985) found that 2 years following treatment, those persons whose spouses had participated in treatment were more successful at maintaining losses. However, by 4 years after treatment there were no significant differences. Other studies, while reporting improved marital adjustment, failed to find increases in weight loss for women whose husbands were involved in the treatment (Weisz & Bucher, 1980). A meta-analysis of 12 studies of the benefit of involving partners in therapy found that this approach resulted in greater weight loss at the end of treatment but not at follow-ups (Black, Gleser, & Kooyers, 1990).

Certainly, the treatment of obese children benefits by the involvement of parents. This involvement sometimes follows a formal family therapy orientation, such as the Fundamental Interpersonal Relations Orientation Model, to assess and assign treatment priorities (Doherty & Harkaway, 1990). Other types of parental participation may also be helpful. Black (1984) found that both parents who played a helper role and parents who followed their own weight loss programs contributed to greater weight loss for their children as compared to a waiting list control. A 5-year follow-up of obese children whose parents had participated in their treatment found that they were less likely to be overweight than children whose parents had not participated (Epstein, Wing, Koeske, & Valoski, 1987).

One study indicated that behavioral techniques can be as effectively implemented through a self-help manual as through extensive contact with a therapist (Pezzot-Pearce, LeBow, & Pearce, 1982). For the moderately obese, commercial weight loss programs such as Weight Watchers, TOPS, or Overeaters Anonymous can be helpful. These programs often combine behavior modification with peer counseling. However, the high dropout rate for these programs makes it difficult to assess their effectiveness. Adding a behavioral element to these programs significantly reduces attrition and increases the amount lost (Levitz & Stunkard, 1974).

While cognitive therapy has shown remarkable success in treating such disorders as depression, the evidence is mixed regarding its effectiveness for treating obesity. Several studies have found behavior therapy alone to be as effective as behavior therapy plus cognitive therapy (Kalodner & DeLucia, 1990).

As with other weight loss programs, the maintenance of the loss following behavioral therapy is often difficult. Evidence suggests that half or more of the lost weight is regained within 3 years following treatment (Kramer, Jeffery, Forster, & Snell, 1989; Lavery, Loewy, Kapadia, Nichaman, Foreyt, & Gee, 1989). Current approaches to weight control emphasize the need for aggressive relapse prevention.

Medical Treatments

Traditionally, medical intervention in weight reduction has often involved the use of anorexigenic drugs. To many people, the idea of taking a pill that reduces appetite and causes weight loss is very appealing. Unfortunately, many of the drugs that suppress the desire for food have side effects that limit their effectiveness. For example, amphetamines reduce appetite, but they also produce undesirable behavioral and physical side effects such as irritability and sleeplessness. More sophisticated drugs have recently been developed that hold promise for weight reduction. Dexfenfluramine, a drug that blocks the reuptake of the neurotransmitter serotonin, suppresses the appetite for carbohydrates (Wurtman & Wurtman, 1986). It also increases the use of glucose by muscles (Duhault, 1973), thus producing weight loss. Craighead, Stunkard, and O'Brien (1981) found that patients who took fenflouramine for 6 months lost an average of 32 pounds. Also, its anorexic properties are not reduced by stress as is the case for amphetamines (Antelman, Caggiula, Black, & Edwards, 1978). Fenfluramine has even been shown to prevent weight gain following smoking cessation (Spring, Wurtman, Gleason, & Wurtman, 1991). Moreover, patients maintain the weight loss for as long as they take the drug (Weintraub, 1992). Unfortunately, once the drug is discontinued, weight tends to be regained quickly (Craighead et al., 1981; Weintraub, 1992).

For persons who are morbidly obese and for whom health risks are severe, surgery is sometimes the treatment of choice. Studies have shown surgically induced weight loss to be effective in ameliorating the effects of both diabetes (Pories, 1992) and hypertension (Foley, 1992).

The early approach of jejunal-ileal bypass has been replaced by procedures that restrict stomach capacity, creating sensations of fullness after relatively small amounts of food have been ingested (Powers & Pappas, 1989). These procedures include gastric stapling and the use of gastric balloons. While the use of balloons is less invasive than gastric banding, the high failure rate associated with this technique makes it less desirable (Mathus-Vleigen & Tytgat, 1990; Kirby et al., 1990). Some researchers feel that jaw wiring, which physically restricts the intake of food, is as successful as surgery (Garrow, 1987) and has fewer risks. The difficulty with this technique is the possibility of relapse once the wires are removed.

The use of surgical techniques to treat morbid obesity remains controversial. Albert Stunkard and his colleagues (1983; 1986) contend that for severe obesity, gastric surgery is the most effective treatment in producing major weight loss, improved psychosocial functioning, and emotional adjustment. Critics disagree that such operations are safe and relatively free from complications (Ernsberger, 1987), citing postoperative depression (Powers, Rosemurgy, Coovert, & Boyd, 1988), surgical complications, and failure to maintain weight loss (Andersen et al., 1988) as arguments against the use of this operation. A consensus statement by the National Institutes of Health (1991), however, supported the use of gastric surgery for some severely obese patients. Given the risks involved, surgery should be used only when there are compelling medical reasons and when more conservative approaches have failed.

Another medically supervised technique that has gained popularity in recent years is the Very Low Calorie Diet (VLCD), also called a protein-sparing fast. Unlike the liquid diets of the 1970s that did not contain enough protein for adequate muscle function, these diets restrict caloric intake but provide adequate protein. Patients typically consume 400 to 800 calories per day in the form of liquid supplements for 3 or more months. One benefit of this approach is the rapid weight loss, often 3 to 4 pounds per week or more (Blackburn, Lynch, & Wong, 1986; Wadden & Stunkard, 1986) and the concomitant medical improvements, such as significant reductions in blood pressure, decreases in serum cholesterol of 20% to 25%, and dramatically lowered glucose levels in diabetics (Wadden, Stunkard, & Brownell, 1983).

When combined with behavior therapy that helps to reduce attrition and to improve the long-term maintenance of weight loss, VLCDs show promise as an effective treatment for morbid obesity. Wadden and Stunkard (1986) compared a VLCD alone, behavior therapy plus a conventional diet, and a VLCD plus behavior therapy and concluded that the VLCD combined with behavior therapy group had significantly greater weight loss than the other two conditions. One commercial program, Optifast, adds nutritional education and exercise programs to the VLCD, structuring the reintroduction of solid foods following the fast and stressing the importance of a low-fat diet.

While some critics argue that only a well-balanced diet offers a permanent solution to obesity (Paulsen, 1990), there is a consensus that a medically supervised VLCD coupled with behavior therapy, nutritional education, exercise, and counseling can be a safe and effective means of weight reduction for the severely obese (Kirschner, 1990).

RELAPSE PREVENTION

A major advantage of the VLCD plus behavior therapy is its relatively high rate of successful maintenance of weight loss. Following this program, patients typically maintain two thirds of their losses after 1 year (Wadden & Stunkard, 1986) and half of the losses after 3 years (Brownell & Jeffrey, 1987). In contrast, the regain following other diets can be as high as 95% in a 3-year time period (Brownell, 1984).

Some researchers feel this "yo-yo" syndrome where weight is lost and regained actually alters the body's "set point," making it increasingly difficult to maintain a lower body weight. The set point refers to the body's tendency to regulate weight at a certain level and to defend against lowering this level by decreasing metabolic rate when caloric intake is restricted. With each cycle of weight loss and regain, the set point may move higher, making future loss all the more difficult.

For this reason, the current emphasis in weight control is on the maintenance of the weight loss once it has occurred. As with other types of addictive behaviors, relapse prevention is of paramount importance. Several studies have analyzed the behavior of those individuals who were able to successfully maintain most of their weight losses. Leon and Chamberlain (1973) found that the successful maintainers did not snack on high calorie foods and ate less while watching television. Maintainers also ate less in response to emotional states such as boredom or depression (Sternberg, 1985). Marlatt and Gordon (1985) have pioneered behavioral and cognitive techniques for preventing relapse. A relapse prevention program described by Sternberg (1985) included the following elements: analysis of high-risk situations, scheduling some reinforcing activity each day, awareness of apparently irrelevant decisions, training in handling slips and relapses, increasing feelings of self-efficacy, and dealing with emotions associated with the violation of abstinence. At the end of a 2-month follow-up period, those who had received the relapse prevention training maintained significantly more of their weight loss than those who did not receive the relapse prevention training.

The initial slip toward relapse often involves negative emotional states. Feeling angry, depressed, or bored can lead to overeating. Teaching coping strategies through activities such as role playing these high-risk situations can be helpful (Marlatt & Gordon, 1985). It should be noted, however, that the widely accepted idea that emotional eating leads to obesity has recently been challenged. A study by Stanley Heshka and David Allison found that subjects often report eating in response to emotions because they thought the researchers expected them to (Adler, 1992). This result highlights the need for research techniques that do not rely on self-report.

During relapse prevention, patients learn to analyze their actions and to recognize "apparently irrelevant decisions" that result in face-to-face contact with temptation. These high-risk situations should be avoided until the skills to deal with them have been mastered. An apparently irrelevant decision would be driving home past a favorite bakery. A "lapse" is the final link in a chain of behavior beginning with such an apparently irrelevant decision. It is much easier to break the chain earlier rather than later.

The cognitive component to relapse prevention centers on redefining a lapse so that it is not seen as the inevitable beginning of a slide into total relapse. Such cognitions as "I'm doomed to be fat all my life" and "I have no willpower" must be confronted and refuted. Feelings of self-efficacy regarding the ability to successfully maintain the weight loss are critical to successful maintenance (Sternberg, 1985).

Brownell et al. (1986) emphasized the need for developing coping skills for high-risk situations and for the physical pressures to regain weight that may be exceptionally strong. To compensate for high levels of self discipline required for successful weight control, rewards are built into the daily routine. These might include reading a good book, purchasing an article of clothing, or relaxing in a hot bath. Food is never used as a reward, although calories may be "banked" in advance of a special occasion such as a wedding reception.

Perhaps the most effective technique for relapse prevention is continuing therapist contact. Straw and Terre (1983) and Hall, Bass, and Monroe (1978) demonstrated that continued long-term contact with the therapist resulted in greater levels of maintenance of weight loss. Clients were more likely to maintain weight loss if they remained accountable to their therapists. Similarly, required weigh-ins produce better maintenance than optional weigh-ins. These results were supported by Baum, Clark, and Sandler (1991), who reported that patients who receive booster visits with therapists following weight loss showed greater levels of maintenance at 1 year than those who did not continue seeing the therapists.

Exercise has also emerged as an important component to any relapse prevention program (Colvin & Dison, 1983). Obesity has been described as a "positive energy balance," which means caloric intake exceeds caloric expenditure. While weight loss programs have traditionally focused on restricting the intake, increasing the expenditure also affects this balance. A study of people who had successfully maintained their weight for 1 year found that they were more likely to exercise several times per week than the regainers (Marston & Criss, 1984). According to Stern and Lowney (1986), "Exercise can increase the rate of fat loss, decrease the loss of lean body mass, and in some individuals could increase resting metabolic rate, improve glucose tolerance, improve mood, alleviate mild depression, and improve self-concept" (p. 55). Interestingly, the duration and frequency of exercise rather than the amount of effort expended appear to be the crucial determinants of weight loss (Stern, Titchenal, & Johnson, 1987). Moderate exercise three times a week for at least 30 minutes produces good results. Because of the stress it places on the joints, jogging is not normally a good exercise for the obese. Swimming, bicycling, or walking are preferred, although any activity that elevates the heart rate into the target range of 40% to 60% of capacity is acceptable. Walking is often selected as being the least embarrassing and the most convenient for the obese individual. While the person who is badly out of shape may need to begin by walking once around the block slowly, the ultimate goal might be 30 minutes of vigorous walking four times a week (Perri, Lauer, McAdoo, McAllister, & Yancey, 1986).

The person who is able to maintain weight loss is likely to be someone who follows an exercise program religiously, who understands and has plans for coping with high-risk situations, who can cope with a crisis situation, who monitors weight regularly and takes immediate steps to reverse small gains (5 pounds or less), who has developed a sense of self-efficacy with regard to managing weight control, and who practices a set of cognitions consistent with maintaining the weight loss. The present emphasis on relapse prevention stresses the need for permanently adopting a healthy lifestyle, consuming a low-fat diet, and exercising regularly.

Many different methods of treatment result in significant weight loss. Without a commitment to a lifelong weight control program, however, the prospect for maintaining that loss is bleak. Nevertheless, individuals who are dedicated to reducing their weight can, with encouragement and learned skills, be successful in their quest for health.

DISCUSSION QUESTIONS

1 Why is weight loss difficult to maintain?
2 Is it necessary to treat the psychological causes for obesity? Why or why not?
3 Which types of psychopathology decrease the chances of successful weight loss?
4 How does the obese binge eater differ from the obese non-binge eater?
5 What is the role of emotional eating in obesity?
6 Discuss the role of apparently irrelevant decisions in relapse.
7 Why is exercise important in relapse prevention?
8 Does the involvement of family members in therapy help the client lose weight?

Exercises

1 Divide the class into groups of four and brainstorm reasons for failure to lose weight. Groups report to the class, and a consensus on the 10 most important reasons is reached.
2 Groups of two role play a dieter refusing food at a party and a host/hostess who insists that the guest eat. The class discusses the best strategies for the dieter.
3 Students keep week-long food diaries with daily records of types of foods eaten, amounts of food eaten, times and places where eaten, and any emotions associated with eating. In class they compare diaries and look for patterns of overeating.
4 Students analyze 10 television food commercials noting the types of motives each appeals to. For example, an ad showing happy friends eating pizza might be appealing more to a social motive than to hunger.

REFERENCES

Abrams, M. (1991). The Eating Disorder Inventory as a predictor of compliance in a behavioral weight loss program. *International Journal of Eating Disorders, 10,* 355–360.

Adler, T. (1992). Study: Data don't support "emotional eating" theory. *The APA Monitor, 23,* 17.

Agell, G., & Rothblum, E. (1991). Effects of clients' obesity and gender on the therapy judgments of psychologists. *Professional Psychology: Research and Practice, 22,* 223–229.

Allison, D. B., Basile, V. C., & Yuker, H. E. (1991). The measurement of attitudes toward and beliefs about obese persons. *International Journal of Eating Disorders, 10,* 599–607.

Andersen, T., Stokholm, K. H., Backer, O. G., & Quaade, F. (1988). Long-term (five-year) results after either horizontal gastroplasty or very-low-calorie diet for morbid obesity. *International Journal of Obesity, 12,* 277–284.

Antelman, S. M., Caggiula, A. R., Black, C. A., & Edwards, D. J. (1978). Stress reverses the anorexia induced by amphetamine and methylphenidate but not fenfluramine. *Brain Research, 143,* 580–585.

Bandura, A. (1977). Self-efficacy: Toward a unifying theory of behavior change. *Psychological Review, 84,* 191–215.

Bandura, A., & Schunk, D. H. (1981). Cultivating competence, self-efficacy and intrinsic interest through proximal self motivation. *Journal of Personality and Social Psychology, 41,* 586–598.

Baum, J., Clark, H. B., & Sandler, J. (1991). Preventing relapse in obesity through post-treatment maintenance systems: Comparing the relative efficacy of two levels of therapist support. *Journal of Behavioral Medicine, 14,* 287–302.

Beck, A. T. (1978). *Beck Depression Inventory.* San Antonio, TX: The Psychological Corporation, Harcourt Brace Jovanovich.

Black, D. R., Gleser, L. J., & Kooyers, K. J. (1990). A meta-analytic evaluation of couples weight-loss programs. *Health Psychology, 9,* 330–347.

Blackburn, G. L., Lynch, M. E., & Wong, S. L. (1986). The very low calorie diet: A weight reduction technique. In K. D. Brownell & J. P. Foreyt (Eds.), *Handbook of eating disorders* (pp. 198–212). New York: Basic Books.

Bray, G. A. (1986). Effects of obesity on health and happiness. In K. D. Brownell & J. P. Foreyt (Eds.), *Handbook of eating disorders* (pp. 3–44). New York: Basic Books.

Brownell, K. D. (1984). Behavioral, psychological, and environmental predictors of obesity and success at weight reduction. *International Journal of Obesity, 8,* 543–550.

Brownell, K. D., & Jeffery, R. W. (1987). Improving long-term weight loss: Pushing the limits of treatment. *Behavior Therapy, 18,* 353–374.

Brownell, K. D., Marlatt, G. A., Lichtenstein, E., & Wilson, G. T. (1986). Understanding and preventing relapse. *American Psychologist, 41,* 765–782.

Brownell, K. D., Wadden, T. A. (1986). Behavior therapy for obesity: Modern approaches and better results. In K. D. Brownell and J. F. Foreyt (Eds.), *The physiology, psychology, and treatment of eating disorders* (pp. 180–187). New York: Basic Books.

Canning, H., & Mayer, J. (1966). Obesity—its possible effect on college acceptance. *New England Journal of Medicine, 275,* 1172–1174.

Carmody, T. P., & Brischetto, C. S. (1986). Combined behavioral and surgical treatment of morbid obesity: A case of backsliding. *Behavior Therapist, 9,* 79–80.

Castillo, H. R., Soler-Saavedra, M. M., Rivero-Vazauez, G., & Baez-Bermudez, E. (1989). Algunas caracteristicas psicologicas de un grupo sujetos que abandonaron el tratamiento de obesidad [Some psychological characteristics of a group of subjects who abandoned treatment for obesity]. *Revista-del-Hospital-Psiquiatrico-de-la-Habana, 30,* 541–549.

Clark, M. M., Abrams, D. B., Niaura, R. S., Eaton, C. A., & Rossi, J. S. (1991). Self-efficacy in weight management. *Journal of Consulting and Clinical Psychology, 59,* 739–745.

Clifford, P. A., Tan, S., & Gorsuch, R. L. (1991). Efficacy of a self directed behavioral health change program. *Journal of Behavioral Medicine, 14*(3), 303–323.

Colvin, R. H., & Dison, S. B. (1983). A descriptive analysis of men and women who have lost significant weight and are highly successful at maintaining the loss. *Addictive Behaviors, 8,* 287–295.

Craighead, L. W., Stunkard, A. J., & O'Brien, R. M. (1981). Behavior therapy and pharmacotherapy for obesity. *Archives of General Psychiatry, 38,* 1224–1229.

Desmond, S. M., & Price, J. H. (1988). Self-efficacy and weight control. *Health Education, 19,* 12–18.

Devlin, M. J., Walsh, B. T., Spitzer, R. L. & Hasin, D. (1992). Is there another binge eating disorder? A review of the literature on overeating in the absence of bulimia nervosa. *International Journal of Eating Disorders, 11,* 333–340.

Doherty, W. J., & Harkaway, J. E. (1990). Obesity and family systems: A family FIRO approach to assessment and treatment planning. *Journal of Marital and Family Therapy, 16,* 287–298.

Duhault, J. (1973). Pharmacology and biochemistry of fenfluramine. *Vie-medicale-au-Canada-francais, 2,* 141–147.

Epstein, L., Parker, L., McCoy, J., & McGee, G. (1976). Descriptive analysis of eating regulation in obese and nonobese children. *Journal of Applied Behavior Analysis, 9,* 407–415.

Epstein, L. H., Wing, R. R., Koeske, R., & Valoski, A. (1987). The long-term effects of family-based treatment of childhood obesity. *Journal of Consulting and Clinical Psychology, 55,* 91–95.

Ernsberger, P. (1987). Complications of the surgical treatment of obesity. *American Journal of Psychiatry, 144,* 833–834.

Foley, E. F., Benotti, P. N., Borlase, B. C., Hollingshead, J., & Blackburn, B. L. (1992). Impact of gastric restrictive surgery on hypertension in the morbidly obese. *American Journal of Surgery, 163,* 294–297.

Garner, D. M. (1980). Sociocultural factors in the development of anorexia nervosa. *Psychological Medicine, 9,* 695–709.

Garner, D. M. & Olmstead, M. P. (1984). *Manual for the Eating Attitudes Test (EDI).* Odessa, FL: Psychological Assessment Resources, Inc.

Garrow, J. S. (1987). Morbid obesity: Medical or surgical treatment? The case for medical treatment. *International Journal of Obesity, 11,* 1–4.

Hall, S., Bass, A., & Monroe, J. (1978). Continued contact and monitoring as follow-up strategies: A long-term study of obesity treatment. *Addictive Behaviors, 3,* 139–147.

Harris, M. B., Waschull, S., & Walters, L. (1990). Feeling fat: Motivations, knowledge, and attitudes of overweight women and men. *Psychological Reports, 67,* 1191–1202.

Hart, K. E. (1991). Obsessive-compulsiveness in obese weight-loss patients and normal weight adults. *Journal of Clinical Psychology, 47,* 358–361.

Ihanus, J., Keltikangas-Jarcinwen, L., & Mustajoki, P. (1986). Preliminary remarks on the psychodynamics underlying morbid obesity. *British Journal of Projective Psychology and Personality Study, 31,* 16–24.

Israel, A. C. (1984). An evaluation of two methods of parental involvement in treating obese children. *Behavior Therapy, 15,* 266–272.

Kalodner, C. R., & DeLucia, J. L. (1990). Components of effective weight loss program: Theory, research and practice. *Journal of Counseling & Development, 68,* 427–433.

Kirby, D. F., Wade, J. B., Mills, P. R., Sugerman, H. J., Kellum, J. M., Zfass, A. M., Starkey, J. V., Birkenhauer, R., & Hamer, R. M. (1990). A prospective assessment of the Garren-Edwards gastric bubble and bariatric surgery in the treatment of morbid obesity. *American Surgery, 56,* 575–580.

Kirschner, M. A., Schneider, G., Ertel, N., Heins, A., McAleevy, P., & Merrell, M. Responsible weight loss in New Jersey. *New Jersey Medicine, 87,* 901–904.

Kolotkin, R., Revis, E., Kirkley, B., & Janick, L. (1987). Binge eating in obesity: Associated MMPI characteristics. *Journal of Consulting and Clinical Psychology, 55,* 872–876.

Kramer, F. M., Jeffery R. W., Forster, J. L., & Snell, M. F. (1989). Long-term follow-up of behavioral treatment for obesity: Patterns of weight regain among men and women. *International Journal of Obesity, 13,* 123–136.

Larkin, J. C., & Pines, H. A. (1979). No fat persons need apply: Experimental studies of the overweight stereotype and hiring preference. *Sociology of Work and Occupations, 8,* 315–316.

Lavery, M. A., Loewy, J. W., Kapadia, A. S., Nichaman, M. Z., Foreyt, J. P., & Gee, M. (1989). Long-term follow-up of weight status of subjects in a behavioral weight control program. *Journal of the American Dietetic Association, 89,* 1259–1264.

Lecke, E. V., & Withers, R. F. (1967). Obesity and depression. *Journal of Psychosomatic Research, 11,* 107–115.

Leon, G., & Chamberlain, K. (1973). Comparison of daily eating habits and emotional states of overweight persons successful or unsuccessful in maintaining a weight loss. *Journal of Consulting and Clinical Psychology, 41,* 108–115.

Levitz, L. S., & Stunkard, A. J. (1974). A therapeutic coalition for obesity: Behavior modification and patient self-help. *American Journal of Psychiatry, 131,* 423–427.

Lew, E. A., & Garfinkel, L. (1979). Variations in mortality by weight among 750,000 men and women. *Journal of Chronic Diseases, 32,* 563–576.

Marcus, M., & Wing, R. (1987). Binge eating among the obese. *Annals of Behavioral Medicine, 9,* 23–27.

Marcus, M. D., Wing, R. R., & Hopkins, J. (1988). Obese binge eaters: Affect, cognitions, and response to behavioral weight control. *Journal of Consulting and Clinical Psychology, 56,* 433–439.

Marlatt, G. A., & Gordon, J. R. (1985). *Relapse prevention: Maintenance strategies in the treatment of addictive behaviors.* New York: Guilford Press.

Marston, A. R., & Criss, J. (1984). Maintenance of successful weight loss: Incidence and prediction. *International Journal of Obesity, 8,* 435–439.

Mathus-Vliegen, E. M. & Tytgat, G. N. (1990). Intragastric balloons for morbid obesity: Results, tolerance, and balloon life span. *British Journal of Surgery, 77,* 76–79.

McClean, R. A., & Moon, M. (1980). Health, obesity, and earnings. *American Journal of Public Health, 70,* 1006–1009.

McReynolds, W. T. (1982). Toward a psychology of obesity: Review of research on the role of personality and level of adjustment. *International Journal of Eating Disorders, 2,* 37–57.

Mount, R., Neziroglu, F., & Taylor, C. J. (1990). An obsessive-compulsive view of obesity and its treatment. *Journal of Clinical Psychology, 46,* 68–79.

Murphy, J. K., Bruce, B. K., & Williamson, D. A. (1985). A comparison of measured and self-reported weights in a 4-year follow-up of spouse involvement in obesity treatment. *Behavior Therapy, 16,* 524–530.

National Institutes of Health. NIH consensus statement covers treatment of obesity. (1991). *American Family Physicians, 44,* 305–306.

Paulsen, B. K. (1990). Position of the American Dietetic Association: Very-low-calorie weight loss diets. *Journal of the American Dietetic Association, 90,* 722–726.

Pecsok, E. H., & Fremouw, W. J. (1988). Controlling laboratory bingeing among restrained eaters through self-monitoring and cognitive restructuring techniques. *Addictive Behaviors, 13,* 37–44.

Perri, M. G., Lauer, J. B., McAdoo, W. G., McAllister, D. A., & Yancey, D. Z. (1986). Enhancing the efficacy of behavior for obesity: Effects of aerobic exercise, and a multicomponent maintenance program. *Journal of Consulting and Clinical Psychology, 54,* 670–675.

Pezzot-Pearce, T. D., LeBow, M. D., & Pearce, J. W. (1982). Increasing cost effectiveness in obesity treatment through the use of self-help behavioral manuals and decreased therapist contact. *Journal of Consulting and Clinical Psychology, 50,* 448–449.

Pories, W. J. (1992). Surgical treatment of obesity and its effect on diabetes. Ten-year follow-up. *American Journal of Clinical Nutrition, 55,* 5829–5859.

Powers, M. A., & Pappas, T. N. (1989). Physiologic approaches to the control of obesity. *Annals of Surgery, 209,* 255–260.

Powers, P., Rosemurgy, A. S., Coovert, D. L., & Boyd, F. R. (1988). Psychosocial sequelae of bariatric surgery: A pilot study. *Psychosomatics, 29,* 282–288.

Prather, R. C., & Williamson, D. A. (1988). Psychopathology associated with bulimia, binge eating, and obesity. *International Journal of Eating Disorders, 7,* 177–184.

Richardson, S. A., Hastorf, A. H., Goodman, N., & Dornbusch, S. M. (1961). Cultural uniformity in reaction to physical disabilities. *American Sociological Review, 90,* 44–51.

Scott, R. L., & Baroffia, J. R. (1986). An MMPI analysis of similarities and differences in three classifications of eating disorders: Anorexia nervosa, bulimia, and morbid obesity. *Journal of Clinical Psychology, 42,* 708–713.

Sitton, S. C. (1983). The use of behavior modification in the treatment of obesity. Unpublished case study.

Sitton, S. C. (1991). Role of craving for carbohydrates upon completion of a protein-sparing fast. *Psychological Reports, 69,* 683–686.

Sitton, S. C., & Miller, H. G. (1991). The effect of pretreatment eating patterns on the completion of a very low calorie diet. *International Journal of Eating Disorders, 10,* 369–372.

Sitton, S. C., & Weber, M. S. (1987). Diet types: Relation of personality to approaches to dieting. *Psychological Reports, 61,* 923–926.

Spring, B., Wurtman, J., Gleason, R., & Wurtman, R. (1991). Weight gain and withdrawal symptoms after smoking cessation: A preventive intervention using d-fenfluramine. *Health Psychology, 10,* 216–223.

Stern, J., & Lowney, P. (1986). Obesity: The role of physical activity. In Brownell, K. D. & Foreyt, J. P. (Eds.), *Handbook of eating disorders* (pp. 145–158). New York: Basic Books.

Stern, J. S., Titchenal, C. A., & Johnson, P. R. (1987). Obesity: Does exercise make a difference? *Recent advances in obesity Research V.* London: John Libby.

Sternberg, B. (1985). Relapse in weight control. In G. A. Marlatt, & J. R. Gordon (Eds.), *Relapse prevention.* New York: Guilford Press.

Straw, M., & Terre, L. (1983). An evaluation of individualized behavioral obesity treatment and maintenance strategies. *Behavior Therapy, 14,* 255–266.

Striegel-Moore, R., & Rodin, J. (1986). The influence of psychological variables in obesity. In K. D. Brownell & J. P. Foreyt (Eds.). *Handbook of eating disorders* (pp. 99–121). New York: Basic Books.

Stunkard, A. J., Stinnett, J. L., Smoller, J. W. (1986). Psychological and social aspects of the surgical treatment of obesity. *American Journal of Psychiatry, 143,* 417–429.

Telch, C. F., Agras, W. S., & Rossiter, E. M. (1988). Binge eating increases with increasing adiposity. *International Journal of Eating Disorders, 7,* 115–119.

Van Itallie, T. B. (1985). Health implications of overweight and obesity in the United States. *Annals of Internal Medicine, 103,* 983–988.

Wadden, T. A., & Bell, S. T. (1989). Understanding and treating obesity. Unpublished manuscript.

Wadden, T. A., & Stunkard, A. J. (1985). Social and psychological consequences of obesity. *Annals of Internal Medicine, 103,* 1062–1067.

Wadden, T. A., & Stunkard, A. J. (1986). Controlled trial of VLCD, behavior therapy and their combination in the treatment of obesity. *Journal of Consulting and Clinical Psychology, 54,* 482–488.

Wadden, T. A., Stunkard, A. J., & Brownell, K. D. (1983). VLCD's: Their efficacy, safety and future. *Annals of Internal Medicine, 99,* 675–684.

Weintraub, M. (1992). Long-term weight control study: Conclusion. *Clinical Pharmacology and Therapeutics, 52,* 642–646.

Weisz, G., & Bucher, B. (1980). Involving husbands in treatment of obesity-effects on weight loss, depression, and marital satisfaction. *Behavior Therapy, 11,* 643–650.

Williamson, D. A. (1990). *Assessment of eating disorders.* New York: Pergamon Press.

Wiseman, C. V., Gray, J. J., Mosimann, J. E., and Aherns, A. H. (1992). Cultural expectations of thinness in women: An update. *International Journal of Eating Disorders, 11,* 85–89.

Wurtman, R., & Wurtman, J. (1986). *Nutrition and the brain.* New York: Raven Press.

Afterword

Each of the three eating disorders discussed in this volume has its own set of distinctive signs and symptoms. Anorexia nervosa was recognized as a psychiatric syndrome more than 100 years ago. In 1980, the *Diagnostic and Statistical Manual of Mental Disorders (DSM-III)* recognized anorexia nervosa as a mental disorder. Bulimia, often thought to be an atypical form of anorexia nervosa, was recognized in *DSM-III* as a distinctive diagnostic category and then renamed bulimia nervosa in *DSM-III-R,* the revised edition of *DSM-III.* Neither compulsive overeating nor obesity has been recognized as a distinct form of eating disorder, yet the *DSM-IV* most likely will include a new diagnostic category, binge-eating disorder, that addresses people with overeating disturbances—compulsive over-eaters—who binge but do not purge. Those in this category would not fit the diagnostic criteria for bulimia nervosa.

On a very general level, those individuals who are anorexic, bulimic, or obese appear to engage in very different behaviors; as a result, their physical appearances are distinct. The anorexic eats too little and thus becomes thin and even emaciated. The bulimic eats too much at one time (and perhaps too little at others), but usually manages to sustain a normal or near normal weight and appearance because of purging behaviors. Compulsive overeaters eat too much, or at least they consume more energy than they expend, which over a prolonged period of time results in obesity.

In discussions of eating disorders, anorexia nervosa and bulimia nervosa are frequently paired. This makes sense since anorexia nervosa and bulimia nervosa share certain clinical features, certain etiological components, and some aspects of treatment. As mentioned above, it was only in 1980 in *DSM-III* when the American Psychiatric Association distinguished bulimia as a distinct syndrome separate from anorexia nervosa.

The differences among anorexia nervosa, bulimia nervosa, and compulsive overeating/obesity are numerous and significant. However, anorexics, bulimics, and compulsive overeaters have much in common, and the conditions themselves are related. These areas of commonality that are of interest to both the clinician and the researcher are reflected in the chapters in this volume.

The multidetermined nature of the eating disorders is a theme that surfaces throughout the chapters. The complex nature of the eating disorders does not allow for simple explanations of etiology; eating disorders are determined by the interaction of a number of diverse factors. Sociocultural, familial, environmental, psychological, biological, and genetic factors function as possible precursors and determinants of eating disorders.

The importance of social factors is an issue common to all eating disorders. Almost all of the chapters underscore the importance of social and cultural influences. Since World War II, society has placed an increasing value on thinness, especially among women.

This emphasis on thinness has been especially apparent in the last two decades, with the ideal body type becoming progressively skinnier. This sociocultural emphasis on thinness has resulted in a societal preoccupation with dieting and weight loss, and thus can be viewed as a significant factor in the current increasing incidence of anorexia nervosa and bulimia nervosa. Whereas sociocultural factors have been viewed as central to the etiology of anorexia nervosa and bulimia nervosa, attention in the area of obesity has focused more on demographic correlates such as age, gender, ethnicity, and socioeconomic status. The prevalence of obesity varies as a function of these demographic correlates. However, sociocultural factors play an important role in both the causes and the consequences of obesity. For example, the increasing cultural obsession with thinness has contributed to overweight individuals feeling more pressure to lose weight in order to fit a societal ideal. Sometimes the cultural stigma of being overweight provides as powerful an impetus for losing weight as do the fears associated with the increased risk of disease associated with obesity. Obese persons, particularly women, are at risk not only for stigmatization, but also for discrimination.

Another area common to all eating disorders involves health issues. Those who suffer with eating disorders—no matter which category—risk their physical well-being and, in some cases, their lives. It has been estimated that as many as

10% to 15% of patients with anorexia nervosa die as the result of their illness. Anorexia nervosa, if left untreated, results in patients literally "starving" themselves to death. Cardiac dysrhythmia results in the sudden death of anorexic patients. Health concerns include volume depletion, electrolyte abnormalities, vitamin and mineral deficiencies, and organ dysfunction. Gastrointestinal disturbances are common; osteoporosis may occur due to protein-calorie malnutrition, diminished mineral intake, and amenorrhea. Poor nutrition and self-induced vomiting result in dental problems.

The medical problems associated with bulimia nervosa are numerous, with electrolyte imbalances being the most common. Unlike the starvation-related medical concerns in anorexia nervosa, the complications in bulimia nervosa result in part from binge eating (which could result in gastric rupture or pancreatitis in rare cases), but more often from weight-control efforts such as self-induced vomiting, laxative abuse, diuretic and stimulant use, and exercise that follow a binge-eating episode. Dental problems are frequent. Parotid gland enlargement, esophageal lacerations, and acute gastric dilatation may occur as well as cardiac irregularities.

Similarly, obesity carries with it significant medical concerns that are caused by or exacerbated by extreme overweight, including diabetes, arthritis, hypertension, cardiovascular disease, sleep apnea, varicose veins, gout, gall bladder disease, asthma, and menstrual abnormalities. Some researchers consider obesity to be predisposing to some cancers.

All eating disorders carry with them the risk of physical and medical complications that range from fairly mild to fatal. Treatment for the eating disorders focuses on these health issues and medical concerns. However, treatment must focus not only on the physical consequences, but also on the underlying problems that have played a role in the development and maintenance of the eating disorders.

Behavioral approaches are at the core of a number of treatments for eating disorders. These approaches focus on evaluating and modifying behavioral patterns. In anorexia nervosa, weight restoration is one of the primary treatment components. In order to achieve this goal, behavioral interventions such as operant reinforcement methods using "privileges" as positive reinforcers are often used. Many treatment programs for bulimia nervosa focus on replacing binge eating with more stable, consistent eating patterns. Other behavioral techniques have included exposure and response prevention, use of alternative behaviors, and cue restriction to avoid binge eating. Delaying the vomiting response is another behavioral approach. Traditionally, obesity has been treated with behavioral approaches. Most current therapies also focus on eating behavior. These behavioral approaches emphasize breaking old habits and replacing them with patterns more consistent with normal weight. One aspect of behavior therapy is identification of antecedents to overeating by self-monitoring. Another aspect, stimulus control, helps to reduce the number of stimuli associated with overeating.

Cognitive-behavioral therapy is another aspect of treatment that is common to the eating disorders. In anorexia, the promotion of healthy eating attitudes, behavior, and activity levels is a primary treatment component. The application of cognitive-behavioral principles and practices has been successful in helping anorexics achieve this goal. Since the foundation of this therapy is the acknowledgment of the importance of personal meaning systems and cognitive sets in influencing affect and behavior, efforts are directed toward revising cognitive processes. The anorexic's cognitive sets are examined and challenged, and healthier replacements are sought. For example, a new cognitive set is adopted in which the importance of a thin body shape is diminished and value attached to other aspirations is increased. Cognitive-behavioral therapy, the most commonly used treatment for bulimia nervosa, focuses initially on interrupting the bulimic behavior. Patients examine the relationship between cognitions and eating behaviors. They monitor eating behaviors and learn to examine patterns that lead to binge eating so they can recognize cues that trigger behavior. Cues and responses are examined, and the consequences of bulimic behavior are reviewed. Also, with the exposure of sequences, cues, thoughts, and consequences, erroneous thoughts can be examined and challenged. In obesity treatment, current behavioral therapies emphasize not only increased exercise and social support, but also cognitive restructuring. This cognitive component is particularly helpful in restructuring attitudes that set the stage for relapse.

Relapse prevention is another element that is common to the eating disorders. Treatment for anorexia nervosa involves cognitive intervention that restructures attitudes and beliefs that might lead to relapse into unhealthy behaviors and thought patterns. Treatment approaches for bulimia nervosa emphasize relapse prevention. Identification of situations that provide a high risk for recurrence of symptoms and relapse are made, and patients develop plans for dealing with them. Similarly, current approaches in obesity treatment emphasize relapse prevention since maintenance of weight loss after behavior therapy is often difficult. Patients learn to recognize high-risk situations and are taught coping strategies and skills to deal with them effectively. Patients learn to redefine lapses so they do not begin a slide into relapse.

Other areas of commonality exist in the treatment of eating disorders. Treatment of all three focuses on so much more than pathological eating patterns. Treatment requires integration of numerous factors including behavioral, cognitive, psychological, emotional, and social. The eating disorders are multidetermined; thus, a comprehensive treatment program that includes multiple components is necessary. The chapters in this volume reflect this theme.

In the preface, we mentioned that awareness of the eating disorders has increased, resulting in a surge of research and literature. However, the prevalence of the eating disorders has also increased, leading to more patients needing and seeking treatment. The eating disorders field is advancing rapidly. Much has been accomplished in the study of the etiology of eating disorders. Numerous causal models have been advanced that have helped in the understanding of the multiple and diverse factors that interact to function as precursors and determinants of eating disorders. Because definitions of the eating disorders have become more precise, communication among those working in the eating disorders field is easier and more productive. The diagnostic criteria currently used for eating disorders give evidence of the more precise definitions. These criteria have been reviewed constantly and revised in an attempt to keep pace with current research and to improve understanding of the eating disorders. Similarly, techniques for assessment have been improved. Inpatient and outpatient facilities designed specifically to treat eating disorders have increased dramatically, and comprehensive, multicomponent treatment programs have been developed. The quality of scientific research continues to increase. Studies on the outcome of treatment programs will be assessed, and programs can then be redesigned if necessary to meet the needs of the ever-increasing numbers of those who suffer with eating disorders.

More advancements will follow. The contributors to this volume have identified current research areas and in most cases have suggested topics for future research. In chapter 2, Smolak and Levine suggest that the principles of developmental psychology and developmental psychopathology will provide significant paradigms to guide future work in the area of the etiology of eating disorders. Most importantly, the application of developmental principles will provide much-needed guidance into the neglected area of prevention. Theorists and clinicians have identified core personality and cognitive features of eating disorders. The critical next step is the documentation of what the early forms of these features look like, what their roots are, and how they evolve toward or away from the development of eating disorders.

In chapter 3, Waller and Calam suggest numerous areas for further research. They also offer two broad questions that should be used as guidelines for future research: Is it possible to establish continuity between parenting in childhood and the eating disorders of later life, or should we treat the two periods as separate? Is it possible to develop family therapies that successfully address unhealthy family functioning in appropriate cases of eating problems, or is the apparent effect of family therapy due simply to its addressing relationship issues?

In chapter 4, Waller, Everill, and Calam suggest that the entire field of sexual abuse and the eating disorders is a fruitful area for research; however, they identify conclusions that should be used to guide future research. First, a relationship between sexual abuse and eating problems exists at the crude, phenomenological level. In particular, the association between bulimic symptoms and the nature of any abuse merits further investigation. Second, to add to the already developing understanding of psychological and practical factors that mediate between sexual abuse and eating disorders, the authors suggest that the psychological factors of self-denigration and dissociation merit further research. Personality disorders should be considered in terms of symptoms rather than at the syndrome level. Also, practical factors such as developmental level and experiences of disclosure need further investigation. Although the relevance of sexual abuse to the eating disorders can be understood in terms of the formulation of individual cases, psychological measures need to be developed to validate these formulations and to evaluate the effectiveness of treatment. The authors suggest that to guide future research into the relevance of sexual abuse to the treatment of eating disorders, the two topics should be addressed in parallel rather than sequentially.

In chapter 5 several areas that merit future research are identified: the relationship between anorexia nervosa and other forms of dieting/weight preoccupation and the relationship between anorexia nervosa and other forms of psychiatric illness, particularly obsessive-compulsive disorder and affective disorder. In addition, the division of anorexia nervosa into bulimic and restricter subtypes as included in *DSM-IV* merits further attention.

In chapter 6, Marx suggests that much remains to be learned about the causes of anorexia nervosa, particularly in the area of family interaction. One particular issue often neglected in studies of etiology involves male anorexic patients; this is a fruitful area for further investigation.

In chapter 7, Goldner and Birmingham note a new development in treatment that is based on the goal of promoting healthy eating attitudes and behavior in eating-disordered patients; group psychoeducation programs promote a nondieting approach to eating and an acceptance of each individual's natural body weight set point. At present, the efficacy of such programs has only been tested in the treatment of bulimia nervosa; such treatment may prove to be effective in promoting change in eating attitudes and behavior in anorexia nervosa. The authors also note the few controlled studies of treatment outcome in anorexia nervosa; perhaps more studies in this area would lead to more effective treatment interventions.

Weiss, Katzman, and Wolchik suggest two areas for further research in chapter 8. Additional research in the relatedness of bulimia nervosa and depression is needed before conclusions are drawn as to whether (a) bulimics are depressed because of their condition, or (b) depression underlies or puts them at risk for bingeing and purging. Additional research is also needed before different causal models of bulimia nervosa can be integrated into a comprehensive theory of etiology.

In chapter 9, Sansone and Sansone outline an area for additional research. The authors report two cases of adenocarcinoma of the esophagus in bulimic women, supposedly related to the epithelial change in the esophagus, resulting from the repeated reflux of digestive juices. This relationship, theorized about in the past, warrants further investigation.

Crow and Mitchell suggest in chapter 10 that attempts to date to examine the relative effects of psychopharmacologic and psychotherapeutic treatments for bulimia nervosa have been limited; only three studies have attempted to do so. More studies are needed.

Rand outlines the direction of current therapy in the study of the epidemiology of eating disorders in chapter 11. The focus is on genetic and environmental/

behavioral factors of populations studied in determining relationships between health and obesity.

In chapter 12, Yuker and Allison note several areas for research. For one, more data are needed to determine gender differences in attitudes toward obese persons. In family studies of obesity, the effects of the family's reaction to the child's obesity should be examined as opposed to merely focusing on the effects of the child's obesity on the family. Further research is needed in the area of relationships between attitudes of health workers and professional competence, particularly in the effects that negative attitudes have on patient care and outcome. New measuring instruments are needed to help assess attitudes toward the obese and obesity. In addition, researchers investigating such attitudes should move beyond simply documenting negative attitudes; instead, they should investigate moderators of the effects of these attitudes and examine theory-based interventions that improve attitudes.

In chapter 13, Sitton calls for new research techniques to be used in obesity treatment that do not rely on self-reports. Patients who reported eating in response to emotions did so because they thought researchers wanted them to do so. Thus, there is a need for new research techniques.

The research areas are numerous and diverse. However, they all point to the unmistakable fact that although tremendous progress has been made in the eating disorders field, more work needs to be done. It is our hope that this volume will be of value to the academician and clinician; that it will foster a greater understanding of anorexia nervosa, bulimia nervosa, and compulsive overeating/obesity; and that it will contribute to the progress of the eating disorders field.

LeeAnn Alexander-Mott
D. Barry Lumsden

Index